The American Quest

1790–1860

A VOLUME IN THE SERIES

The Founding of the American Republic

Planned and initiated by CLINTON ROSSITER

BOOKS PUBLISHED TO DATE

Slavery in the Structure of
American Politics, 1765–1820
BY DONALD L. ROBINSON

The American Quest

1790–1860

An Emerging Nation in Search of
Identity, Unity, and Modernity

CLINTON ROSSITER

Harcourt Brace Jovanovich, Inc.

New York

FOR EDITH

promise made, promise kept

Preface

THIS book deals with a drawn-out, many-sided, indeed sprawling event of American history in a focused, systematic, and yet, I trust, not deceptively ordered way.

The event was the emergence of the United States of America as a modern nation in the years between the Revolution and the Civil War, between the ordeal of blood that brought the Republic to life and the ordeal of blood that saved it for posterity. Into these years was packed an abundance of happenings that invite the attention of all students of development: good deeds for national unity and repeated erosions of it, good deeds for personal liberty and cruel deprivations of it, governmental actions and inactions, the birth and death and rebirth of political parties, economic advances and financial crises, wars and rumors of war, diplomatic coups and fumblings, applications of technology to agriculture and industry, improvements in transportation and communication, migrations of multitudes from abroad and to the West and to the cities, social gains and ethnic tensions, public and private attempts to subdue or rearrange nature, intellectual rumblings and flowerings, spiritual awakenings and traumas, the founding of movements eager to reform America and the reinforcing of obstacles to the success of these movements.

The sum of these happenings, which was greater than the parts, was one of the few truly notable periods of national development in the history of any people; and both the bright victories and the deplorable failures that make up the sum surely deserve the kind of broad-gauged scrutiny they have hitherto been denied. They deserve it doubly because these seven decades were a time of purpose as well as of achievement, of aspiration as well as of movement, of self-conscious striving as well as of aimless wandering. In recognition of this fact I have sought to interpret the development of the United States as a search for progress, both personal and national, rather than simply a course of change made possible by a conjunction of circumstances unusually favorable to innovation, growth, and expansion. In homage to the purposeful men and women who aspired and strove in the young Republic, I call the event, sympathetically yet also objectively, The Quest.

In the past few years historians of every aspect of American life during the Quest—from architecture to transportation, from agriculture to medicine, from immigration to slavery—have borne impressive witness to the notability of these decades by pouring out consensus-challenging monographs, myth-dispelling articles, fresh compilations of statistics, and cleverly arranged collections of documentary sources in such profusion that it is no longer possible, even on a selective basis, for any one person intent on observing the event as a whole to honor Bacon's memorable admonition about chewing and digesting. I subscribe unreservedly, with feelings of frustration inflamed by painful experience, to Thomas A. Bailey's lamentations about the Digestion Gap that worries every conscientious teacher and recorder of our history. Again and again in the course of writing this book I thought I had covered the documentation and interpretation of a particular problem and was therefore licensed to make judgments, however wrongheaded they might seem to other toilers in this bustling vineyard, about its origin and impact. Again and again a book or string of articles or compilation of statistics or collection of sources erupted unexpectedly to question old conclusions by producing new evidence or to generate new conclusions by reworking old evidence, and I was compelled either to recast the judgments or to find more convincing reasons to shore them up. Even in the final revision of this study, other studies have kept on erupting so plentifully as to make me suspect that my hard-earned knowledge of some event or decision or man is not knowledge at all, that it is, rather, deceitful half-knowledge. Yet, if there was ever to be a book called *The American Quest,* I simply had to call a halt at some point; and, except for a few books and articles that forced their way ruthlessly through my defenses, that point was reached on January 1, 1970.

My way, therefore, has been to present a compressed analytical essay rather than an all-encompassing chronological survey. Pleasantly amazed by how much we know of these years, I have chosen to contemplate the whole range of American national development, place explicit emphasis on its broad dimensions, and not be afraid of synthesis or generalization. Seriously dismayed by how much we do not know or know only poorly, I have sought to suggest areas in which other and younger historians might dig deeper for evidence or spin out their own generalizations. At the same time, I have not hesitated to pass judgment on trends and issues for which substantial evidence already exists or toward which an informed hunch might occasionally be directed with profit. And aware of how much we will never know (as well as how certain it is that the more we know, the more we seem fated to quarrel about some of the biggest trends and issues), I have tried to stay within the boundaries of a historical method that is solid if not always colorful: I have done my best to steer clear of dogma and malicious disputations, to respect the legitimacy of points of view other than my own, and to confess ignorance in matters for which no one has or may ever have evidence—and of which it is therefore no sin to be ignorant so long as one knows that in fact he knows not.

Two interests lured me into this study of national development in the young Republic. One was the interest of a historian: a long-standing fascination with the politics and ideas of the American Revolution and its immediate aftermath, about which I sometimes think I have taught and written too much. The other was the interest of a political scientist: a more recently acquired curiosity about the course of modernization in contemporary Asia, Africa, and South America aroused by a series of visits to some of the most hopeful and the most hopeless of the emerging nations. Sooner or later, I remember telling myself as far back as 1961 in New Delhi (or was it 1959 in Maseru?), I would like to make an attempt, however modest, to look systematically at the early history of the United States from the observation post of political science, more specifically, to approach the first years of American independence armed with the concepts of national development first worked out (or since elaborated) in the writings of such men as Almond, Apter, Ashford, Bendix, Binder, Black,

Coleman, Deutsch, Eisenstadt, Emerson, Geertz, Hoselitz, Huntington, Janowitz, LaPalombara, Lerner, Levy, McClelland, Mc-
Cord, Moore, Organski, Pye, Riggs, Rostow, Rustow, Shils, Silvert,
and Weiner.

After some years of irregular speculation, the goad to intensive
creation for which I had been waiting materialized suddenly in
the form of an invitation to deliver the Edward Douglass White
Lectures at Louisiana State University; and the lectures I gave
in response on March 13–15, 1967 remain the skeleton of this
book. I cannot imagine a kinder or more attentive audience than
I had for all of them. Both the kindness, which one would have
expected in those surroundings, and the attentiveness, of which
one can never be sure in any surroundings, reached a peak at
the end of the third and last lecture. Having put forth, not puck-
ishly but serious-mindedly, an essentially Yankee interpretation
of the Civil War to a gathering in Baton Rouge, I was thanked
warmly and exuberantly if not for the interpretation at least for
the effort.

While I can never pay I can at least acknowledge the outstanding debts that have accumulated in these years. Let unstinting
gratitude to these institutions and persons be hereby recorded:

the sponsors and managers of the White Lectures, especially
René Williamson and Wayne Shannon, for providing the goad
as well as their hospitality;

several faculty members of Southern University, especially Jewel
Prestage, for encouraging me to look through a very special
window at the panorama of the American Union;

the guardians of the John L. Senior and Psi Upsilon Funds in
Cornell University, especially James A. Perkins and Paul Mc-
Keegan, for supporting my researches and respecting my liberties;

the officers of the Rockefeller Foundation, especially Kenneth
W. Thompson and Joseph E. Black, for making it possible for
me to devote a full sabbatical year to further contemplation of
the phenomena of nationalism and modernization;

the officers of the Bureau of Educational and Cultural Affairs
in the Department of State, especially John P. Kennedy, for giving
me an unfettered opportunity over the past decade to travel
through more than two dozen newly independent nations and
look for myself upon their successes and agonies;

Preface

the officers and staff of the Institute of United States Studies, University of London, especially Harry C. Allen and Howell Daniels, for inviting me to squat at 31 Tavistock Square during the spring of 1968, there to meditate contrapuntally about the Africa my eyes had just seen and the America in which my spirit had long been dwelling;

the sponsors of the Lectures in American Civilization at the State University College, Fredonia, New York, especially Milton Klein and William Chazanoff, for offering me yet another chance to discourse upon this subject in the spring of 1969;

the undergraduates in History 471, Cornell University, for teaching me more in the fall term of 1969 than I taught them;

Andrew Hacker, Joel Silbey, Donald Robinson, and Walter LaFeber, each of whom read my manuscript in both a friendly and a critical manner—no mean feat;

Jane P. Weld and Carolyn S. Church, for whom the words "manuscript," "bibliography," and "index" have, I fear, forever lost appeal;

and, finally, an admirable array of friends, colleagues, students, and assistants for helping me to transform the thoughts of 1961 into the lectures of 1967, the lectures of 1967 into the lectures and class of 1969, and all together into the book of 1971. The most helpful of this array in addition to those already mentioned have been Mary Crane Rossiter, Charlotte Hildebrand, Janet Moore, Leiper Freeman, Robert Johnstone, Stewart Farnell, and John M. Lewis. For reasons that were in large part out of my control, the process of writing this book turned out to be a longer and tougher journey than I had anticipated; without the help of these generous persons I might not have been able to finish it.

CLINTON ROSSITER

Ithaca, New York
June 1970

NOTE: Clinton Rossiter died July 10, 1970 as he was completing the final revision of this book. He had fifty-eight manuscript pages left for stylistic review, two weeks' work. With the help of Carolyn S. Church and William B. Goodman I have made minor

xiii

stylistic changes. These changes are confined almost entirely to the last three chapters and follow the pattern firmly indicated by the author.

MARY C. ROSSITER

August 1970

Contents

Contents

The American Quest

1790–1860

1

Precursory Musings

on Nationhood, Modernity, and

the Study of History

IN the summer of 1879 Henry James sat down at his desk in London and put his mind to the delicate task of explaining Nathaniel Hawthorne without explaining him away. In a few moments he was gazing with the eye of imagination across the ocean and back forty years at the United States of America in which Hawthorne had begun to write as a young man. Having decided to turn the flank of the unyielding fact that many entries in the early journals were "crude and simple," James pondered a few more moments, then turned loose a barrage of critical fire not upon the man, for whom his admiration ran high, but upon the country, of which he was himself a recent and still uneasy expatriate. How, he asked, could one expect even the most talented author to think deep thoughts in "the coldness, the thinness, the blankness" of American society?

The negative side of the spectacle on which Hawthorne looked out, in his contemplative saunterings and reveries, might, indeed, with a little ingenuity, be made almost ludicrous; one might enumerate the items of high civilization, as it exists in other countries, which are absent from the texture of American life, until it should become a wonder to know what was left. No State, in the European sense of the word, and indeed barely a specific national name. No sovereign, no court, no personal loyalty, no aristocracy, no church, no clergy, no army, no diplomatic service, no country gentlemen, no palaces, no castles, nor manors, nor old country houses, nor parsonages, nor thatched cottages, nor ivied ruins; no cathedrals, nor abbeys, nor little Norman churches; no great Universities nor public schools—no Oxford, nor Eton, nor Harrow; no literature, no novels, no museums, no pictures, no political society, no sporting class—no Epsom nor Ascot! [1]

If some elements that James found missing in American life during Hawthorne's youth were hardly essential to a condition of mature nationhood (pretentious buildings, institutionalized snobbery, poor schools for rich children, a sporting class), others were (the disciplined core of an army, a competent diplomatic service, a respectable culture); and they were still missing two decades later when James began to think his own deep thoughts. From the Jamesian point of vantage, which an articulate minority of Americans has always occupied more or less truculently, we can ourselves look back to the United States on the edge of civil war and discover a nation that, by British or French standards, barely deserved the name almost but not quite denied in this indictment.*

From another point of vantage, however, one occupied more tolerantly by men interested in new departures rather than old establishments, in life-improving production for the many rather than life-embellishing consumption by the few, the United States in 1860 appears as a quite different and more impressive spectacle: a young giant of a nation that had just passed through an unprecedented experience of economic and social development. In seventy years its territory had expanded from 890,000 to 3 million square miles, its population had grown from 3.9 to 31.5 million, and its cities of more than 25,000 inhabitants had soared from two to thirty-five. In fifty years it had built more than 3,500 miles of canals, in thirty years more than 30,000 miles of railroad, in only sixteen years more than 50,000 miles of telegraph. Thanks to these improvements, as well as to the building of ever more numerous, speedy, and reliable steamboats, the country had undergone, in the words of George R. Taylor, a "transportation revolution," [3] which in its turn had helped to

---

1. Notes are on pages 361–384.

* It may please some gracious neighbors in upstate New York to learn that a fellow citizen anticipated Henry James's lament over the fuzziness of the "national name" by a full sixty years, suggesting Fredonia as both "sonorous" in quality and worthy of free men.[2]

trigger revolutions in manufacturing, commerce, finance, and agriculture. The value of American manufactures had risen tenfold since 1810, the amount of currency in circulation had increased almost twentyfold since 1790, and, to pluck only one meaningful statistic from a jumble that tell us of rapid industrial development, more than 15 million tons of coal were mined in 1860, while less than 250,000 had been mined only thirty years before.[4]

Men like Henry James could lament or deride the increased capacity of the American people to engage profitably in the vulgar business of getting and spending, but they could not ignore such signs of civilized improvement as sixty-five medical schools in a country that in 1810 had supported five, and a platoon of noteworthy authors in a country that in 1810 could have mustered none. In sum, the American Republic was a nation, although its nationhood was soon to be grievously tested; American society had begun to display some of the "items of high civilization," although on many the paint was fresh and thin; and the American economy had crossed the threshold of modernity, although several million men still lived like miserable peasants because of ignorance, inertia, isolation, fear, or oppression. While we may grimace over the boastful pronouncements of a man like James K. Polk that the United States was "a sublime moral spectacle to the world" and Americans "the most favored people on the face of the earth," [5] we may wish to give at least qualified support to the quiet judgment of Hawthorne himself: that "a commonplace prosperity" made it possible for most dwellers in his "dear native land" to live in "broad and simple daylight" such as no land had ever enjoyed.[6]

What was the record of the American people in the seven decades of the Quest? What were the successes, and how remarkable were they? What were the failures, and how dismal? What techniques did Americans use in pursuit of their loudly trumpeted national purposes of independence, unity, liberty, prosperity, self-improvement, expansion, and power? What techniques did they shun out of prejudice or timidity or lack of imagination? What circumstances smiled upon their efforts to raise the better part of an entire continent to the power and glory of which the founding generation had dreamed? What obstacles tripped them as they raced up the road of national development? And why was the "broad and simple daylight" of young America about to be darkened by the smoke of thousands of cannons? These are some of the questions this study seeks to answer.

It is important to answer them, and thus to think systematically and broadly about the progress of the United States toward modern nationhood, for several compelling reasons.

In the first place, the phenomenon we call the nation is flourishing today as a political, legal, and emotional community more vigorously than at any time in all history. While many of those who were under thirty in the 1930's still mumble ritualistically about the obsolescence of the nation, those of any age who must deal in either a peaceful or a warlike way with, to pick a dozen or so examples quite at random, Peru, Mexico, Canada, Spain, Rumania, Czechoslovakia, South Africa, Israel, the Palestine guerrillas, two Germanies, three Vietnams, General Suharto, and President Kenyatta, not to forget China, the Soviet Union, and the United States, can testify soberly to the truth of this sweeping yet not inflated statement. The nation has emerged, for better or worse, as the critical community of the world in which we live, the largest viable and also the smallest effective aggregate of sovereignty over the activities of men. If we are to arrive at a better understanding of this harsh world and the kindlier one we would like to build, we must study the history of nations just as intensively as we study the behavior of individuals; and it should go without saying, although many otherwise alert Americans are apparently deaf to the message, that the manner in which the United States emerged and endured as a nation is one of the most interesting case studies of well-nigh universal development.

The revival of the nation as an entity has meant, of course, the revival of nationalism as an idea. Of all the isms, not excluding Marxism, socialism, individualism, tribalism, sadism, masochism, eroticism, vegetarianism, and militarism, nationalism has the most universal and compelling appeal in the world today. So full of life is this phoenix of ideas as both creator and destroyer that we must examine it carefully wherever we find it. In few countries do we find it assuming more striking configurations than in the Republic of Washington, Jefferson, Jackson, and Lincoln.

A second reason is that the nation, again for better or worse, is the principal arena in which the process of economic and social development is expected to go forward on every continent. It is, in a related metaphor, the high road of modernization along which most men have proclaimed their readiness to move. The old empires have fallen to pieces or live on doggedly in a state of moral and material poverty; the new empires are racked with dissension and interested only superficially in broad-scale development beyond the boundaries of the master power; smaller units like city-states cannot muster the resources for such development; and larger ones like supranational communities are confined by fears and jealousies, most of them strongly nationalistic in character, to a narrow range of economic or military tasks. What we are left with in every area of collective concern from the pursuit of diplomacy to the application of technology is, quite bluntly, the nation, and leaders of nations are understandably pleased about this turn of events, especially if they do their leading in those parts of the world where "catching up with the West" is, next to soccer, politics, and baiting the West, the favorite sport. One has only to set the list of members of the United Nations at the founding side by side with the list of 1970 in order to understand why so thoughtful a scholar as S. N. Eisenstadt chooses to call this century "The Age of the New Nation." [7]

Wherever the process of modernization leads in the foreseeable future to the condition of modernity, the nation will almost certainly be, as it has been for the past two or three hundred years, the vehicle of success. Wherever the process leads to frustration and failure, the nation will simply become the villain rather than the hero of the piece. It is discouraging to hear the politically active modernizers of this world talk so often and enthusiastically of national rather than regional or continental or universal development, but that is the way their clients seem to want them to talk, and that is the way they are sure to keep right on talking. No one knows where the world is heading; everyone knows that, whether it goes up or down or completely out, it will go for many years to come as a collection of nations. The durability of this type of community has been reinforced in the past quarter-century by the dissolution of old-style imperialism, the emergence of two great powers (it may yet be three) against whose smothering embraces nationalism seems to be the most effective defense,[8] and the world-encompassing rage for modernization. The nation, it bears repeating, is the principal arena of modernization; nationalism, whether fiercely competitive or gently cooperative, is the principal inspiration of most men who have entered it in order to work for a better future.

This observation invites us to pause for a moment to consider the relationship of nationhood and modernity as states of being and thus of nation-building and modernization as processes of becoming. The relationship is, in four pairs of carefully chosen words, extremely close, mutually nourishing, surprisingly enduring, and apparently necessary. Logic and idealism alike proclaim that the two are and should be two; the records of recent history and the practices of the contemporary world alike proclaim that the two are and must be one. While there is plainly no law of history or axiom of political science that forbids a people to hope for one in the absence of the other, evidence abounds that the two states (and thus the two processes) go hand in hand in the world we have known and can reasonably foresee: *To be modern a community needs to grow into a self-conscious nation; to be an established nation it needs to cross the threshold of modernity.* It was exactly here, at the critical point of connection between nationhood and modernity, that the United States had succeeded notably yet was also in danger of failing desperately in 1860, which is reason enough for studying and restudying the circumstances of the American Quest. The circumstances, we shall learn, were so special and largely favorable, so peculiar to time and place, indeed so unique in the best sense of a much abused word, that no thoughtful American would offer the early experience of his country as a blueprint for the nation-builders and modernizers of Asia, Africa, and South America. Still, if this experience cannot and therefore ought not be imitated, it does provide a few words of both encouragement and caution that leaders of the new nations may ponder usefully. While many of them do not like us, and while those who do cannot copy us no matter how hard they try, all nations would profit greatly by learning more about us.

Finally, the plain but hardly simple fact of the existence of the United States of America as a major industrial and military power invites thoughtful attention to the process through which it arose, developed, expanded, faltered, began to crack, and then was saved from dissolution by desperate action. In a world of nations and would-be nations the most important truth about the most powerful nation is not that it is rich or strong or independent or inventive, not that it is blessed with most advantages and plagued by most problems of modernity, but that it is a nation at all. A single nation, which could display any one of several characters and still be important in this sense, covers an expanse of territory where two or five or ten nations might easily have been spawned to push and squabble and make small wars and eat the meager fare of disunity. The world would be an even more chaotic scene and the North American continent harbor a less developed society if the men of the Quest had failed to recognize that their one great purpose had two dimensions, if they had refused to search for nationhood as zestfully as they searched for modernity, indeed if they had not, in the final reckoning, been successful in both of their efforts.

This is a study of history undertaken by a dues-paying member of the profession of political science. The phenomenon occurs infrequently these days, and a few words of explanation may be in order. While the next few pages are sure to strike some readers as too personal in style—as a matter of fact, this is the way they strike me—I am ready to take the risk of stating several propositions about political science and history more openly and explicitly than the norms of professionalism and taste generally advise because I would not want any reader to have any doubts about the nature of this study. These propositions are a key to the mind of the man who undertook it; the man is willing if not overjoyed to make the key available in the hope that even those who disagree most strenuously with his methods and conclusions will be clear in their own minds about the directions he followed in reaching them.

Let me begin by aiming two propositions at my colleagues, whether dues-paying or otherwise, in political science.

First, the study of history is essential to the good health of political science. It seems almost bizarre to have to make such a statement, but the fact is that history, like normative theory, has fallen into disrepute in American political science. Some of the most creative minds in the profession have dedicated themselves so joyfully to behavioralism that, despite their protestations to the contrary, they have become unhistorical, even antihistorical, in mood and method. As one who plies his trade in the smoggy fallout of the behavioral explosion, I am bound to contemplate this development with alarm as well as with discomfort. Those who shun or denigrate history are guilty of throwing away one of the most versatile tools of their own trade, and they, not the discipline of history, are the losers. The search for genuine understanding of the nature, motivation, activity, and destiny of men and their communities must be pressed just as vigorously along the historical as along the behavioral, statistical, empirical, theoretical, or normative dimension. This observation is especially true of political scientists whose specialty is modernization. Surely they cannot expect to measure success or failure in a developing society if they know nothing of when and how and why it began to develop or nothing of the stages through which it has passed.

Second, the history studied by political scientists, while focusing primarily on the processes and instruments of government, must pay a decent respect to all the varieties of history, for there is no variety that cannot teach us something about the ways and wants of political man. It is not just political, constitutional, or legal history that the historical-minded political scientist should call to the attention of his unhistorical or antihistorical brethren, but also the "tunnels" we like to describe as intellectual, cultural, social, economic, religious, military, or diplomatic.[9] He might also wish to point out that these tunnels are becoming ever more numerous and broad of bore, that the walls between them may someday crumble, and that we are likely as not to be left standing in a vast, well-lighted cavern called, very simply, history. A decent respect for such disparate fields as economics, anthropology, psychology, and geography may also hasten the day of doom for intellectual tunnels in the fragmented discipline of history and the even more fragmented discipline of political science.

To these simple but, I have learned, vexatious propositions about political science let me add another four just as simple, and apparently even more vexatious, about history. They are aimed at whoever may wish to contemplate them.

The first places me openly where I have hitherto been placed offhandedly: in the consensus school of students of American history. While I have listened thoughtfully to the message of the historians of conflict, I remain convinced that the most important single fact about our development as a modern nation has been an unusually broad and deep-seated agreement on fundamental ideas and institutions.[10] While this fact may not hold true forever in the United States (and has certainly been taking a beating in recent years), it was true, I think, from the earliest planting to our emergence as a world power, and as such is the principal if by no means only key to an understanding of the years of development between 1789 and 1861.

To the sticky argument that the American Quest for nationhood and modernity was set in motion by a bloodletting revolution, my reply is that the Revolution was primarily a war of political liberation, a strike for independence against a mother country so reluctant in origin, limited in purpose, cautious in conduct, and mild in economic and social consequence that it can hardly be classed with such other famous revolutions as the French, Russian, Chinese, and Cuban. To the even stickier argument that the Quest led to a blood-spouting civil war, my reply is that the Civil War was an event as notable for the speed and completeness with which the conquered were restored to grace, at least to political grace, as for the fury of all those passions summoned up to conquer them. In any case, the aspect of the years between the two sacrifices of blood that impresses me most vividly is how little fundamental political, social, and ideological conflict accompanied a furious pace of change and expansion, which ought, one sometimes thinks, to have pulled the American people apart in a dozen directions and at a dozen levels.

The most significant of the broad developments that invite the historian to choose consensus over conflict as the primary pattern in which to group and analyze the events of the first decades of the Republic are these: the emergence of a political system to which men who had abandoned monarchy and were inoculated against plebiscitary democracy could pledge their faith in common, the evolution of an economy in which the ownership of private property was supplemented and occasionally regulated but never effectively challenged, the establishment of a political tradition that steered a Liberal course between the Conservatism of Burke and the Radicalism of Rousseau and won the allegiance of all but a handful of Americans, and the absence of any social upheaval that Marx himself would have classified as an authentic class struggle. No consensus-oriented historian can deny that the new nation had its share of tensions and squabbles over political power, social style, religious principle, and economic reward. Yet, by the same token, no conflict-oriented historian can deny that the share might easily have been a great deal larger, not unless he shuts his eyes obstinately to the contrast between the three or four Frances that tore at each other's throats and the one America that hustled its way into the future. No historian, of any orientation, let it be added hastily, can pass lightly over the incontestable fact that *this one America was a white America,* that a sizable chunk of the price of political and social consensus was the exclusion of almost all Negroes, whether held in slavery or set free or born free, as well as almost all Indians from the main arena of American life. Whether the new nation ever really thought seriously about paying the price is a disturbing question to which we must return in due course.

Second, the process of sifting through the findings of hundreds of dedicated "tunnel historians"—most of whom knew they were mining a single lode, a few of whom insisted that their peripheral tunnel was really the main shaft—has persuaded me of the soundness of the multidimensional approach to all major periods, problems, and events of American history. An event like the coming of the Revolution provides an interesting case in point. In my own time I have watched with fascination as men of integrity and learning pressed the search for the causes of the American Revolution through ideas to economics to constitutional interpretations to social forces to politics to geography to religion and back again to ideas, and I have been left with a strong feeling that the study of these causes simply does not have a main shaft. No attempt to explain what happened in England and the American colonies between 1765 and 1776 can be taken seriously unless it gives a sizable amount of weight to each of these and still other areas of human concern and endeavor. The historian, to be sure, must be on his guard lest a commitment to the multidimensional approach freeze him in a stance of passive relativism or timid neutrality, for there are times when a single force like religion or economics or politics or ideology or even a chain of accidents has dominated a course of events, and thus demands rudely that he put special emphasis upon it. The emphasis, however, must not be so special as to become exclusive. The patterns of social organization and individual action in this world are much too complicated to permit men to interpret the past, however brilliantly and grandly, in a unidimensional frame of mind. If there is one sin worse than paying equal respect to every reasonable explanation of a great event or epoch it is the act of seeking, finding, and proclaiming the One Big Explanation. While it may seem that I am beating a very dead horse, the horse (or is it a hedgehog?) has come back to life so repeatedly and suddenly under the proddings of sentimental Turnerians, pseudo-Beardians, crypto-Marxists, and second-generation Toynbeeans that I feel obliged to go right on with the beating.

My third point has to do with the time relationship between the historian and the history he seeks to interpret. It is no secret that many otherwise sound and instructive scholars put too much emphasis on the present, chiefly by reading the interests or fashions of their own age into the age they are studying or by searching for "lessons" that might prove "relevant" for current political and social purposes or by bewailing the sins and ignoring the accomplishments of the generations that have gone before. At the same time, they put too little emphasis on the past itself by failing to heed Maitland's memorable admonition to "think ourselves back into a twilight" in order to understand clearly and judge fairly the behavior of men long dead. I am by no means entirely opposed to the occasional injection of a dose of present-mindedness into the writing of history, and have succumbed more than once myself to the splendid temptation of summoning the past to acclaim or denounce the present. To put the matter in terms both concrete and serious, no one, surely, can fault a first-class scholar who is moved by the present crisis in race relations to turn his attention to the history of the Negro in America, who draws upon his findings as historian to inform his opinions as citizen, and who ends by reading the rest of us a lesson for today that is in essence the lesson he learned from yesterday. The danger always exists, of course, that a historian may think himself back so completely as to abdicate one of the duties of every self-respecting scholar: to pass an essentially moral judgment, however contingently and infrequently, on the men and events with which he has become familiar. Still, we cannot treat the past merely as prologue to the present; we cannot beg off the extra effort of imagination that is needed in order to see the world, in this instance the American world of 1790 or 1830 or 1860, through the eyes of the men who had to apply *their* knowledge and experience rather than *ours* to the problems they faced. If we cannot think ourselves back, we cannot begin to understand, as understand we must, what a stupendous feat the builders of the Erie Canal brought off or why speculation in public lands was not quite the sin it is today or why many men of good will could see no way to bring a peaceful end to slavery. Most important for our purposes, we cannot understand that the United States in 1860, in which even the grandest men lived under what present-minded men would judge to have been rude conditions, had in fact reached the level of modernity toward which it had been aiming from the beginning.

The fourth and final proposition is this: Although *The American Quest* is the product of an attempt to measure the growth of a nation in the largest possible dimensions, I began and ended the attempt in the conviction that history is the study of men, not of forces or factors. While I have used, as it were, a telescope rather than a microscope in my search for an understanding of a critical period of American history, and thus have found it impossible to banish forces and factors completely from these pages, I like to think that the telescope was directed at the comings and goings of millions of ordinary persons and the decisions and driftings of thousands of other persons, both ordinary and extraordinary, who scrambled, fell, or were catapulted into positions of leadership. In any case, I know from several unpleasant experiences that too vigorous a search for forces or factors leads not merely to the sin of proclaiming the One Big Explanation but also to the misdemeanor (or is it too a sin?) of explaining everything, and therefore nothing, in terms of historical determinism.

The freedom of action of the most assertive leaders of men is reduced, to be sure, by the political, economic, social, and intellectual situations of their time. Not even such movers-and-shakers as Napoleon and Lenin could leap over the barriers of circumstance, parade around the stage giving whatever orders they pleased, and have them carried out satisfactorily. Yet inside the barriers there is almost always room to maneuver, and even less assertive men than Napoleon and Lenin can "make history" by ranging as widely as possible and thus winning for themselves a number of options. The rudeness with which one great event or development like the triumph of Christianity or the rise of the House of Commons or the production of the first atomic bomb cuts off retreat into the past and gives general directions into the future makes certain that the number of options is never large, yet once in a while it is large enough to permit men of power to be masters of the fate of a nation and to command men of contemplation to describe them in terms of mastery rather than puppetry. In this rather semideterministic view, some roads are opened up even as most are closed off by the actions or inactions of those who have gone before, and masterful men are invited to inspect these roads and choose one over the others with boldness and foresight.

To draw upon a celebrated example of choice-within-limits, the events of 1775–1783 in North America put a flat prohibition on many courses of action such as a return to colonial status or the importation of a monarch or the erasing of state boundaries. They did not, however, settle the central issue of whether the Union of states was to become more perfect or less perfect or no union at all, which means that the delegates to the Convention of 1787 were more at liberty than many of them realized to decide whether the United States was to be a federal union, a federation, a confederation, or a confederacy, and thus, in addition, to decide in the long run whether its parts might dissolve and regroup into three or more clusters of states. The year 1787, I have tried to explain elsewhere,[11] was clearly the natural child of 1776, but 1776 was just as clearly the father of three or four possible

15

1787's. Nothing in the previous ten or fifty or 200 years had determined that the Constitution would be adopted as a charter of federal union or the Northwest Ordinance as a charter of republican expansion, and any other kind of constitution or ordinance (as well as a failure to adopt one or the other or both) would have led in time to another kind of North America. Historical determinism is a false guide to the events of the 1780's; it is only slightly more trustworthy a guide to the events of the first half of the nineteenth century.

Beyond these propositions, which may prove useful to those who intend to give a careful reading to this study, it would be presumptuous to go on and on expounding an obviously yet also designedly rough-hewn philosophy of history. Suffice it to conclude by asserting a strong belief in the historian's obligation to be objective but not fecklessly relativistic, to be systematic but not neo-Scholastic, to stick close to the evidence but not so close as to forswear the hunch entirely, to write as a moral man but not as a moralizer, to describe what happened at a decisive moment of history as exactly as possible but also to say what could have happened and guess what would have been the consequences, and above all to insist that the discipline of history can be both a rigorous branch of social science and a stylish form of the humanities. In this spirit I have made an attempt to reduce to some kind of comprehensible order the confusing swirl of American activity from the first years of Washington to the last of Buchanan. If some readers judge the attempt a failure, let them blame the author rather than the spirit that moved him.

It might be helpful to trace a preliminary sketch of the broad outlines of this inquiry into the early years of the American experiment.

Chapters 2–4 present a modest yet, for the purposes of the inquiry, essential theory of national development against which the performance of every country from the Britain of George III to the Lesotho of Moshoeshoe II can be usefully and fair-mindedly tested. While chapter 2 deals primarily with the goals of nationhood and chapter 3 with the goals of modernity, the record of the past several hundred years makes clear that pursuit of one set of goals invites, perhaps even commands, pursuit of the other, and that the grand prize of the double-barreled pursuit is the modern nation. Chapter 4 then sets out to isolate and examine the essentials of development, that is to say, the circumstances that make possible and the aspirations that make imperative the search for nationhood and modernity. It goes on to survey the principal techniques, ranging from all-encompassing political manipulation to all-forgiving political inaction, through which the search has been pressed in every part of the world.

Armed with a general theory of the goals and techniques of national development, we thereupon turn to the specific case of the United States in the first seven decades under the Constitution —a point at which, I recognize ruefully, some persons may choose to begin reading this book. Chapter 5 focuses on progress toward full nationhood, chapter 6 on political, social, economic, and cultural achievement. Before we can move ahead, in chapter 8, to a review of the techniques that were used in this period, we must understand why they were chosen and how well they worked, and for that purpose we must give some attention to other techniques, used only halfheartedly or not at all. The burden of chapter 7 is that two major "models" of national growth and expansion—one identified with Alexander Hamilton and John Quincy Adams, the other with Thomas Jefferson—were cast aside uncharitably by a race of enterprising men who had discovered, so they thought, a more effective and rewarding one. In this chapter and several of those that follow a reasonable amount of speculation may be in order, for we are bound to wonder what kind of America would have existed in 1860 if either of the two discarded sets of instructions had held sway, and also what price the nation paid in 1861–1865 and has been paying ever since for its refusal to submit to the political, social, and moral discipline they demanded in vain.

Chapters 9 and 10 attempt to put the American achievement in the perspective of both comparative history and comparative politics by laying out the pluses and minuses of the situation of the young Republic. It was, after all, the conjunction of favorable circumstances such as a common language and unfavorable ones such as the size of the enterprise that made the development of the United States unique and impossible to imitate. If this inspection of the American ambience compels us to re-examine the sorrowful circumstance of Negro slavery, so must it be. We cannot brush aside the harsh truth that the inability of American democracy to bring a peaceful, effective end to the institution of slavery slowed down the course of modernization and almost destroyed the nation. More than that, the insistence of all but a handful of whites, in the North as well as the South, upon treating Negroes as "strangers in the land," men who could never be accepted as first-class, fully participating members of the national community, thwarted some of their highest aspirations, just as it continues to thwart our highest aspirations more than a century later.

The study ends with a chapter on the Civil War, an ordeal of nationhood and a crisis of modernity toward which, alas, the Quest seems to have been leading inexorably for two or three or even more of these seven decades. So closely related were the ordeal and the crisis as the critical components of our first and still most dreadful national calamity that I feel no qualms about putting this whole matter in the form of an uncompromising message to all students of American history: Those who do not grasp the meaning of the war as such an ordeal cannot hope to measure the pace of development in the 1840's and 1850's; those who have not taken the trouble to measure the pace cannot hope to grasp the full meaning of the war, or perhaps, as more than one respected historian has confessed, to find any meaning in it at all.

This study bears witness to a firm belief that the Civil War had more than its share of meaning. It was the kind of war that had to be fought, the kind, moreover, that had to be fought until one side or the other could claim a clear-cut victory. There is almost a surfeit of thought in the vexing truth that the intensity of the American Quest for nationhood and modernity had rendered irrepressible in 1860—indeed, as early as 1830, some historians would argue—a conflict that might have been forestalled by large-minded compromise in 1787, 1808, or 1820.

This introductory chapter should not end without a guileless confession on my own part of mixed feelings about both nationalism as a spirit and modernity as a way of life. The former is a two-edged sword available to liberators and tyrants alike. To vary the metaphor but not change the meaning, it is a fire that can warm if kept under the control of civility, a fire that will devour if allowed to rage out of such control. The latter, as the pages that follow should make clear, is a condition at which the luckiest nation arrives only at the price of dislocation and disorder, and in which the most disciplined nation finds itself beset by a new range of problems (including the problems of overdevelopment or overmodernity) that it must solve boldly or pay for wastefully in the coin of violence, corruption, boredom, and despair. Men more sanguine than Matthew Arnold have wondered aloud about "this strange disease of modern life." [12]

Yet deplore as we may the excesses of both the spirit of nationalism and the longing for modernity, we cannot pretend that they do not exist or deny their contributions to human progress. Men insist upon organizing themselves into nations, and even those who still dream of larger and more peaceful communities recognize that they will have to be constructed slowly out of the building blocks of nations. Men insist, Rimbaud wrote sorrowfully, upon being "absolutely modern," [13] upon having, Mark Twain wrote acidly, "all the modern inconveniences"; [14] and even those who prefer to get along without television and an automobile recognize that hot water, electricity, sewage disposal, fertilizer, and penicillin have something to be said for them.

In any case, both the spirit and the longing are no different from all sorts of emotions and ideas that can be driven beyond the bounds of reason and turned into ugly caricatures, and we must be careful not to damn them out of hand because of the excesses they have spawned. We do not deplore righteousness because some people are self-righteous, morality because some are prigs, frugality because some are misers, piety because some are zealots, loyalty to a principle because some are dogmatists, love because some are consumed by lust. So must we not tar patriotism with the brush of arrogant chauvinism or the commitment to progress with the brush of mindless avarice. If patriotism and the commitment to progress are, in some historically endemic sense, socially and psychologically unhealthy sentiments, then no one should waste much time studying a period of American history in which they held sway over the minds of men great and small. I hope to make clear in the pages to come that a man who works hard at thinking his way back into this period does not waste his time but, to the contrary, spends it well. The Quest was an epic in the history of mankind; like all epics it invites the kind of painstaking, fair-minded attention that leads to a deeper understanding of both the possibilities and the predicaments, both the opportunities and the ambiguities, of the human condition.

I

A Theory of
National Development

2

The Goals of Nationhood

"Qu'est-ce qu'une nation?"—"What is a nation?"—Ernest Renan, in a transport of patriotic eloquence, asked a transfixed audience at the Sorbonne in 1882.[1] The mystical rhetoric of his own answer brought solace to troubled Frenchmen called upon to accept, temporarily, they hoped, the loss of Alsace and Lorraine; it brought no relief to bemused historians and confused political scientists called upon to wrestle, endlessly, it would seem, with a problem in which they already shared, and will doubtless share so long as they exist, a lively interest.

The question lives on to bemuse and confuse because, as Renan himself was aware in those rare moments when he permitted cool reflection to get the upper hand of deep conviction, the nation is a phenomenon of which every concrete example is special in comparison with all other examples, and also in comparison with itself at different stages of development. Every nation worthy of scholarly attention is, moreover, an immensely complicated aggregate of persons, parcels of land, institutions, laws, economic and social arrangements, patterns of behavior, customs, rituals, treasures, traditions, ideas, memories, myths, and hopes. Most elements in the aggregate are so replete with dimensions yet so resistant to measurement that students of the phenomenon, even the most anxious to be systematic and unsentimental in their search for understanding, find themselves disagreeing fundamentally over the simplest definitions.

Since it would serve no useful purpose to add one more shovelful of slag to the gigantic pile of definitions of nationhood and nationalism,[2] I prefer to answer Renan's question by pointing to one concrete example in each of three widely separated parts of the world. Surely one need not play more than a few minutes with such criteria as language, territory, history, political authority, and ethnic composition to recognize that France, Japan, and Chile are genuine nations. Each meets the standard tests of nationhood with room to spare; each is a community of persons who, except for a small and politically manageable percentage of eccentrics or outcasts or disaffected aspirants to special consideration, think they form a nation, most with satisfaction and many with pride; each is considered to be a nation and is dealt with as a nation by other nations and combinations of nations. If we go on to meditate about such pairings as the Soviet Union and Malta, Britain and Lesotho, Sweden and the Arab world, the Netherlands and Haiti, Switzerland and Germany, and Guyana and India, we should have little trouble understanding that the nation is like any other kind of human organization; it can be gigantic or tiny,* old or new, neat or formless, healthy or sick, united by choice or divided by chance, straining for life or fearful of death. And if our thoughts can be extended to take in such groups as the Boers of 1902, the Czechs of 1914, the Quebec separatists and Palestinian Arabs of today, and the Basques and Welsh since time out of mind, we may grasp the important truth that some nations are hardly more than images in the minds of men—in a few cases the schemes of dogged men as likely as not to succeed, in most cases the fantasies of angry or misguided men doomed to fail.

This rehearsal of the varieties of nationhood may lead us to consider one of the most interesting aspects of the phenomenon: *the nation not as it is but what men are making of it, not as a static entity but as a more or less dynamic process, not as being but as becoming.* One of the few characteristics that nations of every description in the twentieth century have in common is *change:* They are all in passage, in fact or fancy, from old to new patterns of community and from old to new ways of life. They move at different speeds, are spurred by different compulsions, and taste success or failure in vastly different portions, but they all move (or pretend to move) and are all headed (or claim to be headed) in one direction. Indeed, for several hundred years

---

* It can be so tiny, indeed, as in the venerable instance of Andorra or the fresh one of Nauru, that it constitutes a mini-nation or, in U Thant's more cautious language, a micro-state.

the nations and would-be nations of the world have had very similar collective goals. One way to know whether a region or tribe or traditional society or former colony has become or is on the road to becoming a full-fledged nation is to appraise its success in reaching these goals. The fact of ceaseless change within the boundaries of every nation, however slow and too often confined to peripheral matters, is the principal reason why no serious student of this phenomenon can permit himself to be casually unhistorical or truculently antihistorical.

If every nation is special and, at the same time, all are moving or want to get moving in the same direction, we have some reason to make comparisons among them. Working with bunches of comparisons we may occasionally produce a generalization. The brave generalization, however conjectural, is one of the handiest tools available to men who want to study the performance of particular nations in particular periods. The performance of the United States in the first stage of independent existence is the specific subject of this study; and, if we are to assess it at all accurately and usefully, we must have in our possession a general "model" (a word henceforth to be used without those somewhat skeptical quotation marks) of national development.

The model I propose for our purpose is simple to the point of austerity, because the use of complicated analyses, indices, and designs, all of them verbalized—I mean no disrespect—in Parsonian or Deutschian or Eastonian terminology, often makes more rather than less difficult the achievement of the kind of broad-gauged understanding of national development for which we should be seeking.* Karl Deutsch himself has written that "no

* To those social scientists who have stumbled, been lured, been ordered, or rushed joyfully across the shot-torn field from behavioralism-the-useful-observation-post to behavioralism-the-bristling-fortress I recommend an open-minded reading of chapters 3 and 4 of Barrington Moore, Jr.'s message in *Political Power and Social Theory*. Behavioral science, whether the behavioral science of comparative politics or of quantitative history, must be modest, cautious, conscious of limits, respectful of other attitudes and approaches in disciplines whose paramount strength lies in diversity, wary of the temptation to imitate the natural sciences, and realistic about the prospects of discovering "laws" as certain as those of Newton, Mendel, or Darwin (how certain are some of them any longer?). Above all it must recognize that politics is often unpredictable and history often inexplicable, that the hardest questions to answer conclusively are the biggest ones, and that the real world of human behavior defies most attempts at quantification. New words and phrases do

terminology should try to be more accurate than life." [4] I agree without reservation, and therefore seek to bring meaningful order out of apparent chaos by shunning presumptuous words and labored concepts. The theory of national development expressed in this model (to be precise, in this pair of models) is more logical and taxonomic than the incongruous phenomenon it seeks to encompass. That, however, is the way of theory—and where would we all be without it? Both theory and models focus on only one of several dozen aspects of the phenomenon of modern nationhood: *the setting and achieving of collective goals.* Since this is the aspect most likely to persuade us to think of nations of diverse sizes, origins, conditions, and prospects as communities of men who share an experience with all other men, there is no need to worry our heads about thus singling it out.

This theory of national development is composed of a series of generalized abstractions that took shape slowly in the course of an examination, intense in some instances while necessarily only transient in others, of four categories of social and historical reality:

old developed nations like England and France;

more recently developed nations like Turkey and Japan;

emerging would-be nations like India and Indonesia;

and, lest we overlook the historical dimension, all nations in the world at various meaningful checkpoints of development, like Britain in 1763, France in 1848, Canada in 1867, or—the case on which we concentrate—the United States in both 1790 and 1860.

By seeking out information in charters, laws, reports, documents, tables of statistics, newspapers, articles, and monographs, and also by probing for more than a decade into the aspirations of living men all over the world, I have been encouraged to think of these reality-based, reality-oriented abstractions—the goals of nationhood and thus, by historical necessity, the goals of modernity—as an experience shared in fact or desire by all but a few

---

not necessarily create new knowledge; the system of theory may distort the order (or disorder) of reality; the modest norm is still as powerful as the boastful number. In short, let behavioralism be a helpful servant but not a jealous tyrant; let us resolve to use it sensibly but not surrender to it abjectly.[3]

handfuls of men in the world today as well as by hundreds of millions of men who have lived since the opening phase of the transformation of feudal Britain and feudal France into the first modern nations. Whether one approaches the French mercantilists of the seventeenth century or the British manufacturers and squires of the eighteenth century or the American delegates to the Convention of 1787 in imagination, or whether one approaches university students in Santiago or civil servants in Accra or army officers in New Delhi in reality, one hears talk, usually very serious talk, of the hopes and strategies of national development.

The goals toward which all hopes and strategies point can be reduced without too much distortion of the confused realities of human existence to a comprehensible eight. Four are primarily goals of nationhood: *independence, territorial integrity, popular cohesion,* and *self-identity,* and to these the remainder of this chapter is devoted. The other four are primarily goals of modernity: *political efficacy, economic viability, social integration,* and *cultural maturity,* and these are discussed in the next chapter. While I have divided them somewhat arbitrarily into two sets in order to make clear that nationhood and modernity can be studied separately, let us again recognize that these phenomena are historically and functionally related. Indeed, so close has been their connection in the past several hundred years, and so close will it probably remain in the next several hundred, that they form, as it were, two sides of one coin.

The goals of national development are, let me repeat, not merely comprehensible, but also common: the publicly proclaimed targets of the vast majority of political communities and the privately recognized aspirations of the vast majority of politically conscious persons in the world today. If enough men in a community hope and work for these eight goals, it is on its way to nationhood and modernity. If enough men have hoped and worked for them with visible success over a long period of time, the community has become a modern nation.

A few moments spent in candid observation of the successful examples of the pursuit of modern nationhood should be enough to remind us that these goals are never fully achieved in the world of reality, that a nation can slide backward as well as toil

27

upward, and that achievement of one or all of the goals opens up a new range of problems of nation-preserving and life-improving for the heirs of those who played the great game of national development so successfully. There never has been such a thing as a perfect nation, a community that has come as close as any organization of human beings can be expected to come to matching the standards of this or any other model of modern nationhood. While the standards of these chapters may be based on real victories in the past and oriented to real hopes for the future, they are framed—let this point be noted carefully —as ideals; and the essence of an ideal, if I am not mistaken, is that it can be honored but never attained. Even if a perfect nation were to arise and flourish, the relentless compulsion of change would soon begin to alter its aspect, precipitate its decay, or transform it into some other kind of community. To the pursuit of the goals of nationhood, and also to those of modernity, there seems to be no end in sight. While the goals, so we read in the records of history and the intentions of men, are apparently to be pursued as a kind of moral duty from which few living persons may claim total exemption, they promise far more delicious prizes than they can possibly bestow.

The first goal of nationhood, not always in point of time but always in the catalogue of desire, is *independence.* The winning of independence solves few problems for a community, indeed may set back development by breeding an abundance of new problems with which it is quite unprepared to cope unassisted; yet exactly because we live in a world of nations, independence is the necessary beginning for a group of men determined to move vigorously toward the other goals. Sooner or later such men must feel that, to the extent their destiny can be controlled, they and not the leaders of some empire or great power or overbearing neighbor or alliance or company are doing the controlling; sooner or later, moreover, they must heed the wise counsel of George Washington that "the nation which indulges toward another . . . an habitual fondness"—or, for that matter, "an habitual hatred"—is "in some degree a slave." [5] The risks of a premature lunge into independence are admittedly high, yet the time has long since passed, in the Communist world just as surely as in the former colonies of the West, when one community with memories or premonitions of nationhood could be expected to go on forever in a state of dependence upon another.

This primary goal of nationhood can be divided, on historical as well as functional grounds, into three principal categories. The first is as appealing to Kenya and Singapore today as it was to the American states in the Revolution and the Confederacy in the Civil War: *political* independence. To be independent in this sense a community need not withdraw into a shell of defiant isolation, which is no longer possible, or go on a rampage of arrogant aggression, which is no longer tolerable. It must seek, rather, to establish a situation in which the holders of power have the kind of control over the processes of decision, policy, and administration that brooks no interference from any external authority, be it a nation or combination of nations, a cartel or corporation, a revolutionary apparatus or counterrevolutionary conspiracy of interests. The government of an independent nation is not in the habit of looking for orders beyond the boundaries of its sovereign reach; it is responsible for particular decisions and over-all performance only to the citizens of the nation, however they may be organized to pass judgment; it cannot be coerced against its will except in the wake of crushing defeat in a war—and then, very probably, at the price of any claim to legitimacy. One kind of political decision an independent government can make in these days of increasing co-operation among nations (for both good ends and bad) is to accept assistance from other governments, yet such a decision need involve no reduction in freedom of action so long as its leaders have consulted the national interest and have decided for themselves to what extent and on what terms assistance will be accepted.

Many nations have found it far more difficult a task to gain and then maintain *economic* than political independence. This is true not simply because every nation, however rich and developed, is a member of the international economy, and is thus dependent to some degree on the decisions of leaders in other nations. It is, rather, because the world has been a long time learning how rich nations can help poor nations without reaping too large a profit or wielding too much power over them. To take an interesting case in point,[6] Chile won its war of political

29

liberation from Spain in 1818, and ever since has been celebrated as a nation that can be neither persuaded nor bullied against its will. On the other hand, Chile is still struggling to emerge from the status of an economic colony of the United States and Europe into which it was swept, with few protests and not entirely without reward, by the inward rush of foreign capital and technology in the late nineteenth and early twentieth centuries. While the policy known as Chileanization may visit hardship temporarily upon the nation, most Chileans consider this a price worth paying for economic independence. The economics of nationhood, I have heard several of them argue with conviction, has an important psychological as well as moral content. Profitability is good but ownership is better, and who, for that matter, can be sure that profitability will not increase over the long run when the nation, be it socialist or capitalist or pragmatically hybrid, owns and thus controls its own economy?

In modern times the flow of capital from nation to nation has built up such a head of pressure that even so developed and self-directing a country as Canada or Australia must be extremely careful not to let control of its economic, social, and political destiny slip into the hands of men who, however respectful their intentions and scrupulous their behavior, are not citizens of Canada or Australia. While it may be suicidal for a poor nation like Ghana or Guinea not to accept foreign investment and instruction on a large scale, the terms of any acceptance should leave no doubt of the nation's determination over the long run to press for home ownership of resources and means of production, and also to maintain freedom of political decision at every stage of development. Several eminent Americans of the founding generation have been credited with the remark that those who "own the country ought to govern it." Perhaps the time has come for the rich nations of the world to tack on the words "and vice versa," then add this two-part slogan to the small but precious store of wisdom of international politics. A country whose economy is largely owned and controlled from abroad is grievously defective in a principal mark of nationhood. The long continuance of such a state of affairs is a standing invitation to political meddling, and that, as the most conspicuous targets of meddling all over the world can testify, has a built-in urge to escalate into political dictation.

We come, finally, to the tricky question of *cultural* independence. To be a full-fledged nation a country must have a culture that it can call its own; yet most nations of the world are branches or subdivisions of an older, more extensive, more prestigious community of language, ideas, customs, talents, religious beliefs, and life styles. Even if one of them were to choose the cultivation of intellectual and artistic excellence as the primary national activity, it could never hope to accumulate a storehouse of good taste full of poems, paintings, plays, symphonies, and architectural triumphs one-tenth as splendid as that of the larger culture. More to the point, no country, except perhaps the new China (and the new South Africa?), would want or be able to wall itself off against the flow of ideas among national and supranational cultures that the revolution in communication has turned into a torrent. Every country, however, will move closer to full nationhood if it can create a special version of the larger culture, make contributions of everything from new words to new forms of art, and guard its way of life against the debasing influence of cheap tastes and fashions that intrude from abroad. No nation can escape from its cultural past, as that amazing nation-within-a-nation, the Russian people, learned to the dismay of dogmatic revolutionaries in the 1920's and to the delight of everyone from Stalin on down to the lowliest peasant in World War II. Some nations are obviously in a less favorable position than others to achieve this special kind of independence, seem destined by size or chronology or geography to be targets rather than sources of intellectual and artistic influence, and must make an extra effort (which is never extra enough for their superpatriots) to cut down the flow of culture, whether tasteful or degraded, from a smothering neighbor. One thinks in particular of Canada up against the United States, Belgium up against France, and Switzerland up against all the richly endowed nations that surround it.

The mention of Canada, Belgium, and Switzerland raises the interesting problem of language, which has been known both to build and to destroy nations almost singlehandedly. Since linguistic community is a tie that binds men together, and is often the only way that an ingroup can distinguish itself from other groups around or amidst it, the ideal solution to this problem would seem to be for all the citizens of a nation to speak the same language and to have the satisfaction of knowing that it is spoken nowhere else in the world. The circumstances of nationhood, like those of manhood, are never ideal, however, and a nation like Switzerland is simply required to work harder than a nation like Japan to dampen the potentially divisive conflicts of language as well as to guard against drifting into the easy orbit of the cultural satellite, in the case of Switzerland three orbits. In spite of the presence of dogged Basques and fanatical Bretons in its midst, France is clearly a more perfect nation than Switzerland in terms of cultural independence and also unity, yet it cannot be denied that a Swiss nation endures—and, more than incidentally, is less likely than France to be ravaged by civil war.

Independence is a condition that is never fully realized, and even those nations that have experienced it in the highest degree may find themselves growing more dependent on other nations for one of two reasons. The first is largely involuntary and more often than not lamentable: a process of backsliding, especially in the economic and cultural spheres. Canada, once again, comes immediately to mind as an example of the nation that needs to erect special defenses against eager money and titillating magazines that threaten to sweep in too fast for it to absorb on a selective basis while preserving all that is best in its own way of life. The other is largely voluntary and more often than not commendable: a process of piecemeal surrender of sovereignty, especially in the economic sphere, to supranational communities designed to pool resources and reach co-operative decisions. A nation that enters into a military alliance takes another kind of step that may lead to a reduction in independence. So mixed is the record of the military alliance as an influence upon the quality of nations large and small, however, that no conclusive and useful generalization can be made about it.

To turn aside for a few remarks of general relevance, independence is also a condition that is hard to contemplate objectively and impossible to measure precisely. The special character of all nations, the fluctuations in their circumstances, the difficulty of establishing indices of independence and dependence, the further difficulty of digging up and arranging reliable statistics, and the largely and understandably normative tone of the debate over the value of independence are some of the discouraging obstacles in the path of the social scientist who would like to be more scientific in dealing with this critical aspect of nationhood. He can work at the "macro" level in a systematic manner by describing and evaluating the steps in an instance of effective control by one country of a major decision in another, but what lesson will he then be able to announce that has universal validity? He can work at the "micro" level in a quantifying manner by making a content analysis, let us say, of a sample of Canadian editorials in the past decade for words and ideas of clearly American origin, but what conclusion will he then draw that is broad, solid, and persuasive enough to justify all those man-hours spent on the computer? Even a hundred systematic descriptions or a hundred quantitative analyses of editorials will not take him far in the direction of the kind of science that deals with significant phenomena and makes reliable predictions. The way of the social scientist and of his quantifying, system-building cousin in history is never harder than when he turns to grapple with a many-sided problem like the extent and consequences of independence in a country such as Brazil or Algeria or Cyprus. Here is one area in which, I predict with no sense of daring, most things that really matter will never be measured except crudely, and may never even be covered under the terms of a generally accepted theory. We must continue to probe the phenomenon of national independence with tools that are something less than scientific; we must do it modestly, tentatively, and with a feeling, respectful yet not despairing, for the limitations under which we all work.

The second goal is *territorial integrity*. Every nation is "rooted" in fact or hope, Frederick Hertz asserted in behalf of scores of other students of the phenomenon, in a "homeland" that is "an integral part of its whole existence." [7] Every nation has therefore had to face, at one or more times in its history, the problem of boundaries: to decide what pieces of land (and, rather more difficult to handle, what people living in disputed pieces) to incorporate by conquest, negotiation, purchase, absorption, or migration, or otherwise to leave outside to become parts, however unwilling, of another nation. The problem is the kind that is "buried finally" by one self-congratulating generation and then rises from the grave to torment the next. Those leaders of the emerging nations who are trying to stabilize or redraw boundaries marked out long ago in the chanceries of Europe with scant regard for the distribution of tribes and entire peoples may gain comfort from the knowledge that Europe, too, has boundaries not as stable as they might be.

The ideal solution in this instance would be a large island inhabited by people who speak one language and have one way of life, and who look out over the water to find no other communities that speak their language or pursue their way of life. The ideal, once again, is no more than an ideal. Even the advanced nation known variously as Britain, Great Britain, England, or the United Kingdom has never been able to digest sizable numbers of Scots and Welshmen (who are becoming, in fact, steadily less digestible), finds its cities filling up with strange-sounding newcomers from Dublin and Karachi, aims the telescope of myth and emotion at Vancouver or Wellington or the Falkland Islands and salutes the denizens of those distant places as "brothers in the British nation," and draws a line between itself and Eire that is a good deal less likely to endure than the line between the United States and Mexico.

The best that any nation can hope for is a set of boundaries that are geographically sensible, politically stable, diplomatically viable, militarily defensible (or at least not completely indefensible), and demographically both inclusive and exclusive. While natural boundaries such as a channel or a great river or a mountain range are doubtless the easiest to justify in law and maintain in life, this whole area is one in which the accidents and incidents of history play a commanding role. Nothing could be less natural than the Forty-ninth Parallel between the United States and Canada, yet the passage of time has converted a boundary largely artificial into one overwhelmingly legitimate. Some men, of course, refuse to permit the passage of time to solve this problem of boundaries. In the minds of Theodor Herzl and his colleagues in Zionism, the eleven or more centuries before A.D. 70 gave Jews an undoubted moral and legal right to create a sovereign nation in a land where no Jews had governed and only a scatter had lived furtively for the next eighteen centuries. While the nation of Israel has been created and then saved three times from sudden death, no arrangement of its boundaries, whether of 1947, 1948, 1949, 1956, or 1967, is recognized by the enemies that surround it. To live indefinitely in such a situation is to live with tensions that bring out both the best and the worst in the character of a nation.

Territorial integrity has *internal* as well as *external* dimensions. Even if all neighbors respect the boundaries of a nation, even if it is so homogeneous as to enjoy immunity from conflicts of race, language, religion, ideology, culture, class, and ethnic origin, one can be certain, assuming it to be modest in size, that it will be plagued from time to time by regional tensions. If a nation is large in size, and if the apparently universal suspicion of central political authority takes hold, it may find itself weakened by regional disaffection or even threatened with dismemberment. While diversity of regions gives added interest to a nation, and while a shrewd decentralization of authority may lead to government at once more respectful of the liberties of the people and more efficient in performance, the centralized or consolidated nation is generally more capable of commanding political allegiance than the federal or confederated one. Some countries, of course, have been left no choice by geography or history except to seek national unity by making a virtue of regional diversity. Never, on the other hand, can they let the play of diversity get out of hand. A final stability of boundaries against all neighbors and a final unity of authority in matters of common concern against all regions are twin goals of every self-respecting nation. The fact that some countries have paid for external stability in the coin of conquest and for internal unity in the coin of coercion reminds us again that the phenomenon of nationhood can wear many different faces.

Intimately related to territorial integrity is the perplexing goal of *popular cohesion*. I choose this phrase in order to indicate that, in addition to the burdens imposed by diversities of class and region, most nations are faced with the problem of incorporating sizable groups of cultural, linguistic, religious, or ethnic outsiders —minorities, tribes, lowly castes, ethnic relics, clusters of immigrants—in the main body of the people. The problem lies both with the main body, which must learn that it constitutes something less than a full-fledged nation so long as entire descriptions of human beings live inside its geographic boundaries but outside the civic community, and with each group, which, if it truly wishes to be incorporated, must not only adopt new ways of living and thinking but also promise loyalty to a community that may have mistreated it shamefully since time out of mind. Yet sooner or later, if the quest for both nationhood and modernity is seriously under way in a country most persons who dwell in it as members of a minority have to develop a genuine sense of belonging, and most persons who hold sway in it as the majority have to look upon them as participating fellow citizens. I say "most" rather than "all" because every nation of historical consequence and moral stature has tried its best to adjust laws, attitudes, and customs to the existence of small, obdurate groups of come-outers like the true Gypsies of Britain and the hard-line Amish of the United States.

Every nation conscious of the problem pursues the goal of popular cohesion in a way which is necessarily different from that of any other nation. For some nations the problem is the fairly simple one of absorbing a flow of immigrants who, however outlandish they may appear upon arrival, are of the same race as the native-born citizenry and are ready (and if they are not ready, their children will be) to generate new loyalties: Argentina and its Italians, Australia and its Slavs, Canada and its swarms of East Europeans. For others it is the stickier problem of accepting minorities whose ancestors may have arrived fifty or a hundred or even more years ago yet are of a different race, have different religious and secular values, have chosen or been forced to be clannish, have chosen or been forced to cherish the old country a little too fondly, and, in some notable instances, have been too successful for their own good: the nations of Southeast Asia and their Chinese, the nations of East Africa and their Indians, Kenya and its white settlers. In almost all the new countries created by mass immigration from the old countries of Europe, native populations have been conquered, shoved aside, decimated, or simply ignored by the more numerous and "civilized" newcomers: the aborigines of Australia, the Araucanians of Chile, the Indian tribes of North America, the primitive peoples of the Amazon. And in a few of the new nations—one really has good reason to describe them as "would-be nations"—the problem is simply the nonexistence of a main body around which other racial, religious, or tribal groups can be arranged in various states of absorption, respect, tolerance, or adjustment: Nigeria, the former Belgian Congo, Guyana. The varieties are endless: Japan and its Eta, an unloved, uncounted, and almost unacknowledged minority of 2 to 3 million persons, as well as its 20,000 or so Ainoko, the beleaguered offspring of American servicemen and Japanese women; Britain and its West Indians, Pakistani, and other men of color from the Commonwealth; France and its own men of color from a range of ex-colonies stretching from Senegal to Vietnam; the bewildering kaleidoscope of the countries of Southeast Asia; and, of course, the United States and its Negroes and Indians, not to overlook its still not quite first-class citizens of Japanese, Chinese, and Mexican descent. When one goes on to think of Switzerland, Canada, Lebanon, Jamaica, Iraq, Iran, Belgium, the Soviet Union, India, South Africa, Yugoslavia, Cyprus, Fiji, Israel, a dozen countries of Central and South America, and two dozen of black Africa, one begins to wonder if cohesion is an attainable or even desirable goal.

Attainable, no—certainly not in the case of dozens of communities that enjoy the legal status of nationhood, including active membership in the United Nations. The world is too full of tribes that straddle both sides of a national boundary, of men who have migrated from one continent to another with no intention of requesting or hope of receiving a full welcome, of cultural minorities that have lived for centuries within the boundaries of a nation yet feel no twinge of national loyalty, and of racial minorities that are consigned indefinitely to second-class citizenship by prejudice, tradition, self-pity, cultural disparity, or lack of empathy and imagination on the part of first-class citizens. While Switzerland, Canada, Lebanon, and Fiji are examples of how some degree of popular cohesion can be achieved in the face of apparently insurmountable obstacles, Nigeria and India seem destined to make ever more clear that membership in the United

Nations and the will-to-nationhood of an elite are not enough to do the job. If they and any other emerging nations finally do fall apart, or simply stumble along as legally recognized but not politically or socially functional entities, the chief source of their troubles will have been the failure to manage an exaggerated problem of popular cohesion.

Desirable, yes—certainly in the case of every community in quest of nationhood and modernity. Popular cohesion is desirable on practical grounds because the tensions of diversity, if they are not contained, can lead to alienation, mistrust, disorder, violence, repression, and crippling diversion of political and emotional energy, and, beyond all these social troubles, to dissolution or civil war. It is desirable on moral grounds because these tensions, even when they are contained, breed arrogance or indifference in the majority and shame or fear in the minority. The people of a would-be nation that is racked by jealousies among tribes or sects, or among groups fiercely attached to different cultures or ideologies or languages, will never get far on the road to modernity. The people of an established nation that treats one or another minority as hopelessly inferior will sooner or later suffer a loss of civility in its own soul and of prestige in the eyes of the world, and might find itself facing nasty problems of disaffection and insurrection.

This has not been an argument for popular cohesion as an end in itself but as a means to the two ends of nationhood and modernity. It has not been advocacy, even if such a course were feasible, of any process of total absorption or synthesis that produces a homogeneous people. It has been, rather, a statement of historical and sociological fact: The more homogeneous the people of a sovereign community may be in terms of origin, life style, language, political values, and religion, the more easily can it attain and thereafter maintain the status of nationhood as well as the condition of modernity. Since most nations are something less than homogeneous, the search for popular cohesion must be directed toward the more limited ends of toleration, respect, and acceptance of diversity, and be pressed through law, justice, education, and, if necessary, subsidy. In the good nation the symbols and substance of first-class citizenship are the rightful patrimony of all inhabitants; to the good nation all but the most stubborn or eccentric inhabitants pledge the kind of allegiance that first-class citizenship generates.

Independence, territorial integrity, and popular cohesion are the principal ingredients of nationhood. They are not enough in themselves, however, to bring a nation to life and then help it to endure. The members of a sovereign community that enjoys these blessings must also engage in a continuing process of *self-identity:* To *be* a nation they must *think* they are a nation. They must think so in the beginning stage by passing successfully through a kind of Eriksonian crisis of self-identification as a nation; they must continue to think so lest they lose sight of their identity. And for both the discovery and the rediscovery of the fact of their nationhood these men will sooner or later find it essential to construct a large apparatus of myth, symbol, slogan, and ceremony. Once constructed, of course, it must be shored up repeatedly. No one can study the history of nations large or small, old or new, quiescent or aggressive, emerging or stillborn, vibrant or despairing, self-confident or self-deceiving, mature or strangled in the cradle, without recognizing this as an area of human experience in which ideas are as powerful as facts, indeed in which the idea of some persons that they formed a nation has been known more than once to defy, ignore, or transform the facts. We need not go all the way with Renan's definition of a nation as "a soul, a spiritual principal" in order to concede that he was right to insist upon the importance of the idea of patriotism in building and preserving the most successful nations in history.

While nationalism has proved on occasion to be so powerful a sentiment in the minds of dedicated men that apparently established facts were transformed into their opposites—division into cohesion, defeat into victory, apathy into zeal, poverty into prosperity—it usually bows to reality, even as it helps to shape reality, and flourishes most hardily as an authentic reflection of the eager, uncoerced loyalty of large numbers of men to a political and social community that deserves such loyalty. A nationalism that cannot be related to a zestfully emerging or doggedly established nation is likely to be nothing better than a shrill, intoxicating ideology. In some instances in history a people has found a new, more fitting identity before it could win the status of nationhood.

In others the sequence has been reversed: Only upon winning the status did a people realize that it had become a nation. Whichever has priority in the development of any particular community, however, the idea of nationalism and the reality of nationhood will eventually interact to keep one another in good health.

Nationalism, let us never forget, is potentially a dangerous human sentiment, and the men of every nation must work hard to keep their sense of identity under tight rein if they are to enjoy it as a blessing and not lament it as a curse. When it encourages them to fight for independence long overdue or to sacrifice in the present in order to build a good society in the future, nationalism wears an aspect of benevolence. When it blinds them to reality, as too many in ill-formed Indonesia were blinded by Sukarno's acronymic oratory, or goads them into aggression and cruelty, as too many in highly developed Germany were goaded by Hitler's rantings about Teutonic superiority, it wears an aspect so malevolent that some persons of good will have forsworn it forever. Yet most men, I repeat, insist upon organizing themselves into nations, and for that task they need to draw deeply upon the spirit of nationalism. The business of the student of nationalism is not to deplore but to understand the power of this spirit, and to search for ways to keep it from raging out of control.

How does the process of self-identification take place? What persuades an aggregation of men to think of themselves as a nation? Language, religion, territory, political skill, and economic necessity can all help a nation first come into being and thereafter endure. So much has been written about these forces, however, that I propose to place emphasis on several other less tangible yet no less influential elements which have been known to contribute to the rise of self-conscious nationalism.

The first is *history,* which takes the form of a widespread sense of shared experiences. In Renan's words, "the possession in common of a rich legacy of remembrances" is an enduring element of every instance of healthy nationalism. The founding generation of a nation must usually be content with "instant history," which it learns to believe in more easily—an interesting trait common to founding generations—by talking bravely about a glorious future. The generations that follow draw strength and comfort from celebrating the achievements of the founders and add their own experiences to the treasury of memory and tradition. One need think only of the history of Britain to recognize that a "rich legacy of remembrances" of earth-shaking events, myth-encrusted documents, and heroic men can contribute powerfully to the awareness of nationhood. The sometimes touching, sometimes bizarre efforts of the leaders of many would-be nations of Africa and Asia to re-create a past that never was offer convincing testimony of the significance of history in the process of nation-building; the sometimes ridiculous efforts of Americans and Europeans to dress up their own pasts demonstrate that it also has a role to play in the process of nation-preserving. While some nations are notorious for clinging to the realities or legends of their yesterdays, whether as a way of rationalizing a sordid present or refusing to think about an uncertain future, most seem to understand that, while they cannot live without history, they must not live too much in it. Neither the heroic parts of the history of Spain nor the trumped-up parts of the history of Ghana nor the borrowed parts of the history of Indonesia contribute substantially to unity or progress in those countries.

A second element of nationalism is *interest,* which may be defined as the assumption of most citizens of a nation that they have gained and will continue to gain substantial benefits, both material and psychological, from membership in it. They have come to believe that many of their vital interests as persons are linked with the purposes of the nation as a community; they show the nation the gratitude it deserves, sometimes far more than it deserves, by being proud of its past, loyal to its traditions, and obedient to its commands. Renan was one of the first students of nationalism to put his finger on interest, and it is instructive to note that, having asserted that interest disposes right-thinking men to live, work, and perhaps "sacrifice" together, he tied in this element with history as a major support of nationalism.

To have common glories in the past, a common will in the present; to have accomplished great things together, to wish to do so again, that is the essential condition for being a nation.[8]

Another critical element is *consensus,* especially the kind that wells up freely from below rather than the kind that is imposed coercively from above. Surely it cannot be denied that a nation is more perfect, and thus more satisfying a community to live in, if most citizens are in broad agreement on basic values, institutions, and purposes, and less perfect, and thus less likely to command uncoerced obedience, if it is ravaged by conflicts of opinion over such issues as the relation between church and state, the ownership of property, the distribution of political power, the organization of the economy, or the role of the family. France and Switzerland are perhaps the most persuasive pair of examples of the importance of consensus in making and preserving nations. Only the lack of a broad consensus on political and social issues prevents France from being in fact what it was in General De Gaulle's fancy: just about the most perfect nation in history. Only the presence of such a consensus, spawned by history and nursed by interest, brings Switzerland into the select circle of the successful nations of the world. Patriotism is a sentiment that may be cultivated almost effortlessly in a nation whose citizens are for the most part content in both the material and the psychological senses with the system under which they live, and who thus are deaf to appeals for acts of either revolutionary or reactionary disaffection. In a nation divided by ideology and interest, it must be cultivated intensely; yet that kind of patriotism, the world knows to its regret, has a way of turning into chauvinism and then running amuck.

The Swiss experience is proof of a somewhat distasteful yet undeniable truth: There is nothing like an enemy, or simply a neighbor seen as unpleasantly different in political values and social arrangements, to speed a nation along the course of self-identification or put it back on course whenever it begins to stray. While reactive nationalism can get out of hand and set an entire people to hating, brooding, and plotting, and while more than one leader in the twentieth century has persuaded his fellow citizens to forget their troubles by teaching them to despise some other (the leader of Nazi Germany discovered that other nation right in the midst of his fellow citizens), it cannot be doubted that the act of *comparison,* whether tolerant or snobbish or downright odious, contributes greatly to the growth and maintenance of national consciousness. If the United States did not exist, Canada might have to invent it; and, to turn from a healthy to a pathological example of self-identification through comparison, Arab nationalism would hardly be the force it is if there were no Israel to hate, no Israeli thrashings to brood over, no ultimate obliteration of Israel to plot.

To history, interest, consensus, and comparison let me add one other element of thriving nationalism: *individualism*. The idea of a functional connection between individualism and nationalism is put forward largely as a suggestion, for it is one of the most beckoning yet still-unexplored areas of human existence in which both the new and old techniques of social science might be employed with great profit. For what it may be worth, my own hypothesis runs as follows: In the most stable, successful, and loyalty-commanding nations, whatever may be their pattern of social organization, the person of the individual is most respected. The search of a country for self-identity is, of course, a search conducted by individuals, some of whom lead, most of whom follow, all but a fraction of whom come in time to feel a sense of both personal and collective worth, a belief in themselves as worthy men and in their nation as a worthy community. The worthy nation invites allegiance; the worthy man, the citizen whose person is respected, rights honored, and needs filled, bestows that allegiance gladly. An exasperated definition of exaggerated nationalism is "pooled self-esteem." [9] We should ignore the exasperation and applaud the definition because it makes the necessary connection between the person as individual and the person as citizen. The achievement of a sense of self-esteem is an act of individualism; the pooling of that esteem with the similar senses of many other men is an act of community. One explanation for the flourishing condition of the nation today is that it pays more attention than any other form of political community to the rights and needs of persons. By teaching its citizens to believe in themselves, the nation teaches them to believe in it; and so by the most solitary and most crowded of roads, through the search of each man alone and of all men together, it attains the goal of self-identity. In the true nation, as that giant figure in the history of nationalism Rousseau pointed out long ago, men are patriots by "inclination, passion, and necessity." [10]

Nationalism reaches its zenith in the concept of *mission*. The belief that God or Providence or Fate has singled out a nation for a destiny higher than its own security and well-being is a striking example of the power of ideas in history. While other kinds of communities—empires, ethnic groups, socioreligious cultures, tribes, dynasties, and, above all, religions—have been united or sustained or driven by a sense of mission, the nation seems to be the most fertile ground in which this idea has flourished.

All self-conscious nations develop a sense of peculiar worth and importance, and thus like to think that success in pursuing their own purposes will bring benefits, just as failure will do harm, to men of other nations, even to men in every part of the world for generations to come. A select few, however, have been especially persuaded by such factors as time, geography, size, success, ideology, and necessity to think and act seriously as nations that have been granted special blessings and are therefore bound by special obligations. England, France, Germany, the old Spain, the new China, the old and new Israel, the Soviet Union, and, we shall learn, the young United States are perhaps the most instructive examples of nations in which a belief in high destiny has been, whether persistently or only discontinuously, a forceful presence in the lives of men great and small.

While the concept of mission is basically an expression of a highly developed sense of nationalism, it must be understood as an idea that ranges far beyond the boundaries of the nation to encompass the whole world. At the same time, it can focus upon a single man and influence his behavior. This powerful phenomenon of nationalism, that is to say, has both an international and an individual dimension. The belief in mission works *up and out* by helping a nation to search for identity, to order relations with neighbors and clients, and to find its proper place in a world of nations. The belief in mission works *down and in* by encouraging each citizen of a nation to find a special meaning in his life, by telling him of one important way in which he and his compatriots are different from citizens of all other nations, and by exhorting him to labor with extra diligence and creativity lest he fail this nation that must not fail the world. The belief, indeed, is a persuasive reminder that we cannot properly define nationalism itself except in terms of the two directions in which it faces.

The idea of mission, like the idea of nationalism it expresses, is another of mankind's mixed blessings. It has been known to raise cities in deserts and make deserts of cities, build cathedrals and burn books, chasten some men and drive others mad, force the pace of progress and freeze entire peoples in their tracks, feed and starve, heal and wound, bring life and spread death. It is, in any case, a phenomenon to be reckoned with so long as the nation endures as the community to which most men pledge their primary political allegiance; and that, one suspects, will be a very long time.

3

The Goals of Modernity

MEN intent on building or preserving a nation in our times need to act imaginatively in the spirit of modernity. If the national structure of independence, territorial integrity, popular cohesion, and self-identity is to be more than a hollow shell of pretension, this spirit should induce them to pursue four additional goals vigorously: political efficacy, economic viability, social integration, and cultural maturity.

These four spacious goals are not inventions and are not a monopoly of modern nations. Communities throughout history—premodern nations, city-states, leagues, empires, large and enterprising tribes—have also yearned for them. They have become the special if not exclusive province of modernity principally because a nation now finds it virtually obligatory to attack them, or pretend to attack them, with the help and in behalf of *the whole people*. Ideology and practical considerations alike call for inclusion of the mass of ordinary men in the process of modernization and the distribution of its fruits. There is a manifestly democratic cast to the definition of national success in each of these areas of hope and endeavor in the twentieth century. Almost every nation and would-be nation in the world has a firm commitment to some kind of democracy in the realms of intention, activity, and results.

Although I speak once again out of necessity in the vocabulary of the ideal, I do this in confidence that my readers will recognize the connection between the ideal of pure theory and the reality of imperfect history, especially in this vital matter of democracy. There are, in any case, enough nations in which most or all of the aspects of modernity we are about to examine have been approximated, if never fully realized, to permit me to describe them in apparently abstract and admittedly ideal terms.

The Goals of Modernity

. . .

No goal of modernity beckons more insistently yet is more difficult for nations of every description to attain than *political efficacy*. This fact is especially true in the twentieth century because an efficacious government is both an end in itself and the chief means for attaining the other ends of economic, social, and cultural development; and, until the end of political efficacy is at least partly achieved, how useful a means can men expect it to be? Leaders of emerging nations proclaim with one voice the need for efficacious government to help them raise the edifice of modernity, yet everywhere they find themselves grappling with problems for the solution of which homemade tools of political management have not been wrought and imported tools will not work. To create a government able to bring the purposes of a nation into focus, identify social needs that may be dealt with on the political level, generate policies that go far to meet these needs, and sustain an administrative effort that converts policy into reality is a staggering task. Once created, moreover, such a government can begin almost immediately to atrophy or decay. The goal of political efficacy, like all the goals of nationhood and modernity, is the kind that a country may reach only to learn that maturity has a way of leading to flabbiness and beyond that to senility.

So dissimilar are the traditions, resources, circumstances, and expectations of the nations of the world that it is next to impossible to generalize in a manner both profitable and convincing about the forms, functions, and techniques of a conspicuously efficacious government. Indeed, one brave or simply foolhardy enough to build a detailed model of such a government would promptly learn to his discomfort that he had revealed more about his assumptions as builder than about the facts of the universal human activity we still call, in homage to Aristotle, politics.* For the purposes of this study it should suffice to set down a short list of the marks or signs of a modern government. Sooner or later, in obedience to the dictates of one philosophy or another, men who respond to the challenge of modernity will construct a polity with

---

* Except on rare occasions, which I signal as clearly as I can, the word "politics" is used in the broad sense throughout this book, and is therefore to be read as a synonym for "the polity," "the political system," and "government."

certain visible and also roughly measurable qualities. These qualities must be substantial projections of accomplishment rather than merely nominal expressions of aspiration. Like the qualities of nationhood, they are most usefully described in ideal terms, yet some nations have gone a surprisingly long way toward transforming these glittering ideals into solid realities.

The first mark is *legitimacy*. No matter whose hands may be temporarily at the controls, the legal and moral validity of the political system itself is acknowledged by an overflowing majority of citizens. They prove the existence of an operative pattern of political socialization by tendering largely uncoerced obedience to the mandates of the system as a matter of habit.[1] In the words of the old phrase, which has never seemed more freshly pertinent than in an age when dozens of governments are struggling to establish or preserve their political authority, "the writ runs" throughout the land: Men vote, pay taxes, perform public duties, and obey laws with no more grumbling than becomes them as men. They may not like, indeed in a healthy polity many of them will not and should not like, the programs and personalities of the governors of the moment. They do not, however, transfer their displeasure with the *men* in power to the *system* of power, which they see as rational, responsible, responsive, functional, enduring, achieving, and, if it has endured long and achieved much, venerable.

The most revealing sign of political legitimacy at the personal level is the capacity of a system to collect taxes, at the national level to effect an orderly transfer of authority, especially under conditions that might tempt men to feel resentful and flirt with thoughts of bypassing normal channels. While the assassination of John F. Kennedy stirred agonizing uncertainties about the character and destiny of the American nation in the minds of all thinking citizens, no uncertainty was voiced or even entertained about the constitutional and moral right of Lyndon B. Johnson to succeed to the vacant Presidency. An event that kindled widespread despair was also, paradoxically, a vivid demonstration of the legitimacy of the polity of a great nation.

The second mark of a modern government is the possession of *sanctions*. The government has an arsenal of effective techniques for securing obedience, whether in the negative sense of being acknowledged by citizens who do not break laws or the positive sense of being assisted by citizens who are interested in making laws work: proclamation, example, persuasion, administrative order, judicial edict, subsidy, informal threat, formal coercion, and, if necessary, military force. The more modern the government, the less it needs to rely on the techniques grouped toward the end of this brief list. A persistent resort to threat, coercion, and outright force, as well as to the kind of subsidy that is no better than bribery, sooner or later begins to erode the foundations of legitimacy. A government that cannot muster the moral, rhetorical, legal, and administrative strength to make its commands operational is the shadow, not the substance, of political modernity.

A political system can hope for neither legitimacy nor strength if it does not display the quality of *representativeness*. It may, of course, represent its constituency, which in a modern nation means the entire citizenry, in many different ways. The common and critical tests are whether the representation is broad rather than narrow, real rather than make-believe, and vital rather than —another old, yet pertinent word—virtual. I agree with Gabriel Almond and James Coleman that every worthwhile system must be able both to "articulate" and to "aggregate" the "interests," "claims," and "demands for political action" which arise in the community,[2] and would add only that the more open, orderly, inclusive, and noncoercive the process of interest-articulation and interest-aggregation can be made, the more fully modern the system becomes. This is why an elected legislature that is not just a pageant, two or more political parties (or one party with two or more wings), organized interest groups not subsidized and controlled by the government, a loyal opposition both in and out of the legislature, judicial guaranties and social supports of freedom of expression, and a bureaucracy both responsive and responsible —the varieties of these phenomena are numerous if not quite infinite—are important and, in the long run, necessary instruments of the modern polity. While the danger of failing to hear the voice of the public interest amid the babble of individual and group interests is always present, the hardest problem facing both long-established and newly created nations is to compensate for the long-standing underrepresentation of citizens who have been taught to expect the sympathetic attention of their governments.

It is not enough for a government to be legitimate, equipped with sanctions, and broadly representative in order to win the obedience and support of modern men. In the twentieth century, whether persons of conservative temper like the fact or not, a political system must also show signs of *activeness.* Drawing upon David Apter's handy distinction between reconciliating and mobilizing forms of government as a point of departure,[3] I suggest that most governments of our time, while they continue to avail themselves of the techniques of reconciliation for the sake of legitimacy and representativeness, are expected to perform tasks of social and economic mobilization, of decision-making and problem-solving and plan-pursuing, that would have been unthinkable in any part of the world as recently as one hundred years ago. The government of a nation that seeks or has attained the condition of modernity cannot be content with the role of passive spectator of the comings and goings of active citizens. It must be active itself—creative, anticipatory, decisive, vigilant—or fall into disrepute; it must be active in deed, not simply in word. As the sad and mixed-up case of independent Burma illustrates,[4] the appearance of activeness is a poor and ultimately disastrous substitute for the fact. For this reason most students of comparative politics assume that a party system of some kind is a necessary appurtenance of modern government.[5] While parties are potentially dangerous agents of the popular will, especially monopolistic ones that suppress loyal dissent and sectarian ones that paralyze the process of decision, they are as important to the mobilizing as to the reconciliating polity.

Efficiency is yet another mark of the modern government. Like the large-scale, machine-oriented factory or large-scale, science-based agricultural enterprise, it performs its assigned tasks in a professional manner or runs the risk of being put out of business. By means of differentiation of role, specialization of function, establishment and constant refinement of standards, creation of techniques for recruiting and training competent personnel, creation of other techniques for rewarding high-level performance, and adoption of new and more sophisticated ways of educating public opinion and acknowledging the public interest, the government of a modern nation may reach a level of administrative efficiency on which it can begin to provide such services as publication of dependable statistics or inspection of meat and medicines or supervision of business practices or cheap, reliable, speedy delivery of the mail in place of slogans that pall, monuments that crumble, and secular passion plays that befuddle.* An educated, hard-working, flexible, imaginative, cost-conscious, and responsible core of civil servants is a functional necessity of the modern polity.

Efficiency in turn may lead to *capability,* the principal mark and ultimate test of the modernity of a political system. The question "who governs?" has proved so appealing to social scientists determined to understand the structure and functioning of the polity that too often they forget to ask the no less significant questions "what is governed?" and "what is governable?" What is governed in every nation depends to a large extent, of course, on what is governable; and that, the outermost reach of public authority, depends upon the state of the political culture—the context of traditions, values, standards, expectations, and prejudices within which the political system operates[6]—as well as upon such nonpolitical facts of national life as the scarcity of a resource like water or the presence of an overpowering neighbor or the inheritance of religious values obstinately opposed to birth control or the flowering of an ethic of industry and frugality.

The capable government, it seems to me, is one that, first, has the good fortune to operate in an ambience in which many important aspects of social and economic development are in fact governable; second, finds support in a political culture that encourages men to expect efficient activity rather than bumbling quiescence; and third, has the will and skill to face up to problems, decide to govern them, enact laws that command popular support, and convert these laws into patterns of administrative action that prompt men to live in ways they have not lived in before. While it is impossible to assess the capability of any one government with precision, and dangerous to compare the capability of one with that of another except in the most general

* Nowhere has the United States revealed some of the pains associated with the condition of overmodernity more vividly than in the decline of efficiency in its postal service, largely under the ponderous weight of too much mail moving at too low a cost in too many directions.

terms, we must recognize that the successful polities of the modern world are those that *work,* rather than *play,* at the business of governing men. In the words of a Ghanaian civil servant who was unusually frank and perceptive in talking with me, a supposedly modern government is a truly modern government and not just feeble pageant when it can "lay taxes with imagination and a regard for equity, collect the bulk of these taxes and do it without too much snooping and coercing, and spend them honestly and efficiently on the public purposes for which they were laid in the first place." When I reminded him that tax evasion was one of the three national pastimes in Italy, he, armed with a refreshingly African opinion of Europe, asked mischievously: "But who ever said that Italy was modern?" When I then suggested that, over the long run, a modern government would spend no more than it could raise and earn, he, faithful to his Christian upbringing, commented solemnly: "Amen!" We agreed that *solvency,* a happy condition that does not forbid deficit spending for short terms and special needs, is a mark of the capable government.

Although I open myself to the charge of bias, both normative and emotional, in favor of the political culture of the West, I am bound to state the considered opinion that both *democracy* and *constitutionalism* are also essentials of political efficacy.

Democracy, whether real or alleged, exists in unexpected places and queer forms in the modern world, and surely nobody insists any longer that Ghana be governed like Sweden or South Korea like Australia in order to be judged democratic. Yet the governments of such countries, and indeed of countries like the Soviet Union and Yugoslavia, will fail the tests of legitimacy, representativeness, and capability if they are not democratic in the generic sense of aiming at the political socialization of the mass of ordinary men, insisting upon a rough equality of political and social rights, providing for popular participation at various levels and stages, and offering the benefits of economic development to the entire citizenry. While it may be too much to ask all the governments of the world to be "of the people, by the people, for the people," not even Castro would dare—and, if he dared, would not last for long—to throw out "of" and "for" along with "by."

Constitutionalism is an even rarer growth than democracy, not least because an increase in the capacity of a government to mobilize men and resources for development usually leads to a reduction in the respect paid to legal and administrative niceties. Several scholars have argued vehemently, indeed, that mobilization and constitutionalism simply do not go together. In this matter, nevertheless, there is also a minimum level at which governments of all descriptions ought to aim, if not sooner, then later. Some aspects of a generic constitutionalism that every efficacious government will come in time to display are these: the infusion of large amounts of regularity and predictability into the procedures of bureaucracy, the amassing of precedents of due process in the courts, the tolerance of dissenting ideas and opinions, the publication and dissemination of statutes and ordinances, and a widespread understanding of the limited usefulness of outbursts of parapolitical behavior like riots and demonstrations in a highly organized and thus interdependent society. Some political scientists, including Kalman Silvert and David Apter, have suggested the existence of a direct correlation between the circulation of information in a country and its capacity for development. Apter himself has made the point forcefully in negative terms: If the leaders of an emerging nation "apply excessive coercion" to the public, "they minimize the production" of the information needed to keep the nation emerging upward and onward.[7] The systematic analysis of these scholars has strengthened my own impressionistic opinion that a political system must begin to show some signs of both democracy and constitutionalism before it can shift self-confidently into high gear. Whatever apparent miracles political repression may be able to bring off in the short run, it works in the long run to stifle the spirit of innovation so essential to economic development, social readjustment, and cultural achievement. This is one of the principal lessons to be learned in a thoughtful study of both the huge successes and the dismal failures of the Soviet Union in the past two decades. It is a lesson of encouragement to the friends of constitutional democracy.

Another primary goal of modernity is *economic viability*. A modern nation has an economy that permits it to strike a posture of independence toward other nations and makes it an object of loyalty in the sight of its own citizens. No awakened nation has ever been as economically healthy as its leaders have wanted and citizens expected it to be. The history and present condition of the healthiest and wealthiest of national economies, that of the United States, are evidence enough that development in this critical area will bring a distressing measure of dislocation and waste, that pockets of backwardness and poverty will dot the landscape of progress and affluence, and that the attainment of economic modernity will surely produce a crop of new problems for any nation that has been counting upon the technology of abundance to provide the answer to just about every social question. Yet the goal must be attacked as vigorously as the goal of political efficacy, which is why many students of development would reverse the order of this study and put it first on the list. Economic viability is an end in itself; it is also, like political efficacy, a means to a host of longed-for ends ranging from social justice to the flowering of the arts. Economic development, it seems hardly necessary to add, not only shapes but is shaped by all other aspects of a nation's life. Ideology, tradition, learning, religion, culture, politics, and social relations feed into it just as it feeds back into them, often with astonishing and unforeseen consequences—a consideration that leads me inexorably to observe that the most absurd mistake men of economic power can make is to assume their power to be virginally economic.

A nation may be judged to have reached this goal when it owns an economy that exhibits certain visible marks of robust maturity.

The first is another of those worldly phenomena in which the will of men is every bit as important a component in the formula for success as are circumstances and institutions: a built-in *capacity for growth*. The fundamental rule of economic growth seems to be this: Although a modernizing or already modern nation may suffer temporary setbacks or halt to take bearings, it must keep moving ahead on the exhilarating track of innovation or sink back into the sour pool of stagnation.[8] While the harsh truth of this rule is not easy for traditionalists to digest (and not much easier for progressives who fear that the disposition to grow may escalate into a rage destructive of values, skills, institutions, and treasures they, too, are anxious to preserve), every modern and modernizing nation must learn to live with it bravely. If the nation is truly modern, it will look beyond the institutionalization of such essentials of economic growth as the urge for innovation, the accumulation of capital, and the provision for so-called social overhead to the creation of primarily political techniques designed to help farsighted men plan for efficiency, allocate resources and energies, preserve what ought to be preserved (if necessary, at the expense of the fullest possible realization of modernity), slow down the pace of economic change when it threatens to get out of hand, and in general transmute the quantitative fact of *growth* into the qualitative fact of *development.** It must display some ability to select targets on which to expend extra amounts of energy, capital, and skill because an enterprise is productive of an ingredient of a more humane way of life. It must have a similar ability to favor an enterprise with wide-ranging linkages, that is to say, unusual capacities to induce both growth and development in other types of enterprise by growing itself.[10]

Economic modernity is a condition in which *stability* is awarded a high value, and in which, therefore, the nation has a number of mechanisms with which to accelerate or decelerate the rate of growth, prevent demoralizing inflation and deflation, anticipate the social consequences of technological innovation, and put a brake on the wildest upsurges and downturns that all economies seem fated to suffer. While no nation has learned how or can probably expect to modernize its economy without experiencing social and political convulsions, some nations are coming to realize that they have both the skills and the funds to reduce the impact of further convulsions, and that the most effective general method of doing this is to resolve to grow at a steady rather than heady pace.

Another way to maintain stability is to guard an economy as far as possible against dangers like natural disasters, hard times or social upheavals or cataclysms in other nations,† exhaustion of

---

* Although it is impossible to be absolutely precise and consistent in making this distinction between growth and development, I agree unreservedly with Louis Hacker and others that the two are not (and must not be judged to be) the same phenomenon, and would add only the observation that, while there certainly can be growth without development, there can probably be no development without growth.[9]

† Perhaps the most astonishing example in recent years of the distress that can occur in one nation because of distress in another was the severe blow

resources, overconcentration of skills, glutting of markets, and long-range shifts in the tastes of clients at home and abroad. Perhaps the most useful of all guards is *diversification*. This is an especially important objective for the primarily agrarian or extractive economy. The commitment to one crop or natural resource, which carries with it a commitment to the role of wheedling exporter, places the well-being of a people at the mercy of men and events they cannot control. It holds out, moreover, the uninviting prospect of all those tensions that beset a nation which boasts political independence yet remains an economic colony of another nation or array of nations. A country with a diversified economy, like a corporation with a diversified line of products or an investor with a diversified portfolio, has a hard-core capacity to withstand the demoralizing effects of change or crisis.

A fourth mark of economic viability is a high level and rising rate of *productivity*, whether of individual worker, unit of organization, sector of enterprise, or entire nation. While productivity is very much a relative condition, we have in hand enough hard information about individual and collective performances in the front-running nations of the past several hundred years to set rough standards against which to measure the performance, and thus the proximity to modernity, of other nations, whether in 1800 or 1850 or 1900 or 1970. The critical point at which to look for evidence of high and rising productivity is the relation between the input of time, skill, resources, and capital and the output of goods to be consumed at home or marketed abroad. In the backward economy the input is relatively large and the output relatively small. The modern economy has managed to reverse the order of the ages; and, if it continues to modernize, the favorable gap between input and output in the productive process will continue to widen. While most students of modernization agree that the "great ascent," of which Robert Heilbroner has written vividly,[11] must begin in the fields, that is, with the transformation of agriculture, the experience of the Soviet Union warns us not to

---

to the economy of Iceland dealt by the civil war in Nigeria. Iceland had been exporting large quantities of stockfish to the Eastern Region, and the blockade of rebellious Biafra resulted in a disaster for the fishing industry and thus for the whole nation.

lay down overly rigid specifications for building a modern economy. The gains in productivity of Soviet industry have been spectacular; Soviet agriculture remains an obstinate undertaking in which determined input should have begun long ago to produce a much larger output.[12]

The modern economy is notable for an ability to create a *surplus of capital* that may be used to purchase resources, talents, and goods the nation cannot or will not produce itself, build up the structure of social overhead (facilities for transportation and communication, public services, the whole apparatus of education, and other equipment and enterprises that are not directly productive of materials and manufactures), replace outworn methods and machines, encourage the invention of new ones, and generally increase the rate of productivity. A formidable problem of the modernizing nation is, in the terse phrase of William McCord, "finding the money." [13] The modern nation has found the money, and all but a fraction at its command has been generated at home rather than borrowed from abroad. Few nations have achieved genuine economic progress in the past, none of the underdeveloped nations can hope for it today, without the assistance, whether massive or shrewdly selective, of imported capital. Progress toward economic modernity, however, should in time breed enough domestic capital to render a heavy reliance on foreign investment quite unnecessary.

It is notable also for a high rate of *flow*. A modern economy circulates goods, money, ideas, managers, workers, and innovations so swiftly and powerfully that a nation must be careful not to let the many flows become one monstrous torrent, for such a torrent will sweep away cherished patterns of living and leave men stranded on the shore of disaffection. Still, it cannot have arrived at a state of modernity in the realm of technology, or hope to remain modern by engaging in the endless process of self-repair and self-improvement, unless it opens up and keeps dredging the channels of flow. The flow of ideas is especially vital: Men yearn and then learn to be agents of economic modernity chiefly through the example or instruction of other men. One need not swallow whole Karl Deutsch's thought-provoking definition of a nation as, in essence, a "community of social communication" to recognize the importance of this special kind of flow to the development of a self-renewing economy that serves a self-conscious nation.[14]

After all that has been said about capacity for growth, stability, diversification, productivity, surplus of capital, and flow, it seems hardly necessary to isolate and consider *sophistication* as a prerequisite of economic viability. Yet some of the most able practitioners of economic growth and development have a way of overlooking this aspect of modernity, and I would rather be slightly repetitious than let the aspect pass by unnoticed. The sophisticated economies of the world are known not merely by the familiar signs of specialization of function, differentiation of role, rationalization of order, and an ever more favorable relation between input and output, but also by such devices of development as large-scale investment in the generation of new knowledge, the same kind of investment in the transmission of knowledge both new and old, accumulation and analysis of reliable data, and maintenance of a large stable of independent-minded economists and other social scientists. No less important are arrangements for efficient marketing, techniques for spotting evidence of cancerous growth or wasting decay, and other techniques for planning in both the public and private sectors. The nation that cannot make plans imaginatively and then execute them flexibly is economically unsophisticated and therefore politically unmodern. The truly sophisticated economies are further known by the provisions they have made for public control of what the political culture defines as the public's business and for humane efforts to reduce the unpleasant side effects of modern technology. Men with consciences as well as brains are the managers of the economy of modernity.

In the end, all other aspects of the goal of economic viability wait upon the attainment of the old-fashioned condition of *solvency*. No nation that is perpetually broke, whether because of austere circumstances or wasteful ways or hard luck or perverse policies, can hope to develop its economy at a pace that will satisfy popular expectations. It cannot buy or borrow what it needs from abroad; it cannot accumulate the capital of innovation and improvement at home; it cannot set aside the large sums for both social overhead and social services that men of the twentieth century assume to be their birthright. Worst of all, a nation with an insolvent economy is a nation with an insolvent government, and such a government is in constant danger of losing its legitimacy and independence. Such a government has also been known to lose its life.

Two points may be useful to ponder as we conclude this analysis of economic viability. The first is simple to make but hard, I have learned, to grasp and accept: While every nation needs to develop economically in order to cross the threshold of modernity, it does not have to travel the road of all-out industrialization. A large nation, perhaps yes; a small one, most certainly not—unless, of course, we classify New Zealand as a backward country or Kenya as one doomed to remain backward because it chooses consciously to concentrate attention upon agriculture and tourism. If the basically nonindustrial nation like the New Zealand-that-is or the Kenya-that-hopes-to-be can manage its nonindustrial enterprises with the aid of industrial values, farm and mine in a sophisticated manner, sell a diversity of products to the world at large, and build up large credits abroad in order to purchase the machinery for further innovation of its agrarian-extractive-commercial economy (as well as the consumer goods it prefers not to make itself), it has every right to think that it lives in a modern way in the modern world. The way may be a bit more precarious than that of the industrialized nation, chiefly because the principal markets of the economy lie always beyond the boundaries of the polity, yet it may also be a good deal more robust. A nation of farmers, miners, repairmen, and salesmen is likely to have all the satisfactions and many fewer of the anxieties of a nation of steelworkers, car manufacturers, computer technicians, and public-relations men. Psychiatry is a luxury in the one, a necessity in the other—or do I have the whole thing 180 degrees out of phase?

The second point is that while economic viability is a goal commanding nations to toil and spin without rest, it is neither a panacea for old ills nor a vaccine against new ones. It helps one nation to prosper and live in peace, goads another to plunder and delight in war. It serves one as the foundation of democracy, provides another with the armory of dictatorship. If the modern economy makes possible the eradication of social ills that have plagued mankind since the beginning of recorded history, it also brings, we have already learned, new and unimagined ills in its train—and the worst of these may well be the mindlessness and corruption of overmodernity. Most important for our purposes, this economy does not work automatically, as one may learn by studying the successes and failures of several highly developed countries in South America, to create genuinely national loyalties and institutions.[15] Economic viability opens up the road to nationhood; men must then demonstrate, year in and year out, the will to travel it.

The interplay of political efficacy and economic viability with custom and circumstance leads toward the prize of *social integration*. In every nation there exists a sphere of human endeavor that is primarily neither political nor economic in character; in almost every one its separate if related existence is a sign of health, and efforts are made to give it positive support. In a few, notably China, this sphere is acknowledged in a backhanded way by the ferocious efforts of the political authorities to bend it to their will, reshape it, or if necessary engulf it. In social relations as in politics or economics many patterns of modernity flourish, yet the most disparate of developed societies share certain characteristics. Before reviewing them, let me speak a word of caution: The modern nation in all its complexity should be compared neither with the most comforting of the tightly knit primitive tribes so dear to the heart of sentimental anthropologists nor to the most serene communities of the Golden Age, whether situated in the legendary past or the utopian future, so useful for the purposes of disillusioned political theorists. The social orders of the best of nations are shot through with imperfections, and I write therefore once again of ideals that may be approached but never fully realized. They should not, however, be classed as silly abstractions, for these characteristics, while stated perforce in a kind of perfectionist vocabulary, are based on and can be related to real achievements in the histories of real peoples.

One such characteristic is a *rational social order* made up of men who can guide and plan and innovate, fill the posts of a sophisticated economy, and offer largely uncoerced obedience to the commands of political authority. It is impossible or self-deluding to imagine a developed society that is not structured into classes, by whatever label they are known or explained away. It is possible and extremely important to assert, however, that the classes in such a society will be functional, that they will be descriptions of men rather than castes, and that the elite, which is indispensable, will be accessible and the laboring class, which is inevitable, will enjoy the full privileges and opportunities of citizenship, including the opportunity for individuals and families and entire callings to move upward on the ladder. The last point calls for special emphasis, since a social order without scalable ladders is a social order without modernity.

The two cardinal features of a rationally organized society are *centrality* and *proximity*. The first word proclaims the significant role of that class of men—let us be unafraid, let us call it the middle class—who are something more than dependent laborers and something less than absentee landlords, who have skills, property, education, confidence, security, and independence to make them a force both for stability and for progress. The size and power of the middle class in such countries as the United States, France, Britain, Switzerland, Japan, and, amusing but not surprising to relate (certainly not in Peking), the Soviet Union are compelling evidence of the existence of the condition of modernity which this class may love so dearly because it has pursued the condition so eagerly. One must agree unreservedly with Kalman Silvert's observation that, while "the drive to include all social groups within new societies" is or should be a mark of nation-building in the twentieth century, "a social class *at the center* may still be essential to a free and independent constitutional state." [16] The italics are mine, yet Professor Silvert, I feel certain, would give them his blessing.

The second indicates that the gap between any two classes or layers in a modern society is narrow and thus conducive to interchange and respect aimed in both directions. The elite, in particular, is not isolated or alienated from the ranks and classes below it by reason of unseemly wealth or esoteric knowledge or cosmopolitan ideology. It is, rather, legitimate, functional, and responsible; it adheres comfortably to the values of the whole nation; like the whole nation, it has developed, in Eisenstadt's words, an "almost unconscious ability to absorb change." [17] The poor, too, are not isolated or alienated. In the fully modern nation, which is still to come, they are so few that they invite our selective sympathy as human beings but not our broad concern as social scientists. Unfortunately for the serenity of all mankind (including human beings and social scientists), the drive toward modernity has a way of breeding new kinds of poverty.

A major aim of those who seek a rational social order is the *reconciliation of classes,* which they attain principally by mixing equality and equity in a formula that provides a satisfactory pay-off—economic, political, cultural, and psychological—for men of every description. A community that can make good on the promises of equality of opportunity, equality of suffrage, equality before the law, and equality of consideration can learn to live with those other inequalities that appear to be a persistent fact of civilized existence. Except in unusual circumstances, the notion of a class struggle is an enemy of modernity. Once this notion enters in force into the minds of a large part of the citizenry, a nation is in serious danger of dividing into Disraeli's two nations, thence splitting into three or four or more, then coming apart at the seams. A social order that breeds arrogance at the top and envy at the bottom forfeits all claims to fairness; and the tensions that plague it will lead sooner or later to a politics of suspicion, disaffection, and disruption. A social order that keeps a floor of self-respect under the bottom and a lid of self-restraint on the top presents a very different and more wholesome picture. It is the best imitation men of good will can create of that ancient and still-enticing vision: the just society.

Perhaps the most useful contribution to the reconciliation of classes, and thus the most important element in the pattern of social harmony that sustains an orderly politics and productive economy, is a long-term *rise in the standard of living* of men in both their private and their public capacities. The rise must be real: an upward movement of the level of pay-off that can be experienced and not just read on a graph. It must also be general: an onward movement that sweeps up the mass of men. When I called attention, earlier in this chapter, to the primary role of economic growth in the process of modernization, I did not wish to imply that the only test of such growth lies in the cold-blooded statistics of large-scale industry. To the contrary, an ever-expanding gross national product is a curse upon the land if its fruits are not wholesome, and are not well and widely distributed among the people of the nation in the form of consumer goods and public services. Here again it may be useful for us to make a distinction between quantitative growth and qualitative development.

The danger always exists, of course, that expectation will outstrip achievement, turn the fact of substantial progress into the illusion of failure, and embitter men who ought to enjoy peace of mind. Yet the danger is the sort that nation-builders are ready to live with as one of the hazards of their profession—and so they should be. In a mature social order most men know that the payoff is larger today than it was yesterday and have reason to hope that it will be still larger tomorrow. That fact, more than incidentally, is one of several reasons why a humane system of medicine, which provides the best kind of personal care for those who are sick and maintains the highest standards of public health for those who are not, is a critical aspect of the attempt to modernize. The medicine of modernity assures men that their tomorrows will be more numerous, secure, and enjoyable.

If we shift our gaze away from classes, we may notice other signs of health in the social order of a modern nation. One is a flourishing *infrastructure* of groups and subgroups organized for every conceivable end: *Gemeinschaften* and *Gesellschaften* that get much of the work of society done and serve as buffers between the otherwise defenseless individual and otherwise encompassing community. The American churches provide a useful example of the manner in which such groups may differ widely in structure, function, purpose, and principle yet may reinforce rather than weaken the community by sharing finally in the national consensus. The more modern a society, the more capacity it will have to cement small groups into larger ones and thereby create complicated and flexible forms of organization. The essential group, it would appear, remains the family, and one has trouble imagining what could ever take its place in a modern society, even when both communalism and the differentiation of roles for the individual have been driven to the uttermost limits. While the family may assume many forms and functions, and certainly becomes more loose-jointed and less extended as a modern nation develops, only a brash student of society would advocate its elimination or an ignorant one predict its disappearance. The tenacity of the family in the Soviet Union is legendary; the "children of the dream," of whom Bruno Bettelheim writes,[18] have found a place for some sort of family structure and entertain surprisingly intense family feelings in the ongoing kibbutz.

A second is a *balance of abodes* that reflects the customs and tastes of the nation as well as the realities of efficacious politics and viable economics. Modern man is man uprooted, whether by chance or choice. Neither spear-carrier in a horde nor solitary trapper, he loses or leaves his job and moves on with his kin in search of a better life. For most of the breed the pilgrimage is from the village and countryside to the city and thereupon, not just in the United States, out of the city and into the suburb. Urbanization is a principal if not always reliable index of social and economic development, and the reason is simple: In an economy growing more sophisticated, the input of labor in agriculture goes downward as the output rises. Men must head for the cities lest they starve in the fields. The city, always a center of civilization, has a special role to play in the developed society; the leaders of such a society have a special responsibility to make their cities places in which people can live and work in decent circumstances. This responsibility is, of course, a very large order, especially in a country like the United States, where the displaced of the land are both forced and invited to flow into the cities, the successful (or merely fearful) of the cities free to flow out to the suburbs. I am compelled to repeat my observation that the achievement of modernity creates new problems for the heirs of the achievers. Indeed, it remains to be seen whether overmodernity in the American style, which threatens to disembowel many of our cities, will lead to a decline of American civilization.

Yet another sign of social health, as well as an engine of both political efficacy and economic viability, is a far-ranging, sophisticated, and truth-presenting (not truth-distorting or truth-suppressing) *system of communication*. In the modern society the signals of inquiry, advice, and decision move "loud and clear" in every direction, which is one reason why Britain and the United States, despite their imperfections in this matter, are more modern than the Soviet Union, and why the Soviet Union, which has progressed beyond wall posters, is more modern than China. As

Karl Deutsch has pointed out in his "functional definition of nationalism," the more directly and self-consciously a society communicates within its own boundaries and concerning its own issues, the more likely it is to be a cohesive nation. The real or potential nation, in his view, is notable for a "wide complementarity of social communication," an "ability to communicate more effectively, and over a wider range of subjects, with members of one large group than with outsiders." [19]

Perhaps even more essential to modern nationhood is an enduring dedication to the task of building and rebuilding the many parts of the one indispensable asset of social overhead: an inclusive and effective *system of education*. The men of a community must learn and learn and learn again if they are to be alert citizens of a democratic polity, useful role-players in a productive economy, and decent members of a humane society. They must also learn that they form a nation. Education is another of mankind's two-edged swords, a blunt truth to which the memory of Hitler's Germany, perhaps the most literate and also chauvinistic nation in history, bears shocking witness. Yet if it can teach some men to be arrogant or unreasonably self-seeking and some to be miserable or unreasonably self-doubting, it can teach others to be intelligent, skillful, contributing members of the community. It can, moreover, help them to realize their better natures. Education cannot do the job of civilizing men all by itself, yet it has now become our "last, best hope" of breeding tolerance, reducing violence, and eliminating antisocial behavior. The high incidence of intolerance, symbolic and often authentic violence, and contemptuously antisocial behavior on university campuses throughout the modern and modernizing world (except, of course, in the Soviet Union) is one of those enigmas of history which command an extra measure of scrutiny. Perhaps it is not an enigma at all; perhaps there are good reasons why the focal points of civilization should have become the scenes for uncivilized acts on a broad and persistent scale; perhaps in time we shall discover the reasons, which up to now have defied all our probings.

In conclusion to these observations on social integration in the modern nation, I confess a reluctance to take a firm stand about the role of *religion*. The question is one about which I am far too uncertain to pose as an objective social scientist. Let me therefore record only a few generally irrefutable observations about the place of religion in any quest for modern nationhood.

The first is a consequence of looking at religion with the eye of a historian. Like language, it has been a mighty force in liberating, building, preserving, dissolving, and destroying nations. Like language, it is still hard at work—liberating, building, preserving, dissolving, and destroying.

A second, which also leaps out of the records of history, is that religious faith declines or becomes more questioning as a nation moves toward modernity. The modern society is ever more secular; its pattern of religion is ever more hostile to filigreed dogmatism or simple-minded fundamentalism.

A third is rather more anthropological in character: The churches remain, except where religion has been proscribed (and sometimes even there), an important part of the social infrastructure. They contribute significantly to the good order (and sometimes self-purging disorder) of even the most ideologically secular countries by providing a haven for lonely individuals and working a moderating influence on the political process.

Finally, if we look at the phenomenon of religion from a broadly psychological point of view, we must recognize the endurance and near universality of man's need to reach beyond the sensate boundaries of the physical world in order to seek meaning or comfort in the mysteries of the spirit. Most men feel the need to worship, however sporadically or informally, and it is almost certainly better for a man, both as private person and as citizen, to worship some version of divine providence rather than his nation or race, an ideology or charismatic leader, history or science.

About the role of *science* itself a firm if not rigid stand is easier to take. While we must be careful not to transform its modest and still reviewable laws into insolent and final dogmas or, in effect, to canonize its most famous practitioners, are we not bound to recognize that this spacious area of human endeavor is the essence of modernity—just as it was, according to Herbert Butterfield, "the real origin of the modern world and of the modern mentality"? [20] Let us consider briefly the most conspicuous aspects of the established science of the advanced nations of the twentieth century, forgetting not that some of them were aspects of the prophetic science of city-states and empires that flourished centuries before the birth of Jesus:

The purposes of science are to probe, discover, understand, and explain; to order, invent, create, and predict; to accumulate knowledge that cuts us loose from the superstitions of the past; to put systematic, verifiable reason in first place among man's ways of knowing about the world and making decisions in it.

The methods of science are to think tough-mindedly, guess daringly, experiment meticulously, replicate objectively, and to suspend every judgment until there can be no doubt of its validity— and even then not to close the book tightly and forever.

The spirit of science is hopeful, and this element of hope has sent forth the best of scientists on an unflagging search for the hard-core truths of both the physical and the social environments in which we live.

The direction of science is toward the future.

The organization of science (I speak primarily of the modern age) is rational, efficient, sophisticated, and impersonal often to the point of ruthlessness.

In human terms, the chief product of science is a technology that has altered the lives of ordinary men in a half-century more drastically than in all the centuries that had gone before.

In social terms, the chief consequence of science is ceaseless change, especially when it works in harness with an achievement-oriented ethic, a bountiful supply of skilled men and daring money, and a loving politics. The fact that a shocking proportion of this change can hardly be classified as progress is not so much the fault of scientists themselves as of those who have given them wrong directions or none at all, and of those who misuse the wonders for which, so they think, they have paid lavishly.

The least perceptive person who scans this catalogue can understand at once that science is a major force in the process of modernization and is therefore, on almost every count, the essence of modernity; the most perceptive cannot assess its impact upon the quality of nationhood in any part of the world with confidence in the accuracy of his results. While science, like the great religions it has sought to supplement or supplant, is an inherently supranational or even antinational pattern of thought

and activity, it has been pressed into service by arrogant nationalism too often—not as often as supposedly supranational religions
but often enough—to leave us suspicious of the loudly asserted
claims of many scientists that they constitute the one "republic"
that ignores all boundaries and unites all men. The most we can
say for science is that it is historically and logically less suited
than religion for the purposes of those who do not build but preserve nations. It has, in any case, no compelling social imperatives
of its own to which men must submit in unison whether they like
to submit or not. It is, as we have learned from living with combinations of letters like NASA and DNA and DDT, an unexampled
agent of modernization in every part of the world and now, it
seems, outside it. Yet modernization, we must again remind ourselves, is not synonymous with salvation—for the body any more
than it is for the mind and spirit. The indiscriminate use of DDT
will be proving that point conclusively for generations to come.

A final goal of modernity is a pattern of *cultural maturity* in
which all citizens can find meaning. While it may be argued that
this is a marginal purpose, that a community need not create and
re-create a rich and broadly founded culture in order to be a
modern nation, I will not be the one to argue it. A true nation
relies so heavily on language and letters, as well as on treasures of
art, architecture, and music, to support the endless quest for self-
identity that neither a sterile nor an antidemocratic culture is
one with which modern-minded patriots of taste and intelligence
can be happy. They know, and they must teach their fellow countrymen to know, too, that the life of a philistine is a life only half
lived, that all the arts can be introduced in hundreds of subtle
ways to enrich the daily comings and goings of the most humble
persons, and that there is no public pride to match that of citizenship in a nation the world takes seriously as a fountain of arts and
letters.

To build a culture both elevated and popular, enduring and
self-replenishing, preservative of old beauty and productive of
new genius is therefore a matter of national concern. While cultural maturity may not have top priority and must wait patiently
upon the achievement of other goals, even the poorest nation can
be well served by small beginnings. And while the fullest

achievement of this goal is no guaranty of national self-consciousness, a rich culture is one of the most influential rallying-points for those who enjoy its fruits in common. Henry James was correct in looking beyond factories and railroads for the essentially nonutilitarian possessions that weld a nation together and make it an object of profound interest. Where he went astray, being Henry James, was that he looked too airily in the wrong places and came up with a list of possessions that had little or no appeal for most men.

Cultural maturity is a condition about which it is next to impossible to be objective. Moreover, the standards for measuring the achievements of any one nation must of necessity be so rough as to strike many social scientists and historians as next to useless. Rough standards, however, are better than none at all. If I may fix attention upon the all-important field of literature, I would suggest a half-dozen or so measurements with which we may assess the quality of a nation's achievement. These, briefly, are the marks of a national literature that is both mature and vital:

It is *rich* and, if it has endured for centuries, *grand:* an accumulation of masterpieces in all or most of the recognized forms of literary endeavor—the epic, the novel, lyric poetry, belles-lettres, drama (including the cinema), history, biography, oratory, and criticism (an area of human endeavor that may be the quintessence of modernity).

It is *distinctive:* a reflection of the special realities and values of the nation, a product of creative writers who have turned loose their imaginations on native materials—the qualities, triumphs, failures, dilemmas, and tensions of their own people.

It is *self-conscious:* evidence of an awareness, neither chauvinistic nor unduly apologetic, of the peculiar worth of a whole range of national life that joins both creators and consumers, whether living or dead, in some kind of inclusive-exclusive fraternity.

It is, to whatever extent possible, *original:* a product of writers who are independent or at least not pitifully imitative of forms and styles of other national or supranational literatures.

It is, in the best sense of the word, *popular:* a storehouse of precious and semiprecious treasures of which the ordinary citizens of the nation are conscious and rightly proud, and in which they can find, each citizen at his own level of awareness and competence, such joys as instruction, inspiration, entertainment, solace, and self-identity.

It is both *deserving and capable of transmission:* a chorus of voices that, like a great school of political thought, tells us of the experiences and aspirations of one community yet speaks across the boundaries of language and culture to other communities. To those who might accuse me of trying to have the best of two conflicting worlds I would reply simply by pointing to the mighty figures of Shakespeare, Flaubert, and Dostoevsky. Is the first not English, the second not French, the third not Russian to the marrow of his bones? Yet does each not speak to all men with ears to listen? A self-consciously nationalistic literature needs the discipline of universal applicability to keep from sliding into arid provincialism.

It is, finally, *self-renewing:* a pattern of national endeavor that, like the political system or the economy, must not encourage men to linger forever savoring past achievements lest, as Lewis Mumford once put the matter, "in sheer defense" they convert their storehouse of treasures into a museum of fossils. The progress of a national literature through history moves, obviously and indeed necessarily, in cycles: Some generations are destined to do more receiving than giving. Sooner or later, however, if the culture of the nation is basically sound, a new capacity for creative giving will emerge, and the nation will be in the happy situation of replenishing the storehouse.

Cultural maturity, I repeat, is a marginal goal when contrasted with the peremptory need for political efficacy, economic viability, and social integration. Still, a country without a culture it can call its own, and do so with seemly pride, is not yet a nation that Ernest Renan would recognize as fully formed or Karl Deutsch as fully functional.

Let me conclude this examination of the goals of modernity by confessing an awareness, born of bewildering experience, of the difficulties confronting the student of a major phenomenon of history that is so obviously relative in character. One longs for absolute standards with which to take measurements; one realizes that time and circumstance make such standards impossible to establish. In an important sense, the United States or even the Great Britain of 1860 displays a dismally unmodern appearance when examined from the perspective of 1970, and we who boast of our modernity or worry about the unpleasant consequences of overmodernity may seem like primitive tribesmen to those who look back from the perspective of 2070—assuming that 2070 rolls around. There is, nevertheless, in the long view of history, a stage of political, economic, social, and cultural development that we have a right to call modernity, a situation in which the men of several dozen nations have known a way of life that has been, in effect, a "great leap forward" from the ways of life of all the men who went before them—not necessarily better, one hastens to add, but different, so different in kind that we can look back ourselves upon the crossing of the threshold of modernity, first by Britain and thereafter by other nations, as one of the truly momentous events in the history of the world. If the men of 2070 fulfill the prophecies of our most sanguine seers and build a completely automated, antiseptic, painless, and abundant civilization, one that is both collectively peaceful and personally serene, we may still lay claim to have been the agents and subjects of the era of modernity, leaving to them the task of coining some other word to describe their own situation.

But what of ours, which a few nations have enjoyed for decades and all nations, so wise men have informed me on every continent, want desperately to attain? How can we tell that a nation has crossed the threshold over which the Britain of the Industrial Revolution led the way? While I do not wish to rehash everything that has been said in this chapter, I have a promise to keep to that exemplary Ghanaian civil servant, who was anxious to inform his fellow citizens in the most practical terms how they would know that their own country had crossed the threshold. I offer therefore a list that we concocted together and labeled "assorted nononsense tests of modernity." These, we felt, are criteria that an average man can apply to his own nation in an attempt to decide whether it has moved into this historic stage in fact as well as in rhetoric. The list is by no means inclusive or exclusive, yet most of these questions, which form the cutting edge of the tests, demand an affirmative answer before we can speak seriously of a nation that has toiled its own way or been pushed by other nations into the stage of modernity:

Are most persons—let us say, more than 50 per cent of the work force—employed in nonagricultural enterprises?

Are most persons—let us say, not less than 95 per cent of the work force—employed, and also decently rewarded?

Do most persons live in and around cities?

Do most live, let us say, more than fifty miles from where they were born or raised?

Do most get away from time to time from where they live?

Do those employed in agricultural enterprises work not for subsistence but to produce a cash crop?

Is there plenty of cash (or solid credit) circulating in the nation, and does the average man's portion buy more than it did twenty-five years ago?

Is the soil improved scientifically rather than exhausted mindlessly?

Are almost all persons literate—educationally, politically, and economically?

Are almost all children under fourteen in school?

Is there a solid core of university-educated men and women?

Have most of them been able to get their education in their own country?

Do most persons, whether they pay or not, have access to the benefits of up-to-date medicine?

Can most persons, barring accident, look forward to a span of years both extended and rewarding?

Do the years at the end of this span offer most persons comfort and dignity?

Are all persons protected by instruments of public health against historic mass-killers such as malaria, cholera, and yellow fever, and also against historic mass-debilitators (and too often killers) such as tuberculosis and dysentery?

Does a baby stand better than a hundred-to-one chance of living through its first week of life?

Is the machine, however ponderous, supreme over the tool, however subtle?

Is the amount of power fed into the economy by the muscles of men and beasts a small portion of the total supply?

Are the average man's hours of leisure at least equal to his hours of work?

Does he have the personal means and public facilities to make the most of these hours of leisure?

Does he have a safe and, wherever possible, tasteful setting for these hours of work?

Can this man learn from the media of communication all he wants or needs to know about the problems of his society and the policies of his government?

Is he required by a representative body to pay taxes?

Does he pay at least 80 per cent of them?

Are they used for the purposes for which, so he was told, they were required of him?

Does he vote or, if he does not, has he been able to choose freely and consciously not to vote?

Is the most important agency in this man's government one-half as efficient as the most productive enterprise in his economy?

Is he able to live in the climate of his country and be both comfortable and active throughout the year?

Does he have a higher standard of living than did his father at the same age?

Is he secure in his person, rights, and property?

Does he have a sense of personal worth?

Does he, unlike most men in history, depend on the services of other men, most of whom he will never see, in order to stay alive?

Does he, unlike most men in history, not merely *endure* his span of years but *enjoy* it, not merely *exist* but *live?*

I hope my readers understand that the most apparently facetious of these questions is not meant to be a joke. To the contrary, each of them, like each of the others we might have concocted, is a serious projection of some critical feature of the over-all pattern of modernity. If it be argued that we might also have raised a few questions about the tendency toward obesity, the need for psychiatry, the decay of teeth, and the decline of a commitment to any other-worldly or even this-worldly faith—not to overlook rootlessness, alienation, conspicuous consumption, pollution, waste, the often dehumanizing effects of specialization of role, and the emergence of patterns of inhumanity and apathy that would mystify premodern man—I would assert simply, along with my Ghanaian friend, as I have tried to assert throughout this book, that the human condition described as modernity, especially as it speeds up in the direction of overmodernity, has its own share of disorder and folly. Before apple-tasting became all the rage, the Garden of Eden, let no one forget, was the most secure yet also the most backward community ever to catch the attention of historians. I still think it preferable to look forward to seventy years of tension than to seventeen of attrition—or to seven of a feeble, vegetable-like existence.

Two final words: First, in presenting this two-part model of nationhood and modernity I have been, as one who seeks to understand the nature of complicated social phenomena almost certainly must be, too taxonomic; and now I hasten to fit the two parts and all their dozens of pieces back together into the totality of the historical phenomenon of national development. This is done not merely to push the limits of our understanding even farther outward, but also because the eight goals form a tough if not quite seamless web of ambition and achievement. The pursuit of any one goal by a community has repercussions, sometimes benevolent and sometimes not, on the pursuit of all. Achievement in one area waits upon achievement in the others; failure in one, especially when it has been a scene of self-conscious aspiration, can spill over the banks of confidence and pollute the whole life and spirit of a people.

For this reason more clearly than for any other, both the inheritors of a developed nation and the builders of a developing nation must push their efforts in every major area of endeavor and leave none neglected out of indolence or ignorance. While uneven rates of development will always occur between one area and another, and also inside the boundaries of each area, sooner or later these men must strike some kind of rough balance of achievement among them. All areas will thrive or none will thrive: That, it would seem, is a primary condition of success in the quest for nationhood and modernity. It is especially important in a time of zealous concentration upon economic development to remind ourselves that real or apparent advances along this one line do not carry a perceptive national self-identity or capable polity or just society or flowering culture in their train— or even, for that matter, a higher standard of living for ordinary men. What is more, even if they do, they will not bring the people of a nation into some earthly paradise, no longer backward but wondrously secure, where they can henceforth find both opportunity and repose. Development, I repeat at peril of exasperating many readers, is a troublesome experience, modernity a condition in which plenty of men are left to rot or are awakened to grumble, and nationhood a phenomenon that has gone sour enough times to warn us all to keep our nationalism in check.

In the end, all the goals of national development merge into one supreme goal that nations share in common with all human organizations: *survival*. Once a modern nation has come into existence, its first intention must be to go on existing, to guard itself against conquest, fission, decay, and death. So long as ours remains a world of nations, each nation must look first of all to its own resources for the great work of self-preservation. While this may very well mean, as we noted in chapter 2, co-operation with other nations and the acceptance of economic, educational, and military assistance, the leaders of the nation should enter into plans and alliances or follow the instructions of supranational organizations with open eyes and on favorable terms. They must tolerate no weakening of the final power of the nation to control its destiny and defend its existence. Until that far-off day when the modern nation is no longer the most functional expression of political will and capable agent of social and economic development, and begins to lose sizable amounts of identity and authority to some larger community, it must stand ready to pay the high cost of survival.

4

The Techniques of
National Development

HOW does a modern nation come into being? How are the visions of a sprinkle of German philosophers, the manifestoes of a handful of Zionists, the plots of several generations of Russian revolutionaries, or the programs of a threatened Japanese elite converted into the realities of the most complicated of all forms of human organization? How do men go about achieving the goals of nationhood and modernity in life, not just on paper? These are the broad questions of method, as distinguished from purpose, that I hope to answer in this last preliminary chapter.

In answering them I hope also to make clear a crucial point about the modern nation: It is not simply the product of a long train of accidents that took place in and around a formless, paralyzed, dependent, unaware community and turned it into a structured, innovative, independent, self-conscious one. In reviewing the history of every nation, we happen upon pivotal stages in which the unanticipated consequences of erratic events worked an immense influence on the pace of progress. Yet the events would have had no such influence if men had not been disposed to accept the consequences and work with them, and only a community with achievement on its agenda or already on record would harbor enough outstanding men of adventurous spirit to transform accident into opportunity. The modern nation is essentially an *achievement*. However much significance we grant to accident-as-happening or accident-as-circumstance, "achievement" is the word, encompassing as it does the notions of purpose, effort, and accomplishment, that is emphasized in this chapter. Once again I find myself drawing, selectively to be sure, on Ernest Renan's elo·

quence. In the making of a nation, he insisted, "Man, sirs, does not improvise. The nation, like the individual, is the product of a long period of work, sacrifice, and devotion." [1]

Confident that Renan would understand and forgive, I also find myself proposing a second generalized, unpretentious, reality-based, and reality-oriented theory, in this instance a theory of national development that makes room for both the universally applicable prerequisites of achievement and the major alternative paths to it.

The reality on which these observations are based is the world-wide scatter of visibly modern nations, each of which is most certainly "the product of a long period of work, sacrifice, and devotion," not to forget ambition, adventure, thirst for profit, migration, disruption, exploitation, and, in almost every case, a few or perhaps several acts of aggression. We are learning more each year about such notable examples as Britain (which first became a viable nation or nation-state and thereafter went in quest of modernity, a road no longer open in a world held captive by the ideology of egalitarian democracy), Germany (which, in a peculiar way, reversed this order), Japan (in which the two quests rolled forward together under a compulsion that telescoped twenty generations into three and led to the brink of self-immolation), and Argentina (where the quest for full modernity remains bogged down in the swamp of imperfect nationhood), as well as France, Switzerland, Sweden, Turkey, Australia, Canada, Italy, Israel, and several dozen others. And as we learn, we are coming to a new sense of both the uses and the limits of comparative history, and thus are showing a resurgent yet measured bravery about drawing general conclusions from an assortment of special cases.

The reality to which this modest theory is oriented is the world of today and of the foreseeable future. In this world the modern nations strain to preserve their achievements and to deal with the problems of middle or old age, the emerging nations rush to catch up (many, alas, to no avail), and all sensible nations and would-be nations, however delicious the air of independence they sniff, look around for lessons, warnings, schemes of assistance, and opportunities for co-operation that may help them to achieve and reachieve the goals of development. It may not be the "best of all possible worlds," but it is one in which a better world for hundreds of millions of people is still within the reach of the nations that constitute it.

Before we turn to the main business of scrutinizing the major techniques of national development, let me suggest that no one of them alone (or, as is more likely to be the case, no combination of techniques shaped by choice and chance to the traditions and needs of a particular people) can be expected to work effectively if certain prerequisites are not present in force. To put the matter another way, and also to offer an exact count, the process of national development will not go forward successfully under any auspices, in fealty to any ideology, in any part of the contemporary world unless four situations or properties or, as I prefer to call them, *essentials* exist or can somehow be generated.

The first essential would hardly seem worth ticking off except that too many men with understandably high hopes have a habit of overlooking it: *opportunity*. A modern nation will never arise on the foundation of a traditional society or liberated colony or adventurous settlement if the circumstances are not promising. They must be positively favorable in terms of resources, skills, geography, and timing; they must be negatively tolerable in terms of the absence or at least manageability of tribal tensions, feudal strongholds, religious and linguistic divisions, the threat of aggressive or subversive or exploitative neighbors, and the sheer weight of a surging population, all problems that plague the existence and corrode the dreams of some of the most admirable of the emerging nations.

One should not be too rigid in setting general standards of opportunity and then announcing that some new nations have a good chance to develop successfully, others only a bare chance, and still others no chance at all, doomed as they are by stubbornly unpleasant circumstances to remain mired in a swamp of decaying tradition or to disintegrate into marauding fragments. The opportunity for nationhood and modernity is by no means a panorama of mindless accident. If it is not present at the birth of a nation to an extent that promises substance to the hopes of the founders, they and their heirs may make up the difference by conscious effort, as the development of Japan has proved conclusively on one side of the world and the endurance of Switzerland on the other. An adequate stock of natural resources is a consequence as well as a cause of economic growth. The strikingly different aspect of the land of Canaan today from that of only two generations ago is proof of this neglected truth. And many a nation has imported everything from iron ore to capital and from locomotives to people in order to overcome deficiencies that had seemed a portent of failure. As "the sense of greatness keeps a nation great," [2] the sense of opportunity gives a nation the sort of opportunity denied to would-be nations that are trapped in a state of senseless torpor.

These observations lead to identification of a second essential: *will*. The word is simple; the reality it seeks to express is subtle and perplexing. Some of the most diligent students of modernization have confessed that we understand very little, and have difficulty getting even crude measurements, of the contours of the lively sense of intellectual and spiritual purpose displayed by the citizenry of a developed or developing nation, by the people of what David McClelland calls "the achieving society." [3] Yet often the only difference of consequence between a nation on the move and a nation left to rot lies in the realm of character and attitude: in the lessons children are taught, the purposes leading men pursue, the virtues ordinary men celebrate, the individual and social energies the whole community seems to have at its command. In the nation on the move restlessness and hope and effort combine to produce a genuinely "modern spirit," in the words of G. Lowes Dickinson, a "dissatisfaction with the world in which we live" and a "determination to realize one that shall be better," [4] and that spirit may well be a more powerful influence in the progress of the nation than the accidental possession of fertile soil or bubbling oil.

In the form of awareness—a feeling of belonging, a readiness to obey, a capacity to sacrifice—the widespread, persistent exercise of will is needed to create and preserve a nation. The sign of nationhood is a widespread, self-conscious sense of the rightness of nationalism, and that, Hans Kohn has insisted correctly, is a "state of mind." [5] In the form of ambition—a delight in effort, a readiness to take risks, a capacity to innovate—the similar exercise of will is needed to achieve political efficacy, economic viability, social integration, and cultural maturity. The sign of modernity is a widespread, self-conscious sense of the necessity of change, and that, too, is a state of mind. Since nationhood and modernity have now merged into one grand purpose of men all over the world, perhaps we can consider these two wills as one, which is internalized in the citizen as a set of value-grounded expectations that men in a traditional society would never harbor and is institutionalized in the community as a set of value-transmitting arrangements that teach these men from earliest childhood to be loyal to the nation and rejoice in progress.

I am speaking for the most part, as I have chosen knowingly to speak throughout these preliminary chapters, in terms of an ideal, and I am perfectly aware that the most eagerly achieving societies in history have had their share of nonachievers who were indifferent alike to the calls of civic duty and to the rewards of personal effort. Such societies could tolerate their presence but go right on achieving largely because of the existence in force of an *elite,* a third essential of development I choose to tag with a label that frightens some persons and misleads others, yet may still be used in a soberly empirical, nonpejorative sense. While this proposition takes us onto dangerous ground, it does seem clear that nations are born, develop, modernize, and endure only under the leadership of skilled and dedicated men. When we identify a group of men who have invented new forms of political decision or discovered new sources of energy or devised new ways of caring for the aged, above all when we read about or meet a group that played the game of nationalism so hard as to bring a nation to life, we should not be afraid to call it an elite: a cluster or series of clusters of extraordinary persons inoculated wtih extraordinary doses of skill and will that have enabled them to shape the lives of countless other persons in an outsized manner.

The elite of a would-be nation may be unified and clear-minded, dispersed and contrary-minded, even divided and bloody-minded, yet unless it exists to provide alert and functional leadership, no real progress will be made in the direction of political, social, economic, or cultural development. To some extent, all this talk of the necessity of an elite is a string of truisms, for the stark fact of human organization is a call for the exercise of leadership. Beyond that, we learn two things from every page of social history: First, the more sophisticated the organization, the more imperative is the call; and, second, the more successful it is in achieving its collective purposes, the more rewarded and respected are those upon whom the responsibilities of leadership have devolved. Yet I venture to suggest that the gigantic, drawn-out, collective act of building a modern nation, which means the transformation or consolidation or integration of an entire way of life, demands and, wherever the act is successful, has nurtured a special kind and degree of leadership.

Membership in the elite is by no means restricted to the cluster of power-wielders or style-setters at the top of each sector of national endeavor. While such men may give marching orders to the whole society, they must sense what orders are possible to give and have confidence that the orders will be carried out effectively. For that purpose, as also for the higher purposes of transforming will into effort and giving cohesion to the nation, men of better-than-average imagination, skill, dependability, and resolution— Alexander Hamilton saluted them as "choice spirits" [6]—must be present in sizable numbers up and down the ladder of every calling.

Massachusetts in the throes of fighting a war of liberation along with its sister states and, at the same time, of writing a constitution for itself (1776–1780) furnishes an admirable demonstration of the case in point: For every General Knox it loaned General Washington to command the Continental artillery, it mustered hundreds of resilient soldiers for the Marblehead regiment that thrice gave Washington a chance to fight another day; for every John Adams it asked to write a constitution, it harbored thousands of plain citizens who knew enough to insist on the viable charter Adams and his colleagues finally produced. Revolutionary Massachusetts was a community in which uncommon men flourished in every walk of life and at every level, and we should not be surprised to learn that this state held a commanding position in the American Quest over the next seventy or eighty years. We have enough other examples in history to prove that a nation is cohesive and progressive in rough proportion to the numbers and devotion of the principal elites, especially at the top and in the middle of the social structure, and also in proportion to the incidence of understanding, respect, ease of communication, and opportunity for passage between the two. In the vibrant society one finds strong links among the groups at the top as well as a steady surge upward of fresh talent from the main body of the people. The two-tiered elite (if thus we may describe and applaud it) is a central value in the equation of modern nationhood.

To opportunity, will, and extraordinary leadership let us add one last essential of national development: *politics*—a word, let me recall, that I have chosen to use in the Aristotelian sense of public affairs and public service. The search for unity and development must be pressed, we have seen, in many fields and for many, often conflicting, purposes. The achievement of an efficacious national polity is only one aspect of a much larger, more complicated process. Yet the political system has repeatedly, with few notable exceptions, proved itself the chief means of fostering a widespread sense of nationalism among the men of an unsure community and of focusing their energies on the tasks of economic, social, and intellectual progress. All the techniques of national development we examine in the next few pages are, in a fundamental sense, political in character.

Not a subjective sense of allegiance to the discipline of political science, but an objective contemplation of dozens of instances of national development leads me, in fact somewhat against the grain of inclination, to assign this important role to politics—although I would add quickly that I am talking about the politics of reason, freedom, progress, and efficiency, not the politics of fanaticism, oppression, stagnation, and incompetence. While much of the good life of the citizens in a modern nation is lived in a spirit of indifference or even defiance toward the political system, while the system itself cannot (and in a constitutional democracy should not) be asked to govern the ungovernable, and while it is often as likely to arrest as to promote development, politics is the key that men must sooner or later turn energetically if a modern nation is to come into being and then to be preserved. Since the point may be excessively unpalatable to some readers, let me make the act of swallowing easier by putting it in terms of the persons who serve the nation in a public capacity: cabinet ministers, diplomats, parliamentarians, civil servants, politicians, judges, juries, councilmen, soldiers, inspectors, welfare workers, city planners, schoolteachers, scientists hired or supported by government, policemen, postmen, firemen—and the list could run on and on through tax collectors to spacemen. Perhaps I should cut it off with the simple reminder that in a modern nation every citizen is expected to vote and inquire and lend support and express grievances, and thus to act himself from time to time in a public capacity.

A few last words designed to forestall criticism before we begin the run through the catalogue of the major techniques of national development:

First, each is at best a rough category of intentions and activities, a general description of a phenomenon that can show itself in a variety of forms.

Next, none has ever existed in an entirely pure form. To the contrary, we isolate one technique and examine its operation only as an exercise in abstraction for the sake of deeper understanding. In the world of reality the use of one technique invites the intrusion of ideas and arrangements generated by several others, and the overlap between any two of them may appear more significant than the distinction.

It might be useful to carry this observation a step farther by noting that most cases of successful development have been celebrated for the way in which several techniques were put together and then transformed into a special, even unique method suited to the circumstances and purposes of one people at one stage in its history. Every nation follows its own road to self-identity and modernity, and thus makes use of a combination of techniques unlike the method of any other nation. Every modern nation that endures over a long period of time will almost certainly be compelled to reshape its method to changes in circumstance and purpose—to abandon a technique that has served it well, to adopt one it has hitherto shunned out of distaste or fear, perhaps to invent a new one that has never been tested.

This last observation is a backhanded way of stating the obvious truth that nations are not entirely at liberty to pick and choose among all the simple techniques and intricate combinations that may be known to exist at any one time. For each nation, indeed, some are simply not available: To adopt them even in a modified form would be to defy wholesome tradition or ignore overpowering circumstance, and thus to invite disaffection and, in due course, disaster. The conditions and traditions of every nation forbid flatly the use of some techniques of development, and also dictate that one or two will have priority over all others that might possibly be used.

Finally, it is essential to recognize that each of these techniques, while described primarily as a road to modernity, has also been with few exceptions a road to nationhood. Whether by working directly to generate a feeling of patriotism or indirectly to create a humane society in which the feeling comes naturally, it can in fact serve the twin ends of modernity and nationhood in one grand gesture. Since the two, I repeat, have been tied inextricably together in the history of the past several centuries, any confusion about this matter that emerges in the next few pages may prove more apparent than real.

The first major technique of national development, which has lost much prestige as a primary pattern of activity yet has a knack of hanging on or reappearing as a secondary force in the most unlikely places, is *private enterprise*. Having defined this technique as the striving, whether competitive or co-operative, of individuals and groups basically nonpolitical in character, I would move on to assert that it is theoretically possible—I say "theoretically" with confidence because I could just as easily have said "historically"—for a nation to be born and then make rapid progress socially, economically, and intellectually in the absence of any conspicuous care and feeding by the political system. In this matter, it might be useful to make a distinction, which is usually and probably necessarily blurred, between *national development* and *nation-building*. Since building carries with it the notion of conscious political direction, this first technique, which might also be called, *the nongovernmental impulse,* has only limited appeal to the emerging nations of our generation, although, to tell the untellable truth, many of them would be well advised to encourage it more vigorously.

The appeal is limited because, to tell another such truth, only a few nations in history have had the time, resources, values, discipline, and sense of security to allow this technique to take priority over all others and work its wonders at its own pace. More important, only a few began their experiments in independence with an existing and thereafter self-replenishing supply of entrepreneurs, administrators, engineers, scientists, inventors, explorers, artists, reformers, craftsmen, teachers, preachers, and poets who could pursue their own careers without political direction or oversight and help to develop the capacities and shape the loyalties of a self-knowing, self-sustaining nation. The nonpolitical elite as an expression of the nongovernmental impulse has had only scattered opportunities to dominate the life of any nation for more than a few years. The simple fact of success in its endeavors creates new instruments of social and economic power that require policing and often support, and raises problems to which politics seems to offer the most effective, tidy, and speedy solutions. Still, the opportunities for far-ranging private enterprise have existed in the histories of many nations; when ingenious men have seized them with determination—most dramatically in eighteenth-century England, nineteenth-century America, and twentieth-century Japan—the result has been both a boost to national self-consciousness and a transformation of society.

The scrutiny of this technique leads once again to an assessment of the role of accident in national development, and I restate the conviction, to which I came only after contemplating dozens of examples ranging from England under the Tudors to Indonesia under Sukarno and Suharto, that nations are achievements and not accidents. Accident has its place in the total array of influences that bring a modern nation to life. Indeed, if we think of it in terms of long-run circumstances as distinguished from short-term happenings, no one can deny that some geographic or demographic or political or social condition completely beyond the control of the nation at one or every stage of development may help mightily to determine the extent of independence, the quality of patriotism, the form of the polity, the productivity of the economy, the structure of society, or the level of culture. Britain is a different kind of nation than it would have been if no Channel had divided it from Europe, Switzerland different because it has great mountains at its core, Japan different because it lacks most of the ingredients to make steel (except the ingredient of will), the United States different because it speaks English, Canada different because the United States exists, the Low Countries different because they have always been a convenient place for other countries to make war, the Congo (Kinshasa) different because Leopold II of Belgium was an alert, greedy, and durable man, a score of nations different because Karl Marx forgot to fall overboard and be drowned in the waters of the Channel. Nevertheless, however much influence we grant to the unforeseen consequences of obdurate circumstances, unexpected events, and erratic men, we must give first place in both the founding and developing of modern nations to the skill of determined men who knew something if not everything of what they were doing.

I do not mean to thrust politics entirely out of the picture being traced of this first technique. Individuals and groups cannot compete or co-operate to develop a modern nation if a political system does not exist to provide, at the very least, for keeping domestic peace, discouraging foreign aggression, administering equitable justice, and serving as the focus of patriotic sentiment. Effective private enterprise of every description needs the protection if not the support of public authority. In all those nations in which the nongovernmental impulse has been an important technique of development, government has been forced to step in from time to time in order to clear away the debris left by the men of the past or to open up a fair field to the men of the future. Still, if this technique has never existed in unadulterated form, and has never had the amount of benevolent influence attributed to it by the ideologues of laissez faire, it has been historically and remains potentially a powerful engine of progress and a rich source of patriotism. Private enterprise may yet be given a chance to prove its worth in countries whose leaders now profess to shun it as obsolescent, irrelevant, or downright evil.

A sizable step beyond the situation in which government is confined to the roles of watchman and symbol is *political response,* a technique that invites it to fill the added role of favor-dispenser. "Interests," James Madison and others have reminded us, spring up in every posttraditional society. The men who share them quite naturally demand representation in the political system; and, once they win it, they go on to ask for supports, subsidies, and special protections. If they are determined, clever, and strategically placed in the economy and society, they get much of what they ask for. One of the most useful things they get is over-representation, which makes it easier for them to ask and get the next time around. They seek their favors in a mood of self-deluding patriotism: It is not their special interest but the national interest that will be served by a helpful response from the political system, not their profits or privileges but the wealth or health of the nation that will be increased. The men of political power who dispense the favors usually respond, unless they are case-hardened cynics, in a similar mood. They know they are helping one particular interest; they have little trouble convincing themselves that what is good for the interest will be good for the country.

Neither favor-seekers nor favor-dispensers are always and entirely wrong. While government may respond to the pleas of special interest, even to the blandishments of powerful men, in a manner that corrodes the loyalty of other men or delays the progress of the community, it can also contribute impressively to overall national development, for example, to economic viability by laying a selective tariff that stimulates expansion in an industry with exaggerated linkages, to social integration by instituting a viable program of care for the aged, to popular cohesion by forbidding discrimination against a despised minority, and to cultural maturity by bestowing imaginative grants on artists and scholars. Governments of every description engage in actions such as these. What distinguishes the technique of political response is that the action is essentially the result of a plea for special consideration by (and occasionally for) a special interest, that it aims at subsidy and protection rather than regulation and direction, and that it does not fit into a general scheme of national development.

Political response is primarily, if by no means exclusively, a technique used by nations in which private enterprise has held sway as the spur of activity. This technique seems to have the most noticeable impact on the economy, first to help it grow, then to rescue the victims of growth (those who shout loud enough for help), then to keep it growing and also to make it more humane by transforming mere growth into development. While political response may seem a rough and tortuous road to economic viability, it does have spectacular achievements to its credit. While it, like every technique described in this chapter, can be a drag on national development, especially when groups unmindful of the

general interest or fearful of social change manage to get the ear
of government, it can also be a powerful stimulus. The contributions of political response to the progress of industry, commerce,
transportation, and agriculture in some of the most advanced and
stable nations deserve to be more openly acknowledged.

If the political system goes on long enough granting boons to
special interests, and if, at the same time, the political culture
grows more egalitarian, a demand will surely arise for a *rationalization of response,* that is to say, for a more conscious and persistent effort to strike a roughly evenhanded balance of favors, to
assess each new petition to a special interest more candidly in
terms of the public interest, and to give preferred treatment to
economic, social, and cultural undertakings that contribute visibly to the health, good order, and progress of the entire nation.
Beyond rationalization of response lies *regulation of enterprise,*
and beyond that we need take just one more step, although a
fateful one, to the belief that conscious, over-all political direction is essential to beget and preserve national unity as well as to
increase and parcel out fairly the rewards of modernity. If it is
also assumed that such direction need not be autocratic, arbitrary, and irresponsible, we arrive finally at a point where we may
isolate and identify a third major technique: *democratic oversight.* Britain, New Zealand, and the Scandinavian monarchies
are the most instructive examples of modern nations that have, in
effect, shifted emphasis over the years from private enterprise and
political response to this third technique, of which shrewd, flexible, responsible planning is quite clearly the essence. India is the
most anxiously observed example of an emerging nation that
searches for nationhood and modernity primarily with a method
grounded on democratic oversight.

The Indian experiment is especially relevant for our purposes,[7]
for here is a nation whose governing elite believes that both democracy and oversight are cardinal political virtues, that the one
in no way threatens the other, indeed that democracy will never
be attained unless there is oversight—and oversight turns sour
unless it operates from a democratic base. In short, the world is
witness to the interesting spectacle of at least one government in
its underdeveloped half that proposes to advance rapidly toward

the goals of nationhood and modernity with special reliance on a technique of directed nation-building rather than of aimless national development, and that insists it can and must attain them as a genuine democracy. In defiance of harrowing circumstances and almost intolerable pressures, the Indian political system continues to be notable for fairness of elections, fullness of public discussion of issues, openness of decision-making, representation of all legitimate interests (with legitimacy defined in broadly permissive terms), accountability of officials, predictability of judicial and administrative procedures, subordination of the armed forces to civilian control, the scope of rights enjoyed by citizens, and an emphasis on persuasion rather than coercion as the principal means of winning obedience. Although India is plagued by illiteracy, it extends the vote to all men and women; although India is poor and still twisted by the tensions of caste, it tries to allocate resources and energies for the benefit of all the people.

It is much too possible, we are constantly reminded, that the Indian experiment will fail, and that one of the death-dealing causes will be the quixotic attempt to survive as a democratic island in an autocratic sea. Many economists and political scientists in the United States and Europe insist, some happily but others grimly, that both growth and development in the modern world command all-out mobilization of the national community. A mobilizing nation faced with problems like those of India, they tell us, cannot afford the luxury of constitutional democracy even if the political system is structured to permit large-scale planning. Democracy exists in India, they add, only because the system has not really come to grips with the staggering issues of poverty, caste, language, religion, and overpopulation. Let us hope that we shall have to wait a long time to find out if these prophets of disaster are right, and let us insist that even if they are, even if India sinks into a torpor or explodes into a dozen or more Biafras, this one instance of failure will not prove conclusively that democratic oversight is simply the plaything of the Western world: a conscience-relieving toy for established nations but a paralyzing contrivance for emerging ones. Democratic oversight has already scored enough victories to demonstrate both efficacy and humaneness. It has, moreover, appeared in tandem with enough different economies, ranging from the near side of old-fashioned capitalism to the near side of all-encompassing social-ism, to demonstrate a flair for flexibility. Perhaps in the next decades it will also display a flair for adaptability. If democratic oversight cannot be transplanted without rejection into the living body of every nation of the world, every nation would certainly profit by importing some of its ideas and procedures on a selective basis.

The most likely alternative for India today, as it was a generation ago, is *autocratic control*. The leading examples of both the capacities and the limits of this major technique remain the Japan of the Meiji Restoration and the Turkey of Kemal Atatürk. What I am talking of in this instance is a political system that also makes nationhood and modernity its principal goals and proposes to advance toward them rapidly in a spirit of conscious nation-building, yet assumes that it can never reach them as a Western-style democracy—although such democracy is often held out as the grand prize to be bestowed upon the people of the modernized nation once autocracy has done the work that it alone can do. Leadership in the system rests in the hands of a small, hardened, dedicated, and, in the technical sense of the word, irresponsible elite of nation-builders for whom discipline-oriented planning is the key to the future. This elite is more concerned with the needs of society than with the rights of individuals. It likes to hold elections; the elections are managed so as to produce the correct results. It likes to encourage public discussions of issues; the discussions are largely a one-way affair in which the leaders tell the led to tighten their belts and have faith in them and their plans. Decisions are made (and made final) behind ministerial or bureaucratic doors rather than in parliamentary arenas; the elite represents, or so it professes to think, the nation as a body of like-minded individuals rather than as a sprawl of other-minded interests; and neither accountability of officials nor predictability of procedures gets much more than lip service as a political value. While the autocrats of the nation-building elite prefer to win obedience to their orders through the inducements of persuasion, they are perfectly willing to resort to coercion.

In most countries that choose this technique, coercion is the principal sanction for three reasons: first, because autocracy ap-

The Techniques of National Development

pears to the autocrats, many of them surprisingly immune to the temptation of posing as democrats, to be the only path to the twin ends of nationhood and modernity; second, because autocracy in one form or another is the inherited way of life; and third, because the armed forces, such as they are, have better training, higher morale, higher morals, fewer scruples, and more effective tools of winning obedience than any other group or institution. The number of military or semimilitary regimes in the underdeveloped world increases with each year as one army after another decides that the civilian leaders of the political system cannot keep the peace, cannot make good on their grandiose plans, or cannot even hold the line against the lethargic tendency to slide back. Many of these countries have no tradition of civilian control of the armed forces; many, thanks to the priority the rich nations have given to military assistance, have an army (and also, more often than not, a police force) visibly more modern than society as a whole. We should therefore not be surprised to learn that the harsh responsibilities of modernization have been seized by or handed over to an elite whose bag of values is full of words like "command," "loyalty," "obedience," "sacrifice," "plan," "strategy," "discipline," and "mobilization."

Although the ruling armies of the underdeveloped countries are dedicated fiercely to the virtues of nationalism, many are quite uninterested in modernizing the economy and social order across the board, and are probably as incapable of bringing off this exacting historical task as the civil governments they have replaced.[8] Still, if we know of armies that are reactionary, brutal, and self-serving, and know of others that are timid, incompetent, and feckless, we have enough examples of modernization under military direction—the achievement of the Turkish army under Atatürk, however flawed, remains the most conspicuous[9]—to persuade us that this is one of several roads to a better future. Men of good will must not close it off abruptly as an alternate route for emerging nations with large hopes but only a small potential for unity and modernity. As a device for recruiting new and often lowborn candidates into the elite, for injecting a "strong sense of realism and detachment" into the attitudes of a people led astray by the rantings of demagogues,[10] of teaching men to decide and manage as well as to read and write, for allocating scarce resources in an effort to build a small but sturdy industrial base, and above all as a school for nationalism, the army may well serve as the most effective institution in an emerging nation.[11] If the nation is ever to become truly modern, however, this army will have to renounce power and take its place as only one of many strong, functional, and integrated institutions. Since even a modest degree of economic and social attainment lies far in the future for most emerging nations, students of modernization will have plenty of time to think of ways to shift both the delights and the burdens of governing from the hands of colonels and sergeants to those of politicians and bureaucrats. Whether the latter will then prove more attentive than the former to the reasonably voiced wishes of the people is a question to which no sure and simple answer can now be made.

A long step beyond autocracy is the awesome technique or, more correctly, array of techniques of *totalitarian manipulation.* China and Cuba—totalitarianism comes in several shapes and sizes—have also applauded the goals of nationhood and modernity, in China's case, to be sure, a masochistically austere modernity. They propose to advance toward them rapidly in a spirit of world-transforming as well as nation-building; in their planning they assume that the political system must engulf every aspect of economy, society, and culture. Although China in particular is not eager to acknowledge the debt, the model of success is the Soviet Union; and although the leaders of every totalitarian and pseudo-totalitarian country may react angrily to an assertion of the haunting truth, they should not be allowed to forget that Nazi Germany displayed all characteristics and most institutions of the model of success it could never quite manage to destroy by force of arms.

The essential characteristics of totalitarianism are, in the subjective opinion of a dogged nontotalitarian, four in number:[12]

the obliteration of all restraints on the activities of the political system: direct restraints like legal prescriptions, indirect restraints like free associations for social or cultural purposes, customary restraints like the family as hitherto organized;

the penetration of every nook of the exposed and defenseless society by the restless, protean, dynamic exercise of political power, that is, the politicizing of every aspect of human endeavor;

the ubiquitous control of the exposed and defenseless person, who must demonstrate his loyalty to the nation and its political system actively and repeatedly;

the pledging of unquestioning allegiance to an ideology so millennial and all-explaining that it takes the form of a secular religion as well as a militant nationalism.

These characteristics are institutionalized in a staggering complex of instruments, procedures, and arrangements. Since this is a study of the growth and expansion of a nation in a period when totalitarianism, a phenomenon of the twentieth century, had not yet emerged in full and noxious flower, I will point to only a few institutions of special relevance for our purposes, then move on to scrutinize other techniques of national development. One is the monolithic party, which identifies itself with the whole nation and provides the spark for each new departure in each area of endeavor. Another is a monopoly of the media of communication so effective that no voices, not even the voices of silence, are heard to dissent. A third appears to be an intricate system of organized terror for purging society of disaffection. And a fourth is an elaborate display of many of the trappings of democracy through which the party and the political system work together to create the mass support so necessary to govern efficiently in the age of mass man. The result is the atomization of society, the creation of an order devoid of buffers between the individual person and the political system. In appearance staunchly rooted in neighborhood, factory, union, and political cell, in reality each man is rootless in the face of the smothering power the system can muster.

Totalitarianism is, in effect, the political expression of a zealous commitment to mobilization as the only certain path to modernity and nationhood. From the point of view of constitutional democracy, as also of benevolent or simply cantankerous autocracy, the label "political" is quite misleading, for the system busies itself with every aspect of life from the care of children to the feeding of poets—poets, it need hardly be added, who celebrate the virtues of the system in lines easy to understand, memorize, and recite. Such a system has a special need for a strong, diligent, confident elite, and such an elite will arise, according to the teachings of the orthodox Lenin—and also of the dissident

93

Mao, the deviant Hitler, and the vagrant Mussolini—out of the disciplined ranks of the monolithic party. Totalitarians believe altogether sincerely in the possibility of the great leap forward, and they know from Lenin, the father of them all (as Marx was the grandfather), that a revolutionary party with "a small, compact core, consisting of reliable, experienced, and hardened workers" is the only force that can be counted on to goad the mass of men into the leap.[13]

Let me conclude this survey of the major techniques of national development with the proposal that Apter's useful distinction between reconciling and mobilizing forms of government be further refined by identifying a third form, the *energizing* system, that is located somewhere between the other two. It is more purposeful, anticipatory, active, and coercive than a government of reconciliation; it is less purposeful, anticipatory, active, and coercive than a government of mobilization. National development, which is a matter of indifference to reconciliators and a holy grail to mobilizers, is a central but not consuming value of the energizing government. Politics, which is a game of give-and-take to reconciliators and an all-purpose machine to mobilizers, serves principally to prime the pumps of economic, social, and cultural development. While the fit is rough, I would suggest that the center of gravity of a reconciling government can be located on either private enterprise or political response, of an energizing government on democratic oversight, of a mobilizing government on either autocratic control or totalitarian manipulation.

To the five techniques that have been isolated and examined I now add two others that are secondary in rank yet often primary in influence. The first is *model-imitating*, an old and tested technique that has been used in fruitful association with all other techniques. The world is full of instruments of economic and social development that have scored celebrated victories, and each is a model for nation-builders to try on for size. There are general political models, which range in magnitude from the Soviet Union on down to Sweden or Cuba; special political models, of which the Royal Military Academy (Sandhurst), the Academy of Sciences of the Soviet Union, and the Tennessee Valley Authority

The Techniques of National Development

are three alluring samples currently on display; and special nonpolitical models, of which the patterns of computer technology in
dozens of American industries are the most intriguing to observe
and expensive to imitate. The most famous model of all is the
nation itself, in present form an original creation of the West.
Every continent brims with nationalists who claim to speak for
real or presumptive or still-inchoate nations and who have found
a new and reassuring identity principally by imitating the ways
of former masters. England, France, and Spain have been the
most influential models in this respect, although the men who
made these models work did not intend them to be so attractive
and the men who learned their lessons in nationalism by imitating them now prefer to deny it.

While some nations are trapped by circumstances of ideology
or geography in a situation in which the political, economic, social, and cultural models of a colossal neighbor or partner are
virtually rammed down their throats, most are reasonably free to
shop around for institutions, processes, and ideas that, having
worked wonders of unification or modernization in one country,
might work wonders in theirs. The difficulty is that too many
nations beg, steal, borrow, or purchase models they cannot afford,
cannot learn to operate, or cannot introduce without corroding
indigenous institutions and values of solid merit. The most successful example of the use of this technique was the Japan of the
Meiji Restoration, which imitated the West relentlessly without
selling more than a small portion of its birthright.

Model-imitating beckons to nations of every description, developed as well as emerging, democratic as well as autocratic or totalitarian. The resort to this technique can be conscious or unconscious, broad or narrow, indiscriminate or selective, public or
private, gladly proclaimed or shamefully covered up, engaged in
by a whole nation or practiced by a few ambitious men. The
model—an electoral procedure, an industrial process, an automated factory, a school curriculum, a system of social security, a
military academy, a pattern of access to a large city, even an array
of shrewd strategies for getting hitherto indifferent persons to be
strong nationalists and willing agents of modernization—can be
studied on its home grounds or imported in the form of manuals,
blueprints, ideas in the minds of clever men, or physical proper-

95

ties. Almost every emerging nation is strongly attracted by proximity, ideology, or the pull of a shared history to an established nation (or to several), and it may well find that imitation is the shortest of short cuts to the goals it has set for itself. The technique is also available to established nations, which have plenty of lessons to learn from each other, and perhaps occasionally from "backward" friends and neighbors.

When a nation imports operators along with a model, it makes use of the related technique of *tutelage*. While this technique has achieved remarkable successes in countries that had not yet achieved or even anticipated independence—the consequence of the British presence in India, whatever the motives and expectations, is the most renowned case in point—I refer in this instance to the conscious acceptance or retention of experts from abroad *after* the winning of independence. The responsibilities of tutelage may be assigned to an old imperial master, as several emerging nations of Africa have assigned them candidly to France. The tutors may come, whether the tutored nation bids them welcome or not, from a new "friend," especially one that promises payments and protection along with instruction. They may be as well-intentioned as Peace Corpsmen in Ghana, oblivious to consequences as missionaries in the old China, committed narrowly to the interest of their own nation as Soviet officers in the new Egypt, or malicious as Chinese "diplomats" in Congo (Brazzaville), but all act as tutelary agents of modernization. It might be better for the morale and independence of the tutored nation if assistance came (this is true of capital as well as of personnel) from multinational groups such as arms of the United Nations or specially created consortiums. It might also be better if the nation requiring assistance recognized that the technique of tutelage produces healthier results in an area of public endeavor like education than in one like politics.

Tutelage is a dangerous technique that may lead not only to the feeling of inferiority and the fact of dependence but also to the raising of expectations that can never be satisfied, to the abrupt abandonment of old ways that could have made rich contributions to development, and to the stunting of the growth of new skills and leadership. In that special instance of tutelage, the export of young people to study abroad, a new nation faces the added dangers of feeding the famous (or infamous?) brain drain, creating a cosmopolitan and disaffected elite, and yielding to the temptation to abandon efforts to build its own institutions of higher education. Yet the developed world has too many excellent models for the underdeveloped to ignore them, and mere imitation may not be an effective enough technique to get copies of these models to run smoothly in an environment devoid of men with the will and talent to make them run. Although it may pain the new nations to admit the fact, they must accept instruction in the ways of modernity; and that fact almost always means the importing of instructors who operate as well as teach. If the technique works as it is supposed to work, both teachers and taught, both operators and apprentices, can look forward to the day when rehearsal becomes reality and the need for wholesale tutelage vanishes.

It might be useful to end this chapter with a few general observations. Three have already been made and are repeated only in order to lend them special emphasis:

First, every nation combines, whether by intention or accident, two or more techniques in a method that seems best suited to its own circumstances, values, and purposes.

Second, no general method or special technique can be expected to contribute effectively to progress in the absence of favorable conditions, a deep-seated will to achieve, a persistent display of skilled leadership, and a political system that fosters loyalty among all men and, at the very least, provides a fair field for most.

Third, the process of development, however healthy the motives that generated it and however modern the nation to which it finally leads, is not a jolly excursion but a disruptive experience.

To these I tack on the proposition, which is slowly being tested and found valid, that national development in any major field moves not steadily but fitfully, not in measured steps but in erratic bursts. While one should hesitate to transfer a concept from physical to social science, it does seem that something like Max Planck's quantum theory of the irregular emission of energy is basic to an understanding of the progress of nations as political, social, economic, cultural, and spiritual entities. The path of a successful nation leads visibly onward and upward to self-identity, unity, and modernity, yet the march along the path moves at an uneven rate. It moves, moreover, through thickets, mudholes, and rough spots that men can map in advance only vaguely and understand in retrospect only crudely.

And to that, finally, I add the opinion, which need not be tested in order to be judged valid, that development should be qualitative as well as quantitative. The building of a modern nation is an endeavor in which men ought not presume to engage unless they are prepared to be selective about techniques and purposes. Within the limits of natural and inherited circumstances they should make choices on moral, political, and esthetic grounds, and their choices should add up to a version of the good life that holds out dignity, hope, and opportunity to those who follow after. It is not enough, to take one critical example, for an economy simply to grow more productive. The question must be posed: productive of what and for whom? The only answer a modern nation can make is this: productive of the appurtenances of a truly human existence for every citizen. In deciding what those appurtenances are and how they can be produced, a nation chooses, in the last reckoning, whether it will *develop* as well as *grow*, whether it will be exciting, just, and civilized or dull, cruel, and boorish. Not simply survival, but *civilized survival* is the ultimate goal that gives meaning to the pursuit of all other goals of national development.

II

The American Achievement

1790–1860

5

The Quest for Nationhood:

Successes and Failures

THOSE who write history must be selective and schematic, and thus, of pitiless necessity, are condemned to distort it. Those who read history, if they are to understand what they read, should therefore stand fast against temptation and refuse to equate necessary distortion with obstinate reality, the neatness of what men write with the untidiness of what they write about. This is, I think, an especially useful message of caution to persons who read about a period or age or stage in the life of a civilization, religion, nation, political party, social movement, trail-blazing idea, or famous man. They are bound to remind themselves constantly, as are those who seek to instruct them, that history is written but not made in chapters. At the outset of an appraisal of the exuberant pilgrimage of the American people from 1790 to 1860, I confess without qualms that the selection of these two dates as the beginning and end of a chapter in our history is to some extent arbitrary, artificial, and thus distorting. The chapter, after all, began well before 1790; the end of the chapter is not in sight.

At the same time, these seven decades were very much a unit, a period of American history notable both for the sharpness of the break at either end, as sharp as we have ever experienced in the United States, and for the persistence of trends, problems, and national purposes through all these years of growth, expansion, and development. Indeed, it is a good deal more difficult to fix dates for the Great Awakening, the Age of Jackson, the Progressive Movement, or the Jazz Age than for the chapter of national development we seek to understand. The launching of the more perfect Union under the Constitution in 1789 set the United

States on a course that was impossible to reverse and difficult to deflect; the course led, at first somewhat absent-mindedly and at last harshly, to a bloody dispute about the next set of directions for the American people. A strong line of continuity runs from the first year of President Washington to the election of President Lincoln. What makes the line unusually strong is the easily forgotten fact that it emerged from a moment of exceptional discontinuity in American history and led almost inexorably to another.

Let us therefore consider this period as a unit and deal with it topically and analytically rather than chronologically. To be specific, I propose to take the political, economic, social, and intellectual measurements of the United States of America that catapulted Lincoln into Washington's office and thereupon fell victim to agonies which had been long imagined but never quite expected. I take them in a manner both orderl and rough: orderly because the record of American endeavor in this period is appraised in terms of the theory of national development sketched out in chapters 2 and 3, rough because it is plainly impossible— no matter how many Congressional roll calls, fluctuations in wholesale prices, circulation figures of newspapers, and statistics of immigration or taxation or railroad-building we can dig out, sort, trust, and punch on cards—to be exact and also unassailable about such vital questions as the amount of unused political capability, the degree of popular cohesion, or the range of technological literacy in the Republic of 1860. Yet if one's judgments of the record of an entire people in a memorable stage of their history can be neither exact nor unassailable, they can be systematic, objective, and at least occasionally conclusive. Thanks to the existence of a small mountain of primary evidence and secondary evaluation, they can, moreover, be assessed to a degree that, while considerably less than exact, is something more than vague.

When dealing with grand and controversial phenomena one finds them much easier to classify than to quantify, yet I am consoled by three thoughts: The resistance of trends and events to meaningful quantification does not excuse historians from the duty to study them systematically; the system of classification chosen for this survey is based squarely on the realities of recent history and contemporary politics; those who rejoice to quantify still need those who prefer to classify in order to get moving in the right direction. Perhaps some useful directions may emerge from the analysis that follows. And as one last word of preliminary caution: Although this analysis makes the distinction of chapters 2 and 3 between nationhood and modernity, I implore all readers to remember that history has merged these two phenomena into one: the modern nation. This is an essential point for students of the young Republic to keep in mind, for in the seven decades that stretched from Washington to Lincoln, the Quest was pressed largely by men who were certain that *America could not be a nation unless it was modern and could not be modern unless it was a nation.*

Since *independence* is the first goal of nationhood, we may well judge that the United States got off to one of the fastest starts of any new nation in history: It threw off the controls of its mother country abruptly, refused to look back in remorse, and never strayed from the path of self-reliance. This judgment is especially true of the political system. It would be hard to imagine a nation more oblivious to the commands or impervious to the influence of men of power in other nations than the headstrong Republic (made up, let us recall, of headstrong states) of the first half of the nineteenth century. While Americans of the 1850's felt command of their destiny slipping from their hands, they knew that this command was dissipating, as it were, into thin air, not passing into the hands of any other nation or combination of nations. The point about American independence was made with excessive clarity both at the beginning of this period, when the Treaty of Alliance of 1778 with France was repudiated, and at the end, when Lord Palmerston found it impossible to respond favorably to the plea of the Confederacy for recognition. From Yorktown to Appomattox the United States "went it alone" as few nations of the modern world had the good fortune and resources to go.

The American people had always had plenty of practice in going it alone politically. Massachusetts was virtually a self-directing commonwealth during the first half-century of its existence; Connecticut and Rhode Island, according to a sour yet perceptive Tory who wrote in 1775, were colonies in which the King and Parliament had about "as much influence . . . as in the wilds of Tartary";[1] all the colonies, even newly founded Georgia, with its fussy rule-makers in London, contested or flouted or ignored British authority with relative impunity. When the time finally came for the leaders of the mother country to assert their authority with vigor, they found themselves face to face with thirteen rebellious children who, while they might not always get along too happily with each other, now decided rather suddenly, as such decisions go, that they could get along rather well without their mother. Although the idea of independence may seem to have burst full grown from the bold minds of men like Paine, Jefferson, Franklin, the Adamses, and Washington, it had been in gestation since the first plantings in Virginia and Massachusetts.

In the early years of independence some doubt festered in less resolute minds about the immunity of the United States against foreign influence in the political process. Few Americans gave a thought to the possibility that their country might lose independence by losing a war, not even if Britain, France, and Spain were to forget their antipathies, hire Hessians by the boatload, and plan a united effort to smash the upstart. More than a few were worried that intriguing men or disaffected sections might be bought for a good price, and enough Spanish gold flowed malevolently through the specie-starved Southwest to give substance to the worry. In the years of Aaron Burr's disgrace, Andrew Jackson's victory at New Orleans, and John Quincy Adams's purchase of Florida, however, this worry born of the knowledge of European practice and nourished on the time-honored conspiratorial theory of history dear to Whiggish hearts began to decline and finally vanished.[2] As the sun of American nationalism rose steadily higher, the confidence of Americans in an independent destiny grew steadily stronger.

This is not to say that America huddled or swaggered in isolation behind the great ocean. The ocean was a barrier, and Americans were thankful for the security it bestowed upon their experiment. It was also a highway, a broad and ever more passable channel of commerce in goods, money, skills, techniques, ideas, and men. From the very beginning, despite the attempts of a few austere souls to turn their backs on Europe, most Americans were hardly less thankful for the opportunity the Atlantic gave them to trade busily with other nations without submitting to their political dictates.

The connection with Great Britain was especially close, a connection, be it recalled, with the most developed, sophisticated, productive nation in the world—and, moreover, the "cradle" in which, as even men far out on the advancing frontier in Arkansas had to admit, the "principles of civil and religious freedom" had first been "rocked." [3] So commanding was the position of Britain in the early years, so essential was the existence of Britain for the health of the American economy,[4] that we are forced to wonder just how much real independence the Republic had won in the War of Independence. From one point of vantage, the junior partner, the circumstances of whose agrarian-extractive-commercial economy summoned Americans to export or die, seems to have been pitifully dependent on British markets for the sale of raw materials, British factories for tools and trinkets, British industry for techniques and technicians, British capital for financing the export trade and the development of transportation (and also, at a pivotal moment, for the purchase of the Louisiana Territory), and thus British approval, however grudging, for the success of the whole enterprise. There can be no doubt that the Republic was far less economically than politically independent in, let us say, 1790 or 1810 or 1830, and that important decisions about the American future were being made by men who had no love for America and no responsibility to its people. "It is absurdity to celebrate the 4th of July as the birthday of Independence," a New Englander lamented in 1787; "until we manufacture more . . . we are still a dependent people." [5]

In the end, the Americans had the best of both worlds: an *economic* connection with Britain, and to a lesser extent with other countries, that offered the markets, tools, materials, skills, innovations, and capital necessary to stimulate rapid development, and a *political* stance that immunized it against the kind of coercion or persuasion too often visited upon the fledgling or even established country that reaches out for help in its efforts to catch up with the outriders of modernity. There are two principal reasons why the United States was able to preserve political independence and, at the same time, gain steadily in economic independence in these decades of national development.

The first was the fact of development itself: The growth in productivity and sophistication of the American economy carried diversification in its train; the result of this growth was a wholesome increase in both flexibility and stability. It took men and women off the land and lured them into factories to make tools and trinkets that would no longer have to be imported from Britain and Europe; it produced, ever more cheaply and in ever more abundance, exportable stuffs and goods for Britain and other countries to purchase ever more eagerly; it generated rising surpluses of native capital for Americans to invest in American undertakings; it placed the United States in a situation of long-term solvency that made shrewd bargaining with the world a paying proposition. Perhaps more important, the development of the economy ran inward as well as upward: The percentage of total American production consumed at home rather than peddled abroad climbed impressively throughout this period.[6] While the export trade remained vital for the health of the economy, the steadily more inviting domestic market received steadily more profitable attention from farmers, merchants, and entrepreneurs. The consequence was a stiffening of independence against both the calculated decisions and uncontrollable vagaries of the British and European economies. While the Panic of 1857 proved painfully that the United States was still immersed in the world economy, the shock was nothing compared with what it would have been under similar circumstances thirty or forty years earlier. The Americans were able to fight their own way out of many troubles that had not been of their making. By 1860 the junior partner was junior no longer; America's years as an economic colony were drawing to a close.[7]

The other reason for the preservation of political independence and the increase in economic independence was somewhat more fortuitous: the blunt truth that British and European bankers who steered capital into American enterprise had a difficult time following up investment with control. While some credit must be given to the doughty, often defiant spirit of American politicians and businessmen, the peculiar nature of the political system of the United States, about which many things will be said in the chapters that follow, seems to have been decisive in this matter. The small range of tasks demanded of the national government reduced its own reliance on foreign capital to near zero, and the flow of such capital simply bypassed Washington. By the time this flow had reached its far-flung destinations, the power of British and European investors to exercise continuing supervision or to bring the authority of their own governments to bear was also near zero, and many high-placed foreigners learned the hard way what low-placed Americans knew in their bones: The political system had been designed—diabolically designed, some of these foreigners lamented—to prevent rather than encourage coercive or even persuasive action against states, enterprises, and entrepreneurs. When an Englishman or Frenchman put money in a canal-building venture in Indiana, he put it on terms that were set and, if necessary, altered unilaterally in Indiana. Most of the $7 million in New York's bonds for building the Erie Canal ended up in London; the canal itself was run in New York for the benefit of New York and its neighbors.

Cultural independence lagged as far behind economic independence as did economic behind political. The most obvious example of continued American dependence on the Old World, and especially on one country in it, is to be found in the related fields of language and letters.[8] Despite the pleas of such red-white-and-blue men as Noah Webster, Charles J. Ingersoll, William Ellery Channing, and Ralph Waldo Emerson for a "distinct" and "pure" American literature,[9] the facts of this special case were simply too obdurate: The language of America was the language of England, even if many Englishmen claimed not to understand it;[10] England had been a bubbling fountain of literature in the common language for centuries; the fountain continued to bubble lavishly and seductively; most Americans saw no reason why they should not go right on drinking at it; few Americans expected their own fountain to start bubbling on a competitive basis until more pressing tasks of national development had been accomplished. Yet patriotic Americans were outraged by John Bradbury's blast of 1818 at the pretensions of their literature,[11] not least by his supposedly friendly prediction that when Americans had "got to the Pacific Ocean," they might "set down to amuse themselves" and produce "epic poems, plays, pleasures of memory, and all the elegant gratifications proper to an ancient people."

In the meantime, their principal business was, in Bradbury's words, to "tame the wild earth." Even though Americans knew the meaning of this truth far more clearly than Bradbury, some nevertheless hoped that they would not be required to wait until their nation was "ancient," that as the business of growth and expansion went on apace they would find themselves in an increasingly strong position to tame and create at the same time. To a meaningful if not overly dramatic extent, they did not hope in vain. Toward the middle of the century, just when adventurous Americans were reaching the Pacific Ocean in large numbers, contemplative Americans—talented writers, as well as orators, painters, architects, and actors—became active in respectable numbers. Yet then as now the reasonably contented victim of several major accidents of history, cultural America remained a sort of semi-independent outpost of Britain, and also, of course, of all Europe.[12] It took vastly more than it gave back, and much of what it chose to take was insipid, tawdry, or puerile.

One may argue plausibly that most citizens of the United States passed up the challenge of cultural independence by placing culture near the bottom of their list of national and personal aspirations. The argument, although plausible, does nothing to reverse the judgment that most of what was elevated and sophisticated about life in mid-century America had been borrowed rather than created. The best one can do is to soften the judgment by noting that Americans of this period carried forward a tradition of the colonial years by picking and choosing freely among the intellectual and esthetic offerings of the Old World, and that as time went by they turned increasingly to countries other than Britain for instruction and entertainment. Edward Everett and George Ticknor struck a famous blow for the kind of cultural independence that arises out of a diversity of relations with other nations when, with the unsolicited assistance of the Duke of Wellington and Marshall Blücher, they went off in 1815 to become the first of a line of distinguished Americans to study at German universities. No one who met these fine young men could doubt for a moment that they were citizens of a proudly independent nation. In the course of their long and useful lives they were destined to see the emotional, political, economic, and cultural defenses of American independence rise steadily higher. By the middle of the century, one could say, the United States had become almost too independent for its own good.

Territorial integrity was a question of absorbing interest to Americans from the first days of independence, as it had been to their ancestors from the first days of settlement. In 1854 they saw, not all of them happily, the book closed peacefully on the *external* half of this universal question:[13] The purchase of the Gadsden Strip from Mexico rounded out the boundaries of the contiguous area of the continental United States,* and an astonishingly far-flung set of boundaries they were. In the same year they saw, most of them apprehensively, the book reopened abruptly on the *internal* half: The passage of the ill-starred Kansas-Nebraska Act transformed the possibility of secession into something much closer to a probability. The Gadsden Purchase, it should be noted, did its part to arouse Northern hostility toward the South. Men of clear mind understood well that the only reason for buying an apparently worthless piece of land in the remote Southwest was to gain a passable right of way for the widely anticipated railroad to the Pacific that would take off from and thus favor the South, one that would run westward in imperial splendor to the sun and smog from New Orleans or Memphis rather than from Chicago or St. Louis.

While most Americans believed from the beginning of the Quest that expansion to the West was their destiny and thus their duty as *one people,* not until the 1830's did they begin to think clearly of *one nation* that would stretch from ocean to ocean across a land where the sun would be "four hours in its passage." [14] Much talk of separate but friendly confederacies was heard in the years immediately after the Louisiana Purchase, and in 1825 Senator Thomas Hart Benton of Missouri, who wanted the Far West for Americans but not necessarily for America, insisted eloquently that "the western limit of this Republic" be

* In describing the United States of the Quest as continental, or making its expanse coterminous with a continent, I do not mean to overlook the existence or mangle the sensitivities of patriotic Canadians and Mexicans. I use these words with few qualms because they were the stock in trade of our ancestors, and because the habitable area of the United States—200 years ago in prophecy, today in fact—has distinctly *continental,* as contrasted with *regional* or *insular,* dimensions.

fixed at the Rocky Mountain barrier. "The statue of the fabled god, Terminus," he declaimed, "should be raised upon its highest peak, never to be thrown down." [15]

Fortunately for Benton's reputation as prophet and patriot, the statue of Terminus was never raised. The eagerness of men to settle Oregon and California, their assumption that they would continue to enjoy the status of full-fledged Americans, the prospect of a railroad to the Pacific, and the invention of the telegraph all helped put an end to talk about "a boundary in the mountains" or "sister republics on the Pacific slope." So, too, did the long-range determination of American diplomacy to push Britain, Spain, and Mexico as far out of the hemisphere as they would go without having to resort to potentially disastrous fighting. Most of the time Benton himself talked as if the destiny of the Republic was to be a Union of states from Maine to California. This still left him far behind John Quincy Adams, who had staked out a preliminary claim to the Pacific Northwest in the Adams-Onís Treaty of 1819 with Spain, had told Congressman William Lowndes, of South Carolina, in the same year that for "the United States and North America" to become "identical" was a "law of nature" as certain "as that the Mississippi should flow to the sea," [16] and had joined with John C. Calhoun (of all people) in 1824 to persuade President Monroe not to send a message to Congress calculated to discourage "territorial settlement on the Pacific." Adams refused flatly to give in to Monroe's Jeffersonian argument that the men who went out "would necessarily soon separate from this Union." [17] The daring continental vision of the man from cooped-up New England was one of the many precious gifts he bestowed without thought of reward on his fellow citizens. "The achieved West," as Bernard De Voto called it, gave "the United States something that no people had ever had before, an internal, domestic empire." [18] How pleasant therefore it is to record that Adams lived long enough to see the vision become an article of national faith.

Along with the question "how far west the nation?" went the rather more explosive questions "how far north?" and "how far south?" Sooner or later, men realized, secure and stable lines would have to be drawn between their nation and whatever neighbors it might bump into in pursuit of the manifest destiny of continental empire. As John Randolph had pointed out sarcastically in 1812, the Union was not "like space, indefinite in its extent." [19] Yet no two of Adams's fellow citizens would have agreed in 1819 upon the proper boundaries of this North America which, obedient to a dictate of the law of nature, was to be identical with the United States, and even after 1854 some Americans believed that their government had been unnecessarily timid and self-denying in dealing with Mexico to the south* and the Canadians and their British protectors to the north. For most, however, the problem had been solved about as effectively and advantageously as any that had confronted the young Republic.[21] The Rio Grande seemed a sensible place to halt, for both geographic and demographic reasons, while the Forty-ninth Parallel, the product of decades of give-and-take with the most skilled diplomats in the world, had already begun to look as if it had been on the map forever,[22] even to men whose hearts had danced only a few years before to the extravagant music of "54°40' or Fight."

While negotiation, purchase, threat, counterthreat, force, innovation, ambition, and happy accident each played a part in the long process through which the United States achieved the first or external half of the goal of territorial integrity, all together were no match for the mighty power of *migration*. To put the matter as simply as possible, the Republic expanded in two generations from an entity of 890,000 square miles with unstable boundaries to one of 3 million square miles with stable boundaries because it was full of men and women who were ready to pull up stakes and carry the course of empire westward—no matter what obstacles nature or politics or circumstance might place in their paths. Just as important, when they had got to such faraway places as Texas, Oregon, California, the Dakotas, and even Utah,† these men and women assumed that they were still Americans and

---

* Including, one must assume, a gentleman from Arkansas who advocated vigorous expansion into Texas far back in 1825 in order to provide a dumping ground for "failures and ne'er-do-wells from the United States." [20]

† The forgotten epic of the so-called Mormon Battalion of 1846–1847 should be proof enough of the point that most members of this persecuted church were looking for an isolated refuge *from* the intolerance of Americans yet, in some undefined way, *within* the jurisdiction of America.[24]

therefore expected the American flag to follow them in due course. "A rage for emigrating to the western country prevails," John Jay wrote in 1785,[23] and a principal consequence of this rage, which still shows signs of life, was to give substance to the dreams and muscle to the diplomacy of continentalists like John Quincy Adams. Not the farsighted policies of government or the exploitative schemes of entrepreneurs, but the restless impulses of the people made the young United States one of the most expansion-minded nations in history. From the eruption into Kentucky in search of land during and after the Revolution to the rush for California in search of gold in 1849, the sharpest goad to the achievement of territorial integrity on a continental scale was the self-generating horizontal mobility of the citizenry of the new nation.

The painful, sporadically ill-tempered effort of the American people to come up with a viable answer to the second half of the question of territorial integrity was, we must never forget, a very different story. The problem of internal adjustment proved far tougher to solve than that of external demarcation; the solution, upon which the last chapter of this book is focused, was cruel to the point of tragedy. In any case, it must have seemed a grim joke of fate to all men of good will in the 1850's that, at the exact moment the nation achieved the final stability of boundaries against all neighbors, which was described as a worthy end in chapter 2, they came face to face with a desperate challenge to the final unity of authority in matters of common concern against all regions, an equally worthy end of national development. An intimate connection existed, of course, between the achievement and the challenge, between the fact of expansion and the prospect of disunion; the joke could not be passed off as an accident or coincidence. The surge to the West had upset forever the traditional balance of slave states and free, and the South had been left to learn the humbling lesson of how to live, and also how to act politically, as a conscious and permanent minority. The South, a region in which humility has never been a virtue, was in no mood to learn the lesson.

Tensions among regions, distrust and often defiance of the national government by "sovereign" states and stiff-necked people, and the specter of dissolution all plagued the American experiment from the outset. The Union was huge, in an important sense far more huge than it is today, because of the slowness of transportation and communication. It was also an experiment quite without precedent, for no people sprawled over so far-ranging a country had ever attempted to govern themselves on principles of republicanism and individual liberty. Nature and circumstance had divided America into regions; the regions were certain to multiply as Americans moved ever westward. History and emotion had divided it further into states; each state, while not quite a candidate for nationhood entirely on its own, was an indestructible entity within the American system. The states, too, thanks to the spacious decision of the Framers to build a republican empire in which new territories would grow up to full equality, were certain to multiply. If we recall the size of the stakes and recognize the toughness of the problem, we should not be surprised that a train of heated controversy over the nature of the Union led from Philadelphia in 1787 to Washington in 1819 and 1854 and on to Montgomery in 1861. We should also recall that the South had no monopoly on disruptive sentiment through all these years. Those who deplore the Virginia and Kentucky Resolutions of 1798–1799 or are scandalized by the behavior of the South Carolina Nullifiers of 1828–1833 would do well to contemplate the antics of the Hartford Convention of 1814–1815 or the "personal liberty" laws through which many northern and western states sought to render the obnoxious Fugitive Slave Act of 1850 null and void within their borders.[25]

What, for that matter, was the nature of the Union that had been forged in the Revolution and rendered "more perfect" in the Constitution? The passage of time would have to answer this transcendent question to the satisfaction of most Americans, and answer it in one reasonably clear way, before the goal of internal balance could be achieved.

Roughly six plausible interpretations came up for consideration in this period. Although each was essentially constitutional in form, behind constitutional interpretation one stumbles upon economic myth and reality, political purpose and principle, geography, social forces, ethnic strains, and cultural disparities, not to forget the memories, ambitions, and fears of millions of individuals. In an order ranging from the more perfect to the less, the six interpretations were:

an indestructible, organic Union of persons (the cherished but largely quixotic view of Alexander Hamilton);[26]

an indestructible, progressively more organic Union of persons fortuitously and, on balance, happily organized into indestructible yet hardly sacred states (the final position of Abraham Lincoln);[27]

an indestructible, contractual, yet also progressively more organic Union of states at one level of definition and of persons at another (the final position of Daniel Webster);[28]

an indestructible, contractual Union of persons who had chosen to be grouped in states (the painfully worked-out opinion of Joseph Story);[29]

an "indestructible Union, composed of indestructible states" (the formula with which Chief Justice Salmon P. Chase was later to justify the waging and winning of the Civil War to all Americans);[30] and

a Union that, however solemnly contracted, useful, and bolstered by tradition, could be eroded piecemeal by single states or demolished totally by combinations of states, since every state had entered it as a sovereign entity whose right to withdraw *in extremis* was the one constant weight in the federal balance (the harshly logical interpretation of John C. Calhoun).[31]

The Union was also, Paul Nagel has pointed out,[32] other and differing things to Americans: experiment, polity, spirit, symbol, convenience, and, at the bitter end of this period of trial, a "yoke" that millions of them sought to throw off angrily. The core of this great question about the nature of the Union was one of definition and thus of identity: Was the *Union* a *nation*— and, if it was, what kind of nation? We shall return to the question at the end of this chapter, but it should be understood clearly as a conclusion to this discussion that all Americans between Hamilton at his most quixotic and Calhoun at his most logical would have answered the first part of the question "yes" (as Hamilton always did emphatically) and the second "a federal nation" (as he never did except reluctantly). *Federalism* was a given of American life that the men of the new Republic inherited without protest and believed in without qualm. Indeed, most of them professed to be thoroughly grateful for the inheritance, since only such a nation, united yet not consolidated, could expect to maintain a republican form of government over the vast expanse of land they proposed to occupy.

Whether federalism, as contrasted with regionalism or localism, is still the stout bulwark of American liberty in which our fathers placed their trust is a question that invites probing debate. What need not be debated, since it cannot be denied, is that *the division of the Union into states was absolutely necessary for the birth, rise, and extension of the American nation.* While in this respect the Republic was less perfect a nation than England or France in, let us say, the year 1840, only because of this imperfection, the division into states, was it a nation of any description. All the original states would have refused to enter the Union in the first place if they had expected the common government to drain away their power and redraw or erase internal boundaries; all the new territories that grew into states would surely have defied such a government and established new unions or confederacies on their own. There was then and remains now nothing sacred and eternal about every boundary of every state; there was then and remains now something imperative and coeval with the American continental nation about the existence of the states as indestructible entities.

Federalism, in sum, played an oddly double role in this notable period of national development. It gave a new kind of nation the opportunity to emerge and expand, yet it always posed a threat of dismemberment and extinction. At the end of the Quest, we shall see, the role of federalism was to become even more complicated than that, for it helped mightily to meet the open challenge of this threat and preserve the nation. From this point of view, perhaps, the American search for unity of authority in matters of common concern appears not to have been such a failure after all.

At one level of social existence and individual status the United States of America in 1860 was, in the light of its brief and checkered history, a model of *popular cohesion* with remarkably few imperfections. At another level, however, achievement of this third goal of nationhood lay generations in the future; only a handful of apparently eccentric Americans had recognized the full dimensions of the problem and begun to think of ways to solve it. If America was an amazing offshoot of Britain and, to a lesser extent, the countries of northwestern Europe, which most Americans assumed as effortlessly as they breathed, it presented a picture of remarkable homogeneity at the core of society and of easily tolerated diversity around the edges that caught the admiring attention of most observers from abroad. If it was a country belonging to all men who lived in it, the picture was marred by one large flaw and several smaller ones that some observers described with pity and others with malice.

The offshoot of Britain and one related part of Europe had come close to achieving the goal of popular cohesion largely because of three happy circumstances. The last of these, to be sure, was a source of unhappiness to many Americans of the Quest.

The first was the notable degree of ethnic homogeneity in the colonies that united to declare their independence in 1776. Whatever the uses of the metaphor *the melting pot* in discussing the problem of popular cohesion in late nineteenth-century and early twentieth-century America, we cannot apply it to the young Republic without torturing the truth. The metaphor that best expresses the realities of early American demography is not that of a melting pot of men from many nations but of *a solid trunk of men from one nation* onto which branches of men from a few other and closely related nations were constantly being grafted with comparative success. While ethnic tensions had been a fact of American colonial life almost from the beginning, as Dixon R. Fox and others have demonstrated,[33] they were never so severe in character as to transform political bickering or social mistrust into outright civil strife. In any case, these central demographic facts of early American history must constantly be kept in mind: At the time of the Revolution something like seventy of every hundred white Americans were of English blood; another fifteen to twenty looked back to other parts of the British Isles; the rest were men whose ancestors had lived in countries that shared with Britain the origins and ways of northwestern Europe, such as the Netherlands, France, Switzerland, Germany, and Sweden.[34] Perhaps 1,500 Jews, most of whom seem to have been Spanish or

Portuguese in immediate or less immediate origin, added a touch of spice to the pattern of American homogeneity while enjoying more genuine acceptance than would have been their lot in almost any country in Europe.

The Republic of 1815 was even more homogeneous. Forty years of turmoil in the Atlantic world had cut down sharply on immigration; as a result, the processes of absorption, adaptation, toleration, and synthesis were given a longer time and freer hand to do their work than ever before or after in our history. With the coming of peace came a new flow of immigrants; yet most of them, too, were natives of the northwestern part of Europe. From the moment of disembarkation they were, even the mistrusted newcomers from the southern counties of Ireland, candidates for admission to the main body of the American citizenry, and the terms of admission were reasonable and surprisingly mild: Pledge primary allegiance to this new nation of asylum and opportunity, learn to speak its language tolerably well, practice at least a few of its ways, subscribe to its republican principles, raise children to be patriotic and fully participating Americans. Most newcomers agreed to the terms readily. Those who did not, such as the inward-turning religious colonies of Germans that dotted the landscape of Pennsylvania and several Midwestern states, were for the most part left in peace by a society with few techniques and even fewer compulsions to lure or coerce men into conformity.

The second circumstance, about which much evidence remains to be gathered and interpreted, was the notable capacity of the main body of society to make good Americans out of Englishmen, Scotsmen, Germans, Scandinavians, Irishmen, and others (including the five Poles who arrived in 1850)[35] without visiting cruelties upon them, diluting its own strength, or straining the bonds of nationhood. While chief credit must be given to the simple truth that a large majority of immigrants came from the same parts of the world Americans had always come from, some can also be given to other factors: the fairly easy and restrained flow of immigration, which did not turn into a torrent until the late 1840's;[36] the migration of native Americans westward, which left places for newcomers to fill; the skill and perseverance of the vast majority of these newcomers; the sweep of the land itself, which bade welcome, stern but alluring, to those who also chose to go west and dig or peddle to the diggers; the permissiveness and competitiveness of American politics, which thousands of immigrants could thank for the amazing opportunity to vote almost before they had collected their belongings and got off the boat; the diversity and fluidity of the American scene, which enabled immigrants to settle among men and women of their own kind; the broad-mindedness of American constitutions and laws, which held out the promise of every right of first-class citizenship except that of running for President; the desire of immigrants themselves to learn the ways of their new country; and the pattern of education, which was being asked, even in those narrow and backward days, to teach the children of immigrants how to be better Americans than their fathers.

Not until the second quarter of the century did the menace to popular cohesion known as *nativism* begin to work a sizable and unpleasant influence on American social life.[37] Even then it seems to have been differences in religion rather than national origin or life style that brought the Know-Nothing impulse and all its malicious or simply fearful variants out into the open. If the Irish of the sweeping influx of 1847–1854 suffered the indignity of being warned in blatant signs not to "apply," as countless thousands of them did, it was not so much because they were Irish as because they were Irish Catholics. The United States of the early years was a *Protestant as well as a white country*.[38] American Protestantism had been feeding for too many generations on the fear of "Papism" as a political as well as religious threat to permit the casual absorption of more than a million men and women who were doggedly Catholic. Not just bigots, but Americans of good will and liberal views were troubled by the suspicion that it was impossible for a man to be both a devout Catholic and a patriotic American, and the suspicion has been a long time dying. The influx of German Catholics, it might be added, was second only to that of Irish Catholics in arousing fears for the safety and character of republican virtues and institutions.

Finally, we should pay our respects to the interesting yet strangely neglected truth that the United States spared itself much social and political grief by refusing to heed the advice of many leading citizens to push hard and far to both the north and south. The good sense or capacity for self-denial of some Americans and the timidity or irresolution of others helped confine the expansionist impulse to the present boundaries of the contiguous area of the United States, and thus left the many parts of Canada, the northern provinces of Mexico, and the whole of Cuba outside the jurisdiction of a nation that was consistently prodded to gobble all of them up. If to these aspects of *a destiny that was manifest but not unlimited* we add the divisive influence of slavery, the legendary skill of British diplomacy, the forbidding aridity of Mexican soil, the apparently hostile climate of western Canada, and the proud refusal of several million people—Mexicans, Cubans, English-speaking Canadians (many of them the children of Loyalists), the men and women of self-contained Quebec—to engage in the act of cohabitation with the overbearing Americans, we arrive at a solution, perhaps fortuitous but nevertheless substantial, to the problem of territorial integrity that was also a solution to what could easily have become a nasty problem of popular cohesion. Since the problem would indeed have been both territorial and popular (and, as a result, distinctly political), one may envision it in terms of two Senators from Nova Scotia, two from Quebec, two from Ontario, two from Sonora, two from Chihuahua, two from Matanzas, and so on and on until the Senate of the United States would resemble, if it were still to exist, the General Assembly of the United Nations or the Supreme Soviet. The "empire of liberty" of which John Adams, Thomas Jefferson, and their colleagues dreamed,* and for which John Quincy Adams and his successors haggled successfully, might have turned out to be an empire forced to choose between chaos and coercion; and such an empire, even if it could have been held together, would not have been a cohesive nation. The United States of the Quest acted more sensibly than it realized by deciding, in effect, that such places as Cuba and Quebec consisted of indigestible lumps of people if not of land.

At the second level, the one on which even the scatter of immigrants from Quebec, Mexico, and Cuba (as well as purchased mi-

* Adams wrote to Count Sarsfield in February 1786 of an "empire of liberty" on the American continent counting "two or three hundred millions of freemen." Jefferson's own phrase was an "empire for liberty," which he incorporated in a letter to Madison, April 27, 1809.[39]

norities like the Creoles of Louisiana and Spanish-speaking inhabitants of old California) did not have to dwell for long as outsiders unless they chose, the United States had solved the problem of popular cohesion by delimiting it, ignoring it, or rationalizing it out of existence. In less polite words, *the United States had not solved the problem at all;* it had been left, rather, to lie in wait and gather strength for an assault in force upon later generations. The problem, we know to our sorrow, has proved harsh to the point of intractability, and at least some blame for the monstrous character it has assumed in recent years must be laid at the door of both the leaders and the led of white America, wherever they may have lived in the empire of liberty, of the first decades of national development. In this matter above all others we must think ourselves as understanding students of history back into the twilight in which the new nation lived throughout this period, and thus not belabor the main body of Americans too blithely or viciously. We must also admit, however, that the process of explaining a large-scale historical failure does not necessarily explain it away. Such a failure should be called by its right name even as its agents are judged with the charity of distance.

A few incontestable statistics and a few nearly incontestable words of generalization may serve to demonstrate the extent and nature of this failure. Out of a total of 31.4 million persons counted in the census of 1860, 4.4 million were Negroes, men all or partly black. Four million of this number lived in the South in a state of character-wasting bondage, some 400,000 in both the South and the North in a state of nominal but certainly not real freedom.[40] All were assumed to be a lesser breed of human being, and were therefore permanently unwelcome candidates for full admission to the American community even in those parts of the country that had the most use for their labor or the least need to worry about their presence. The involuntary residence of these millions of persons of color in a white man's country, which had been looked upon as such from the first planting,[41] was an ever more visible drag on the pursuit of almost every goal of national development. In no instance—this is the point of the moment— was the drag more stultifying than in the immense and otherwise successful American endeavor to achieve the goal of popular cohesion.

If for this same moment we can put aside all feelings of indignation about the injustice of the affair as a collective experience in American and African history or about the demeaning frustrations of the Negroes as individuals, we may see more clearly (not too clinically, I trust) how black presence and white arrogance or indifference combined to produce this unfortunate situation. We can also, if we try, cast our gaze back to 1860 and look right over the exotic heads of the 35,000 Chinese who had been lured more or less permanently to the United States to compensate for the shortage of unskilled labor in California.[42] It is somewhat harder, yet also possible for the sake of this particular line of argument, to look over the heads of the several hundred thousand Indians who lived meanly within the pale or defiantly outside it, and thus to write off the insoluble if not unmanageable problem of cohesion presented by the stunned Onondagas and the menacing Sioux. Only a few Indians had ever "wanted in" to American society, nor, to tell the harsh truth, did more than a few white Americans want them in. Australia is not a failure as a cohesive nation because it has never managed to bring its aborigines into society as fully welcome, fully participating citizens; and almost every nation, we noted in chapter 2, has more or less permanently unaccepted or unwilling minorities living in its midst. The white Americans of the young Republic may be judged severely for their methods of dealing with the Indians—the Cherokee Removal of 1838 was an act worthy (or unworthy?) of czarist Russia[43]—but only leniently for failing to incorporate them into society. Limits exist, after all, in life and in nature to the most imaginative efforts of men of good will to blend two mutually antipathetic strains of race and culture into one, and such efforts were, in any case, not even on the agenda of the Quest.

One person in seven, in the southern part of the United States one person in three—that, surely, is a problem of quite different dimensions. Along with the other tensions and agonies it has since brought upon the land, the refusal of white men to deal with black men as Americans—and if Negroes were not Americans 240 years after the first of them were unloaded in Virginia, what were they?—was a failure in the pursuit of an elementary goal of national development. In this failure to treat them as persons who might sooner or later qualify for all the rights and privileges of membership in the community, the Negro-shunning white men of Cincinnati or Albany or Boston were just as clearly implicated as the slaveholding white men of Charleston or Nashville or the Delta. No one can pick his way through the evidence piled up in Leon Litwack's impressive study of the condition of Negroes in the North without concluding that, whether slave or free, black or brown or nearly white, picking cotton in Alabama or shining shoes in Philadelphia,[44] these unfortunate people remained strangers in the land (for most of them the land of their birth) throughout these decades of a wondrous search for nationhood and modernity.

To tell the whole corroding truth, the nation moved backward rather than forward in its treatment of free Negroes during this period. One of the truly discouraging stories in American social history teaches of the way in which such Negroes, including *freeborn* Negroes, lost rather than gained ground in such areas as admission to schools and churches, eligibility for the suffrage, and enjoyment of elementary political and legal rights, including the right, precious alike to both citizens and aliens, to move without restriction into the freest of the free states.[45] The story seems all the more discouraging if we project it against the larger background of the triumph of democracy as the American way of life and politics. The fact that free Negroes lost most ground to discrimination, segregation, and nagging restriction in exactly those states that were most boastfully democratic—New York can serve as a northern example, Mississippi as a southern—may give pause to those who assume, as do most Americans most of the time, that the people and their representatives can generally be counted on to do the right and just thing.

This, then, was the mixed record of the Republic in pursuit of the goal of popular cohesion in these decades: at one level, where six out of seven Americans dwelled, an over-all success that was to stand the nation in good stead when called upon to absorb waves of strange immigrants in the years just before and after 1900; at another level, where six Americans dwelled and a seventh hung on, an accountable but nonetheless bitter failure that would rise from the grave to plague generation after generation. There is, more than incidentally, a large streak of historical irony in the fact that the mere existence of a submerged black America promoted popular cohesion in dominant white America.

Through all the years from Washington to Lincoln the American people were engaged in an industrious search for *self-identity*. The search, we know to our sorrow, led in the end to a shattering crisis, so shattering and therefore decisive for the future that I feel compelled to discuss it separately, especially in the last two chapters, and to concentrate for the moment on the record up to 1850. The record was one of unusual achievement, and we must not let the events of the 1850's and 1860's blind us to this truth. If this had not been so, if there had been no solid sense of continental nationhood both inclusive and exclusive,[46] the North would never have gone to war to preserve the Union, and both victorious North and conquered South would not have moved on together toward a new, more solid sense of such nationhood. The foundations of American nationalism, as they were to prove in the hour of reckoning, had been well and truly laid by the middle of the nineteenth century, and by all odds the most important of these foundations was the nation itself—for whose endurance I hope to account more pointedly than I can at this stage in chapter 11.

Long before the coming of the Revolution, preachers, poets, and pamphleteers were telling fellow colonists that they were "a new Jerusalem sent down from heav'n," [47] a different and better race of men with a special destiny to cherish. The winning of independence transformed this kind of prophetic exhortation into a settled article of American faith. Yet while Americans saw and identified themselves as a new people on the face of the earth, two fateful questions remained to be answered:

First, were they different and better enough to rejoice confidently in the fact—and, if they were, in what ways?

Second, was the fate of America to be a country, that is, one sovereign nation like Britain and France, or a "country," that is, a parcel of related yet basically sovereign half-nations, city-states, and provinces like Germany and Italy?

In the process of answering the first question "yes" with the aid of words like "republicanism," "liberty," "opportunity," "morality," "improvement," and, finally, "democracy," and the second also "yes" with the portentous qualification expressed in the word "federal," the people of the United States found an identity that permitted the Union to develop and expand in unprecedented ways. Perhaps more important, this sense of identity then encouraged it to stand up successfully to the most severe test a nation can ever meet.

In chapter 2 it was mentioned in passing that language, religion, territory, political skill, and economic necessity can help a nation come into being and thereafter endure. Since we are here, as we were there, more concerned with the idea of nationalism than with the natural, accidental, and man-made underpinnings of nationhood, and since the influence of our own underpinnings will be examined in other chapters, let me pass them by again with only a mention. I do this in confidence that readers will not accuse me of downgrading the importance, to be specific, of the English language, the Christian (and largely Protestant) religion, the western lands, the Convention of 1787, and the quickening flow of domestic trade in developing and uniting the American nation. Let us concentrate on the condition in 1850 of those less concrete yet no less real elements of nationalism: history, interest, consensus, comparison, and individualism. What contribution had each made to the vibrant patriotism displayed by most Americans of that time?

If the legacy of remembrances at the service of orators and schoolteachers was skimpy compared with that of Britain or France, the young Republic drew enough sustenance from the memory of the founding generation alone to make *history* a nourishing support of the sense of an American nationalism. Then as now the Hampdens, and also the Village Hampdens, of America liked to "look back with reverence" as keenly as forward with anticipation;[48] as a result, the apparatus of myth, symbol, slogan, and ceremony designed to emphasize the uniqueness and unity of the American people grew more impressive with each passing year. The invocations of a heroic past and visions of a glorious future indulged in by men as different in style as David Ramsay, Jedidiah Morse, Parson Weems, Jared Sparks, John Quincy

Adams, William Holmes McGuffey, Rembrandt Peale, John Trumbull, Daniel Webster, John Marshall, and, pre-eminent among historians who felt the hand of God laid upon America, George Bancroft kept the apparatus working at full blast. It is interesting and highly pertinent to note that the first major public oration of an ambitious young lawyer named Abraham Lincoln—the date was January 27, 1838, the audience the Young Men's Lyceum of Springfield—referred reverently to the Founding Fathers (a few of whom were still walking around unburied) as if they were heroes who had sailed with Jason and sketched plans with Solon. In describing his own generation as the "legal inheritors" of the "fundamental blessings" of an unexampled system of personal liberty, he paid homage to a *"once* hardy, brave, and patriotic, but now lamented and departed race of ancestors," [49] and the young men of Springfield doubtless nodded solemn approval of the description. Here was one new nation, it would seem, that had a special talent for creating and exploiting instant history, and also for believing in it. Twenty-three years later, in his Inaugural Address as President of a temporarily disunited United States, Lincoln summoned history once again to support the cause of American nationalism. "The mystic chords of memory, stretching from every battle-field, and patriot grave, will yet swell the chorus of the Union," [50] he insisted doggedly— and how right he was to insist upon the power of common memory to reunite the nation.

While some scholars seem to have taken the cue from Henry James and written sadly of the poverty of the American legacy and crudeness of the techniques used to exploit it,[51] their collective judgment strikes the mind as either precious or irrelevant. The kind of nation most Americans hoped for in the future demanded a legacy that would liberate energy without paralyzing will; at the same time, the techniques of national devotion needed to express the American character as something simple, sincere, zestful, and democratic. As to the legacy, one may well ask: Did a new nation ever have heroes quite so satisfying as the Pilgrim Fathers, the men of Jamestown, the Signers, the Framers, Benjamin Franklin, Daniel Boone, and the semidivine Cincinnatus of the West, George Washington? [52] And as to the techniques, one may go on to ask: Are our hearts ever stirred today, as were those of our ancestors, with feelings of joyful patriotism by the oratory of thousands of ordinary men on the Fourth of July and of scores of larger-than-life men like Daniel Webster on occasions like the celebration at Plymouth in 1820 and the laying of the cornerstone at Bunker Hill in 1825? Such feelings have gone out of fashion; yet in the days of our youth they were the intellectual fertilizer of the flowering of American nationalism.

Interest also played a part, as northern men like Gouverneur Morris and southern men like John C. Calhoun proved rather forcefully in a left-handed way. Unblushing nationalists in their early years when the Union was a source of emotional nourishment to them and practical benefits to friends and neighbors, they lost their faith in later years when the waters from the source began to have a brackish taste. For most Americans between 1815 and 1850, however, the more perfect Union was a new kind of nation in which membership bestowed a range of rights, privileges, immunities, opportunities, and protections that no sensible man would wish to surrender. Those Americans who set off bravely for territory that was not yet American—Florida, Texas, California, Oregon—and expected the flag to follow in the fullness of time proved this point about the services of interest to nationhood even more forcefully than did the disillusioned Morris and the disgruntled Calhoun. They knew, as those also knew who stayed at home, that everybody would be a loser if the Union were to divide or dissolve, or if it were to permit other sovereign nations of Americans to spring up on its southwestern, Pacific, and northwestern flanks.

Although it is sometimes hard to glimpse through the dust stirred up by the fury of political debate, the violent acts committed by persons and crowds, and the unceasing tussle of North and South, a notable *consensus* of political, economic, and social principle added greatly to the vitality of American nationalism in this period. The collapse of Federalism and the rejection of English and European Radicalism left a fair field for American-style Liberalism. By 1850 the principles of bourgeois democracy had become a national tradition with no serious competition from the right, the left, the past, the future, or even from the South.[53] Dissenters hung on, to be sure, in stately mansions in Philadelphia and Charleston, immigrant hovels in New York and Boston, socialist studies in Milwaukee and Cincinnati, and utopian communities all over the land. Most Americans, however, were dedicated in common to the beauties of personal liberty, the security of constitutionalism, the rightness of democracy, the wrongness of class distinctions, the virtue of private property, the moral necessity of hard work, the certainty of progress, and above all the uniqueness, superiority, and high destiny of the United States of America. Detractors of democracy and prophets of doom were unpopular in a land whose national character expressed itself in disbelieving laughter at the dismal proclamation of Fisher Ames in 1803 that the United States was "too big for union, too sordid for patriotism, too democratic for liberty." [54] When it did, in the end, prove almost too big for union, the men of the South demonstrated a peculiar allegiance to the political consensus by adopting a constitution copied, with only a sprinkle of generally sensible changes, from the Constitution of 1787.

Few young nations have been more lavishly blessed, if that is the right word, by the existence of an enemy than the United States in the early years of independence; few have made more effective use of the techniques of *comparison* in the search for identity. Whether this enemy was Europe as a whole, as it was symbolically in much writing and orating of the time, or that special corner of Europe called Britain or England, as it was literally in 1812 and prospectively in 1845, its mere presence in the world helped speed up the course of self-identification in the United States. I agree with Cushing Strout that "for much of their history Americans have defined themselves through a deeply felt conflict with Europe," [55] and would add only that in no period has this conflict been carried on more energetically, self-righteously, and, all things considered, fruitfully than in the decades of the Quest. Reactive nationalism was an unusually powerful sentiment in the days of Monroe, Adams, and Jackson. Indeed, one sometimes gets the impression that men were content to define America simply as *anti-Europe* or, on certain anniversaries, *anti-England*. Washington Irving spoke for most Americans in 1832 when, after seventeen years of working at literature and playing at diplomacy in Europe, he told an audience of distinguished citizens who had assembled to welcome him home to native soil and native themes:

I come from gloomier climates to one of brilliant sunshine and inspiring purity. I come from countries lowering with doubt and danger, where the rich man trembles and the poor man frowns—where all repine at the present and dread the future. I come from these to a country where all is life and animation; where I hear on every side the sound of exultation; where every one speaks of the past with triumph, the present with delight, the future with glowing and confident anticipation.[56]

For all but a few fastidious or supremely self-confident Americans the comparison between the New World and the Old ranged from the invidious to the odious. America was free, fresh, democratic, virtuous, and progressive; Europe, in particular that "dissolute old whore England," was oppressive, tired, crippled by class distinction, corrupt, and decaying. Tradition, heritage, language, literature, travel, trade, immigration, the borrowing of ideas, and the transit of inventions injected a sizable amount of ambivalence into the attitudes of educated Americans toward Britain and Europe. The attitudes were further scrambled because America, like many a new nation that has struggled to its feet and scored a few successes, was the prisoner of a superiority-inferiority complex of monumental proportions. Having told themselves that they were the greatest people on earth and in history, Americans were thereupon told by a long line of travelers (who usually waited until safe at home before opening fire) that they were nothing of the sort; rather, that they were boastful, mean, ill-taught, ill-mannered, dishonest, hypocritical, and boorish. They were "addicted," Henry James wrote in an effort to explain Hawthorne's "exaggerated, painful, morbid national consciousness," to "the belief that the other nations" of the world were "in a conspiracy to undervalue them." [57] The addiction, if such it was, seemed to comfort Americans rather than demoralize them. Those who were born in the United States, like those who had come to stay, knew in their hearts that this country was different and better, and with the help of that knowledge they discovered their identity.

Finally, the dedication to *individualism* of an entire people worked in ways mysterious in nature yet plain in result to encourage America to recognize itself as a nation. The fact of American individualism antedated the use of the word by several generations; it was, by any name, one of a half-dozen distinctive characteristics of the young civilization. There could be no more dramatic testimony to the width of the gulf between Europe and America than the transformation in meaning that took place when the word was finally imported for popular use around 1840. In the school of Saint-Simon, Yehoshua Arieli has pointed out, individualism was "almost synonymous with selfishness, social anarchy, and individual self-assertion"; in the pages of John O'Sullivan's *Democratic Review* it "connoted self-determination, moral freedom, the rule of liberty, and the dignity of man." [58]

American individualism in the time of O'Sullivan was not, of course, as simple a concept and gentle an influence as all that, for it covered a span of personal principle and conduct ranging from the kindly self-reliance of a philosopher like Emerson to the ruthless self-advancement of an entrepreneur like Commodore Vanderbilt by way of the doughty self-removal of a mountain man like Bill Williams. In later years it was to be twisted into strange and often ugly forms; in recent years it has been transformed into an ideology of self-deception with which to mask the decline of both the privacy and the independence of the person. Yet in those early, simpler years individualism was a governing principle of American life, and as such it made a rich if still neither measurable nor quite comprehensible contribution to the progress and unity of the nation. By freeing a race of ambitious men from the institutional shackles of the European past it set them to digging, tinkering, migrating, playing politics, generating visions, and taking risks at a pace that surprised, even if it often dismayed, those who came from Europe to see for themselves what the fuss was all about. By stripping these men of membership in most groups and orders of traditional society it focused a large portion of their loyalties on the most exciting object in sight: the nation. And since the nation itself seemed so permissive in practice and liberty-oriented in doctrine, those groups and orders that endured or sprang up—families, neighborhoods, churches, schools, colleges, associations, professional groups—could command the loyalties of individuals for their own purposes and then, as it were, reinforce and pass them on upward to serve the great Republic. Whether as an individual going it alone or co-operating freely with others, the American of the first half of the nineteenth century found much of his own identity precisely in being a free American.

One other loyalty-commanding order existed, we have already taken note, between the individual and the nation; and, however necessary to the growth of a continental republic, it posed a persistent, occasionally passion-provoking threat to unity. That order was the state or, in a larger sense, the region. Men pledged their allegiance, I repeat, to a *federal* nation; the allegiance was therefore of a kind that had never been known before. Although it had been tested severely in 1798–1799, 1814–1815, and 1828–1833 (and, in the judgment of many Americans, found weaker than they had expected), the allegiance gathered strength as the years passed and history, interest, consensus, comparison, and individualism all did their good work along with more tangible or visible forces such as the English language, the Constitution, and a party system seemingly designed to suppress passions and resolve crises.

By 1850 most men were convinced that to be a loyal American one had to emulate Washington, Jefferson, and John Adams, and thus also be a loyal son of state and region. Two giants of the earliest years had been undiluted nationalists, Benjamin Franklin and Alexander Hamilton, but they were obviously special cases. In the middle of the nineteenth century only an immigrant with the principles of a Francis Lieber (and with no political ambitions) could emulate them.[59] Every important American nationalist stood with feet planted firmly in some part of the country in which he had been raised or to which he had migrated; to that part he directed a sizable portion of his public fealty. Henry Clay, John Quincy Adams, Daniel Webster, Andrew Jackson, Stephen A. Douglas, Thomas Hart Benton, Abraham Lincoln—all had love for the Union, all had love for their states and regions, all saw no conflict, rather, a mutually nourishing connection, between the two loves. These famous men and the millions of followers for whom they spoke were patriots who had met every test set by Rousseau—inclination, passion, necessity—and had attached their ultimate patriotism to a nation so huge and loose-jointed that the sight of it would have sent Rousseau, not to forget Montesquieu, into a state of shock.

. . .

The Quest for Nationhood: Successes and Failures

The pursuit of an American identity led many citizens, not at all surprisingly, to think and speak of a "nation singled out by the searching eye and sustained by the protecting arm of a kind and beneficent Providence" for the purpose of changing "the whole aspect of human affairs on this globe." [60] The idea of *an American mission* had taken root in the colonies as far back as 1630 when John Winthrop proclaimed Massachusetts a "city upon a hill," and in the forcing bed of the Revolution it burst into full flower. The belief in a high destiny encouraged resistance, rationalized rebellion, legitimized independence, and justified an often apparently senseless war in which Americans shed the blood of Americans as well as of Englishmen, Irishmen, Scots, and Hessians. Then, when all these astonishing events had come to pass, it moved a few choice spirits to take the lead in reconstituting the political system on the basis of a new unity forged out of the realities of an old diversity. Thereupon an entire people took up the theme of the United States as both guardian and beneficiary of a cosmic trust.

While several variations on the theme of a national mission won popular acceptance during and after the Revolution—America as asylum, America as redeemer, America as exporter of the spirit of liberty,[61] America as the "seat of another golden age," even America as an "all powerful commonwealth" in which the countries of Europe would find their place as "colonies" [62]—the primary destiny of these settlements-turned-republic remained constant throughout the early decades of independence, and thereby gave the United States a penetrating sense of self-identity and an exhilarating sense of self-confidence that were to support the Union nobly in its hour of trial. If the concept of mission was useful both to the incipient nation that fought the Revolution and to the fledgling nation that went in search of unity and modernity, it was indispensable to the uncertain nation that found its unity denied and modernity challenged in 1861. From well before the Revolution to well after the Civil War the dedication to a mission was as important for the rise of the American nation as ever it was for the triumph of the Israel of Joshua or was later to prove for the modernization of the Soviet Union.

Stripped of all excrescences and elaborations, the true American mission commanded the United States to stand before the

131

world, neither boastfully nor meekly, as a model republic. It was
a simple belief; and, by reason of this simplicity, it was comprehensible, viable, and endlessly serviceable. At a desperate stage in
the march of history, Americans believed, God had called forth
certain hardy, liberty-loving souls from the privilege-ridden nations of the Old World; He had carried these precious few to a
fresh scene, thus presenting them and their descendants with the
best of all possible environments for the development of a free
and progressive nation; and in bestowing this special grace He had
also bestowed a special obligation for the success of the special
nation. Were the Americans to fail in their experiment in republican self-government, they would fail not only themselves and
their posterity but also all men everywhere who deserved to be
free. If such government could work here, it might also work in
other parts of the world; if it could not work here, it would never
work anywhere.

The final and perhaps fundamental point about this concept of
mission was that *a successful America would serve literally as an
experiment or model:* It would invite men of other nations to
admire and imitate; it would not go into the business of exporting ideas and institutions with the sword and the dollar. The
principal force for carrying the American message to a doubting
world was, quite simply, the force of good example.

These pages could be filled with thousands of heartfelt declara-
tions of faith in the mission of the independent United States as
it was framed in this first, unspoiled version. Let us be content
with a scatter in which remembered men declaimed in behalf of
forgotten compatriots:[63]

John Adams to himself and a few friends (1765):

I always consider the settlement of America with reverence and
wonder, as the opening of a grand scene and design in Providence
for the illumination of the ignorant, and the emancipation of the
slavish part of mankind all over the earth.

James Madison to his fellow delegates at Philadelphia (1787):

It is more than probable we are now digesting a plan which in its
operation will decide forever the fate of republican government.

Alexander Hamilton to the same gentlemen a few minutes
later:

I concur with Mr. Madison in thinking we are now to decide forever the fate of republican government. If we do not give to that form due stability and wisdom, it will be disgraced and lost among ourselves, disgraced and lost to mankind forever.[64]

George Washington to the dignitaries assembled to hear his first inaugural address (1789):

The preservation of the sacred fire of liberty and the destiny of the republican model of government are justly considered, perhaps, as *deeply*, as *finally*, staked on the experiment intrusted to the hands of the American people.[65]

Thomas Jefferson to Dr. Priestley (1802):

We feel that we are acting under obligations not confined to the limits of our society. It is impossible not to be sensible that we are acting for all mankind; that circumstances denied to others, but indulged to us, have imposed on us the duty of proving what is the degree of freedom and self-government in which society may venture to leave its individual members.[66]

Joseph Story to an assembly at Cambridge celebrating the fiftieth anniversary, not of independence, but of Phi Beta Kappa (1826):

We stand, the latest, and if we fail, probably the last experiment of self-government by the people.[67]

Andrew Jackson, no friend of Story's, to the nation in his Farewell Address (1837):

Providence has showered on this favored land blessings without number, and has chosen you as the guardians of freedom, to preserve it for the benefit of the human race.[68]

A famous poet, Henry Wadsworth Longfellow, to his extensive audience (1849), which included the even more extensive audience of William H. McGuffey:

> *Thou, too, sail on, O Ship of State!*
> *Sail on, O UNION, strong and great!*
> *Humanity with all its fears,*
> *With all the hopes of future years,*
> *Is hanging breathless on thy fate!* [69]

133

And last, a famous historian and public servant, George Bancroft, to a joint session of Congress gathered to pay tribute to Abraham Lincoln (1866):

In the fullness of time a Republic rose up in the wilderness of America. Thousands of years had passed away before this child of the ages could be born. From whatever there was good in the systems of former centuries she drew her nourishment; the wrecks of the past were her warnings. . . .
The fame of this only daughter of freedom went out into all the lands of the earth; from her the human race drew hope.[70]

Since these words speak eloquently for themselves, let me limit myself to three brief concluding observations:

First, the eloquence seems to have been entirely sincere. I have never found, despite a severe if admittedly remote probing of psyches and motives, any evidence to suggest that these men and those who echoed them throughout the land did not mean exactly what they said.

Second, Washington, Adams, Jefferson, and the rest were not indulging in flights of fancy. They were, rather, expressing a solid belief that almost all Americans carried in their minds and hearts.

And third, the belief seems to have been about as benevolent in influence inside the United States and mild in impact outside as any concept of national mission in modern history. It taught more Americans to be thankful, dutiful, and moderately self-confident than to be arrogant, undisciplined, and blindly self-willed; it pressed upon America's neighbors in every direction without furnishing a license to conquer them. In sum, the American mission stimulated a healthy nationalism that fell short of unthinking chauvinism and an exuberant expansionism that fell short of imperial conquest. Then, at the end of the Quest, it performed, through the perception and eloquence of Lincoln, its last and greatest service: It gave moral justification, which was needed desperately, to the terrible war for the Union.

There were times, to be sure, when the orators of the muscular, combative version of Manifest Destiny came close to converting the American mission from the Republic-as-experiment to the Republic-as-conqueror, but a more restrained if hardly self-denying version managed to prevail.[71] If it was the destiny of the American people to expand until neighbors as well as nature called a halt, it was not their destiny to engulf Canada, Mexico, Central America, and the islands of the Caribbean or to leap over the Pacific (ah, those more simple days!) in search of empire. The concept of mission encouraged expansion into the unsettled or only thinly settled lands of the West, for thus they could be won outright and, in American minds, altogether properly for the cause of republican liberty; it did not give the government of the United States an excuse to lord it over half the world and exact tribute from the rest. In short, the American mission helped to make *a nation with the dimensions but not the trappings of empire.* For that service, if for no other, later generations of Americans should study thoughtfully the purest version of their nation's mission, and perhaps even go to it from time to time for spiritual refreshment.

6

The Quest for Modernity:

Successes and Failures

THE commitment of the young United States to the goals of nationhood carried with it a commitment to the goals of modernity. From the first days of independence most Americans assumed that only if they were willing to abandon stifling old ways, explore liberating new ones, and drive relentlessly forward, upward, and outward might they become the kind of new nation to which the old nations would turn, once their prejudices against the upstart had been laid aside, for the lessons in freedom God had willed the Republic to teach. The sweep of the democratic ideal across the American land in the next two generations made the merging of the two commitments into one historic Quest all the more imperative, since only a nation that had crossed the threshold of modernity could satisfy the wants and thus capture the hardheaded loyalties of a citizenry made up of educated, liberty-loving men and women. The very timing of this experiment in continental republicanism commanded the American people to dare and toil to become a modern nation, or to give up the attempt to be a nation at all.

The size of the experiment reinforced this command. Once the Americans had made their choice for both an empire of liberty and a more perfect Union, which they did with a flourish in the Treaty of Paris, the Northwest Ordinance, the Constitution, and the Louisiana Purchase, they were bound by every consideration of principle and utility to reduce the divisive effects of space so that free men from Maine to Texas and from Georgia to the Rockies (and, in God's good time, "beyond the South Sea") could act and interact as citizens of one nation in the realms of economic and political reality. It was admirable of the founding generation to conceive the dream of a continental republic; it was obligatory for the generations that followed after to give substance to the dream. To frame this point in terms of a major goal of nationhood, the achievement of territorial integrity in both the external and internal dimensions waited upon the development of a network of transportation and communication that would make the United States one huge market place for the easy, unobstructed exchange of produce, raw materials, manufactured goods, skills, credits, ideas, and opinions. Joseph P. Bradley, of New Jersey, an active booster of railroads and later a justice of the Supreme Court, put the matter this way to an approving audience of students at Rutgers in 1849:

What constitutes the indissoluble bond which unites and keeps *us* together as one nation, and one people? What, but the mutuality of interests produced by the great variety of our industrial productions, and the consequent exchanges which the mutual supply of wants requires? It is this which lays down upon the map of our country the complicated net-work of our canals, our rail-roads, and our telegraphs. It is this which interlocks and weaves together all our public lines of communication and transportation; which carries life into all the breathing engines of social prosperity that labor around us, on the sea and on the land, by day and by night, unceasingly.[1]

Let us close the circle of nationhood and modernity by observing how all these good things of which Bradley spoke—mutuality, variety, productivity, exchange, prosperity—worked together to make possible the development of a political as well as an economic nation. When the representatives of the new state of Minnesota arrived in Washington in 1858 they were much nearer to home, and thus more disposed to think of Washington as the capital of a viable nation, than had been the representatives of Kentucky in 1792 or of Illinois in 1818. Even the representatives of California, waiting impatiently for a railroad to be driven through to the Pacific, could manage a smile over the false prophecies of some of their grandfathers that men who had gone off to live by the South Sea could never hope to have active, fraternal, national ties of a political character with men who had chosen to stay in New England or Pennsylvania or South Carolina.

If modernity was the prerequisite of full-fledged American nationhood, how far and successfully had we carried forward the second half of the Quest by 1860? Was the nation politically efficacious, economically viable, socially integrated, and culturally mature? Let me try to answer these questions as systematically, objectively, and exactly as I can—but only after having remarked again that it is considerably easier to be systematic than objective and enormously easier to be objective than exact.

The 1850's were years in which the American political system labored under nearly intolerable pressures. Since both the nature of the pressures and the manner, cruel but effective, in which they were finally released and reordered are to be discussed in due course, it might be more equitable and useful to assess the *political efficacy* of the nation in 1850, at the moment, let us say, when Henry Clay touched off the greatest of Great Debates in the Senate and thereby proved unwittingly yet convincingly that democrats should be careful not to ask too much of the techniques of democratic compromise. While by no means overlooking the role of state and local governments in a designedly federal political system, let us focus attention on the national government. As Alexander Hamilton had foretold far back in 1780 and retold in 1788, this was the one government that had to arise and prosper before the shimmering idea of an American nation could become a durable reality.

So long as it stayed within its appointed bounds (whose location was, to be sure, a subject of always warm and occasionally hot controversy), the *legitimacy* of the national government was clear and unchallengeable. If to this government we apply Max Weber's analysis of three types of "title to rule"—charismatic, traditional, and rational-legal [2]—we discover an interesting mix: at the beginning, in the person of George Washington, a small but helpful portion of charisma;* toward the end, as the Constitution took on the patina of age, a somewhat larger portion of tradition; from beginning to end, from the formation of the more perfect Union in 1787–1789 to the defense of this Union by Webster in 1850, a fifty-times-larger stock of law as reason. If the writ ran at most times and in most places throughout the land, it did

---

* In his *First New Nation,* S. M. Lipset exaggerates, I think, both the amount of charisma Washington possessed and the uses to which it was put. He was not, after all, the ruler of a nation of demoralized serfs.[3]

so principally because of a widespread, assiduously nurtured faith in the Constitution as the best of all possible national charters. An "assembly of demigods" adept at political reasoning put it together painstakingly and then offered it to the people;[4] the people, the most alert and enlightened the world had known, pondered this charter carefully and then, after exacting a promise of ten noble, liberty-defending amendments, accepted it. In this half-true, half-mythical way the instrument of a primarily rational-legal title to rule was given the added dimension of the consent of the people, and who could argue with that kind of legitimacy? Certainly not the Whiskey rebels of 1794 or the Virginia and Kentucky legislatures of 1798–1799 or the New England governors of 1812 or the Virginia judges of 1821, all of whom protested loudly that they had no argument with the system of political power, only with the strange purposes for which the power was being used, and the silencing of whom, one batch of challengers after another, helped to add the final dimension of tradition.

The most impressive evidence of the legitimacy of the national government was the series of peaceful, unchallenged (or only whimsically challenged) successions to the Presidency between 1797 and 1850. The Republic passed safely if not always serenely through a half-dozen transfers of executive authority that would have touched off major convulsions in all but two or three nations then existing: from Washington to John Adams in 1797, from Adams to Jefferson in 1801, from James Monroe to John Quincy Adams (over the angry head of Andrew Jackson) in 1825, and from Adams at last to Jackson in 1829, not to forget two transfers from the dead to the quick, William Henry Harrison to John Tyler in 1841 and Zachary Taylor to Millard Fillmore in 1850. The men of the young United States showed an uncommon respect for the ground rules of republicanism in refusing to be tempted into irregular behavior in these potentially explosive situations.

The *sanctions* available to the national government were numerous and, all things considered, effective—so long, I repeat, as it stayed within the appointed bounds. While it resorted occasionally to the harsher techniques of threat and force, it counted for the most part on proclamation, example, persuasion, and minor-league subsidy, which did the tasks expected of them remarkably well. Historians give too much attention to the success of the government in enforcing its commands in the Whiskey Rebellion of 1794 and the Nullification Crisis of 1832–1833 or, conversely, to the failure to enforce them when faced with the defiance of New England to the Embargo Act of 1807 and the defiance of Georgia to Chief Justice Marshall's decision in *Worcester v. Georgia* (1832).[5] Perhaps more attention might be directed to the relative ease with which the government raised money largely through sales of public land and duties on imports, in many years a good deal more than it was prepared to use, from a people brought up to dislike taxes and fees of any kind and plagued by a persistent dearth of specie. Few new nations as republican, federal, and suspicious of authority as the United States would have put up with Hamilton's daring move in 1790 to organize a small fleet of revenue cutters (the parent of the Coast Guard and the first purely national instrument of the American nation), which he took in order to cut down on smuggling, a favorite American outdoor sport ever since the Molasses Act of 1733. Few of any description have been asked by high authority to consider, in the querulous words of a Senate committee in 1826, the "serious inconvenience of an overflowing Treasury." [6] This complaint, one must admit, would read something like a fairy tale to men in Accra or Jakarta or Rangoon, or even in the city where it was first issued.

One solid reason for both the legitimacy and the authority of the national government was an extraordinary degree of *representativeness,* which became ever more extraordinary as the United States approached the outermost reach of political democracy as then imagined and defined: universal white-manhood suffrage. While problems of malapportionment of offices and underrepresentation of inchoate or inarticulate interests existed in those days as in these, I am prepared to put forward the claim (which waits, to be sure, for full confirmation upon several dozen monographs) that this government was more genuinely representative of the entire citizenry than any other in the world then and all but a half-dozen in the world today.

Among the most important arrangements of a political system

that became, some men feared, almost too representative of the hopes and anxieties of the American people were:

the principles and institutions of constitutional government inherited from the past and adapted, subject to the usual delays in such matters, to the present;

the broadening of the suffrage and consequent increase, sporadic but impressive, in popular interest and participation in politics;

the emergence and then, after a short dry spell of rather casual one-party dominion, re-emergence of the world's first system of competitive political parties organized within the government and throughout the land;[7]

the concurrent emergence in fact and doctrine of the world's first institutionalized and generally acknowledged loyal opposition;[8]

the more timid yet no less portentous groping toward the creation of a network of nationally organized interest groups;

the conversion of the Presidency by Andrew Jackson and, in their own manner, his two pale imitators, Martin Van Buren and James K. Polk, into a popular, indeed tribunitive, office;

the flourishing of a cheap, wide-ranging, free, and sometimes responsible press;

the admission of new states—a full eighteen between 1790 and 1850—on an equal footing with the old.

Even the spoils system, which has been poorly understood and thus egregiously maligned, did its share in developing a government that reflected and guarded the interests of the people. The one genuinely troublesome defect in the American pattern of representation (a defect, in large part, of its virtues) was the steady erosion in popular esteem of the concept of the public interest that had been a touchstone of policy in the years of Washington, Adams, and Jefferson. While pluralism and localism are two characteristics of a truly representative political system, each got quite out of hand in the heady days of Jacksonian democracy.

Another solid reason was the limited range of affairs in which the government engaged. If it had displayed the persistent and expensive *activeness* advocated by Alexander Hamilton and John Quincy Adams, both its legitimacy and its capacity to apply effective sanctions would have been put in severe hazard. So important for the basic line of argument of this study is the question of action and inaction in the American national polity that I wish to give it separate, elaborate, and a whiff of speculative treatment in later chapters. Let it suffice at this point to recite these preliminary conclusions: First, no government of those days, not even the most clever and splendid in Europe, was half as active as most governments, even in some of the most inexperienced and impoverished nations of Africa, are expected to be in these; second, the government of the United States, for reasons of ideology, tradition, nature, and circumstance, was noticeably less active than most regimes with which it could be fairly compared; and third, it became less and less active, in proportion to the population, wealth, and problems of the country, as it moved into the middle of the century.

While it may be thought unnecessary to substantiate the first of these conclusions, one may point to the size of the armed forces in 1850 (just under 21,000 officers and men in a population of just over 23 million)* as evidence for the second, and to the disengagement of the national government (after the demise of the second Bank of the United States) from even a Madisonian pattern of responsibility for central banking as evidence for the third.[10] The United States of America in 1850 provides, indeed, a classic case of the reconciling government, one that invites an extra measure of attention because of three interlocking facts of American history: Despite an immense reserve of experience and talent, the national political system was barely holding its own in the business of give-and-take; it was to go from bad to worse and finally to the edge of dissolution in a bare ten years; and while all this successful, half-successful, and unsuccessful reconciliation was taking place, the country was growing, expanding, and developing at a dizzying pace. *The coexistence of a mobilizing nation and a languishing, in some respects deteriorating polity* is a phenomenon that commands the most thoughtful attention. I hope to give it that kind of attention in the chapters that follow. Suffice it at this point to repeat a distinction I have already made in a general sense: In terms of parties, elections, suffrage, and popular

* Of the 21,000, moreover, something like 10,000 were (or should have been) at sea rather than on land.[9]

participation, politics in America was an ever more zestful undertaking in the years of the Quest; in terms of *governing*, however, of making important public choices for the nation and seeing them through to reality, politics in America was an ever more withered affair. While a zestful political life added immeasurably to the legitimacy and representativeness of the government of the United States, it did not of itself make this government one from which energetic actions could be expected as a matter of course.

While historians have taken much sly pleasure in lamenting the decline of Federalist and Jeffersonian standards of public service under the withering sun of egalitarian democracy, and also in making a depressing contrast between Washington and his Cabinet at the beginning and Fillmore and his Cabinet at the turning point of the Quest, no one, not even the admirable Leonard D. White,[11] has been able to follow lamentation and contrast with a convincing evaluation of the level of *efficiency* displayed by the government of the youthful United States. Someday perhaps this will be done on a systematic, comparative, and, wherever feasible, quantifying basis. Until that day we must be largely content with general impressions. My chief impression, which emerged from endless hours of leafing through reports and of rummaging in diaries of officials from the President to the Commissioner of Patents, is that the government of the United States performed its assigned tasks with hardly less efficiency than did the average private business springing up by the thousands throughout the land. At whatever level one wishes to concentrate his gaze—Presidency, Congress, courts, departments, customs houses, forts and camps, the 20,000 or more local post offices—one discovers a confusion of functions and overlapping of roles that a twentieth-century government would not tolerate. One also discovers signs, however, of the first long strides toward specialization, differentiation, and professionalism, as well as the extrusion, once the spoils system had fulfilled a wasteful yet essential mission for democracy, of partisan politics from those levels of administration at which it manifestly did not belong.

Our concern, be it recalled, is a nineteenth-century government, which appears to have been, at every level, a fair reflection of both the quality of American society and the expectations about public efficiency of the American political culture. We may well stand aghast at the sight of a system that permitted Samuel Swartwout, Collector of the Port of New York from 1829 to 1838, to swindle and steal on a monumental scale; we may also be deeply impressed by the forceful, honorable, frugal, and precedent-setting efficiency of, to cite only a few examples, the Presidency under Andrew Jackson, the Navy Department under George Bancroft, the Coast Survey under Alexander D. Bache, the Patent Office under Henry L. Ellsworth, the Post Office under Amos Kendall, and, of course, the Supreme Court under John Marshall. In many respects, at many times, and in many places high and low, the competence of the government of the United States compared favorably with that of the most celebrated governments of Europe.

Having ruminated this much about the basic inactiveness and modest efficiency of the American national government in the middle of the nineteenth century, we need touch only lightly on the questions of *capability* and *solvency*. So little was asked of the political system, and so progressively crippled did it become at the upper levels as men began to agitate the issue of the extension of slavery in earnest, that we have no way of telling how much forceful governing it might have done. One thing, in any case, seems beyond dispute: However low the level of capability from year to year, this bare-bones government proved on a number of occasions—the reform of the patent system in 1836, the prosecution to victory of the unpopular Mexican War, the granting of federal lands to help build a north-south railroad in 1850, the dispatch of Commodore Perry's expedition to Japan of 1853–1854, the dogged prosecution of its bureaucratic tasks throughout the 1850's—that it could move men and control events. In point of fact, this apparently noncapable government had an immense reserve of unused capability, and the time might come when men more resolute than Millard Fillmore and less frustrated than Henry Clay would be willing and able to draw upon it.

The solvency of the system had also gone largely untested, and no one knew for certain how much money could be extracted from the American people, or by what means, in order to weather a short-term public crisis or grapple with a long-term public need. Three pairs of statistics may give some idea of the untapped money-producing potential of this people: The per-capita debt of the national government, which had been roughly $19 in post-Revolution 1791 and $15 in postwar 1816, stood at 99 cents in prewar 1857; the annual receipts of the national government, which had averaged about $20 million in the 1820's, had risen only to around $60 million in the 1850's.[12] The retirement of the public debt in the 1830's and the tight rein under which it was held in the 1840's and 1850's were, in George R. Taylor's words, an "unparalleled achievement" for a "great modern nation." [13] While much credit for this achievement must be assigned to happy circumstance and a low-keyed political culture, some must also be given to a nation of men and women who "ate their bread"—and good bread it was—in "the sweat of their faces."

Perhaps the longest strides in the development of the American political system in the years of the Quest were taken in the direction of *democracy* and *constitutionalism*. The democracy was flawed, as it seems always and everywhere to be, with imperfections and indecencies; the constitutionalism served too often as a polite screen behind which men wrestled lustily for power and profit. Yet no nation on earth had moved as fast and far in search of the one, and only Britain had scored more solid blows in defense of the other. No nation could stage an election as delightful, noisy, popular, honest, and, in an odd sense, meaningful as the Harrison–Van Buren extravaganza of 1840; no nation except Britain had as much predictability, regularity, and due process in the enactment, administration, and interpretation of the laws. While the two seemed often at odds—ebullient populism threatening to sweep away decorum in politics and to undercut protections for minorities, a fussy concern for procedures and limitations threatening to frustrate the clearly voiced will of the majority—men like Webster, Douglas, and Lincoln, as well as the millions for whom they spoke, understood as sharply as Jefferson himself had ever understood that democracy and constitutionalism were two sides of one precious coin: *liberty under law.*

Before concluding this preliminary analysis of the strengths and weaknesses of the national government of the United States at the mid-point of the nineteenth century, let me again acknowledge that even today this government is only one part, although the dominant and central part, of a large, complicated, self-duplicating, often self-triplicating political system. A century and a quarter ago it was neither dominant nor, for most men, central; and we would do well therefore to pay our respects to the governments of the thirty-one states, of the half-dozen organized or soon-to-be organized territories, and of the thousands of cities, counties, villages, towns, and hamlets that sprawled across the American landscape. All things considered, they seem to have earned these respects. If they were probably less efficient,[14] solvent, and constitutional than the national government, they were certainly, within their own spheres, every bit as legitimate, armed with sanctions, and representative. They were also probably, within those same spheres, more active, capable, and democratic. While most areas of this extensive political system remain unmapped by modern political science, we know enough about the best of the state and local governments to recognize the value of the services they rendered in such fields as education, transportation, public health, and social reform. The University of Michigan and the Massachusetts Board of Education, the Erie Canal and the Georgia Railroad, the water system of New York City and the hospitals of Philadelphia, the model prisons that Tocqueville and his friend Beaumont came to study—here are bits of concrete evidence, which could be multiplied many times over, that the political system as a whole did rather more governing than the ideologues of laissez faire would have us believe. Yet as Louis Hartz has demonstrated in the pivotal case of Pennsylvania,[15] many state and local governments also began to languish, indeed to surrender public responsibilities they had hitherto shouldered, in the years just before the Civil War.

If we turn our attention back to the national government, we scan a balance sheet of success and failure, dedication and doubt, boldness and timidity, confidence and uncertainty. While this government had failed to do many tasks to which it was surely equal, had backed off from some after auspicious beginnings, and had not even imagined others that would become standard responsibilities a half-century later, it did have solid accomplishments on the record, and in due course we shall take a careful look at these as well as at its failures and falterings. If the government did little to mobilize the energies and talents of a lusty young nation, it set a public stage upon which private enterprise was destined to score one of the two most stunning victories of a checkered history. That service alone was greatly to its credit; that service, moreover, may have been the most useful it could have performed for the American people in their peculiar situation.

Lest this discussion of the state of the American polity of 1850 end on too happy a note, let us recall that from the beginning we had been an uncertain nation, then note that such a nation got what it deserved: an uncertain national government. This uncertainty about the nature and future of both the Union and its government catches the attention of the twentieth-century American when he digs into the evidence of two symbolic facts of political life in the middle of the nineteenth century.

One was physical, and thus struck the eye of many Americans and all foreign visitors: the unadorned, helter-skelter, retarded, and crude condition of the nation's capital, which was "little better," according to the fourth generation of the Adams family, "than a poorly administered southern village." [16] In direct contrast to the grand hopes of the men who had founded it, the city of Washington was a cross between a "vast construction site" and an overgrown hamlet.[17] It would be interesting to know if the first sight in early 1861 of an unfinished dome for the Capitol and an unfinished Washington Monument made President-elect Lincoln even more painfully aware than he had been in late 1860 that he was entering upon the leadership of an unfinished nation.

The other fact was juridical, and thus made sense or nonsense chiefly to men with legal minds: the vagueness surrounding the concept of American citizenship, which moved the Attorney General to ask as late as 1862, "Who is a citizen? What constitutes a citizen of the United States?," and then to answer, after a "fruitless search" in lawbooks and public records, that "the question" was as "open to argument and to speculative criticism, as it was at the beginning of the Government." [18] The hesitancy of the Framers, the pride of states old and new, the enduring anxiety about centralized power, the federal principle, the slavery issue, and the problem posed for white America by hundreds of thousands of free Negroes all conspired to produce a political-legal-constitutional-ideological situation in which national citizenship appeared to be secondary to state citizenship and, moreover, derivative from it. Not until this situation was exactly reversed

147

would the government of the United States be truly national; not until such a government was fully alive would the United States be a certain nation.

In the first half of the nineteenth century the United States passed through one of the half-dozen most spectacular stages of economic growth and development of any country at any time in history. So vigorously did it pursue the goal of *economic viability* that by 1860 it was getting ready to challenge England for first place among all nations. The Americans had hit what Walt Rostow calls the take-off as far back as the 1830's;* they had then soared upward so swiftly that the consummation of a full-scale industrial revolution was simply a matter of time; they were, indeed, already enjoying some of the fruits and suffering some of the pains of the "rapidly maturing industrial state." [20] While pockets of backwardness dotted the landscape, so also did harbingers of the technology of the twentieth century. While the South sulked or swaggered to the rear of the procession, the planters, merchants, entrepreneurs, small farmers, and slaves of that still largely agrarian area played their own part (an essential one, we shall see) in the development of a hustling, ever more bountiful national economy.

Of the marks of economic viability none was more impressively on display for all the world to see and also, Americans were sure, to envy than the *capacity for growth*. The consequences of generations of growth were the factories, fields, mines, machines, ships, shipyards, tools, skills, networks of transportation and communication, financial assets and credits, public works, and private possessions that made up the total wealth of the nation. The most rewarding part of this accumulated wealth was a built-in, ever-expanding capacity for still further growth, which was writ large in the mechanisms, motives, and momentum of a dy-

* Rostow places the American take-off in the 1840's, but I agree with Lee Benson that he "tends to give disproportionate emphasis to industrial developments," and would therefore place it myself, as does Benson, a decade earlier. Indeed, Robert W. Fogel has made a plausible case for the 1820's. Louis Hacker, however, will have none of this controversy, for in his most recent book he insists that the take-off did not come until *after* the Civil War. Perhaps he, Fogel, and everyone else who has joined in the debate might agree to peaceful coexistence if we were to substitute "point of no return" for "take-off." [19]

namic economy. Although both the growth and the development of this economy came in bursts, led on three notorious occasions through boom to bust, and were often hampered by state and local governments that either did too much to fan the flames of speculation and overbuilding or too little to set a helpful stage for imaginative enterprise, the American appetite for innovation and output had carried an entire people far along the road from austerity to plenty. No matter what reliable or at least plausible statistics one scoops out of the records—size of national income, value of exports and imports, amount of money in circulation and on deposit, number of factories and banks, mileage of track and canals, tonnage of ships built or already in commission, acreage of cotton, production figures for scores of goods[21]—the evidence is clear that the wealth of the nation was increasing much faster than the population, which surged, we have noted, from 3.9 million in 1790 to 31.5 million in 1860.

As has been the case in all modernizing countries, the growth of the American economy was sectoral: Economic historians agree generally that the sectors of seminal growth were cotton-raising, textile-manufacturing, railroad-building, and ironmaking. They also agree, although the data are scarce and slippery to handle, that average per-capita income rose from something like $80 in 1830 to $140 in 1860,[22] an unusually healthy indication of economic progress in light of the startling fact that a dollar bought as much in the latter year as in the former, and at least ten to fifteen times more than it buys today. The most startling fact of all, it appears to the historian without special training in economics, is that the advances between 1790 and 1860 were achieved without inflation.[23] Prices fluttered from time to time for all the usual reasons of war, peace, depression, and recovery; the over-all index, however, had a habit of returning sooner or later to that of 1790. Perhaps a socially acceptable amount of inflation might have helped the economy to develop even more swiftly in these years, yet the pace was already about as swift as any people has been asked to maintain. The institutional and ideological weakness of organized labor, the lack of national political capacity to influence events in the economic sphere, and the virtual nonexistence of activities and obligations we have come to associate with the welfare state all militated against the chance that economic growth would lead to a wage-price spiral. The workers of those dead days were left largely to their own devices, as were indeed the entrepreneurs, but at least they had the security, now seemingly lost forever, of steady prices.

This growth was not achieved without disorder, waste, and suffering. A more clever and celebratory historian than I would need to be summoned to award the American economy of 1860 high marks for *stability*. An economy expanding as rapidly as that of the young Republic is certain to experience growing pains, especially when risk-taking is part of the way of life and innovation works incessantly to render the wonders of one generation fossils in the next. A notable example is the misery that the coming of the railroad inflicted upon every canal in the nation except the Erie and the Delaware and Hudson. The panic-triggered depressions of 1819–1822, 1837–1843, and 1857–1858 are not so easily shrugged off, however, for the records of those years still make unpleasant reading. Bankruptcies, cuts in production, slashes in wages, foreclosures, repudiations of state bonds, collapses in prices of farm products, bank closings, widespread unemployment—these and other deplorable features of hard times in America brought sorrow to millions of men and women who had hoped and worked for better things; and neither the temper of the political culture nor the state of the political art encouraged government to act, even to think about acting, in order to decelerate boom or mitigate bust. Yet if men suffered, healthy growth was retarded, and government wallowed in a swamp of imperception and indecision, the economy itself managed to get up a new head of steam every time and move once again upward. One comes away from a study of these three distinct periods of disruption and stagnation with immense respect for the self-generating capacity for recovery of the American economy.

A crucial element of this capacity was a marked increase in *diversification*. The American economy grew not only bigger and richer but also more varied in patterns of production and investment. While the South continued to concentrate a disproportionate amount of attention on raising cotton, the rest of the nation moved toward a healthier balance between agrarian, commercial, and industrial pursuits. Within each of these areas, moreover, men went off on the hunt for prosperity in dozens of directions. Wheat and corn were the leading crops throughout this period, yet more and more farmers found it profitable to put their time and money in everything from pigs to hay by way of fruits and vegetables. The manufacture of cloth and clothing (including boots and shoes) held on to first place among nonagrarian pursuits,[24] yet more and more capital and energy were siphoned off to produce machines and tools and to dig for coal and copper. Two immense steps toward diversification, and also toward the national affluence of the future, were taken just before the Civil War. In the 1850's the gold of California became the most valuable of American mineral products; in 1859, at picturesque Oil Creek in Pennsylvania, the first drilled oil well began to flow. It might be mentioned in passing that since the citizenry of the United States was not taxed on income, the Congress of the United States had not yet moved to supply the wealthier or simply more nimble members of the citizenry with an opportunity to hide behind an oil-depletion allowance.

Another such element was a startling increase in productivity. Especially after 1840 the introduction of homemade and imported machinery revolutionized the making of such basic goods as cloth, clothing, shoes, tools, iron rails, weapons, engines, and ships, not to forget nails, newsprint, books, flour, and machinery itself. Two disbelieving visitors from Britain reported back to their fellow countrymen in 1854 that, "as compared with the operations of the most expert spinner in Hindoostan," the average American and his spinning machine could "perform the work of 3,000 men." [25] While much American farming, faithful to a tradition that stemmed from earliest colonial times, was wasteful, slovenly, and shockingly inefficient, much also took off for the future under the impetus of inventions that carried this brash nation to world leadership in the manufacture and use of agricultural machinery.[26] With an instinct for the convincing fact, Thomas Cochran and William Miller have written, "The West grew a wheat crop large enough to feed the nation in 1860, but that crop would have rotted in the fields had there been no machines to harvest it." [27] Cyrus McCormick and his swarm of imitators and competitors had made it possible for wheat-growing to keep pace with cloth-weaving and iron-forging and shoemaking as

151

each endeavor, and along with them the whole economy, climbed dramatically toward an input-output ratio hardly less modern in 1860 than had been achieved in front-running England. This increase in productivity led, as it always does, to the displacement of workers and disappearance of skills, yet it also led to shorter hours, cheaper prices, more numerous choices, and better lives for the mass of the American people.

Almost but not quite needless to add, the United States of 1860 had found the money; and, although the 1850's were a period of accelerated inflow of profit-seeking capital from abroad, most of the money had been found at home. Foreign investment in the United States reached the vicinity of $400 million in 1860, but the sum was just a shade higher than what Americans paid for imports in that single year.[28] Toil, risk, innovation, and good fortune had joined to create the *surplus* of domestic capital that permits a nation to develop a modern economy while at the same time maintaining a posture of sturdy independence.* Some of the techniques men used to find the money for canals, railroads, ships, factories, and cultivation of new lands were crude by our standards and fraudulent by any standards, yet the noticeable increase in overhead at the social level and in possessions at the personal level was the sign of an economy well on the way to the affluence of modernity. Even then, be it noted, American business was a primary source of its own capital needs. In Caroline Ware's study of cotton-manufacturing in early New England she discovered that the principal capital for the expansion of this pace-setting industry was plowed-back profits. Other scholars have called attention to the important role played by men eager to transfer profits from an established field of enterprise such as importing or shipbuilding to a new field such as ironmaking or railroad-building.[29]

Of all developments in the American economy before the Civil War, the most promising of modernity was a rate of *flow* that would have amazed the visionary men of the founding generation. Farm products, manufactures, money, managers, workers, and innovations circulated so vigorously that every part of the

* Two treasures brought to light in this period (and then, to be sure, exploited with awesome effort) will serve to show what I mean by good fortune: the soil of the prairies and the gold of California.

country, even the lagging South, was swept up in a torrrent of economic change.

The basic component of this pattern of flow was the network of transportation: roads, canals, steam-conquered rivers, and, by 1860 firmly seated in the place of honor, more than 30,000 miles of railroad. It would be hard to exaggerate the importance of this network in the growth of the American economy.* The quest for modernity in any nation requires the *conquest of distance*. In a nation the size of the United States the penalty for failure in this struggle with nature would have been deceleration, stagnation, and ultimately death, and farsighted Americans were correct to see that, in George R. Taylor's words, a "transportation revolution" was the first order of business for the nation.[30] The two historians of the American economy quoted several paragraphs above on the impossibility of harvesting the wheat crop in 1860 without machines go on to assert the impossibility of then marketing this crop without steamboats, canals, and railroads. The wheat of the West, they write, "would have overflowed the warehouses had it depended upon old-fashioned wagons and flatboats for distribution." [31]

While a welcome increase in speed and carrying capacity may appear to us to have been the principal result of the transportation revolution, men of those days were more likely to take delight in the sharp decrease in cost. Whether by road, river, canal, or railroad, the charges for shipping profitable freight as well as for transporting ambitious men went down and down through all the years of the Quest. An especially stimulating plunge took place hard upon the opening of that highway of empire, the Erie Canal. The cost per ton-mile of moving goods from Buffalo to New York was roughly 19 cents in 1817, 8/10 of a cent in 1860; and by the latter date farmers and merchants in a hurry could pass up the advantages of the canal and ship their products by rail for about two cents a ton-mile.[32]

If we add the dimension of backward linkage to a pattern of ever more rapid, capacious, efficient, and inexpensive transportation (by noting, for one example, the transformation of iron-

---

* The integration of the network, to be sure, was far from satisfactory, a point that I discuss in chapter 10 in the highly specific terms of the unwillingness of American railroaders to agree on a standard gauge.

making in order to meet the needs of railroad-builders), we have a right to talk soberly about a revolution. And the revolution, we must recall, was not merely economic in character. Ever improving transportation led to ever increasing horizontal mobility, such horizontal mobility to heightened opportunity, such opportunity to accelerated vertical mobility; and all of these together speeded the onward march of democracy. An astute French visitor expressed the true meaning of this development in 1837 when he observed that for Americans (or, indeed, for any people) "to improve" the channels of flow

is to promote a real, positive, and practical liberty; it is to extend to all the members of the human family the power of moving about and using the world which has been given to all as a common patrimony; it is to increase the rights and privileges of the greatest number as truly and as amply as could be done by electoral laws. I would go further— it is to establish equality and democracy.[33]

The most zealous promoter of a railroad from Baltimore to the Ohio could not have made the point more eloquently.

The Americans of this period brought off an equally remarkable and modernizing revolution in the related area of communication. Because of the development of the transportation network itself, the establishment of express service, the expansion of the postal service and adoption of uniform postage rates, the sprouting of journals and newspapers (including the "penny press" of the large cities), and the stringing of 50,000 miles of telegraph wire, they could talk to each other in 1860 as citizens of a modern nation. If much of what they had to say was crude, tawdry, and, on the great issue of the day, inflammatory, the fact remains that the verbal as well as the physical conquest of distance had carried them far, too far ever to turn back, toward economic viability.* To tell the truth, few of them had much interest in turning back. If there was any one thing more impressive than the network of transportation and communication constructed in these years, it was the eagerness of merchants, manufacturers, journalists, farmers, craftsmen, politicians, migrants, and immigrants to make use of it.

* In the case of the telegraph, the king of wire-stringers, Ezra Cornell, went further to call it the "annihilation of space." [34]

The Quest for Modernity: Successes and Failures

If we think ourselves once again back into the twilight of the middle of the nineteenth century, we may see signs of growing economic *sophistication* all about us. While the political culture was one in which such activities as regulation, planning, money-management, statutory protection of workers, and government aid to the distressed were still many years over the horizon of national development, the economy itself was far more complicated, flexible, anticipatory, and professional in outlook than it had been only twenty or thirty years before. The introduction of ingenious and reliable machines into one enterprise after another brought steep rises in productivity. The growth of savings institutions and multiplication of instruments for efficient marketing are two examples of the trend toward specialization of function. The increase in well-trained engineers and emergence of a sizable group of men who concentrated their energies on investment are two examples of the trend toward differentiation of role. Indeed, the old-fashioned, Jack-of-all-trades enterpreneur was disappearing so rapidly that by 1860 Henry Varnum Poor, whose *American Railroad Journal* itself served as an instrument of progress that could not possibly have flourished in a less sophisticated American economy, was voicing the now familiar complaint that managers of railroads did not own and owners did not manage.[35] Nor was this complaint confined to railroads. In more and more fields the corporation was supplanting individual proprietorship, family enterprise, and partnership as the basic form of economic organization.

As enterprises grew larger they became more specialized; specialization, in its turn, led away from charming but costly dispersion toward more impersonal but less costly concentration. An interesting example was the convergence of facilities for handling cargoes on the New England coast: Once-thriving seaports gave up trying to compete with well-placed Boston; Boston itself offered faster, more predictable, and cheaper service to shippers and travelers alike. Cities everywhere went through the dual process of specialization and concentration, and the result was to create more efficient units of production and more dependable channels of flow. Professionalization kept steady pace with this process. Bankers, lawyers, brokers, civil servants, and engineers of all types became better educated and more role-conscious in

The American Quest

the years just before the Civil War. From those years there date—
sure signs and, in the right hands, useful engines of modernity—
some of the most respected professional organizations in the
United States. The men who directed production and distribution were not far behind. Henry Varnum Poor gave an extra dose
of distinction to 1854, a memorable year on many counts, with
his future-invoking decision to turn the attention of the *American Railroad Journal* to the study and celebration of the "science
of management." [36]

We must not pass airily over the abundant evidence of waste,
mediocrity, ignorance, and incompetence in the American economy of the 1850's. It is depressing to note the scarcity of large-
minded political economists like Poor, Mathew Carey and his son
Henry, and J. D. B. De Bow, startling to discover the crudeness
of methods of accounting, astonishing to discover that consumer-
oriented obsolescence of textiles and other manufactured goods
was part of the American style long before the Civil War.[37] And
surely no rapidly industrializing economy could be saluted as
truly sophisticated when it lacked both a system of central banking and a plentiful stock of national currency. The state banks,
wherever they were permitted to exist, were a poor substitute for
the two banks of the United States; state and private notes constituted much too large a portion, something like 80 per cent if
we include demand deposits in state banks, of the money supply
of the country.[38] Yet these were inadequacies certain to be reme-
died in the course of time, and one is rather more impressed by
the spectacle of a young nation bubbling over with largely self-
taught inventors who turned their little worlds, and sometimes
the whole world, upside down with ingenious discoveries: Eli
Whitney with the cotton gin and his method of manufacturing
firearms with standardized, interchangeable parts;[39] Archibald
Binney with patented molds for casting type and Samuel F. B.
Morse with the telegraph; Cyrus McCormick and Obed Hussey
with their reapers; Charles Goodyear with vulcanized rubber and
Elias Howe with his sewing machine; Richard Hoe with his rotary press and Elisha Otis with his passenger elevator; and a host
of men like John A. Roebling, the bridge-builder, Major G. W.
Whistler, the railroad-builder (for both the B. and O. and the
Czar of Russia), and the half-dozen early steamboat-builders who

dreamed, improvised, borrowed, and adapted in behalf of themselves and a nation on the move. And a final word in praise of the growing sophistication of the economy of this nation: As one who has burrowed into every census before the Civil War, I can report with feeling that in variety, imaginativeness, and reliability the census of 1860 is unbelievably superior to, let us say, the census of 1820; it is, indeed, so superior that I have sometimes felt that two entirely different countries were under scrutiny.*

In this discussion of such aspects of the American economy in 1860 as capacity for growth, productivity, surplus, and flow, we have already touched upon the essentials of the fundamental goal of *solvency*. The meeting at a pivotal stage in modern history of a fair land, an ambitious people, a permissive and occasionally helpful polity, and an achievement-oriented system of values had created an economy that might occasionally fall on hard times but would never go broke. Both the total wealth of the nation and the capacity to accumulate still more wealth stayed safely in front of the expectations of the people. Individuals might skid into bankruptcy, enterprises collapse, and headstrong states refuse to honor solemn obligations; yet the nation as a whole was well on the way to becoming the people of plenty of which David Potter has written. This nation had the assets, if not yet all the refined techniques of extraction and appropriation, to pay for any service it might need over the long haul or any charges it might run up in an emergency. No asset looms more impressively as reality and symbol than the gold of California, which was exported in such quantities in the 1850's that the economy had no trouble living (as it had lived almost continuously since 1790) with an unfavorable balance-of-payments situation.[40]

The American economy in 1860 was not merely bigger, lustier, richer, and more viable than it had been in 1790 or 1830; it was also *more national*. All parts of the country, including the foot-dragging South, were bound tightly together by ties of commerce. The West shipped vast quantities of flour, corn, pork, and beef to the South and also to the East; the South shipped cotton, to-

---

* Much credit for this development must go to J. D. B. De Bow, who took time off from his persistent efforts to get the South to modernize, in order to supervise the census of 1850.

bacco, and sugar to the East; the East handled most of the business of exporting cotton across the ocean, thereby extracting money as well as raw materials from the South, and sent its own manufactures and capital in every direction. Although each region planted, extracted, converted, and manufactured for consumption within its own boundaries, each also made important purchases and sales in other regions. Whatever it was politically or psychologically in 1860, the United States was more of a nation economically than many countries of the world are today or can ever hope to be.

The circumstances that contributed to the rise of a national economy in the United States are too numerous and, in many instances, too poorly understood to be reviewed at length in a study of this nature. Nevertheless, it might be useful to mention four about which much is already well understood:

the acceleration of the rate of flow, which brought every part of America into close commercial contact with every other part;

the trend toward diversification, which put every part in a solid position to produce raw materials or finished goods that could be sold for a profit in other parts;

that one masterful act of politics, the adoption of the Constitution, which opened up the prospect of a free-trade area coterminous with the boundaries of the nation;

the willingness of the South to plant cotton, cotton, and yet more cotton.

The last of these circumstances was first in consequence. The more we learn of the growth of the American economy in the opening decades of the nineteenth century, the more clearly we see that cotton was indeed a king whose influence, if not whose sovereignty, extended to all parts of the country. By concentrating so heavily on cotton, by producing the world's most eagerly devoured commodity at the neglect of other forms of agrarian, commercial, and industrial activity, the South fed the mills of England and New England, speeded the accumulation of capital, lured men west to grow crops to sell to other men in the South too obsessed with cotton to grow such crops for themselves, and stimulated both diversification and flow in every part of the country.[41] Emerson was more shrewd and less amusing than he knew when he asserted:

Cotton thread holds the Union together; unites John C. Calhoun and Abbott Lawrence. Patriotism for holidays and summer evenings, with music and rockets, but cotton thread is the Union.[42]

Cotton was more than that: It provided well over half the value of all exports between 1820 and 1860,[43] and thereby made the position of the United States in the world economy both tenable and profitable. Since the South did the growing and the Northeast most of the financing and managing of the export trade, Southerners got far smaller a share of the profits from cotton than they thought (and we today might also think) they had coming. Be that as it may, the central if paradoxical point is clear: Even as the South lagged socially, technologically, and culturally behind the rest of the country, and moved politically and emotionally into a hostile posture, it furnished powerful economic support to the American search for modern nationhood. The planters of cotton, unwittingly and even against their collective will, did almost as much as the builders of railroads to nourish the development of a viable economy and growth of an indestructible Union. Once again we must marvel at the capacity of men to make history—especially when it is not the history they think they are making.

By the middle of the nineteenth century an unprecedented society had risen to flourish on the North American continent. All who paused to record their thoughts about it—enthusiastic or disillusioned citizens, confident or bewildered immigrants, friendly or malicious travelers—agreed that there was, after all, something new under the sun: a new way of life, a new race of men, even perhaps (in the minds of the most enthusiastic, confident, and friendly) the long-promised "new order of the ages." * Far less structured than the posttraditional European societies of those days and the modernized American society of these, the United States had arrived at a condition of *social integration* that was well suited for achieving the primary goals of the nation: independence, growth, expansion, progress, liberty, prosperity, the conquest of nature, the perfection of the Union. American

* The ancient words *Novus Ordo Seclorum* are written boldly on the reverse of the Great Seal of the United States, as one who has a dollar bill may see for himself.

society was crude, bumptious, restless, erratic, and devoid of some of the most elementary safeguards of both individual welfare and the public interest. It was nonetheless highly functional in American terms; and those, we know, were the terms of a bourgeois, liberal-democratic, individualistic people stripped of both the shackles and the defenses of a feudal past and set down to do their own work and the Lord's in a challenging yet also inviting arena.

We know a good deal less about this society than about the political system it starved, the economy it shaped, or the culture it looked at askance, for social history is the stunted stepchild of the family. Yet enough bits of evidence exist, if we can select and arrange them in a think-backish mood, to encourage some suggestive generalizations about life in the United States in the 1850's. Whether the suggestions of today become the conclusions of tomorrow depends upon the willingness of hundreds of young historians to turn away from fields like politics, economics, diplomacy, and literature, in which evidence is abundant and fairly easily gathered, and toward the field of social relations, in which a scholar can spend a lifetime rummaging in the trunks and shelves of local historical societies and have precious little of consequence to show for his labors. What follow, then, are modest hypotheses that must sooner or later be tested and retested if we are to understand the American past "as it really was."

Despite the sneering remarks of fastidious visitors, who found what they were looking for only in enclaves like Boston, New Orleans, and Charleston, the rising nation had a *rational social order*. The most conspicuous feature of this order was a class structure with a high degree of proximity between any one layer of men and that above or below it. Except for the neglected or harried Indians and the enslaved or unaccepted Negroes—a large exception, yet one we must make dispassionately if we are to think back into the twilight of this obstinately white America— the people of the United States were grouped loosely in a social pyramid much broader than it was tall. For those who prefer another familiar metaphor, they were spread up and down the rungs of a social ladder whose top and bottom were far closer together than in any country in Europe and, more to the point, in both the America of fifty years before and the America of fifty years later. The upper elite, which had shifted the focus of its attention from public affairs to private enterprise, was about as legitimate, accessible, functional, and adjusted as an elite can be, and still was distinguished by a lack of men with too much wealth, self-esteem, and economic or political power for the health of a democratic nation. The laboring class, which had begun to move in increasing numbers out of fields and into factories, was a proletariat neither in expectations nor political cast of mind. And the middle class, which had long been the self-acknowledged center of gravity of American life, was busily engaged, except in the hardest of hard times, in recruiting millions of new members from below, propelling thousands of old members upward, and offering the second elite room to maneuver.

Toward the end of the Quest the impact of rapid, undisciplined industrialization began to crack this healthy if never idyllic pattern of proximity: Both millionaires and mendicants, both far-ranging entrepreneurs and hopelessly trapped unskilled workers were counted in larger and larger numbers. Yet even in 1860 perceptive observers from the stratified countries of Europe were more impressed by the equality of condition among Americans than by the conspicuous consumption of the wealthy or the obscure misery of the poor, and so they continued to echo Tocqueville's astonishment over discovering a "whole society" that had "melted into a middle class." [44] As Matthew Arnold observed a few years after the Civil War, "That which in England we call the middle class is in America virtually the nation." [45] That redoubtable pioneer Morris Birkbeck had already seen and reported this point from another perspective when he wrote in 1817 that "refinement is unquestionably far more rare, than in our mature and highly cultivated state of society; but so is extreme vulgarity." [46]

However the Americans of 1860 may have grouped themselves in their own minds or may be grouped in ours, their social order was one in which the *reconciliation of classes* was an accomplished if by no means immutable fact. Writing just before the Civil War in the oldest of American idioms, the economist Henry Carey announced the "true mission of the United States": to prove that a "perfect harmony of interest" could exist among men of all ranks and callings.[47] Although he could not deny the presence of streaks of a new kind of haughtiness at the top, truculence in the middle, and despair at the bottom of American society, he could also take justifiable pride in the fact that classes were more at peace than at war in this country, that nothing resembling a Marxist class struggle was on the agenda of bourgeois America. Property, especially in land, was too widely and equitably distributed, opportunity too visible and pursuable, and the pay-off (a word that, to their credit, they never even thought of using) too inviting and attainable to permit arrogance and envy to take command of American life and to pit class against class in violent political or civil combat. While neither the floor of self-respect under the bottom nor the lid of self-restraint on the top was the product of conscious national effort, they were visible features of a developing yet still largely decentralized economy; and neither the floor nor the lid we have constructed in modern America is much more effective an instrument of social justice than its primitive counterpart of a century ago. If there were in fact two nations edging toward war in the middle of the century, the two, unlike Disraeli's, were divided on grounds that had little to do with class distinctions. If there was more violent behavior than one likes to discover in the workings of a supposedly civilized society, that was largely the product, like cherry pie (or apple?), of natural and nurtured circumstances unique to the continental Republic of North America.

We have so little hard evidence about the relation of wages and hours to prices and choices (and so much of what we have is streaked with self-contradictions) that it is next to impossible to arrive at a happy generalization about a *rise in the standard of living* during this period of rapid economic growth. If, as we noted above, the average per-capita income rose something like 75 per cent in the three decades before the Civil War, this statistic tells nothing about the manner in which the total income of the nation was distributed and then spent. While there is good reason to believe that merchants, manufacturers, professional men, successful farmers, and some descriptions of skilled workers were, taken as a whole, clearly better off in 1860 than in 1830, the same does not hold for peripheral entrepreneurs, displaced craftsmen, poor farmers, and unskilled workers.[48] The whole subject is rendered confusing to the point of chaos by the reduction in the over-all standard of living that took place when restless men

moved west to settle new lands and other men moved in from
Europe, many of them from poorhouses and decayed villages, to
take their places. Still, despite the austerities of migration, the
miseries of immigration, and the dislocations of a process of industrialization that galloped around untamed by the political
system, the standard of living for most Americans, which in most
things was higher than that of the Old World to begin with,
seems to have climbed upward in these years. Visitor after visitor
agreed with Michael Chevalier's comment of 1837 that the "one
thing in the United States" most striking to a "stranger on step-
ping ashore" was the "appearance of general ease in the condition of the people of this country." [49]

As life became more worth living for millions of Americans,
their chance to live it improved visibly. If neither the safeguards
of public health nor the standards of private medical practice had
as modern a look in 1860 as, let us say, the New York money market, the New England shoemaking industry, or the northeastern
railroad network, beginnings that promised a far more sophisticated system of medicine had been made.[50] The few solid statistics we have about life expectancy and infant mortality in this
period, for example, show a slow rise in the former and decline in
the latter. Indeed, the annual infant mortality rate in Massachusetts, which had dropped to something like 125 out of 1,000
live births in the 1850's, went up once again during the Civil War
and never came down to the prewar level until around 1910.[51]

The *infrastructure* of American society in this period was modest and decentralized, yet it, too, with a few glaring exceptions,
was a good servant to an ambitious race of individualists. While
the days of Rotary and P.T.A. were far in the future, a rising
trend toward free co-operation for social, charitable, economic,
educational, religious, cultural, and political purposes was already under way. Tocqueville was one of the earliest observers to
understand that the kind of individualism practiced in America
would lead in due course, not paradoxically but altogether naturally, to acts of voluntary association;[52] and even he might have
been astonished if he had revisited America in 1860 and observed
the proliferation of churches, bible and temperance societies,
professional associations, co-operatives, chambers of commerce,
subscription libraries, institutes for adult education, and dozens

of other types of *Gesellschaften*. These groups brought men together to do much of the work of society, served as buffers between them and the larger community, and for the most part fitted effortlessly into the American scene as supports of the rising nation. No less important than the proliferation of such associations was the movement to organize them on a national basis. Although the founding of the American Bible Society in 1816, the American Peace Society in 1828, and the American Anti-Slavery Society in 1833 receives most attention in standard histories of the United States, the establishment of the American Medical Association in 1846–1848,[53] after several false starts, holds perhaps more significance as a portent of the future.

Far and away the most important form of organization in this developing infrastructure was the enduring American family. If the decline almost to extinction of household manufacturing removed the nonfarming family from the scene as an important economic unit,[54] and if both women and children were generally less at the mercy of paternal dictation than their counterparts in Europe,[55] the family was nonetheless a more influential, close-knit, value-transmitting, educating, disciplining, and contributing organization than we have spawned for many decades. Ralph H. Gabriel has pointed out that both the fact and the spirit of American individualism also led to a new role for the family as a new kind of refuge for otherwise solitary men;[56] and the Americans of the Quest, be it noted, were the most solitary and, in this sense, modern men who had ever been known.

The most grievous flaw in a generally satisfactory portrait of a functional infrastructure was the failure of workingmen of nearly every description to organize themselves into unions that might have offered protection against the worst pressures of industrialization. In both the 1830's and the 1850's strong local and national unions appeared to have emerged as permanent features of society and the economy, but the collapse of pioneering efforts, first in the aftermath of 1837 and next in the aftermath of 1857, left individual workers to bargain on their own throughout the rest of the nineteenth century.[57] Law, tradition, the assumptions of a bourgeois political culture, the imperatives of industrialization, the migration of adventurous men to the West, and the immigration of poor laborers from Europe all conspired to keep the union two or three generations behind the corporation in the race toward modern America. Nevertheless, the short-lived National Trades' Union (1834) and the more tenacious National Typographical Union (1852) were harbingers of the future no less significant than the American Medical Association. So, too, for that matter, was the pitiful failure of the hopeful working-men's parties of the 1830's. Their frustrating experiences suggested that American labor might do better for itself politically by operating within, rather than outside or against, the two-party system, and American labor is still acting on the suggestion.

The most interesting features of the *balance of abodes* in 1860 were, first, the *emergence of the city* as the vital center of economic, social, and cultural life and, second, the unexampled mobility of the American people that rendered the balance of one decade obsolescent in the next. All over the nation men and women were leaving the land, of which they had tired or which had tired of them, and flocking to the cities in search of work. Much of this flocking was done by Americans who headed west. We make too much of those who went over the Appalachians to clear trees in Ohio or grow wheat on the prairies, too little of those who went over to operate lathes in Cincinnati or sell cigars in Chicago.

No esoteric statistics do more to persuade the student of this period that he gazes upon a society moving rapidly toward modernity than these simple and fairly reliable pairings.[58]

Population living in or around urban areas:
  1790: 5 per cent
  1860: 30 per cent
Cities with more than 25,000 inhabitants:
  1790: 2
  1860: 35
Cities with more than 100,000:
  1790: 0
  1860: 10
Cities with more than 1 million:
  1790: 0
  1860: 1 (Fernando Wood's Fun City)
Work force employed in agriculture and related pursuits:

1790: 90 per cent
1860: 50 per cent
Population in territory beyond the boundaries of the original
thirteen states:
1790: 200,000, or 5 per cent
1860: 15.6 million, or almost 50 per cent

Urbanization and *mobility* are writ large in these statistics, to
which should be added two crucial facts: The cities were symbio-
tic rather than parasitic in their relations with the countryside;
the willingness of millions of Americans to pull up stakes and
move on was a powerful stimulus to the Quest for nationhood as
well as for modernity. Much of the American future, men were
beginning to realize, lay in the great cities, including those of the
West, and the future would be quite different from the past. It
cannot be merely coincidental that festering slums and organized
police forces appeared on the American scene at about the
same time.

We have already taken note of the creation during the Quest
of a *system of communication* that was far-ranging, reliable, inexpensive, and popular. At first glance, one finds it hard to apply
any of these adjectives to the *system of education* in 1860, for it
was limited in scope, erratic in operation, too expensive for most
families and communities, and organized to educate only a fraction of the people—and, for the most part, to educate poorly.

In this period of almost reckless economic and social advance,
higher education had, if anything, declined in quality and usefulness to an ambitious nation. While the nine colleges founded before the Revolution (Harvard, William and Mary, Yale, Princeton, Pennsylvania, Columbia, Brown, Rutgers, and Dartmouth)
had been joined by another 175, all together were educating
a smaller percentage of the population in 1860 than in 1800; and
even the best were offering a nit-picking, unimaginative bill of
fare in a mind-shriveling way. Andrew D. White, '53, said of his
days at Yale that instruction "was at the lowest point, so far as I
know, that it has touched in any modern nation"; Louis Agassiz,
professor at Harvard in these same days, described his institution
soberly as a "respectable high school where they taught the dregs
of learning"; Columbia's own board of trustees proclaimed pub-

licly that the college was a "Spectacle mortifying to its friends" and "humiliating to the City." [59] Higher education in 1860 was suffering under many burdens: exaggerated elitism, fossilization of curriculum, lack of creativity, the hostility of zealous populists, sectarian control, and, just as seriously as the railroads and canals, overbuilding. The number 175 is one to warm the heart of the American patriot—until he learns that more than 500 other colleges were founded and then withered away in these years.[60] Primary education had a somewhat better record of achievement; yet even in the most modern parts of the North too many communities were unwilling or unable to support the free schools that state legislatures had ordained airily to rise and flourish. Secondary education was a largely private affair, and most of the famed "academies" were as inaccessible to the children of ordinary parents as were the colleges.[61]

As is so often the case, however, the first glance is misleading. If we look longer, deeper, and with more understanding into the condition of education in the middle of the nineteenth century, we may discover that America had begun to heed the warning of Thomas Jefferson not to expect to be both "ignorant and free, in a state of civilization," [62] and as a result was the beneficiary of many hopeful features of educational modernity: An unprecedented system of free public schools had been well and truly laid in all northern and also some southern states; faith in education had become a settled article of the American creed that needed the good offices of only a few more Horace Manns, Emma Willards, Calvin Stowes, Henry Barnards, Andrew D. Whites, and Justin Morrills to be transformed from idea to reality;[63] the first steps toward a broader, present-minded curriculum had been taken at colleges like Union, the University of Michigan, and Yale (in, of all subjects, agriculture);[64] and institutions for adult education were sprouting all over the land under both private and public auspices. Perhaps most important (and a sobering caution to all of us not to become hypnotized by statistics) was the vast apparatus of informal education that served the American people in those simpler days. Millions of children learned to read and write at home; tens of thousands of lawyers read law in the offices of their seniors; thousands of engineers, including the unlikely geniuses who built the Erie Canal, Benjamin Wright and James

Geddes, learned their skills on the job through the wasteful but compelling experience of trial and error. It is important to note that the ablest practitioners in many professions throughout this period were also the ablest teachers. Thanks to all these formal and informal instruments of education, and also to the widespread cult of self-improvement,[65] the mass of Americans in 1860 was probably as well-educated and certainly as literate as any people in the world. While the backward South dragged the national average down,[66] something like 80 to 90 per cent of the white adult population could be classified as literate.[67] In Massachusetts, the one state that had made a reality of general, free, compulsory education before the Civil War, the figure is said to have approached 100 per cent. I write "said to" because this is one of those fields in which definitions are debatable and evidence thin. A huge amount of research, both painstaking and imaginative, must be undertaken before we can be as certain as we ought to be.

By almost any standard *religion* seems to have been a more vital force in American life in 1860 than in 1790. Despite a careful and, I trust, fair-minded contemplation of the many and confusing aspects of this force, it is impossible for me to judge whether, on balance, religion helped or hindered the American search for modernity. Here are four of several dozen examples of paradox one finds in the record:

The religious impulse led to the founding of most new colleges in this period; too many of them were kept under narrow, dreary sectarian control.

Piety drove millions of plain persons to learn to read and write; "religious intransigence," one scholar has argued persuasively, was the "gravest obstacle to the development of an effective common school system throughout the United States." [68]

The church stood second only to the family as a strong, sheltering, consent-based element in an underdeveloped social infrastructure; millions of churchgoers were caught in the reason-despising grip of fundamentalism.[69]

The Christian religion ignited the antislavery movement; ministers of the same religion furnished slaveholders with comforting arguments for the rightness of their cause.

Perhaps the most sensible course of action would be to toss out a major hypothesis that sooner or later will have to be tested rigorously: Early republican America is a puzzling exception to the rule that nations become more secular as they become more modern. We may then close this discussion with a generalization that has been tested rigorously and judged substantial: Whatever the influence of American religion upon the search for modernity, it contributed richly to the search for nationhood.[70] The more angrily the multiplying American denominations quarreled among themselves over fine points of doctrine, the more assiduously they joined in asserting the heaven-declared, mission-fulfilling nationhood of the American people. Throughout the dizzying years of the Quest the new nation found much of its identity in the practices and preachings of the churches that spilled over the land. When the polite debate over American identity turned at last into a passionate crisis, men of religion in both the South and the North were still serving as outriders of the nationalist drive. The drive, alas, was now headed in two opposite directions.

American *science*, both theoretical and applied, lagged far to the rear of science in Britain and Europe. Upon those supposedly decaying societies it remained critically dependent for ideas, techniques, education, and personnel. Still, in such men as Benjamin Silliman, Joseph Henry, Crawford Long, William T. G. Morton, Jacob Bigelow, William Beaumont, Asa Gray, Nathaniel Bowditch, Matthew Fontaine Maury, James Dwight Dana, the imported Louis Agassiz, and the inventors mentioned above (not to forget that departed genius Benjamin Franklin), the nation had a clutch of scientists who were making modest payments on the American debt to the Old World,[71] and who were also making the New World newer all the time. Silliman and Maury stand out as men of particular merit, the former for his pioneering work at Yale in scientific education and publication, the latter for having created a new branch of science, oceanography.

Mobile, loose-jointed, bourgeois, achievement-oriented, individualistic, family-centered, unsophisticated, confident, boisterous, democratic—these are the adjectives I would use in conclusion to describe American society in the middle of the nineteenth century. If it appeared crude to many visitors and appears understructured to us, it was unusually functional in terms of the political culture, economic necessities, and national purposes of the age. Several scholars, notably Stanley Elkins and Rowland Berthoff, have found so many signs of disorder in this period that they have written forcefully of a shattering "institutional breakdown." [72] Much as their researches command respect, I cannot agree with so dismal a view. They have exaggerated the orderliness of eighteenth-century America, underestimated both the tenacity of the family and importance of voluntary associations in the nineteenth century, made a false equation of proliferation with anarchy (as Elkins does in the case of the churches), and somehow assumed that man on the move is man completely naked and exposed. While it is true that America was an unusually mobile society, it is also true that a high degree of mobility—spatial, occupational, and social—was a vital support of the Quest for continental nationhood and industrial modernity. We should, moreover, recall that this nation of free-swinging individuals had a large potential for associative effort whenever the situation shouted loudly for such effort. The building of the Erie Canal and the trek to Oregon are only two of hundreds of examples one could cite in praise of the talent for voluntary organization so characteristic of American society. We should also recall that migration within the country, like immigration from Europe, was often undertaken by groups of families or by entire villages.

In the long view of history, we are looking at a society in abnormally rapid transition from a structured past, which had been left behind in Europe, to a restructured future, at which we had not fully arrived in 1860, nor have arrived today. Yet in the most unsettled years of this transition America was not all scramble, not all flux, disorder, and formlessness. The new nation had its own definitions of social integration, and we must use them as well as our own in passing judgment on its performance as a community of free men reaching out for modernity.

No honest American living in 1860 would have proclaimed soberly that the Republic had arrived at a state of *cultural maturity,* and that the Old World was henceforth bound to take America seriously, the way it took itself, as a major fountain of arts and letters. Yet if American culture was immature, it was by no means sterile. If the fountain was no gusher, it had begun to flow; and some of its waters were clear, tasteful, and exhilarating. To tell the truth, if the cultured men of the Old World, especially the surprisingly thin-skinned British, had not repeatedly been put off by American boasts that the newest of countries would soon overtake Europe in this area of civilized endeavor as in all others, they might have done less carping and listened more respectfully to what a hitherto unheard national muse had to say.

Let us review briefly the record of American cultural achievement as it might have been read by a fair-minded foreign observer in the years just before the Civil War. Although a few words will be devoted to architecture, music, the theater, and painting, I think it both proper and imperative to concentrate attention on the field of literature—first, because we did so in chapter 3 out of respect for the primacy of literature as a vehicle of national self-identity; second, because creative Americans of the time put their most dedicated and expectant efforts into this field; and third, because the efforts had begun to have laudable results, indeed had nurtured a profusion of blooms in which any nation then existing might have taken pride.

Thoughtful Americans had special cause to take pride in these results, for the obstacles to distinguished literature (or, for that matter, to distinguished art, architecture, drama, and music) had been forbidding. It is a sobering truth of our history, not just a comforting myth, that fierce concentration on economic development shoved cultural development far to the rear of the American procession toward the anticipated glories of the future. If to the low priority assigned by this apparently obdurate circumstance are added the unpropitious effects of the commercial spirit of the age, the suspicions of elevated taste endemic to egalitarian democracy, the contrasting "predilections and prejudices for everything foreign" that unnerved a citizen of Ithaca, New York,[73] the absence of a settled aristocracy that could provide patronage and bolster morale, and the dearth of home-grown themes of which Hawthorne and Cooper complained almost as loudly as Henry James, we may entertain surprise that so many treasures of national literature date from this fledgling period. If we go on to note such restraints as the forced dependence on the Old World for models and training, the tie of language with an ancient and richly endowed country, and the mulish failure of Congress to enact an international copyright law that would have protected foreign authors against pirating and thus American authors against underselling,* surprise becomes wonder. And if, finally, we add the colossal fact of distance, which in the early years of a far-flung, wilderness-assaulting people always plays havoc with the refinements of civilization, wonder gives way to disbelief. The harsh influence of distance finds convincing proof in the fact that almost every one of the literary treasures of the Quest was produced by a man who lived in the old and settled northeastern states.

Of the marks of a mature and vital national literature set forth in chapter 3, all were on display in bright colors in 1860:

If not yet ostentatiously *grand,* American literature was demurely *rich;* and it was growing richer with each passing year thanks to the cumulative efforts of such men as Herman Melville, Nathaniel Hawthorne, Walt Whitman, Ralph Waldo Emerson, Henry D. Thoreau, Henry Wadsworth Longfellow (who also agreed with Henry James, but did it privately, that America was a "deadly country for a poet to live in" [75]), James Russell Lowell, William Cullen Bryant, William Gilmore Simms, John Lothrop Motley, Francis Parkman, George Bancroft, Oliver Wendell Holmes, the departed James Fenimore Cooper and Edgar Allan Poe (both of whom had won acclaim in Europe), and the only recently departed Washington Irving and William H. Prescott. Some of these writers were giants, all were men of talent and perception who had made a mockery of Sydney Smith's sneer of 1820 in the *Edinburgh Review:* "In the four quarters of the globe, who reads an American book?" [76] The fact that masterpieces like *Moby Dick, The Scarlet Letter, Leaves of Grass,* and *Walden* were not bought and read by more than a handful of tasteful persons in the American quarter of the globe says much about the habits of the reading public but nothing, by which I mean nothing to raise any doubts, about the native-born genius of the men who had written them. To tell the truth, those habits have not changed much in the course of a century. *Peyton Place, The Carpetbaggers,* and *Valley of the Dolls* had their titillating, wildly

* An Englishman put the heart of this matter candidly to Ralph Waldo Emerson: "As long as you do not grant us copyright we shall have the teaching of you." [74]

successful forerunners in "Maria Monk's" *Awful Disclosures,* Timothy S. Arthur's *Ten Nights in a Bar-Room,* and Ann Sophia Stephens's pioneering dime novel *Malaeska.*

To achieve genuine merit, of course, American literature had to become *distinctive,* and in this instance its leading figures were not notably successful.[77] Despite the pleas of several generations of cultural patriots, little that could have been written in no other place or time stems from the America of the Quest. A distinctive American literature would have probed deeply into the triumphs and tragedies of distinctive Americans: pioneers and speculators, entrepreneurs and immigrants, Indians and Indian fighters, vapor-prone ladies and stolid bumpkins, river dredgers and riverboat gamblers, slaves dreaming of liberty and slaveowners hoping for profits. Yet most probings of the truly new in the new way of life had been much too cautious and confined to the surface. Each reader, to be sure, will have an exception or two to haul out in order to explode this generalization:* Melville? Hawthorne? Whitman? Bancroft? Cooper? Exceptions, however, are questionable evidence, even if they bear a remembered name like Noah Webster, apostle of an unmistakably American language, or a forgotten one like Alexander Bryan Johnson, trail blazer in the study of semantics.

American literature was nothing if not *self-conscious.* A man had to be an eccentric author in that simpler age not to gain nourishment from awareness that the United States was a country of special worth. So purposefully did men of letters like Irving, James K. Paulding, and Cooper bend to the task of explaining exactly what was special about it that one scholar describes the literary history of nineteenth-century America as a "major and intensive quest for nationality." [78] The Quest led many such men, as it led preachers and politicians, to define the meaning of their nation in terms of a historic destiny. The gentle Emerson, the elegant Lowell (when he chose to be), and the unbuttoned Whitman (as he chose to be) were three of dozens of distinguished authors who sang the grand theme of the American mission in their best writings.

While it was harder for American literature to be *original* than

---

* This reader, wherever he may be, is reminded that Samuel Langhorne Clemens was still a steamboater in 1860.

to be distinctive or self-conscious, in this instance, too, we find men, most notably Poe and Whitman, who went boldly astray from the paths of convention to create forms and styles that had no precedents. Even Emerson, who knew where England and Germany were to be found and how much a man could learn in those delightful countries, had a streak of independence that carried him far beyond tasteful imitation.

One would like to say flatly that the literature of the young Republic was *popular*, yet most of the remembered authors of the Quest were writing for our times rather than for theirs. The devotion of the intelligent reading public to Richardson, Dickens, and, in a class by himself, Sir Walter Scott (all widely available in pirated editions) stands in painful contrast to the indifference of this same public to Whitman, Thoreau, and Melville. We cannot, moreover, ignore the craving of the Peyton Placers of those days for imported trash and for third-rate American novels, of which sentimental ladies had become both the most talented producers and the most grasping consumers in the 1850's. Cooper, Emerson, Irving, and several leading poets and historians enjoyed audiences worthy of their talents. So also did Harriet Beecher Stowe, but her most celebrated work, which exploded upon America in 1852 and Europe immediately thereafter, was a political rather than literary sensation. Most American authors had to content themselves with the hope of better things in a future they would not live to see. "Our native democrat," Thoreau predicted charitably, "whose brains, boots, and bones are spent in composing a free republic and earning money, is growing up to the fine arts, even if at present utility sways the balance." [79]

Although the Old World seemed ready enough to read tales of Iroquois braves by Cooper, Spanish seamen by Irving, or Aztec priests by Prescott, it paid even less attention to the writings of Melville and Whitman than did the countrymen of these giants, which is another way of saying that it paid almost no attention at all. Americans, nevertheless, had created a literature both *deserving and capable of transmission* across the boundaries of language and culture; and the day would come when these men of vision and others, including that unassuming tutor of Gandhi, Henry D. Thoreau, would win worldwide respect for the ability to write about the common burdens and glories of mankind in a characteristically American idiom.

Finally, American literature was intensely *self-renewing.* Like the founding generation of our national politics, the founding generation of our national literature respected the past yet refused to be trapped in it. Aware, indeed, that the past of their country was a tiny part of a huge inheritance, American poets agreed with the New York satirist William Cox that "hope must, in some degree," be to them "what memory is to those of other lands." [80] The hope of an exalted future in which they would be honored richly if posthumously by a tasteful citizenry helped to keep many authors at work through years of neglect; and thus little by little, at a quickening pace, the storehouse began to fill for the delight and instruction of modern America.

About other fields of culture I can be brief. In architecture Americans faced all the problems of the politically independent, intellectually dependent, achievement-oriented, survival-intent new nation in an exaggerated form; yet they managed to score modest successes that promised an exciting future. One may still look upon several of these successes with his own eyes: Joseph-François Mangin's and John McComb's City Hall in New York, Benjamin H. Latrobe's and William Strickland's Bank of the United States in Philadelphia, Charles Bulfinch's State House in Boston, the first and purest examples of the Gothic Revival, and a scatter of admirable homes, public buildings, and monuments that have stood up gallantly to the assaults of the bulldozer. One may also look, although the view is obscured, upon the first cast-iron office buildings in lower Manhattan, drab yet prophetic monuments to the future rather than the past. One wishes he could look upon, but must be content with imagining, the delicate triumphs of landscape architecture achieved by Solomon P. Grindle, who in other times and under more lavish patronage might have been a match for Capability Brown. In music and the theater native-born creativity was simply overpowered by the stored-up might of the Old World, yet in these fields, too—for example, in the plays of John Howard Payne, Nathaniel P. Willis, and George H. Boker as well as in the acting careers of Edwin Forrest, Charlotte Cushman, and Edwin Booth—there were signs of an awakening.

The course of painting throughout this period was symbolic of the ambivalent position of the artist in a raw yet ambitious country. In the early years, when society was more visibly structured, the emphasis was on portraiture: Ralph Earl, Gilbert Stuart, the Peales, and Samuel F. B. Morse carried on in the great tradition of the departed John Singleton Copley. As the old order dissolved and the new nation loomed larger, such men as John Vanderlyn, William Dunlap, Thomas P. Rossiter, and Washington Allston turned their attention to history, whether classical, Biblical, or unabashedly American. Toward the middle of the century the pace of change became so quick that Thomas Doughty, Thomas Cole, John Frederick Kensett, Asher B. Durand, Jasper Cropsey, George Inness, and other painters of unquestioned talent gave up the personal or historical for the natural and focused their romantic compulsions on the landscape as they saw it or wished it to look.[81] While the leading spirits of the Hudson River School are hardly in a class with, let us say, Copley or Winslow Homer, their best canvases remain surprisingly tasteful and refreshing treats for the eye. If to this small galaxy of artists we add the special geniuses of William Sidney Mount, George Catlin, George Caleb Bingham, and John James Audubon, we may judge that painting stood second only to literature in its contributions to the cultural life of the new nation.

By way of conclusion, two things might be said about this cultural life in order to put it in proper perspective, and thus to see it as a panorama of modest achievement and great expectations rather than a shambles of vulgarity, waste, indifference, and mediocrity.

In the first place, let us again make a special effort, for which I have called perhaps too often, to remove ourselves from these times to those of more than a century ago. If we do this constructively, we may discover, for one example, that a huge amount of intellectual energy was poured into a form of intellectual and artistic activity for which America has lost, accountably but sadly, most of its talent and respect. No one has a right to sit in judgment on the culture of the Quest unless he throws the considerable weight of oratory onto the scales. In the minds of Americans of the first half of the nineteenth century, from schoolboys squeaking in front of classmates all the way to Daniel Webster thundering upstairs in the Senate or downstairs in the Supreme Court, oratory was a vital, expressive part of a democratic culture.[82] Part ritual, part theater, part instrument of education, part poetry, the best of American speech was also the source of some of the best of American writing, as Emerson and Lincoln, each in his own way, prove to every generation of their literate descendants.

Second, in culture as in the economy these were years in which the foundation of a more creative future was firmly laid. As I taught myself what little I know about the history of American painting between the Revolution and the Civil War, the one image that impressed itself most vividly upon my consciousness was not Copley fleeing or Morse abdicating or Cole romanticizing or Mount jesting, but all five luminaries of the golden age of American art—Winslow Homer, Thomas Eakins, Albert Ryder, Mary Cassatt, and Major Whistler's son James—poised on or already over the edge of glory in 1860. Here stands an array of talent and imagination that is proof of young America's capacity to offer something to the world other than cotton, wheat, gold, oil, reapers, machine tools, and interchangeable parts—not that these were unimportant products to offer a world which hungers and thirsts more than a century later for a human and thereafter humane way of life. The Republic of 1860 invited wise men everywhere to consider the possibility that a nation could produce soul-stirring paintings and wonder-working tools at one and the same time. This in itself was a notable achievement.

Far back at the beginning of chapter 5 I promised to take the political, economic, social, and cultural measurements of the United States in 1860, and I have tried to keep that promise. Let me now top off all this measuring with one final rendering of the accounts, and do so by taking care not to be overly repetitious, recognizing that all measurements are gross, and begging readers to understand that the human condition, like the human being, is always imperfect. No absolute standards of success exist; the record of achievement of every notable society, and of every notable man in it, is blotched with failures and sorrows. Thus fairly if not viciously or vacuously judged, the record of the United States of the Quest in achieving the goals of nationhood and modernity reads roughly as follows:

Independence: a major plus, especially since the economic and cultural aspects of this primary feature of nationhood had begun to catch up with the political, which was never in doubt.

Territorial integrity: a major plus in America's posture toward other nations, a dubious mixture of pluses and minuses in the attempt to establish a pattern of confident equilibrium within its own far-ranging borders.

Popular cohesion: a major and, under the unprecedented circumstances of the American gamble, remarkable plus. The plus was scarred, however, by one large and two lesser (although hardly less distressing) minuses: the anachronistic, unimaginative, indifferent, too often cruel treatment of the unacceptable Americans, the Negroes, both enslaved and free; the cavalier and also too often cruel treatment of the slightly more acceptable and a good deal more American Indians; and the tide of ethnic suspicion that began to rise hard upon the invasion of Europeans whose customs, standards, religions, values, and languages seemed to threaten the hard-earned cohesiveness of white, Protestant, English-speaking, bourgeois America.

Self-identity: a major plus from ocean to ocean, which began to crumble, however, as one moved southward toward the Gulf.

Political efficacy: many small minuses, a few small pluses, a visible major plus out of the past (the Constitution of Madison, Hamilton, and Marshall), an invisible major plus waiting to burst forth in the future (the untapped capability of the national government). The invisibility of this plus led critics like the Russian historian Mikhail Pogodin to lament that America was "no state, but rather a trading company, like the East India Company which independently owns territory," and which, as a consequence, would "hardly ever bring forth anything great of national, let alone universal, significance." [83] Some men, it seems, are obsessed with symbols of political splendor the way others are with signs of economic activity.

Economic viability: a major, major plus observable in the hustling and bustling of 30 million people on the verge of overtaking the most advanced nations of Europe in capacity for growth, diversification, productivity, flow, solvency, organization, the application of intelligence, the use of machinery, and the accumulation of both national and personal wealth.

Social integration: another major plus in light of the circumstances, although for the first time the pace of industrialization was introducing the very rich and swelling the ranks of the very poor.

Cultural maturity: still a minus when contrasted with France or Germany or Britain despite the display of a scatter of hopeful pluses.

All in all, this is a record of impressive achievement. The difference between the United States of the last days before the Civil War and the United States of the first days after the Revolution was one of kind as well as of degree. While slavery hung on obstinately, the poor were still with us, violence remained an endemic aspect of the social scene, culture was struggling to get off the ground, colleges taught by rote, and thousands of solid citizens perched on hills from time to time to wait exultantly or masochistically for the end of the world, America moved onward and upward toward the goals that are the common dream of twentieth-century men. Above all it moved toward the status of modern nationhood, and did so at a pace that transformed "speculation" repeatedly into "fact." [84] If the political scaffolding of the Republic was in a state of disrepair (and the cultural scaffolding stunted by a lack of funding and caring), the total edifice was a nation that could never go home again to Arcady, never return, except in the fancy of a few dissenters, to a simple, static, traditional way of life. In 1860 the United States was a modern nation; they "didn't come more modern" and were nowhere more pridefully national than the United States.

Negroes, Indians, and some Mexicans—and, of course, many white Americans whose lives had been ruined—could have argued that this status of modern nationhood had been bought at the price of their freedom and well-being. The men of the Quest would have countered, although few were ever moved to do so, that the fate of almost all these exploited or discarded Americans had been sealed long before the Revolution. The dynamics of America, like those of any country launched upon a swift course into the future, were certain to visit distress upon some people.

For the vast majority, however, the dynamics were both stimulating and rewarding. The final judgment would be rendered, in any case, on the basis of the lot of the descendants of the distressed. That judgment, it appears, is yet to be rendered.

The four years after 1860 were to prove a cruel test for the men who had brought about this achievement, and they were to amaze the world by the manner in which they showed themselves equal to it. Their nationhood, however uncertain on the surface, was so tenacious at the core as to survive the most severe challenge a political community can face. Their modernity, however primitive in our eyes (especially in meeting the no-nonsense tests of chapter 3 dealing with public health and private medicine), laid a foundation for further material and intellectual progress that no shock of events would be able to demolish. If the Republic could once resolve the ambiguous legacy of 1787 and at least manage the problem of popular cohesion, what limits could be placed upon its relentless drive toward first place among the powers of the earth?

One of the interesting and still-unexplained features of the opening stage of this drive, the Quest of 1790–1860, is the way in which it accelerated in the 1850's. Wherever one looks in that useful compendium *The Historical Statistics of the United States,* conclusive evidence looms up to prove that a developing nation shifted suddenly, as it were, into high gear, then rushed ahead at a dazzling speed. The speed is all the more dazzling to the eye of the twentieth-century observer because of the contrasting effect of the enfeebling consequences of the North-South confrontation for both the sense of American unity and the capacities of the American political system. The statistics of population, immigration, industrial production, farm income, urbanization, newspaper circulation, and dozens of other phenomena of American development speak eloquently of this sharp rush ahead.[85] In 1850, for example, we traveled on 9,000 miles of railroad, chattered over 12,000 miles of telegraph, exported 166 million dollars' worth of goods and services, issued 2,193 patents, read 254 daily newspapers, and bore the costs of 18,417 post offices; in 1860 the figures were, respectively, 30,000, 50,000, 438 million, 7,653,387, and 28,498.[86] The audacious manner in which the nation came off the floor after the depression of 1857–1858 is more eloquent proof than any collection of statistics that the Americans were a people impossible to hold back. In their pursuit of most of the goals of modern nationhood they were leaving the British provinces to the north and the independent countries of Latin America ever farther behind and, at the same time, closing the gap, which had once upon a time loomed so large, between the advanced countries of Europe and themselves ever more rapidly. In many areas, indeed, the Americans of the Quest had overtaken Britain, France, and the rest, and now stood—or, as they would have preferred to say, *ran*—first among all the nations, empires, confederacies, and colonies of the world.

As the young nation grew, it intruded both its substance and its image upon this world. There had been a time when America attracted a disproportionate amount of attention, especially in Europe, but that was a little America full of small farmers (led by one big farmer and one medium-sized Jack-of-all-trades) who stumbled about firing shots heard around the world. This new America was big: a match for Russia in unified and settled area, more than a match for Britain (and fast overtaking France and all the bits and pieces of Germany) in population.[87] Its celebrated envoys were treated as representative men of a power that was up and doing rather than eccentric products of a settlement that, except for them, would never amount to much. Something more than merely symbolic was the triumphant sail of the yacht *America* against an armada of reluctant contenders around the Isle of Wight in 1851 (a "transcendent" victory, *The Times* of London acknowledged);[88] something more than merely symbolic were the unexpected displays of Yankee ingenuity (with, characteristically American, feeble and reluctant support from the government) at the Crystal Palace in London in the same year and at Paris in 1854,[89] as well as the startling rise of that ill-starred genius Paul Morphy, of New Orleans, to the unofficial yet uncontested championship of the world of chess.

Nor did Americans need to make pilgrimages to Europe to get their due: Hardheaded Europeans were flocking in droves to America, not to patronize or mock, but to learn from a race of upstarts who had performed "miracles" (of which they were inordinately proud),[90] and who therefore had something to teach their former teachers. The visit of a British commission to the

United States in 1853, which resulted in an admiring but still-not-quite-believing report on the American economy to the British Parliament,[91] was only the most prestigious of hundreds of similar visits to a nation that had become, in critical areas of the economy like the machine-tool industry,[92] a model of mechanization and standardization. It had also become, in fewer but perhaps more critical areas of politics like the suffrage, a model of democratization. So far and fast in all these areas had America driven that it had begun to serve other nations as Britain had always served it: *a forcer of the pace of history*.[93] The United States had made so many lunges into the industrial and democratic future that neither it nor any other country with the potential to follow on could now turn back. The Americans, in short, had become an influential nation almost without realizing what they had been doing; and, taken all in all, their influence was benevolent in character. In any case, the plain truth is that in realizing what they had been one cannot write of the shattering or aborted revolutions of Europe, or indeed of the wars of independence fought all through Latin America, without paying homage to the example of the American Revolution; one cannot explain the British North America Act of 1867, in which Canada at last achieved confederation and a large measure of self-government, without rehearsing Canadian and British fears of the huge, reunited, developed, and ambitious Republic to the south; one cannot discuss the rise of political parties or broadening of the suffrage without assessing the performance of the America of the Quest. Long ago, in 1783, at the end of the hard bargaining in Paris that sealed the fact of independence, the American commissioners had written to Congress: "Since we have assumed a place in the political system of the world, let us move like a primary and not like a secondary planet." [94] The men of the Quest had given obstinate substance to the airy hopes of Franklin and his colleagues: The United States had become a primary planet. The only major questions that remained to be answered in the heady days of the 1850's had to do with the capacity of this planet to survive as a continental nation and to wipe out the dark stain of human slavery.

I began chapter 1 on a sour note: the lament of Henry James over the sterility of the America in which Nathaniel Hawthorne grew to maturity. Let me close these two chapters with an observation made by that same Henry James in that same book on Hawthorne. Despite all its sins in offering neither an Eton nor a Harrow nor an Ascot to the world, America had known, James admitted straightforwardly, "immense uninterrupted material development." "When one thinks," he added in words borrowed a bit too casually from Hawthorne himself, "of the scale on which it took place, of the prosperity that walked in its train and waited on its course, of the hopes it fostered and the blessings it conferred," one was bound to speak of it as a time of "broad morning sunshine" in which "all went forward" in an "earthly empire." [95]

By reason of its success, this earthly empire had moved, ironically, from sunshine straight into the fog of disaster. About the elements of this disaster the chapters that follow will have much to say. These chapters, however, should end on the note of triumph sounded by Henry James; for who can deny that in the years of the Quest the United States was, in comparison with all other nations and empires that had ever existed, a country bathed in "broad morning sunshine"?

III

The American Method

1790–1860

7

Circumstances, Aspirations, Models

WHATEVER risks may attach to the enterprise, one who studies and then describes a famous example of national development must go beyond what to how, beyond generalized assessment of achievement in pursuing goals to detailed analysis of the manner in which they were pursued. This is the way I propose to discuss the over-all performance of the young Republic of the United States in the next two chapters.

How did the Americans of the first half of the nineteenth century make their historic bid for republican, continental, federal nationhood and distance-conquering, machine-centered, freedom-expanding modernity? What techniques of individual and associative effort, whether consciously selected or unconsciously adopted, did they use in pursuing their goals? What was the American Method to which all these techniques added up? Was it a special method, unlike that of any other country in those days and forbidden to any in these? Were other techniques and thus other methods available to men of their time, place, situation, and political culture? Would the use of some other method have produced a different kind of nation? If we are to understand what took place in the United States from 1790 through 1860, as well as what then took place in 1861–1865, we must answer these questions as thoughtfully as we can. We must answer them, moreover, in order to understand ourselves. Much of the quality of American life down to this day has been shaped by the choices, and also by the refusals to choose, of the men of the Quest. We are not helpless prisoners of the history they made, yet their hand lies upon us in ways great and small.

. . .

In chapter 4 I picked out four essentials of national development: opportunity, will, elite, and politics. Now we must look closely at the United States in the first decades of independence in an attempt to discover to what extent and in what form these essentials were present.

Few peoples in history have enjoyed a more favorable *opportunity* to become a modern nation than the sparse yet spacious and ambitious community that took three giant political steps toward a more perfect Union between 1787 and 1789: the shrewd labors of the rightly named Grand Convention at Philadelphia, the drawn-out but finally victorious struggle over ratification of the proposals of this convention, and the successful launching of the government anticipated in these proposals by Washington, Hamilton, Jay, John Adams, Madison, Jefferson, and their colleagues. So interesting and fateful were the circumstances of the American experiment that I feel it proper to devote one entire part of this book (chapters 9 and 10) to identifying and assessing them. At this point let me concentrate on two decisive truths about the ambience of the newly independent Republic.

The first is that the United States, despite its heralded independence and isolation, was an important member of the Atlantic community. The commitment of other parts of that community, above all Britain, to the virtues of nationhood and modernity forced the new Republic across the sea to proceed vigorously in the same direction or remain a peripheral colony to be patronized and exploited. Young America, it seems clear, was caught up willy-nilly in an ebullient tide of history that it would ride upon gloriously or sink into feebly. Many American goals were set by men and events beyond American control, indeed by men who had lived and events that had taken place long before the first settlers came to this continent.

The second truth is that, except for a half-dozen medium-sized difficulties and one staggering burden, the institution of slavery and all its consequences, the circumstances of the American experiment were about as rewarding as those of a developing nation can ever be. Drawing on the generalizations proposed in the first pages of chapter 4, I would describe these circumstances as positively favorable in terms of resources, skills, geography, and timing,

negatively tolerable in terms of the absence or at least manageability of tribal hatreds, feudal strongholds, religious and linguistic divisions, the threat of aggressive or subversive or exploitative neighbors, and the sheer weight of a surging population.
*Young America was the luckiest of the lucky countries of modern
history,* and few articulate Americans of the Quest were shy about
proclaiming the fact, whether gratefully in order to exhort their
fellow citizens or smugly in order to win their political support.
From Alexander Hamilton in 1781 ("Never did a nation unite
more circumstances in its favor than we do") to James K. Polk in
1848 ("We are the most favored people on the face of the earth")
and beyond to Abraham Lincoln in 1863 ("No human counsel
hath devised nor hath any hand worked out these great things"),
the theme of the good fortune of an entire nation rang loudly
and, for the most part, jubilantly in American ears.[1] These famous leaders, whenever they paused for breath, could hear themselves echoed by thousands upon thousands of lesser men, who
were apparently prepared in good times or bad to toast "the land
we live in—who would not wish to live in such a land!"[2] A
writer in the *New England Galaxy* styling himself Mendoza put
the point unblushingly in 1822:

I am a true patriot, one who loves my country so well, that I most
potently believe no country exists, ever did exist, or ever will exist,
equal to her in every thing that can render a nation great and glorious;
And I sincerely wish every body to the d——l, who is or ever shall be
of a different opinion.[3]

This theme of good fortune also rang convincingly, for few
peoples in history have displayed a more spirited *will* to take advantage of opportunity than did the first three generations of
independent Americans. The United States of the Quest was very
much an achieving society,[4] a creation yet also a nursery of millions of men intent upon bettering their lot as individuals and, in
the process, helping their nation rise to the heights of glory that
had been reserved for it since the first planting. I have dug long
and pleasurably in the documents of this early America—records
of debates in public assemblies, messages of Presidents and governors, reports of administrators and committees, pamphlets,
poems, commencement addresses, sermons, prospectuses, hand-

bills, political manifestoes, public and private letters, editorials, diaries—and I have been struck by the enthusiasm of its dedication to all the goals of nationhood and modernity. The founding generation, one may learn for himself in the records of the hardheaded Convention of 1787, the records of the equally hardheaded ratifying conventions,[5] and the comments of many ordinary men about an extraordinary moment in history,[6] anticipated confidently that the United States of America would grow into a mighty nation. The way would be hard, as those who opposed the Constitution took grim pleasure in pointing out,[7] yet the way, which "great nature with a bolder hand" had been building for almost two centuries,[8] lay wide open. The prizes might prove so opulent as to end up corrupting the winners; yet not to reach for them would be to break faith with American destiny. For the individual the prizes were unexampled liberty, well-being, safety, and justice; they were, in short, the oldest and fondest dreams of mankind. For the nation the prizes were the appurtenances of a new and pacesetting kind of civilization. The United States that patriots foresaw—and by foreseeing willed and by willing helped to create—would be all these things:

Big in space: No one in the founding generation, we learned in chapter 5, could be certain just where the restless Americans would finally halt their march west, south, and north, or could guess whether they would then form one sovereign nation or two or three or more. At the same time, no one doubted that the march would take place as scheduled, that Americans would push out the boundaries of their civilization forcefully and, in God's good time and theirs, fill in every habitable blank space on the map of a "great and valuable portion of the globe."[9] Most citizens of the new nation seem to have been obsessed with space, and they were confident that sooner or later, by peaceful migration rather than by militant aggression, they would occupy more of it than any people in history. "The proudest empire in Europe," Gouverneur Morris wrote to a friend in 1801, "is but a bauble, compared to what the United States *will* be, *must* be, in the course of two centuries; perhaps one!"[10]

Big in numbers: No one in the founding generation could be any more certain how many persons would dwell in all those filled-in spaces, yet again no one doubted that the new world was destined to outstrip the old. "The fact is," an anonymous Virginian wrote in 1791 while musing about the growth of the United States in population, "that this country is advancing to the sovereignty of the globe with a rapidity that baffles all calculations." [11] Some men, of course, refused to be baffled and talked of "millions," "tens of millions," or "millions upon millions"; and occasionally a man more precise in calculation yet no less exuberant in vision made this kind of guess:

> For 1930, 133,000,000, in round numbers
> For 1940, 177,000,000, in round numbers
> For 1970, 236,000,000, in round numbers
> For 2000, 283,000,000, probably 300,000,000.[12]

The date of the guess was 1815, when the population of the United States was roughly 8 million; the man who did the guessing was Elkanah Watson, of Pittsfield, Massachusetts, of whom we shall learn more in a moment.

Rich: So confident were most Americans that their "spirit of enterprise" would combine with "fortunate circumstances" to produce a "great national prosperity" that a few, including the most eloquent exponent of national prosperity, Alexander Hamilton, were moved to warn that wealth piled upon wealth might easily lead to "insolence, an inordinate ambition, a vicious luxury, licentiousness of morals, and all those vices which corrupt government, enslave the people and precipitate the ruin of a nation." [13] Most Americans, needless to say, were willing to take this chance—as was, after all, Hamilton himself—and to leave the worrying about the vices of the rich to their rich descendants. Those descendants, they were sure, would live in the first country in history in which no one starved or went cold or wallowed in misery—or had to content himself with the vices of the poor. As to the total economic power of the United States to come, what could be more useful and comforting than to quote Edmund Burke's words of 1775?

Young man, there is America—which at this day serves for little more than to amuse you with stories of savage men and uncouth manners; yet shall, before you taste of death, show itself equal to the whole of that commerce which now attracts the envy of the world.[14]

Free: The genius of America—a phrase much favored by the Framers of the Constitution—was republican freedom; an empire of liberty—the phrase, we have learned, was coined by John Adams—would arise and flourish upon the continent of North America. Indeed, the United States would not be the nation God had blessed and challenged were not "liberty, charming liberty" the birthright of every citizen. Americans were bound to choose freedom over all other human conditions, however seductive, because such was the command of the law of nature; they were also bound to choose it because it was the open door to personal well-being and national power. Liberty as an end in itself, liberty as the means to all other good ends in life: this was the way, both warmhearted and hardheaded, Americans looked upon the most precious legacy of their Revolution.

Morally improved: Even the crustiest or most skeptical men of the founding generation—John Adams, Alexander Hamilton, Ezra Stiles, and Timothy Dwight are four outstanding examples[15] —believed that Americans had been granted a unique opportunity to display the benevolent side of an eternally mixed human nature. Most were hardly less confident than was Thomas Jefferson himself that the general level of morals and manners, already far above that of decaying Britain, decayed Spain, debauched France, and incestuous Germany, would move steadily upward with the fortunes of the Republic until "virtue's bright image" would be "instamp'd on the mind" of a whole people.[16] While no American ever went quite as far as Marx and the idealist Marxists were to go in predicting the elimination of all traces of depravity from the character of men, there existed a widespread, deep-seated feeling, punctuated only occasionally by a salvo of dire prophecy from an embittered figure like Fisher Ames, that "the principles of humanity and general benevolence" would reign with ever increasing authority over both public affairs and private relations.[17] Montesquieu and the English moralists had taught America that virtue was the "principle" or "spring" of a republic;[18] the citizens of the model republic therefore had a special reason to cultivate it assiduously. They could cultivate it, moreover, with great expectations, since this form of government, David Ramsay announced, was clearly most "favorable to truth, sincerity, frugality, industry, and simplicity of manners." [19] It was also favorable to other great ends. In 1789 the editor of a newspaper in New Jersey pointed with seemly pride to two splendid accomplishments of the republican way of life: the ornate barge that took General Washington across New York harbor to his inauguration (proof, it appears, of the "great spirit of American MANUFACTURES") and a 536-pound hog butchered by Abraham Anthony (proof of the "great perfection" to which meat could be brought in the new nation).[20]

Culturally elevated: Conscious of the thinly productive, austere, often raw state of the arts in their infant Republic (including the art of living graciously), Americans who cared about such things agreed nevertheless with Franklin that a huge reservoir of talent lay ready to be tapped as soon as the nation could shift some part of its attention away from the "Necessaries" and toward the "Embellishments" of life.[21] When the geographer Jedidiah Morse saluted the "hopeful proofs of genius" in 1789,[22] he expressed no doubt that these proofs would multiply a thousandfold in the next century, and that the artists, writers, and scientists of a mature America would give back richer treasures to Europe than the young one had been compelled to accept. When Americans like John Adams echoed Bishop Berkeley's sentiment that the "course of empire" was set unswervingly westward, they assumed, as did Berkeley,[23] that cultural grandeur would be as visible a mark of this empire as political liberty or economic well-being. Far back in 1758 the second Nathaniel Ames told his large audience that the lands beyond the Appalachian barrier were destined to be "the Garden of the World" in which "Humane Literature" would grow as luxuriantly as corn and wheat.[24] And in 1771 two young orators at the commencement exercises of the College of New Jersey (Princeton) sang this theme along with several others to which we have been listening:

> *This is thy praise, America, thy pow'r*
> *Thou best of climes, by science visited,*
> *By freedom blest and richly stor'd with all*
> *The luxuries of life. Hail, happy land,*
> *The seat of empire, the abode of kings,*
> *The final stage where time shall introduce*
> *Renowned characters, and glorious works*
> *Of high invention and of wond'rous art.*[25]

Great: If the Republic of the future turned out to be all these things—big in space, big in numbers, rich, free, morally improved, culturally elevated—it must also be, John Adams believed "beyond a doubt" in 1785, the "greatest power on earth, and that within the life of man." [26] An anonymous writer in a small newspaper in upstate New York was equally confident in 1819:

Give but the imagination play, and there is no limit to the grandeur we may anticipate for our country. Nay, if arithmetic be true, a very few brief years will find this the most powerful nation on the globe.

And then he added, in a vein reminiscent of Adams and all his colleagues in greatness:

We have only to wish that it may be as enlightened as it will be powerful.[27]

When Americans spoke of the nation to come as an "empire," even as the "queen of empires," [28] they used this now discredited word artlessly to mean a country of outsized dimensions and influence, and they felt that their destiny was to be such a country. The Republic would surely become, as we still like to put it, a *great power.* Since it would avoid entangling alliances and mind its own business, the evidence of power would be tens of millions of self-respecting men plying peaceful trades rather than tens of thousands of self-preening men strutting about in uniforms; yet no nation should make the mistake of underestimating the capacity of the tens of millions to ply another trade—Hamilton called it the "Trade-Militant" [29]—in the event of an attack on the United States. As the youthful Lincoln declaimed in 1838:

Shall we expect some transatlantic military giant, to step the Ocean, and crush us at a blow? Never! All the armies of Europe, Asia and Africa combined, with all the treasure of the earth (our own excepted) in their military chest, with a Buonoparte for commander, could not by force, take a drink from the Ohio . . . in a trial of a thousand years.[30]

To a reminder that a British army had taken a drink in the Potomac only twenty-four years earlier (after boiling the water carefully, one trusts) Lincoln would doubtless have replied that the lesson of the unnecessary humiliation of 1814 would never again be lost on the American people.

The United States, in any case, was destined to be a great power of a new kind. As such a power it would be universally respected, and both Britain and France, the disliked enemy and the mistrusted friend, would have to fall in behind as it led the procession of humanity onward to happier days. Secure in an ever more ascendant position among the nations of the earth, it would change the world not by force or bribery but by mere example. Joel Barlow, one of the most democratic and least doubting prophets of an exalted America, sang of his country in *The Columbiad:*

> *Let me behold her silver beams expand,*
> *To lead all nations, lighten every land,*
> *Instruct the total race, and teach at last,*
> *Their toils to lessen and their chains to cast.*[31]

It seems both astonishing and touching that levelheaded Americans could have entertained such dreams of glory in the first halting years of independence; yet, having worked painstakingly to get inside their minds and hearts, I am convinced that they meant exactly what they said: The dreams were the sort that are expected to come true. I say this with special conviction because so many of the celebrated men who dreamed rhetorically, and also the thousands who echoed them in newspapers, pamphlets, poems, sermons, and orations, acted in the present even as they declaimed about the future. The cutting edge of their faith in a great America was the will to work, dare, decide, innovate, move on, and move up. We know very little of the psychological forces that shape an achieving society. Sooner or later, if we are to know more, sophisticated scholars must probe deeply into the behavior of thousands of persons in the first decades of American independence. Then, perhaps, we may be in a solid position to apportion roughly fair amounts of credit to the forces that are said to have sent us on our way: the Protestant ethic, the frontier, European example and prodding, the profit motive, the drive for personal esteem and national glory, the accumulated energies of a postfeudal society with no feudal relics in its path.

What we do know is that the will to achieve existed in vigorous form well before the eruption of the Revolution, and that to Americans of the founding generation this will was as natural a sentiment as the need to love or be loved. We know, too, that it imparted a momentum to the experiment that ran throughout the period I am describing, and still shows few signs of running down. Hezekiah Niles, himself a convincing example of the power of self-improvement, was only one of thousands to testify to the "almost *universal ambition to get forward*" in early nineteenth-century America; Ralph Waldo Emerson, another breed of individualist, was one of thousands to salute the United States as "a country of beginnings, of projects, of designs, of expectations." [32] This ambition, multiplied millions of times over, must be recognized by us for what it was: *one of the most powerful national wills in history,* the more powerful because it welled up freely from the body of "a sanguine and enterprising people" rather than was imposed autocratically from the top down.[33] Having observed his fellow countrymen in action, young Salmon P. Chase could write confidently in 1832: "The law of man's nature, impressed on him by his God, is onward progress." [34] Such progress could never have taken place if Americans had not had the will for it, and the will itself seemed therefore to be the "law of man's nature," at least as it was to be honored in bountiful North America.

The principal vehicle of this will, and also the principal instrument of this progress, was an extraordinary *elite,* a galaxy of thousands upon thousands of uncommon men—one might well call them *the excellent Americans*—who were active in all areas of endeavor and on both the upper and middle levels of society. What was said in chapter 4 of Massachusetts in the Revolution could be said of almost all the states in the middle of the nineteenth century: The upstart nation was full of individuals of better-than-average imagination, skill, dependability, ambition, and resolution.[35] Let us concentrate our gaze for the moment on the men at the top, on those Americans who had been born or, more likely, had worked themselves upward into the ranks of the first elite.

While the attention of leading Americans had shifted markedly away from public service and toward private enterprise, this was a development to be expected among a people that had been taught to be suspicious of political power, that saluted its founding fathers for having solved most public issues in one ingenious stroke, and that, more than a century before Calvin Coolidge put out the official word, carried on as if the "business of America" was indeed "business." Yet even in the days of Millard Fillmore and Franklin Pierce—not the best days we have known—a political elite possessed of rare skills was a reserve in being if not yet a force mobilized for action. When the time finally came for politics to reassert its primacy for a few earth-shaking years, Lincoln and his Cabinet moved front and center to perform as effectively in saving the Union as did Washington and his collaborators in founding it.

In the intervening years, that is to say, in the half-century between the departure of Jefferson and the arrival of Lincoln, men committed to a politics of earth-smoothing compromise and an economics of earth-shaking innovation took the lead in pursuing the national purpose; and, for every Henry Clay to practice that kind of politics, two dozen Moses Browns and Samuel Slaters emerged to practice that kind of economics. One could fill up hundreds of pages with the names of inventors, builders, engineers, managers, and investors who rose above their contemporaries to contribute with ingenuity to the economic development of the nation; let us rest content with pondering the entries in the *Dictionary of American Biography,* not merely of Brown and Slater, but also, let us say, of Eli Whitney, Simeon North, Cyrus McCormick, Colonel John Stevens, Thomas Handasyd Perkins, Francis Cabot Lowell, John Jacob Astor, Nicholas Biddle, Samuel F. B. Morse, Ezra Cornell, Henry Noble Day, John Perkins Cushing, Benjamin Wright, James Geddes, Elias Hasket Derby, Stephen Girard, Major George Whistler, Dr. Daniel Drake, Henry Varnum Poor, Samuel Colt, William Kelly, Cornelius Vanderbilt, Erastus Corning, and Dr. Jacob Bigelow, the last of whom did more than any other man to impress the word "technology" upon the American consciousness.[36] In the accomplishments of these men we can find solid evidence of the existence of an exceptionally functional economic elite, and the elite, it bears repeating, was not a scatter but a swarm of achievers and improvers. We should also look at the entries of Daniel Boone, Colonel Return Jonathan Meigs, the Reverend Manasseh Cutler, General Stephen W. Kearny, Stephen Austin, General John C. Frémont, Joseph Smith, Brigham Young, and the Reverend Marcus Whitman, for thus we might remind ourselves that a few score uncommon men played a vital part in the settlement of the West by millions of common men. Infinitely more farsighted leadership and skilled organization went into that settlement than most Americans seem to realize. And, while we are about it, we should look at such entries as Wendell Phillips and Susan B. Anthony, for thus we might remind ourselves that not every member of the American elite was a getter-and-spender or even a man. Then, finally, let us ponder the lives of Benjamin Banneker, Paul Cuffe, Richard Allen, James Forten, Charles L. Reason, and Frederick Douglass, for thus we may learn, perhaps for the first time, that a few men who were not white had overcome the cruel handicaps of prejudice to hover manfully as portents of the future on the fringes of the American elite.[37]

In addition to being functional in terms of the social imperatives of this nation at this stage of its history, the elite displayed several other qualities of interest to students of national development. In the first place, it was, we have noted, about as legitimate as an elite in a self-conscious democracy can ever be, principally because most men at the top had earned rather than inherited their places, and also because their activities helped to create additional places for other upwardly mobile men to fill. Second, in an age in which instruments of formal education were few, narrow, and wary of innovation, many members of the elite were, like the mass of men, largely self-taught, which is another reason why their ascendancy was never seriously challenged. Third, as the nation moved toward a more productive economy and more complicated social order, many groups in the elite became more specialized in interest and professional in outlook. Even the democratic suspicion of the wiles of expert men dedicated to high standards of competence could not slow down a broad advance toward sophisticated self-confidence in such fields as law and engineering.[38] Finally, the elite of the 1850's, like that of the Revolution, was *an integral, not an exotic, part of the American community*. It arose out of the body of the people; it shared in the experiences, ideals, and life style of this people; it did not look abroad constantly for instruction or inspiration. Such men as George Bancroft and Edward Everett were only strengthened in their Americanism by sojourns at foreign universities.[39] The elite was, indeed, anything but cosmopolitan or alienated: It found itself, with a few celebrated exceptions, comfortably at home in a land it had done much to build. This assertion is especially true of the entrepreneurial elite. Unlike its counterparts in most countries of the Old World, this elite faced no entrenched aristocracy of the sword, the miter, the coronet, or, except in the South, the land that might contend with it for political power, deny it prestige, and despise it for the character of its endeavors.

I do not mean to paint a collective portrait of American leadership during the Quest in hues too rosy. In those days as in these the nation had its share of charlatans, cowards, obscurantists, and incompetents in high places, and not even the best men could find a solution both workable and moral to the most agonizing problem that faced their country or plan ahead both imaginatively and realistically for the disabilities of overdevelopment. We must give, nevertheless, a sizable amount of credit for the success of the American experiment to the men who hustled and bustled their way to the top. While we need to know more about them—about the origin, upbringing, education, ambitions, values, experiences, efforts, strokes of fortune, and patterns of behavior of thousands of influential men (and of several hundred influential women)—we know enough already to realize that we stand in the presence, imagined yet forceful, of one of the most influential, successful first-level and second-level elites in history. As the elite of a nation dedicated to the proposition that elites are morally wrong and operationally unnecessary, it put on a show that deserves more careful attention than it has hitherto won.

Opportunity, will, elite—these essentials of national development were present in admirable abundance in the first years of the Republic. About the fourth essential we cannot be so full of admiration, for *politics* played a strangely ambivalent role in the Quest.* On one hand, it scored a huge success at the outset. In the span of a single generation a series of consciously political

---

* Let it once again be noted that the word "politics" is used in the broad, Aristotelian sense.

decisions worked in concert with a series of welcome accidents to convert America from a dependent sprawl of "little Englands in the wilderness" into an independent Union of thirteen states in being and another thirteen or more just over the horizon, then opened up the road to continental, republican empire. On the other, the capability of the political system, which was never impressive, began to shrink alarmingly in the aftermath of the success. This shrinkage became ever more visible as the one terrible problem the founding generation had refused to govern positively (by failing to provide somehow for the containment and, in due course, elimination of slavery) became ever more obstinately ungovernable even as it impinged ever more fiercely upon the standard problems of a rapidly developing nation. The result was a lamentable if understandable shift from a politics of creativity to a politics of compromise and, when the spring of compromise began to run dry, beyond to a politics of anger and paralysis. This shift is exceptionally striking to the historian of national development because of the sharp contrast between what happened to the nation as a whole and to politics as one aspect of national life. *The nation boomed; the political system of the nation languished*—that is perhaps the most important generalization one can extract from the record of these seven decades of American development.

So much importance do I attach to this generalization that I propose to isolate it, then scrutinize it with the utmost care. This is the principal burden of chapter 8, in which we must examine the techniques of development that were used in the early decades, and also speculate briefly about the social and economic consequences of a languishing politics. In the interest of both rigorous examination and fruitful speculation, however, let us pause first for a few further thoughts of a preliminary character on the subject of American national development. In particular, I would suggest that a more accurate assessment of the influence of politics in this period may be made, and thus a sharper insight into what was characteristically American about the American Method be gained, if we recognize that the road traveled to power and glory, and also to disorder and tragedy, was not the only one traced out on the map of destiny by the fingers of wise men of the first and second generations. To be exact, three grand methods or systems or, as some would prefer, models of national development were offered, offhandedly yet forcefully, to the American people for their consideration in the span of those generations. The fact that the first was tested gingerly and then rejected, the second never really tested at all, and the third left with an open field in which to run tells much of what needs to be known about the role of politics in the American Quest.

The first model is properly identified with the daring programs of two famous men: Alexander Hamilton, Secretary of the Treasury under Washington, whose Report on Manufactures (December 5, 1791)[40] was a well-structured plan of economic development to be worked out under the direction of a vigorous national government; and John Quincy Adams, sixth President of the United States, whose First Annual Message to Congress (December 6, 1825)[41] was a restatement of the Hamiltonian theme with slightly less emphasis on economic progress and considerably more on intellectual, cultural, and moral improvement. Other leading Americans contributed richly to this model: President Washington himself, who needs no introduction yet ought to be recalled as a man keenly interested in spinning a tough web of factories, canals, turnpikes, and institutions of learning to bind the nation together and keep it from "sinking into chaos";[42] Robert Morris, the Financier of the Revolution, who taught both Hamilton and Washington much of what they knew about money and banking;[43] Tench Coxe, Assistant Secretary of the Treasury under Hamilton, who had an adroit hand in the preparation of the Report on Manufactures;[44] the early and late James Madison, that is to say, the hard-driving nationalist who led the way in 1787 and the resuscitated nationalist who "out-Hamiltoned Hamilton" in 1816;[45] Albert Gallatin, Secretary of the Treasury under both Jefferson and Madison, who took up the cudgels for a national plan of internal improvements in a memorable report to the Senate in 1808;[46] Henry Clay, eloquent partisan of the American System of protective tariffs, internal improvements, and national banking;[47] and intellectual advocates of economic nationalism like Mathew Carey, Daniel Raymond, Hezekiah Niles, Nathaniel A. Ware, Friedrich List (who came and went), and Francis Lieber (who came and stayed).[48]

The second model of national development is properly identified with the prudent hopes of Thomas Jefferson, who also needs no introduction. Throughout his career, in hundreds of public statements and private letters, Jefferson, like Hamilton and the younger Adams, expressed a lively dedication to progress and expansion. He differed, however, from both his enemy (always) and his friend (early and late) in advocating an empire for liberty that would grow up and out on an orderly basis and at a measured pace, would pursue its goals largely through nonpolitical and nonnational means, and would end up, he expected, as a loose group of socially similar and thus mutually tolerant republics. This model is not only properly but exclusively identified with the hopes of Jefferson. Surrounded as he was by leading men who were either more nationalist or less expansionist than he proved to be, Jefferson stood alone in recommending it (somewhat fuzzily and diffidently, to be sure) to the American people. So colossal a figure is this man in the history of the American political tradition, however, that one need feel no hesitation about asking him, as it were, to stand there alone.

The third model, a permissive system of expansion and development in which national politics would have neither a stimulating nor a restraining hand, is not so easy to identify with the words and deeds of any one man or group of men. Having sifted through the credentials of an array of candidates who contributed to it, ranging from Andrew Jackson to Amasa Walker by way of James K. Polk, William Leggett, Martin Van Buren, Amos Kendall, and a dozen entrepreneurs like John Jacob Astor and Colonel John Stevens, I have settled on two men. One is from the founding generation, the other an epigone; both require more elaborate introductions.

The man from the founding generation is Elkanah Watson (1758–1842), merchant, patriot, banker, entrepreneur, booster, reformer, promoter of canals and railroads and mills, scientific agriculturist, political polemicist, and all-round public gadfly. Watson's progress through a life of many rich successes and a few stumbling failures took him from modest origins in Plymouth to an apprenticeship in Providence with the famous merchant John Brown (1773–1779), to France and England to enjoy at first prosperity and to suffer thereafter distress as a merchant

Circumstances, Aspirations, Models

(1779–1784),* back to North Carolina for a repeat performance (1785–1788), then north to Albany to score a lasting success as banker and man of affairs (1789–1807). Retiring from active business, he moved to Pittsfield, then back to Albany (1816), then to Port Kent on the shores of Lake Champlain (1828) for many happy years of farming, promoting, debating, corresponding, lobbying, and traveling. Watson was a resourceful, articulate member of the new American elite. Whether visiting Washington at Mt. Vernon to exchange views on the importance of an extensive system of canals, battling DeWitt Clinton for the honor of paternity of the Erie Canal, prodding the New York legislature to pay attention to everything from turnpikes and railroads to free schools and colleges of agriculture, introducing fresh new strains of tired old animals, proposing factories designed to transform raw products into civilized articles of consumption, or staging the first county fairs in the nation, he was an appealing symbol of a young, self-confident, achieving America as well as a useful agent of its progress toward modernity. In several books (the most important published posthumously in 1856 under the delightful title *Men and Times of the Revolution; or, Memoirs of Elkanah Watson*), a mass of private letters, and a volley of public pronouncements, he voiced his expectations of a grand America with vigor and imagination.[49] In his own attempt to bid this America rise and flourish he had "done enough," he confessed as an old man, "to fill up the space of four lives." [50]

The epigone is Robert John Walker (1801–1869),[51] lawyer, politician, administrator, promoter, speculator, and financier. Born in Northumberland, Pennsylvania, and educated at the University of Pennsylvania, Walker moved from Pittsburgh to Natchez in 1826 and there embarked on a fantastic but by no means atypical career of speculation in plantations, slaves, and unsettled lands. After serving as Senator from Mississippi from 1836 to 1845, he gave four energetic years to President Polk as Secretary of the Treasury, then stayed on in Washington to practice law, advise Presidents, peddle securities, promote railroads, and continue his speculations. As the gulf began to widen between North and South, Walker's deep-seated pro-Union sympathies came to

* And to hear George III announce publicly that American independence was a fact of life.

203

the surface, especially during an unhappy few months when he was governor of the harried Kansas Territory.

During the Civil War this dedicated War Democrat went to Europe on behalf of Secretary of the Treasury Chase in order to push the sale of Union bonds and hurt the sale of Confederate bonds, and in both efforts he seems to have scored a huge success. Throughout his career he was an enthusiastic expansionist, the kind of American who invited Great Britain to join the Union, advocated the incorporation of the whole of Mexico, helped William H. Seward to lobby the Alaska Purchase through Congress, and, in his last, illness-plagued days, wrote an article outlining for citizens of Nova Scotia the benefits to be gained through annexation to the United States. His four reports as Secretary of the Treasury still make interesting reading,[52] especially the report of 1845, which has been rightly described as a "classic of free-trade literature." [53] Walker, like Watson, was both symbol and agent of an achieving society. The only difference between them was that Watson was bent on achievement and Walker hell-bent. What other American of his time could boast that he had gone down in a submarine (while Secretary of the Treasury) and up in a balloon (while on the mission for Chase)? The balloon ascent was typical of Walker's zestful, opportunistic approach to life: He wanted to find out what it was like to be a bird; he also wanted to scatter leaflets upon the citizens of London denouncing Jefferson Davis and the Confederacy. No sooner was he back on the ground from his "celestial journey" than he wrote to Chase imploring him to look carefully into the potential of the balloon as an "engine in war." [54]

One could easily construct other models of American national development out of the principles and hopes of men of the first two generations. I chose to concentrate on these three—the Hamilton-Adams, the Jefferson, and the Watson-Walker models—because all, despite important differences we are about to examine, had two fundamental qualities in common: They were uncompromisingly *continental in scope;* they were vigorously *capitalist in thrust.* These qualities, continentalism and capitalism, were clearly, along with republicanism and the sense of mission, the *immutable givens of the American experiment.* No counsel that advocated a little America policy, as did the disaffected Federalists, or proposed a socialist system, as did several hopeful immigrants (not to forget Orestes Brownson and Albert Brisbane),[55] was viable in terms of the common expectations outlined at the beginning of this chapter. Each of the three primary models encompassed a firm commitment to those expectations; the exponents of each model looked ahead to a far-flung, teeming, prosperous, free, virtuous, cultivated, and powerful America that would set a historic example for all the world. What Jefferson meant by prosperous or powerful was not the same as what Hamilton meant; what Adams understood by virtuous or cultivated was miles over the head of Walker. Yet all these men and their colleagues carried a soaring vision of material and moral greatness for America in their heads. All, even Hamilton, believed that we were a chosen people; all, even Jefferson, expected us to end up the most splendid empire (in the oldest and best sense of the word) since Rome, indeed *the first true empire of liberty in the history of mankind.*

Let us turn now from similarities to dissimilarities, from vague and thus easily agreed-upon expectations to more precise and therefore contentious recommendations, by hearing the answers that the advocates of each model of national development might have made to a series of questions about the future of their fellow countrymen, about what Americans were supposed to hope for and the ways in which their hopes could most effectively be realized.* In this manner, we may be able to trace at least a rough outline of the relevant dimensions of our three models. While the questions are framed deliberately in a style that would have made sense to men of the young Republic, they are also designed to provide a comprehensive understanding of the dedication of the respondents to the enduring goals of nationhood and modernity. Almost but not quite needless to add, one who poses such questions to men long dead runs serious risks: of giving too much order to clusters of ideas noteworthy for charming disorder; of playing down specific ideas of any one man that do not fit neatly

---

* In each instance I base these answers on the whole range of the man's policies and writings. It would be pedantic (and also space-consuming in the extreme) to print all the bits of evidence amassed to support each answer, and I therefore cite chapter and verse only for direct quotations and unusually disputable points.

into the general scheme attributed to him; of granting each man, except perhaps John Quincy Adams, credit for a higher degree of awareness as a model-builder for America than he in fact displayed; and of being much too present-minded, for example, in making use of a word like "model," which has new and special connotations. The risks, I think, are worth taking; readers, I know, are capable of discounting for them as the exposition proceeds. These, in any case, are the questions and answers:

1. *What should be the pattern of the American economy?*

HAMILTON-ADAMS: Balanced, with the balance tipping inexorably but not unrestrictedly away from agriculture and toward commerce and manufacturing.

JEFFERSON: Primarily and, if necessary, obstinately agrarian, with commerce the demure handmaiden of agriculture and manufacturing the barely tolerated servant of each.*

WATSON-WALKER: Balanced, with the balance to be set and reset by the natural forces of economic development. (Both men became less agrarian and more commercial-financial-industrial in orientation as the years passed and America moved toward economic viability.) [57]

2. *What should be the pattern of American society?*

HAMILTON-ADAMS: Largely middle-class, increasingly urban.

JEFFERSON: Largely middle-class, predominantly rural.

WATSON-WALKER: Largely middle-class, balanced and rebalanced between urban and rural by the same play of natural forces.

3. *Is there an American elite?*

HAMILTON-ADAMS: Yes.

JEFFERSON: Yes.

WATSON-WALKER: Yes.

---

* I am mindful, of course, of Jefferson's famous letter to Benjamin Austin of January 9, 1816, but the "manufacturer" he was at last ready to "place by the side of the agriculturist" for the sake of American "independence" was almost certainly one who operated on a small scale, for example, within the limits of his own house.[56]

4. *Who are its most useful members?*

HAMILTON-ADAMS: Statesmen, enterprising public men who are able to work fruitfully with "monied men" (Hamilton's emphasis) or learned men (Adams's).

JEFFERSON: Statesmen, gifted and learned men who join with the sturdiest tillers of the soil, all together forming a natural aristocracy that is the "most precious gift of nature for the instruction, the trust, and government of society." [58]

WATSON-WALKER: Entrepreneurs, risk-taking men who give other men an energetic lead in manufacturing, commerce, finance, agriculture, transportation, and, for that matter, politics.

5. *What is the chief duty of the elite in the process of development?*

HAMILTON-ADAMS: To mobilize the energies of the American people for growth, expansion, economic progress (Hamilton's emphasis), and both moral and intellectual improvement (Adams's).

JEFFERSON: To conciliate and restrain, to speak words of caution to headstrong innovators—except perhaps in moments of exceptional national crisis or opportunity.

WATSON-WALKER: To hustle, boost, grab, clear, plant, dig, extract, invent, spin, import, export, and speculate, whether in dreams or in dollars.

6. *What is the role of government in this process?*

HAMILTON-ADAMS: To foster development actively in almost every sphere of human endeavor.

JEFFERSON: To smile so long as development proceeds at a reasonable pace and toward fitting goals, to frown when it gets out of hand, to steer when it strays off course.

WATSON-WALKER: To set down a few simple ground rules, then stand aside to let development run its course according to the "fixed and certain laws of political economy." [59]

7. *What, then, is the essence of good government?*

HAMILTON-ADAMS: Energy.
JEFFERSON: Austerity.
WATSON-WALKER: Permissiveness.

8. *What is the role of the government of the United States in the process of development?*

HAMILTON-ADAMS: To take charge of the process; for instance, to charter banks and corporations, maintain a national system of banking, lay tariffs that protect vulnerable enterprises and encourage new ones, pay bounties and premiums for the same purposes, prohibit competitive imports, lure foreign capital, invite (and to some extent control) immigration, introduce innovations in technology, reward inventors, elevate standards of production, build (or at least help to build) a distance-conquering network of transportation according to a national plan, stimulate scientific agriculture, establish and nourish a world-renowned national university, maintain professional armed forces on land and sea, own and operate the "manufactories of all the necessary weapons of war" (Hamilton's emphasis),[60] subsidize the whole range of science and art (Adams's), and generally spur the rise of a sophisticated, diversified, productive economy.

JEFFERSON: To assist the process modestly by cutting personnel, costs, and pomp to the bone, more specifically to serve the best interests of the people by performing minimal tasks such as defending our shores and carrying the mails; by refusing firmly to encourage overbuilding, restless migration, speculation, and wildcatting;* by deferring as much as possible to state and local governments;[61] and, for all that, by being realistic when offered a fantastic bargain like the Louisiana Purchase.

WATSON-WALKER: To get out of the way, that is to say, neither to promote nor to restrain the entrepreneurial drive and to act forcefully only when the honor of the Republic is at stake.†

9. *What is the role of the state governments?*

HAMILTON-ADAMS: To be, as it were, miniature national governments, taking care to integrate their activities with the govern-

* Jefferson's negative view of this role prevented him, unfortunately, from going one step farther in order to outline the ways in which the national government might positively *discourage* such activities as overbuilding and wildcatting.

† Watson and Walker parted company in their attitudes toward a protective tariff, the former favoring it as one of the few useful contributions the national government could make.[62]

ment of the United States and neither to obstruct it nor to invade the broad area of its sovereignty.

JEFFERSON: In one direction, to keep a watchful eye on the national government; in the other, to support the cause of local self-government.

WATSON-WALKER: To be more active than the national government, principally by helping entrepreneurs to help themselves through sporadic use of the technique of political response.

10. *How important, then, is local government?*

HAMILTON-ADAMS: Not very important (as a New Englander, Adams would not have been quite so deprecatory or simply uninterested as Hamilton).

JEFFERSON: All-important, since the future happiness of the American people depends upon their willingness to group themselves into a galaxy of compact "ward republics" in which those who do the public business are visible, approachable, and immediately responsible.[63]

WATSON-WALKER: Not nearly as important as local push and pride.

11. *How is the Constitution of the United States to be interpreted?*

HAMILTON-ADAMS: Very broadly, as a grant of powers.

JEFFERSON: Very strictly, as a catalogue of limitations.*

WATSON-WALKER: More or less strictly, as a symbol of the Union.

12. *What should be the foreign policy of the United States?*

HAMILTON-ADAMS: Disengagement from the Old World, hegemony and expansion in the New (in the case of Hamilton *aggressive* expansion if it should become necessary), a brisk trade with all the world.[65]

JEFFERSON: Strenuous isolation from the Old World, non-

---

* The Jefferson of the restrictive opinion on the constitutionality (or, more properly, *unconstitutionality*) of Hamilton's Bank was, in an odd way, never more fully on display than in his twists and turns over the Constitution-stretching purchase of Louisiana.[64]

aggressive expansion in the New (through purchase and migration),* a modest trade with all the world.

WATSON-WALKER: Bluster toward the Old World, hegemony and both aggressive and nonaggressive expansion in the New, a booming trade with all the world (in each of these matters the emphasis is Walker's).

13. *When the American people reach the outer boundaries of their continental destiny, what political front will they present to the world, that is to say, what will be the identity of America?*

HAMILTON-ADAMS: A perfected, organic, indestructible Union —America as a *full-fledged nation.*

JEFFERSON: A harmonious brotherhood,[67] a loose-jointed and tolerant empire for liberty—America as a *confederation* (and thus legally a nation) if all the potential sovereignties and near sovereignties on the continent so chose or America as a *league of peace and friendship* in which as many as five or six nations and confederacies pursue their related yet separate destinies.†

WATSON-WALKER: A useful, contractual Union—America as a *federal nation.*

14. *What aspect of human nature is most conducive to social and economic progress?*

HAMILTON-ADAMS: The spirit of enterprise.
JEFFERSON: The spirit of friendship.
WATSON-WALKER: The spirit of adventure.

15. *What is the most important engine of such progress?*

HAMILTON-ADAMS: Government.
JEFFERSON: Education.
WATSON-WALKER: Business.

---

* To the end of his life the man of the Louisiana Purchase saw no reason why Cuba and Canada should not be brought by payment or persuasion into the empire for liberty.[66]

† This view was especially repugnant to Adams, who told his mother that the choice facing Americans was whether to be "a nation, coextensive with the North American continent, destined by God and nature to be the most powerful people ever combined under one social compact" or to be "an endless multitude of little insignificant clans and tribes at eternal war with one another for a rock, or a fishpond, the sport and fable of European masters and oppressors." [68]

16. *What, finally, should be the pace of American development?*

HAMILTON-ADAMS: Accelerated.

JEFFERSON: Measured.

WATSON-WALKER: Headlong.

By way of conclusion to this chapter and transition to the next, let us note briefly the fate of each grand model of American national development:

The Hamilton-Adams model, it should be plain to see, was thrown out for consideration about 150 years too soon. The citizens of the newly independent United States were simply not prepared, we shall learn in a few pages, for the range and authority, the energy and "consolidating tendency," of Hamilton's program of national development. They would accept grudgingly his recommendations for funding the Revolutionary debt and shoring up the public credit of a government that had been discredited from the hour of its birth, blow hot and cold on the divisive issue of protective tariffs, and even, for a span of about forty years, tolerate a system of central banking that performed some of the functions of the Bank of England. They would have almost nothing to do with the bolder proposals of the Report on Manufactures, which called for a political stirring of the economic pot much too vigorous for their republican tastes.

By 1825 they were so indifferent or hostile to the idea of a nation-building, nation-improving central government, and so increasingly able, they believed, to take care of their own needs (which were not the high-flown needs of John Quincy Adams), that the visionary recommendations of the Annual Message of 1825 were laughed into oblivion and the modest ones ignored. Almost at the outset of his career as President, the farsighted yet also unseeing Adams put an end to much of his own usefulness as a national leader with one magnificent but, alas, mirth-provoking reference to the need for an interlocking system of observatories, for a string of "light-houses of the skies," to serve the American people. His day, like that of Hamilton, was to dawn when he was dust in the grave. One cannot read through this remarkable message of 1825, an unaccountably neglected major document of American political thought, without being impressed by the sweep of his vision and the sincerity of his hopes; one therefore learns much about the temper of the young Republic from the fact that every member of Adams's Cabinet except one, Secretary of the Treasury Richard Rush, advised him to tone his message down lest he commit political suicide.[69] They knew, even if their President did not, that a government as active as the one he proposed would forfeit its claims to legitimacy in the minds of the people it was intended to serve.

The Jefferson model, equally plainly, was inadequate to the needs of the American people as the people understood them, and it requires only the barest of obituaries. If Jefferson, like most of his fellow citizens, was at heart a continentalist, capitalist, anti-statist, and republican, his prescriptions were too austere and restrained—I would like to say Utopian but will settle for Arcadian—to suit the temper of a nation that had already begun to stir, innovate, hawk, gamble, and move on at a forced pace. While the pace had become so forced by the 1830's as to raise discomforting doubts about both its velocity and its direction, and to set many persons to yearning, openly or secretly, for the restoration of "a calm and stable order of republican simplicity,"[70] few voices were raised in places high or low to suggest that the pace might be slowed through a combination of public restraints on wildcatting and private decisions not to be so greedy. At least one of the dozen or more Jeffersons who still command our respect and affection was dead and buried by the date of his retirement to Monticello.

The Watson-Walker model, in a form altered pragmatically to accommodate both the austerities of an admonishing past and challenges of an exuberant future, turned out to be the American Method of national development down to 1861. We turn now to scrutinize this method in detail.

8

The Choice of Techniques

BLESSED by a rare opportunity, driven by a deep-seated will to achieve, following the lead and providing the support of a new kind of elite, the people of the United States ran a spectacular course of development in the first half of the nineteenth century. At a speed and in a manner that startled the nations from which they and their ancestors had come, the Americans moved from apparent insignificance to acknowledged prominence, from shaky beginnings to solid achievements, from the promises of youth to the challenges of maturity. They also moved from an airy faith in inevitable progress and confident expectation of a glorious future to a suspicion that the progress of a nation may have to be paid for in the coin of disorder, the glory of a nation in the coin of tragedy.

For students of twentieth-century national development the most unusual feature of this course was the unassuming, rather than forceful, presence of politics, the fourth essential discussed in chapters 4 and 7. Whether as the chief means of fostering a widespread sense of nationalism among the men of an unsure community or of focusing their energies on the tasks of economic, social, and intellectual progress, the political system of the early Republic, by which I mean the structural and functional sum of every public agency at every level, played an erratic, penurious, and increasingly feebler role in the years of the Quest. While the art of governing had moments of primacy, for example, in 1787–1792, 1803, and 1816, persistent attention to the imperatives of nationhood was a small part and comprehensive mobilization of the forces of modernity no part of the American Method in the middle of the century. Indeed, this method seems to have had less use for government than that of any other developing nation in the past three or four hundred years. The phrase used by Robert L. Thompson to describe the force that powered the opening stage of development of the telegraph—"methodless enthusiasm" [1]—might be applied to all the doings of the young Republic. The American Method was very special, even unique: The essence of the uniqueness, we noted above, was the coexistence of a booming nation and a languishing polity.

The principal technique of national development in the young Republic was, beyond a doubt, *private enterprise.* The consciously public acts of men like Washington, Jefferson, Hamilton, Madison, and Marshall, not to forget the surveyors of Ohio, the explorers of the Louisiana Territory, the canal-builders of New York, the railroad-builders of Georgia, and the hospital-managers of Philadelphia, set a hopeful stage for the double-barreled search of the American people for nationhood and modernity, yet most of those who roamed the stage and left a lasting mark were entrepreneurs of one breed or another. They were *private men acting in private capacities;* they were *subject to no steady direction and only sporadic stimulation from political authority.* The Americans who had most to do with building up the vigorous national economy of 1860, and who thereby added to the residual strength of American nationalism, were men turned loose from both the shackles of a privilege-ridden past and the restraints of a more socially conscious future.

As we should not underestimate the importance of the Framers as stage-setters, or overlook the services of public figures like John Marshall, Andrew Jackson, and Daniel Webster in keeping the fires of a national patriotism burning, so we cannot ignore the evidence of state and municipal participation in economic development piled up by such scholars as the Handlins, Louis Hartz, Nathan Miller, Milton Heath, James N. Primm, Harry Pierce, Harry Scheiber, and Carter Goodrich.[2] Yet the chief impulse to progress and expansion through most of these exciting years was, I am convinced, basically nongovernmental in origin and operation. If this generalization, which cries out for the test of scores of monographs, is only partly valid for the first part of these years, it is overwhelmingly valid for the last part. Whether expanding outward (as in the trek to Oregon) or developing inward (as in the building of New Jersey's canals), the people of the United States ran ever farther ahead of both the vision and the activity generated by their political system. Thereby they created a socio-economic situation in which the system would sooner or later be forced to follow in their ambitious wake or surrender its claims to legitimacy.

These two cases of Oregon and New Jersey,[3] chosen at random from dozens of equally instructive cases, are evidence that the nongovernmental impulse at work in early nineteenth-century America had many more aspects than self-reliance or old-fashioned individualism. They also encourage a denial, which is offered in a suggestive yet fairly confident mood, that the competition of self-starting, free-swinging individuals was principally responsible for the health, wealth, and bright prospects of the American economy of 1860.

The settlement of Oregon may also serve as evidence that only through *associative effort* could most Americans in those days, like most in these, achieve many of their goals as free men in a free country. The more we learn of life on the frontier in both colonial and early republican times, the more obvious it becomes that the co-operating group, not the lonely individual, carried the course of empire westward. Forests were cleared, barns raised, crops grown and marketed, Indians held off or pushed out, towns settled, roads and rivers opened up, and innovations spread across the land by men who associated out of necessity with other men in a host of common endeavors. If this was true of the process of settlement, it was equally true of most other processes of American national development. Immigration, migration, expansion, progress in agriculture and commerce, industrialization, urbanization, extension of education, efforts at social and political reform, and the conquest of distance all called for vastly more co-operation, organization, discipline, and leadership than some mythologists of laissez-faire individualism would have us believe. *Co-operative individualism*—a confusing label, yet the most accurate we have at our disposal to identify a characteristically American phenomenon—was an important subtechnique of private enterprise in this period of what may have been the best days the technique has known on earth.

The case of the building of the Morris and the Delaware and Raritan canals in New Jersey around 1830 leads us faster than might seem advisable to a scrutiny of the second major technique of national development in the context of early America. I am prepared, nevertheless, to hazard a little confusion in the interest of restating sharply the fuzzily perceived fact of American history that *competition,* while a major force in developing the economy, was not primarily the classic contention of free individual against free individual or unsupported enterprise against unsupported enterprise. It was, rather, a vigorous, often angry struggle (which still goes on, vigorously if less angrily, in many parts of America) of *region against region, state against state,* and *city against city* for enterprises, markets, shipments, profits, prosperity, and prestige. While neither the entrepreneurs nor the politicians of those simpler days had the resources of twentieth-century boosters at their command, they had enough—in the form of subsidies, state and municipal loans, schemes for tax relief, mixed incorporations, publicly built facilities such as markets and warehouses, and special privileges, as well as public enterprises pure and simple—to speed up the pace of economic development. This truth finds especially convincing witness in the development of American transportation, an area of enterprise in which, George Taylor has written, the captains of "a sort of metropolitan mercantilism" employed "railroads rather than merchant fleets" as the "chief weapons of warfare." [4] Although the emulative urges of states and cities led to unnecessary waste, inefficiency, controversy, and insolvency, they also led to the far-flung transportation network of 1860 and thus, in an odd, circuitous way, to an economy visibly more national than that of 1790 or 1810 or 1830. When one looks back to the activities, both solid and silly, of the railroad-promoters and railroad-builders of the three decades before the Civil War, one is reminded of Sir Lewis Namier's observation that much of what we call history has been a process in which "small men did things both infinitely smaller and infinitely greater than they knew." [5]

Let me now haul the opinion offered obliquely in the last paragraph out into the open and put it squarely: *Political response* ranked second only to private enterprise as a technique of American development in this period. The entrepreneurs of young America were not simply turned loose to seek their fortunes; they were also given enough pats on the back to send them on the way with heightened expectations of success. In a general sense, the American experience had no unusual flavor about it: Every up-and-coming country has ways of patting innovators and builders on the back. The experience was different, however, from that of other countries in the way it wove such aspects of political response as source, intention, method, rhythm, and inspiration into a unique pattern. To take these aspects in order:

Source: Public assistance to economic development came chiefly from the second level and, as time went by, increasingly from the third level of a three-tiered political system.

Intention: It was designed chiefly to encourage the growth of private enterprise, usually by lessening risks and increasing profits.

Method: It was more concerned to get enterprises started than to keep them going.

Rhythm: It rarely flowed on a steady basis; rather, spilled over into the area of private activity in the form of disconnected, unpredictable bursts of largesse.

Inspiration: Most significant for the purposes of this inquiry, public assistance consisted of spillovers that were, in effect, isolated responses to isolated requests. Some responses were public-spirited and open; too many were narrow and devious.

Assistance of such a character was a faithful reflection of the values prized in the political culture of the age, and almost certainly did more good than harm to the economic and social health of the young Republic. It led often to the distresses of overbuilding, and was occasionally a drag upon, rather than a spur to, progress, yet it also did a job in stirring the pot of private enterprise that Americans refused to have done in any other way. At the same time, it made a mockery of even the most humble hopes for planning by the national government as well as by state and local governments.

The responses of the national government, which seem paltry for a country that expected to become an empire of liberty, added up nonetheless to a useful contribution to the expansion of the Union and the growth of the economy. From the Reverend Manasseh Cutler, who pressed the old Congress to disgorge the Northwest Ordinance in 1787, all the way to the lobbyists who won a massive grant of federal lands to aid in the construction of a north-south railroad system in 1850, determined men found the national government not entirely impervious to pleas for special favors that outraged no important group or region and could be explained away as services to the public interest. While the tariffs of the middle period and the Fugitive Slave Act of 1850 were responses that outraged too many Americans to be explained away quite so easily, only the crankiest ideologues could fault the small but helpful bits of aid Congress handed out from time to time to importuning inventors, fur traders, fishermen, explorers, steamship operators, and road-builders.[6]

From the beginning of this period to the end, the protective tariff, which was advertised as a cheap and effective goad to economic growth, was the one persistent (and highly controversial) activity of this character on the part of the national government. It is therefore instructive to note that many historians who have studied the influence of the tariff consider it to have been next to useless as such a goad.[7] More than one has gone farther to suggest that it may even have had a stultifying effect.[8] Concerning this matter, too, much evidence remains to be sifted and many conclusions to be drawn by the fraternity of American economic historians. While some of these conclusions are sure to be at odds on the principal issue, at least we may move the discussion to a higher plane of confusion.

The responses of state and local governments were more vigorous and numerous throughout this period. At the same time, they were more disconnected and unpredictable, as one may learn by reading the erratic, sometimes almost chaotic record of state banking, which in several intensely agrarian states was—so much for the spirit of modernity—a record of nonbanking.[9] Even so spectacular and public an act as the building of the Erie Canal was neither accompanied nor followed up by other public acts that might have exploited the advantages of this highway of empire far more effectively. The canal was not, as a venture of such magnitude could have been in another political culture, the core of a plan for broad-scale development. It was, rather, a kind of once-in-a-lifetime gift to a people assumed to know how to use it without any additional help or direction. In the instance of the Erie Canal, New Yorkers and their neighbors proved, as did men of other states and regions in hundreds of other instances, that the cycle of enterprise, request, response, stimulation, and yet more enterprise worked a generally healthy influence on the development of the American economy.

While private enterprise and political response joined hands in a fruitful partnership for growth and expansion—and let there be no doubt that the former, both as instigator and as beneficiary of public activity, was the senior of the two—*democratic oversight* was of little importance in this period of American history.

At the national level the stage had been set for generations to come in 1787–1792, and the stage, however bare, seemed adequate to most Americans. Neither the far-ranging visions of Hamilton and John Quincy Adams, the disciplined cautions of Jefferson, nor the relatively modest schemes of Albert Gallatin and Henry Clay made sense to men brought up to deride or defy the instructions of oversight, particularly those that might emerge from a "consolidated government." In special areas of concern, for example, standards of safety for those essential yet literally explosive agents of expansion, the steamboats of the great rivers (first in 1838, most effectively in 1852),[10] this government moved a half-century ahead of itself. The oversight it provided, however, was hardly worthy of the label: erratic in origin, disconnected in purpose, limited in range, timid in execution.

At the state level there was, we have seen, more determined activity of a public nature in support of growth and development. Yet even within the bounds of the most advanced, well-intentioned state (readers may take their choice among Pennsylvania, New York, and Massachusetts), one is hard put to discover any recurring activity that can be called a *rationalization of response* or *regulation of enterprise,* much less a pattern of *democratic oversight.* While the states were ready to crow lustily about their precious rights, they were faint of heart in exerting their undoubted powers.

At the local level, where regulations both redolent of the past and prophetic of the future became ever more conspicuous in the design for common living, boosterism was much too vigorous an

219

urge to encourage men of consequence to pause and think in terms of comprehensive plans for efficient, balanced, and disciplined modernization of economy and society. Planning at any level or on any scale—and shrewd, flexible, responsible planning is, I repeat, the essence of democratic oversight—was an alien value in the political culture and a furtive practice on the public scene of this earlier America.

A major reason for the virtual nonexistence of this technique was the refusal of most Americans to believe that anything in the way of oversight could possibly be democratic. Tradition, principle, experience, and history all taught them to identify grand schemes of civic improvement with autocratic control, with a past they had left behind in Europe and a future they meant to forestall in America. Looked at in the political-intellectual context of those years rather than these, the counsels of Hamilton and Adams do appear too autocratic to have persuaded more than a handful of Americans to weigh them carefully. The great protagonists of nation-building were, one must admit, about as unlikely a pair of persuaders in this matter as could well be imagined; their plans were simply too energetic in nation-conscious republicanism and not permissive enough in individual-conscious democracy. Hamilton's commitment to popular government was, his keenest admirers will confess, fitful and much too expediential.[11] Adams, always more of a nationalist than a democrat, gave the game away completely in one ill-timed move, the Annual Message of 1825, in which, for example, he told the members of Congress that if the Czar of Russia could support "geographical and astronomical science" so could they.[12] This was something like a President telling the members of Congress today that since Brezhnev and Kosygin support ballet so should they.

A word might be introduced at this point on the role of the military in the first stage of American development, and the best word I have been able to dig out is *insignificant*. If we think in terms of war itself, we may note that the War of 1812 was a dangerous time for national feeling (despite the upsurge of nationalism in its aftermath) and a mixed blessing for the process of economic growth, the Mexican War an even more dangerous time for patriotism and no stimulus at all to the economy. If we think in terms of an army and navy keeping the peace and serving as a school for nationalism, we may recall that, since the peace of a large country was never so easily kept, the peace-keepers were barely visible. In 1850, we have learned, the people of the United States numbered just over 23 million, the armed forces just under 21,000.[13] The school was not only tiny but, so far as one can tell from the scant evidence in hand, every bit as ambivalent in attitude about the nature of the Union as the people at large. And if, finally, we think in terms of a military taking the lead in a process of modernization, we are bound to conclude that, despite the usefulness of West Point as a reservoir of trained engineers or the importance of arms production in the development of a technology based on the interchangeability of parts or even the central role of army officers in surveying the West, America went its way to the modernity of 1860 with no direction and at best modest assistance from a source that is dominant in many parts of our own world.[14] Nothing is more revealing of the uniqueness of the American Method than the fact that army engineers were loaned directly to early railroads as surveyors or administrators, that is, to fiercely competitive instruments of local pride and ambition.

Totalitarian manipulation does not, of course, enter this picture of the techniques of national development available to a special people at a special time in history, a time, indeed, when it was available to no people in the world. It nevertheless invites attention because one useful way to understand what the American Method *was* may be to recall what it *was not,* indeed *could not possibly have been.* Not the obliteration but the accumulation of restraints on the activities of the political system, not the restless, protean, dynamic exercise of political power but shabby attrition, not the ubiquitous control of the exposed and defenseless person but unprecedented liberation, not unquestioning allegiance to an all-explaining ideology but a growing awareness that allegiances in a democracy are measured, plural, and often conflicting—these broad trends of early American development may demonstrate how far removed in spirit as well as in time and circumstance this experiment was from the twentieth-century phenomenon of totalitarianism. No monolithic party? No monopoly of the media of communication? No system of organized terror? No disciplined elite? No demonstrations of mass support for the plans of this elite?—one can almost hear Lenin expressing his scorn over the absence of these essentials of totalitarian modernization and wondering how the United States, even under the leadership of a capable if shortsighted bourgeoisie, managed to grow, expand, develop, and prosper. To his shade, as to the living men who try or pretend to honor him, one can say only what has been said several times before: There are as many methods of national development as there are nations that have developed or are in the course of developing; *we must judge the efficacy of a method primarily in terms of results rather than of intentions.*

So jealous were Americans of their independence, so certain were they of their capacity to meet the challenges of modern nationhood, that the technique of *tutelage* was no part of the American Method. While foreign-born experts were busy in many sectors of the economy, they had come not so much to *instruct* America as to *live* in it. Few of them had been invited to come; most of those few were expected to stay on. As for the political system, the men who managed it were unprepared, whether out of fear or out of lack of imagination or self-confidence, to seek advice or guidance from the more experienced nations of the Old World. America taught itself, it may safely be said, how to grow, expand, develop, and prosper. All the tutors in the world could not have taught this headstrong nation how to do the job any more effectively; all the tutors in the world could not have saved it from the mistakes that were made along the way.

One reason for the success of this outsized experiment in self-instruction was the willingness of Americans to make use of the technique of *model-imitating.* While inheritance and improvisation held unchallenged sway over the political system, in 1860 just as surely as in 1790, farsighted men gave a boost to the economy by shopping here and there, most profitably in Britain, for prototypes, skills, inventions, innovations, machines, tools, manuals, processes of education, and patterns of organization.[15] Modern technology had its origins in the Old World, and men in the New World did not hesitate to import bits and pieces in order to build up a technology of their own. By the 1850's they had become so successful in their efforts to combine innovation and extemporization with importation and adaptation that the current of technological progress was running eastward as well as westward.[16] The French government, for example, sent the delightful Michael Chevalier to the United States as early as 1833 to study transportation; the British swallowed their pride in 1853 and dispatched a parliamentary commission to learn about the latest Yankee machines. The reports and commentaries of Chevalier (1840) and the British commissioners (1854) were full of admiration for the technological achievements of the up-and-coming nation.[17]

Perhaps this is to labor a distinction that readers already find obvious, yet I must call pointed attention to an important contrast: *an economy whose leaders resorted repeatedly to the technique of model-imitating, a political system whose leaders had no use for it at all.* When I identify inheritance and improvisation as the sovereign forces of political development, I mean to reinforce the opinion announced at the beginning of chapter 5: The United States was much more politically than economically independent of the rest of the world. Whether drawing on the best colonial and Revolutionary patterns of ordering political power (the source of most key clauses of the Constitution and the Bill of Rights) or pushing ahead in a spirit of trial and error to establish a remarkable number of firsts in the Atlantic world (the Northwest Ordinance, the federal arrangements of the Constitution, the Jacksonian Presidency, and the party system), Americans proved beyond a doubt that they owned or could invent the political instruments they might need for their grand purposes. If the sum of these instruments, the American polity, was somewhat less than effective in the last stages of this chapter of national development, that is because Americans lacked will rather than skill. Except for special cases like Colonel Hamilton's Bank of the United States (modeled disingenuously on the Bank of England) and Colonel Thayer's military academy at West Point (modeled candidly on the Ecole Polytechnique),[18] the political experiences of other countries taught little to Americans. Not one of the models of national development presented in chapter 7—the Hamilton-Adams, the Jefferson, or the Watson-Walker—was a product of the conscious kind of model-imitating so popular today in many parts of the world.

Once again let us be clear in our minds that the United States of the 1850's was *not a product of autogenesis*. It cannot be too often and strenuously emphasized that the Republic began its independent career in possession of a rich legacy of institutions and ideas imported from the Old World and adapted to American circumstances, that it remained tied by bonds of culture and trade with this supposedly decaying world, and that many useful agencies of development, ranging from factories in New England to agricultural periodicals in the South, were faithful if not always grateful imitations of English, French, Dutch, and German prototypes. More than that, it was precisely because several parts of the Old World had moved so far toward nationhood and modernity that the ambitious young Republic was both invited and pushed to move in the same direction. The nationhood of France and the industrialized economy of England were, in this large sense, models the United States was persuaded unconsciously to adapt to its own needs. *By circumstance and choice the United States would be a modern nation of a special kind; by necessity it would be a modern nation of some kind.* The essence of this historical necessity was simply the existence of England and the most advanced nations on the European continent.

Private enterprise that waxed steadily more self-confident, political response that was often helpful yet always haphazard, model-imitating that stimulated the economy but found little favor in the polity—these were the ingredients of the American Method of national development in the years between the Revolution and the Civil War. The first, the nongovernmental impulse, was far and away the primary ingredient; and at least one reason for its primacy was the capacity to harness the other two techniques to its earth-shaking purposes.

Before we come face to face at last with the most perplexing questions posed at the beginning of chapter 7—whether the Americans of the Quest could have chosen or stumbled upon some other method and whether a different kind of nation would then have emerged—we must look more carefully at the role, both real and potential, of the national government in this period. I choose once again to concentrate attention on the topmost level of the American political system because of the persuasiveness of Hamilton's argument, which he stated most eloquently in the last paragraph of the last number of *The Federalist,* that no such thing as a full-fledged nation can exist without a legitimate, capable national government.

Our look at the political realities of the Quest is, by design, a second or even third look. It must be careful; it may also be brief. Four points command attention:

First, the public men of the first generation laid a political foundation for a new kind of nation. From the signing of the Declaration of Independence to the proclaiming of the Monroe Doctrine—this is, I realize, stretching the definition of a first generation to the outermost limits—the leaders of the young Republic were capable of acts of political creativity in which any new nation might find a source of genuine pride. Not all their decisions were wise or fortunate; yet the over-all record, about which the pages that follow are more expansive, was one of solid achievement.

The second is that—we noted this point on the state level in the case of the Erie Canal—the most creative of these decisions generated very little follow-up. Despite the counsels of men like Washington, Hamilton, Gallatin, and John Quincy Adams, no lasting programs encouraged Americans to take advantage of opportunities opened up by nation-building actions; no lasting programs steered or lured them into engagements that might serve the public interest. *Piecemeal response to private requests rather than steady anticipation of public needs* was the style of the national government in all these years. The zigs and zags of the advocates of a protective tariff made this fact dramatically and sometimes drastically manifest.

What the government of the United States chose to do was generally useful to the cause of national development, for example, in chartering the first and second Banks, building (ever so slowly) the National Road, improving rivers and harbors, establishing trading posts for Indians, authorizing hospitals for seamen, granting bounties to codfishermen, paying advances to the small-arms industry, regulating interstate steamboats, and running a postal service at least as efficient as the one we have today. The things it chose to do, however, were few, disconnected, and unpredictable, certainly for a nation on the move to the status of a great power. The conquest of distance, we have learned, was the indispensable component of the American formula for success in the Quest for nationhood and modernity. It is therefore somewhat startling, even to a historian in the most think-backish frame of mind, to contemplate how thin a contribution the national government made to the building, much less to the planning, of the railroad network of 1860. A short-lived reduction of duties on special types of iron (1830–1843),[19] an equally short-lived provision authorizing federal engineers to survey routes at public expense (1824–1838),[20] grants of federal lands to encourage construction in the 1850's (1850, 1852, 1853, 1856, 1857) [21]—this is the sum of what the national government did about the clearly mandatory conquest of distance by rail. It is not exactly the picture of a planning, mobilizing, anticipating, overseeing, or even energizing government.

What the national government chose to do, moreover, became less and less conspicuous or eventful as the United States approached and then passed the mid-century mark. While the population, territory, productivity, wealth, and problems of the country grew at a dizzying pace, the apparatus at Washington poked along far to the rear. Whatever figures of national political activity one counts on a year-to-year basis from, say, 1820 to 1860 —number of civilian employees in and out of Washington (excluding local postmasters), number of officers and men in the armed forces, length of sessions of Congress, statutes passed, cases decided, dollars received and expended by the Treasury[22]—one comes away with an impression of frugality to the point of folly and listlessness to the point of peril. To cite one critical example, the operations of the General Land Office (first in the Department of the Treasury, then in the Department of the Interior) [23] look to the eye of the twentieth-century observer like those of a plodding colony rather than of a bustling empire. I am not, let it be understood, trying to establish some kind of one-to-one correlation between the development of a nation and the activity of its government; I am saying simply that the impressive development of the American nation between 1820 and 1860 went unreflected in the style, reach, or energy of the instruments of the common political system.

The fourth and final point is that the decline in activity of the national polity was absolute as well as relative. *The government at Washington withdrew from obligations it had assumed in ear-*

lier, more constructive years, and turned them over, along with whatever assets and prospects they had, to states, municipalities, corporations, or private citizens—or even, as it were, to no one at all. The Bank of the United States, the National Road, trading posts for Indians, advances to the small-arms industry, surveys of routes for railroads, and subsidies in aid of vital enterprises were only a few of the responsibilities abandoned or obliterated by a government uncertain of its duty, authority, and character. This general retreat of the national government is almost perfectly symbolized in the manner in which it first financed, then owned and operated, and finally tossed away Samuel F. B. Morse's space-annihilating telegraph. Having refused penuriously to purchase the patent, it sold off aimlessly the pioneering line he had built between Washington and Baltimore.[24]

Lest it be assumed that states and cities took up the slack, we should take note of the indisputable fact that they, too, fell less busy in the 1840's and 1850's. Banking and transportation, the two developmental kinds of activity in which states had been most energetic, became increasingly domains of private enterprise; public services and social reforms, which were offered at the local level or not at all, failed miserably to meet the human needs created by the economic successes of American capitalism. In those days, too, the cities of the United States, despite some laudable efforts, could neither control nor anticipate the dislocations of rapid urbanization.

Let us come at the phenomenon of a languishing political system in a mobilizing nation from another direction by scanning a list of some activities in which the national government was not engaging in the 1850's, yet for which men possessed of less vaulting vision and more political shrewdness than either Hamilton or the younger Adams had called again and again. Why did the common government of this rapidly developing country fail to do many useful and politically at least possible things of which it was administratively and financially capable? Why did it not:

maintain a supply of currency adequate to the pressing needs of the people?

bring a modest degree of discipline, such as had been operative during the best years of the two Banks of the United States, to the always confusing, often chaotic pattern of banking throughout the Union?

initiate, subsidize, co-ordinate, and supervise a string of roads, canals, deepened rivers, and railroads that met the rough test of service to a new territory, a group of states, a vital region, or the entire nation?

buy Morse's patent, then build and operate its own telegraph system (as Postmaster General Cave Johnson recommended forcefully in 1845 and 1846), or at least set up a program of licensing private builders and operators engaged in this obviously national "business of transmitting intelligence" across state boundaries? [25]

think out and administer a more consistent, democratic, national, and developmental land policy than the stuttering, often malfunctioning program that, despite a trend toward liberalization after 1820, seemed always to favor speculators at the expense of settlers? [26]

go beyond the modest support of science-in-the-national-interest that it gave, sporadically and stingily and often furtively,[27] to men like Lewis and Clark, Whitney, North, Maury, Morse, Bache, Charles G. Page, Ferdinand Hassler, Lieutenant Charles Wilkes, and Joseph Henry? *

reach beyond the jolly codfishermen and pitiful disabled seamen to give aid or comfort to persons, whether tinkering craftsmen or experimenting farmers or adventurous mappers, whose exertions were especially developmental and public-oriented in character?

heed the advice of the venerated Washington, if not of the controversial Hamilton and Adams, by suppporting a national university that might set the pace in many fields of knowledge yet not undercut the state and private institutions of an already safely pluralistic system of higher education?

pay some attention to the social problems of untamed immigration by supervising the reception of would-be Americans if not controlling their numbers or quality? †

* Henry, be it recorded gratefully, was the man who stood up bravely to the forces of sectionalism, strict construction, timidity, and obscurantism by taking a decisive lead in the conversion of the memorable bequest of James Smithson into a high-level instrument of progress and a special symbol of the Union.[28]

† Congress did attempt, beginning in 1819, to protect immigrants against the

enforce the solemnly adopted but flagrantly violated laws designed to suppress the slave trade forever after January 1, 1808? [30]

maintain a more professional and socially useful army and navy?

make steady, flexible, equitable use of the power granted to Congress in the Constitution to "establish . . . uniform laws on the subject of bankruptcies throughout the United States"? *

To each of these questions a particular answer can be compounded out of a particular assortment of shortsighted men, discouraging events, half-baked ideas, deeply rooted prejudices, unfavorable circumstances, and whimsical accidents; yet every answer, that is to say, the explanation of every instance of inactivity or feebleness in the national government before 1861, comes down in the end to the same domineering forces and situations. The central fact of the political history of the Quest is that *most Americans were not prepared, either intellectually or psychologically, to demand and support a national government any more energetic, expensive, and effective than the one they had.* The fact finds persuasive witness in the establishment of only one new executive department (Interior) in all the years between 1798 and 1889.

For the existence of this central fact let me put forward, not didactically but suggestively, an explanation that takes us into the areas of political culture, social context, geographical environment, and historical compulsion, there to discover a half-dozen reasons.

The first was *ideology* or, as some prefer, *principle,* which had both a negative and a positive aspect. On the negative side, a sullen hostility to energetic use of political power, above all power that emanated from some faraway place, gripped the minds of Americans in this period. While the salad days of laissez faire and Social Darwinism lay a full generation in the future,[32] the conventional wisdom of mid-century American politics was notable for the assumption that even the most democratic form of

---

worst conditions of the Atlantic passage, but the laws were poorly drawn and fitfully enforced.[29]

* Here again Congress did act—yet in much too faltering a manner. In this period it passed two bankruptcy laws (1800–1803, 1841–1843), both of which were halfhearted, discriminatory, and divisive, both of which were rudely put to death.[31]

government was inherently oppressive, irrational, wasteful, corrupt, and corrupting. Born in the colonial experience, nourished on the admonitions of English radicals, legitimized by the Revolution, and confirmed by all good Jeffersonians, this old-fashioned Liberal attitude toward the uses and abuses of political power was reconfirmed by the Jacksonians and accepted at face value by the Whigs, most vocally in the aftermath of the ill-begotten Specie Circular of 1836.[33] Designed to discourage speculation in western lands and reduce dependence on bank notes and credit, this deflationary order of President Jackson, interacting savagely with the inflationary consequences of his spectacular victory over the second Bank of the United States and his determination to distribute surplus revenues, dealt a stupefying blow to an already stumbling economy. It is ironic that an antistatist ideologue like Jackson should have demonstrated so forcefully, if also unwittingly and even ignorantly, the power of a bare-bones government to affect the economic health of the nation. Few Americans stopped to think that if their government had much power to do harm it might possibly have, if placed in the right hands and armed with the right weapons, much power to do good.

The old-fashioned Liberal attitude toward political power did not, of course, prevent pragmatic men from requesting activity in behalf of special interests. Eloquent antistatists lined up every year in Washington—as they still do—to beg for favors like tariffs or land grants or contracts or other subsidies. It did, however, make the kind of broad, rational, and steady activity proposed by Hamilton and Adams seem autocratic and therefore quite unacceptable. It also helped to keep the military in the insignificant place assigned by circumstance. One reason for the shriveled, largely unprofessional character of the armed forces in this period was the triumph of Liberalism as a secular religion, for in essence this famous doctrine, Samuel Huntington has reminded us, "does not understand and is hostile to military institutions and the military function."[34] While American-style Liberalism was anything but pacifist in character, the men who subscribed to its teachings preferred to fight whatever wars might come their way in an amateurish, learn-it-yourself manner.

On the positive side, the American political consensus compensated for the distrust of public authority by expressing faith in the capacity of individuals to direct their own lives and see to their own needs. Whether competing or co-operating, whether going it alone or joining freely with others, the new man who had emerged on the North American continent was supposed to have far less use for coercion or guidance than his cousin in Britain and distant cousin in Europe. While Emerson may have laid it on a bit thick in his hymn to self-reliance, he was expressing a stoutly American belief that placed advocates of capable government in a weak position to persuade their fellow countrymen.

The *rise of democracy* reinforced this belief and thus undercut political creativity at the national level. On one hand, it made respectable the time-honored American sport of pinning the noxious tag of "monarchy"—which in those days served the same purpose as do "Communism" or "fascism" for us—on even mildly active government. As more and more people found their political voices, the ingrained republican dislike of taxes (and therefore of the activities that taxes support) grew to nearly pathological proportions. Austerity in government, particularly in that distant government suspected of an unusual potential for pomp and profligacy, became both the shield and the symbol of democracy in the nation. Fully two-thirds of the members of the House of Representatives learned, to their shamefaced sorrow, all about this suspicion in the election that followed passage of the Compensation Act of 1816.[35] In this law Congress tried for the first time to give itself modest salaries instead of stingy morsels of per diem. The act having been abruptly repealed in the very next session[36]—but not abruptly enough to satisfy the electorate—Congress was not to try again, and to win this modernizing point, until 1856.[37]

On the other hand, the rise of democracy seemed to inject substance into the faith, first proclaimed hopefully by radical workingmen and thereafter taken up joyfully by conservative businessmen, in popular education as a kind of broad, effective, inexpensive substitute for politics. The better educated a people, the less need they have for government—so ran an appealing argument in the years after Jackson, and so it runs to this day. Education-as-panacea became, Rush Welter has demonstrated, the attractive reverse of the coin of limited government, and the two sides formed what he calls, not entirely without hyperbole, a philosophy of "educated anarchy." By "representing both formal and informal education as sufficient instruments for dealing with pressing social problems," [38] the American faith in democracy weakened the governments of nation, state,[39] and city just when they could have used added strength to deal with the worst excesses of the race toward modernity.

Geography, a word used here in its most ample sense, lay at the root of three further reasons for the hard times of the national government in this period.

The first was simply the *size of the country,* which grew relentlessly in outer limits, settled lands, productive factories, national wealth, and achievement-oriented population and thus fulfilled the most exaggerated prophecies of the founding generation. Size, however, has a way of generating sizable problems, as every empire and large nation in history has learned the hard way. Certainly this was true of the first continental republic. While patriots might congratulate one another on the spaciousness of the United States, they suspected—very probably correctly—that a government of 30 million people, which had reaped its own share of benefits from the conquest of distance, might have a capacity for power and splendor, and also for officiousness and extravagance, well over ten times that of a government of 3 million. One effective way to put a tight lid on this capacity, they assumed, was to keep the government in a state of half-starvation, and in such a state they chose to keep it.

The second was *sectionalism,* which was a challenge to nation-minded Americans long before the inauguration of the more perfect Union, and which grew more protean and divisive as adventurous men moved westward to bring new regions into a country already swollen, by traditional republican standards, to the bursting point. It is as hard for the historian writing about 1850 as for the census taker counting in 1970 to carve up the vastness of the United States into neat and demographically logical sections, not least because the sections we love to list have always been busy forming, dissolving, and then re-forming political alliances and economic networks in so puckish a way as to blur the vision of the most clear-eyed observer. One can, nevertheless, identify anywhere from five to fifteen sections in a condition of tension at the mid-point of the nineteenth century; and, however healthy the condition may have been for some purposes of the American people, it made concerted political action of a national character virtually impossible to sustain. The tariff is perhaps the outstanding example of political action designed in theory to serve the entire Union and thereby to cement it ever more tightly, yet operating in fact to delight some parts and send the others into a rage. One comes away from reading the year-in, year-out debates in Congress over the tariff with a feeling that he has been sitting in on the antics of a premature United Nations rather than the deliberations of a mature United States.

The third was jealous *localism,* which almost carried the day against creative nationalism in 1787–1788 and was still around to drive governors crazy, every bit as crazy as governors drove Presidents, sixty and seventy years later. If localism did more than sectionalism to bring roads, canals, and railroads to life, it also did more to prevent the emergence of a transportation system based on a rational response to national needs. The hopes of men like Gallatin, Adams, and Clay for a program of internal improvements under the aegis of an enlightened Congress were as much the victims of local ambitions and fears as they were of the antistatist ideology. To tell the blunt truth, the old states and cities that had built up their own networks of transportation could never quite understand why they should be called upon to do for others what they had done for themselves.

Upon the geographical realities of size of country, sectionalism, and localism was imposed the related reality, largely but not exclusively political-constitutional in character, of *federalism,* which was enough in itself to cramp the public style of an uncertain nation. The unprecedented fact of "an indestructible Union, composed of indestructible states" played an ambivalent role in the drama of American national development, and the ambivalence reached an all-time high in the 1840's and 1850's. A faithful adherence to the federal principle, we learned in chapter 5, made it possible for the Union to grow in dimension and potential, to expand and encompass such outlandish places as Texas, California, and Oregon. At the same time, federalism encouraged every state from Maine (face to face with the Fugitive Slave Act of

1850) to South Carolina (face to face, as it had been off and on from the beginning, with the whole range of national exertion) to look upon the government at Washington as the "very definition of tyranny," and to defy legitimate orders of this government with the confidence that attaches to indestructibility. *Damned without federalism, damned with it*—this, surely, was a crucial political-constitutional aspect of the Quest of the United States for modern nationhood in the first half of the nineteenth century.

For all these mutually reinforcing reasons—a negative hostility to political power, a positive belief in the competence of ordinary men to solve public problems in a nonpolitical manner, the emergence of the first continental democracy, the huge dimensions of the whole experiment, the sections into which the Union was tenaciously divided, the localities into which it was further subdivided, the federal arrangements of 1787 and adjustments of later years—no other method of national development seems to have been available to the American people in these years. Neither the half-mobilizing, half-energizing model of Hamilton and John Quincy Adams nor the half-reconciling, half-disciplining model of Jefferson stood any chance of adoption in such a situation. The circumstances of the American experiment were a cumbersome burden for a national political system to bear; we should not be surprised to learn in retrospect that the system stumbled badly after its first constructive successes. The field was thereupon left open to the erratic yet compelling operation of the permissive Watson-Walker model. That model, be it recalled, gave first priority to private enterprise, had some use for political response (so long as it did not lead to any kind of political oversight), and for the most part left the American people alone to exploit their obvious talents for rewarding and earth-shaking economic activity. *By 1850 the Watson-Walker model was certainly the unchallenged and probably the only viable American Method of national development.*

It is not inconceivable that the political system of the nation could have stood up bravely under this burden of principle, prejudice, geography, tradition, and constitutional restraint, and thus have offered many of the services listed above—except for the one crushing, in the end almost death-dealing, fact of *slavery*.

Chapter 10 gives detailed consideration to the ways in which the institution of slavery, the controversies it generated and the attitudes it encouraged, became ever more dangerous a threat to the nationhood and ever more pronounced a drag on the modernization of the United States. Let me limit this discussion to the always restraining, often crippling, and finally almost paralyzing effect of the existence of slavery upon the national government. From the beginning a divisive issue in politics, in time it became the "Irish Question" of the United States. By the middle of the century public men found it impossible to *debate* any problem of consequence for the nation—land policy, fiscal arrangements, sources of revenue, aims of diplomacy, internal improvements, size and disposition of the armed forces, aid to science and education, the tariff, territorial expansion, admission of new states, even the route of the anticipated railroad to California—without debating, openly or implicitly, the problem of slavery. The problem, indeed, was an Irish Question multiplied tenfold.

Worse than that, they found it impossible to *act* decisively on many of these problems, and much of the blame for a whole range of political impasses must be assigned to the South. Left ever farther behind as a proud yet self-pitying minority, counting ever more heavily on slavery as the institutional basis of a special way of life, forced ever more angrily on the defensive about both the institution and the way of life, the South converted the comforting old doctrine of strict construction into an obsessive new dogma, and the dogma spread out its tentacles to cover the whole range of real or potential activity under the Constitution. Southerners knew better than Northerners that the one threat of consequence to slavery lay not in time or space or sense of guilt or enlightenment but somewhere deep in the national political system. In the course of denying that the system had authority to check the growth or anticipate the demise of this institution, they found it at first expedient and thereafter necessary to deny that the system had authority to do much at all. Like most antistatist ideologues, they were prepared, when tempted by a delicious opportunity, to do the kind of thing they forbade to others. One such opportunity presented itself in 1850 when grants of federal land to Illinois were balanced against grants to Alabama and

Mississippi for the over-all purpose of building a great north-south railroad.[40] Another presented itself in the same year: In the Compromise of 1850 the South extracted a much tougher law on the return of fugitive slaves than the old act of 1793—and one clearly if ironically more national in character, operation, and sanctions.[41] The predictable result of this brazen assertion of central authority was a flurry of states'-rights activity and weakening of political nationalism in the North.

In short and in sum, no matter which way the government of the Quest turned to deal with an issue affecting slavery—and that came in time to encompass just about every issue that faced the nation—it lost both energy and legitimacy. Drawing once again on David Apter's dichotomous categorization of basic types of governments, which was transformed into a trichotomy in chapter 4, I am bound to pass this judgment on the national government of the United States in the middle of the nineteenth century: Never really *mobilizing*, only gingerly and haphazardly *energizing*, it was no longer even a success in the business, so central to the viability of the Watson-Walker model, of *reconciliating*. Whenever this government made life-saving compromises, which it did on several celebrated occasions, it angered some Americans while failing to please many others; whenever it made life-giving decisions, which was not very often, it invited disrespect and defiance. The pressures on the government of the nation, like those on the sense of self-identity of the people it had been contrived to serve, had now become so intolerable that both a dramatic release and a drastic reordering seemed merely a question of time. For this government to stumble, as it did ever more shakily in the 1830's and 1840's, was one thing; for it to be brought to its knees, as it was in the 1850's, was quite another. Not even Watson, by then in his grave in Port Watson, or Walker, still on the loose in Washington, could have approved the twice-staged spectacle of a House of Representatives unable to organize for weeks on end because of the ferocious play of sectional antagonisms.[42] No political system can be as frustrated as that of the United States was in the 1850's and continue to operate indefinitely; no nation can flourish as a spiritual, economic, and social entity under the dreadful weight of the politics of frustration.

. . .

The Choice of Techniques

Yet even as the political system of the United States fell deeper into confusion and inactivity, the people of the United States went right on flourishing. In disregard of the growing threat to nationhood posed by sectional controversy, in defiance of the blows rained upon them in the depression of 1857–1858, in a mood of determination to move ahead no matter how miserly the national government or how cramped its style, the Americans modernized their economy and society at an accelerating pace. By 1860 they had lunged so far over the threshold of modernity that the prospect of turning back or even the choice of slowing down no longer existed; by 1860 they formed a nation that, however uncertain, was to prove equal to the most exacting of all tests of nationhood. To account for this performance would be to rehash so many things said in chapters 5–7, and also to take so much of the edge off chapter 9, that I will pick out only a handful of explanations—two that invite restatement and two that have not been stated before—and then sum up the meaning of the whole experience.

In the first place, we must again remember that rarely in history have three of the four essentials of national development—opportunity, will, elite—joined in a configuration so fortunate for a newly independent country. While historians need to dig more assiduously into the reasons behind the reasons, in particular to find convincing answers to the questions "whence this will?" and "why this elite?," one need not hesitate to pay these essentials the respect they deserve. It was, we may judge, precisely the robustness of this configuration that not only encouraged Americans to downgrade the uses of the fourth essential, politics, but shielded them so long from the bitter consequences of this niggardly attitude.

Second, the unkind things said about the progressive emaciation of authority and prestige in the national government must not be allowed to cast a blinding pall over the services politics did render to the cause of the developing nation: stage-setting services at the national level in the early years, energizing services at the state and local levels in the middle years. Nor can we overlook the fact that the capacity for creative politics was not dead, only on a long leave of absence, in the decade before the Civil War. The amount of unused capability in the national government was far larger than any person imagined—as Abraham Lincoln, his Cabinet, the armed forces, and the Thirty-seventh and Thirty-eighth Congresses were shortly to demonstrate.

Third, it is important to note how many workable substitutes for the nation-building proposals of Hamilton and John Quincy Adams developed to fill potentially dangerous vacuums: The "reckless banking" of the 1840's and 1850's made an erratic yet useful contribution to the accumulation of capital;[43] the New York money market, having taken over first place from Philadelphia, performed the functions of a system of central banking for some parts of the country; regional and local rivalries built up arteries to the West along the exact routes advocated in Gallatin's report of 1808;[44] and, just before the outbreak of the Civil War, blatant sectionalism forged a link for the Union in the form of the longest railroad in the world, the combined Illinois Central and Mobile and Ohio.* The best of the colleges, the service academies, the Smithsonian Institution, the military surveys of the West ("the great graduate schools for a whole generation of naturalists" [45]), the expeditions of Wilkes and Maury, and other hand-to-mouth scientific activities added up, one might argue, to the national university dear to the heart of George Washington. And dedicated men achieved several of Adams's scientific goals through roundabout, even devious means. An amusing example was the building of "light-houses of the skies" by junior officers as necessary properties of what was called, in order to soothe or hoodwink strict constructionists in Congress, the Depot of Charts and Instruments in the Navy Department. When the new Naval Observatory was built in the early 1840's, the man of many talents, then sitting in the House of Representatives, could not resist the temptation to tell his colleagues that he was "delighted that an astronomical observatory—not perhaps so great as it should have been—had been smuggled into the number of institutions of the country, under the mask of a small depot for charts, etc." [46]

Hand in hand with this process of *providential substitution* went one that might be called *cluster nationalism:* New procedures and institutions in dozens of fields of American endeavor presented the same face in every part of the Union, and thereby

---

* It is characteristic of the political culture of the Quest that a tiny gap was left between the two parts.

helped to create an unforced sense of national unity. Thanks to common language, memories, and intentions, and thanks also to the ease with which fresh ideas flooded across boundaries, men in states as far apart in space and temper as New Hampshire, New Jersey, North Carolina, and Wisconsin went about the business of getting and spending, and also of governing and developing, in the same manner and with the help of the same techniques. The process of spontaneous, roughly simultaneous uniform development had run in America since earliest colonial times, and it kept on running throughout the period we are surveying. Sometimes the clusters were left to bloom in healthy isolation, as in the broadening of the American suffrage; sometimes they were linked together to form half-federal, half-national systems, as in the building of a railroad network, the organization of major and minor parties, and the founding of nationwide professional societies. In all these instances and hundreds like them the result was a more unified nation. The result of that development was perhaps a tougher nationalism than might otherwise have existed: a sense of common destiny in the hearts of men in all parts of the Union that had grown from the bottom up rather than been imposed from the top down. For the needs of this people in this stage of their search for a new way of life a more functional and resilient nationalism did not exist in fact and could not have existed in imagination. The "cunning of history" was hard at work for the American nation in the most querulous years of the Quest.

Far back in chapter 1 a promise was made: to indulge in a reasonable amount of speculation about the kind of America that would have existed in 1860 if some other method of national development, one in which politics played a more active role, had held sway during these years. Since it has now been suggested that no other method stood any chance of adoption under the obdurate circumstances of the experiment, ranging from an antistatist ideology to the Southern fear of emancipation by order of Congress, the dictates of reasonableness in fulfilling the promise would appear to be brevity and restraint. Because the Americans of the Quest backed off from the effort to control events with the aid of a strong national government, events took their own course, and the brash, fast-moving, hopeful, and yet uncertain nation of 1860 seems almost to have been the only America that could have existed at the end of the course.

That "almost" is thrown in because I refuse to be tempted by the comforts of historical determinism into slamming the door on the possibility that somewhat less obdurate circumstances could have emerged, that these circumstances would have permitted a somewhat more energetic polity to flourish, and that the activities of such a polity would have shaped a somewhat different nation. Less disruption of institutions and values, less waste of resources and energies, less instability in the economy and unpredictability in society, less suffering in the lives of men and women who toiled hopefully and yet were ruined—these might have been welcome consequences of a polity only half as forceful, anticipatory, and large-minded as Alexander Hamilton and John Quincy Adams had recommended to their fellow countrymen. More order in expansion, more discipline in growth, more concern for the quality of life, and thus more light and less heat in the controversy over slavery—these might have been welcome consequences of a Jeffersonian polity modified under the direction of the Madison of 1816. And any polity more full of vigor at the national level, where Hamilton and Adams put their fondest hopes, or at the local level, where Jefferson believed that popular government was most useful and responsible, would have been more effectively armed to deal with the commotions and dislocations that were to befall America in the Gilded Age.

Yet one cannot suppress the suspicion that there would also have been a good deal less economic progress, and perhaps a good deal more uncertainty about the Union, if even a modest Hamilton-Adams or modified Jefferson model had reigned victorious as the American Method. The ambitions of the great mobilizers and energizers might have bankrupted the country by luring Americans into prematurely grand schemes of development; they might have stirred fatal disaffection in parts of the Union that these men, especially Hamilton, never really understood. The cautions of the great teacher and restrainer might have slowed the drive for economic independence by persuading Americans of the timeless validity of the agrarian dream; they might have failed, moreover, to make the Union coterminous with America by putting the conquest of distance near the bottom of the list of national priorities. Certainly no one of these giants gave a significant enough place in his system to that sharp goad to expansion and progress in the young Republic: the insistence of an adventurous people on running ahead of the national government into new areas, enterprises, values, and modes of life.

All these considerations lead to a conclusion that the United States in 1860 was the product of a dispersed process of *national development* rather than of a focused attempt at *nation-building*. The configuration of a rare opportunity, a widespread will to achieve, a functional elite, and a languishing politics was unique; so, therefore, was the character of the American Quest for nationhood and modernity. The desire to go upon this quest welled up spontaneously in the vast body of the people. A multitude of personal ambitions added up to a national purpose, which in turn gave the ambitions a new dimension of legitimacy. A multitude of personal achievements added up to a record of collective progress, which in turn gave the achievements a special place in history. In the creative interaction of individualism and nationalism is to be found the central meaning of the American experience in these seven decades of relentless transformation.[47]

IV

The American Ambience

1790–1860

9

The American Situation: Pluses

"Amerika, du hast es besser als unser Kontinent, das alte"— "America, you have it better than our continent, the old one"— the aged Goethe sang in 1827 of a nation whose prospects had interested him and whose best literary minds had honored him all through the last years of a splendid life.[1] In proclaiming America the clear-cut winner over Europe in the lists of nature and history, he put an end, at least in the ranks of his own large following, to a debate that had agitated intellectuals on both sides of the Atlantic for two generations.[2] Certainly in the United States itself few men of common sense and patriotism doubted any longer that their country, despite unfortunate blemishes and laughable bluffings, enjoyed a head start toward glory that was the envy of all hopeful and unprejudiced minds in the Old World. Today, a century and a half later, the descendants of these men, having observed the gap between the bold reach and the feeble grasp of most new nations of Africa and Asia, may look back to the America that captivated Goethe and agree to this large proposition: *No newly independent country ever began the long drive toward modern nationhood in an ambience so promising* as that which smiled upon the citizenry of the young Republic.

If we agree that America, as chapter 7 suggested, was the luckiest of the lucky countries in modern history, we must move on to face the challenging questions: How lucky? In what ways lucky? To what extent unlucky amidst all this luckiness? The next two chapters attempt to answer these questions. This chapter addresses itself to the *pluses,* the quite fortuitous, the largely inherited, and the more or less consciously willed advantages of nature and history that were the lot of Americans in this period; chapter

10 ponders the *minuses*, the fortuitous, inherited, and willed disadvantages that muddied the stream of national development, and in the day of reckoning almost turned the stream aside into a sink of self-destruction. At the end of the next chapter the pluses will be set summarily against the minuses as a way of restating the central proposition about the especially favorable circumstances of a memorable yet only faintly remembered search of a new country for the attributes of nationhood and the prizes of modernity.

In this listing of the most influential of the fortuitous pluses of the American experiment, *accident as a force in history* gets rather more credit than it got in the opening pages of chapter 4. This is a consequence of examining one phenomenon from two angles of vision. There I was concerned to emphasize the fact of the modern nation as an achievement, here to emphasize two qualifying facts: An achievement like the England of 1800, the France of 1850, the United States of 1860, the Japan of 1900, or the Soviet Union of 1950 takes place in a context, not in a vacuum; essential parts of any generally favorable context are accidents of nature and history that encourage men to dare, then reward them for daring successfully. A half-dozen or more such accidents, that is to say, happy circumstances for which the first three generations of independent Americans could take no credit, come effortlessly to mind. The more realistically we bring ourselves to contemplate the bad luck of most would-be modern nations on one or several or all of these counts, the more certain we can be that good luck in abundance was the accidental situation of the young Republic.

The first happy circumstance was the *geography* of the United States. Despite the originally huge and prospectively far more huge dimensions that troubled a few of its citizens, the new nation was internally a viable, manageable, and thus governable entity. Unlike modern India or South Korea, it had room, seemingly almost infinite room, to expand; unlike modern Indonesia or Pakistan, the different parts of the room were contiguous— which they would not have been if some expansion-minded Americans of this period had won a point or two by purchasing Cuba, seducing Nova Scotia, or forcing the northern areas of Mexico into the Union. Perhaps more important, unlike modern countries more numerous than one can count on fingers and toes, it was broken up by no barriers to internal accessibility that might discourage efforts to set the essential of national development we have identified as *flow* in vigorous motion: no impenetrable ranges, no endless deserts, no vast areas crisscrossed by shallow, swampy rivers. Even if the railroad had never been invented, the Americans had both the navigable rivers and the passable or breachable stretches of terrain, not to overlook a coastline punctured by a string of beckoning ports, to make a reality of the far-flung yet interdependent economy envisioned by Washington, Hamilton, and Gallatin.

Externally, the geographical situation of the United States was equally fortunate, particularly in relation to the part of the world that had been the exploring, colonizing, extracting, exploiting, and governing source in the decades of infancy through which the ancestors of the independent Americans had been required to pass. Both a moat and a door—everything depended on how the independent descendants chose to view and use it—the great *ocean* was the one fact of geography that had the most wholesome influence on the course of national development. What the Channel had been for centuries to the English the Atlantic was now to become—even more decisively because of its awesome dimensions —to the Americans. As a moat the ocean kept the might of Europe at an ever more discouraging and therefore secure distance. As a door it could be opened to the inward movement of goods, capital, ideas, innovations, and men, as well as to the outward movement of those raw and refined agricultural exports on which the health of the American economy largely depended. The ocean permitted Americans to be both *political isolationists* and *economic participants* within the Anglo-European system. At the same time, it persuaded them to think as a race of separatist come-outers and thus hastened the day of self-identity as the new order of the ages, as the first nation in many centuries to rise from the mire of imperial exploitation.

The situation of the *Old World* helped this ambitious part of the New World move ahead swiftly in other ways. The quarrels of Europe, stretching from more than twenty years before 1776 to almost forty years after, gave Americans the chance to win independence and then, despite dangers and discomforts, to consolidate it. They also gave countless Fourth of July orators the chance to toast their country as a "rock amid the billows of a tempestuous world," [3] and thus to encourage the growth of a widespread sense of mission. These same quarrels cut down drastically on the flow of immigration,[4] and the breathing space lasted just long enough for an unformed nation to develop a solid core of political, social, and cultural cohesion. Thanks to this cohesion, which had happened rather than been willed, the United States could receive the torrent of immigrants that burst upon it in the 1840's and 1850's without too many shocks, then begin to absorb them without too many ill effects. Finally, as we learned in chapter 7, the commitment of Britain and other countries of the Old World to the virtues of nationhood and modernity forced the new Republic, not without effort yet also willy-nilly, to proceed more energetically in the same direction than it might have proceeded if left to its own devices. Europe, in sum, was as much the unwilling yet life-shaping nurse of America as it had been the absent-minded yet life-giving mother.

This review of the geographical blessings lavished upon the young Republic may best be closed with a brief notice—such notice is all that need be taken by an American who travels, let us say, fifty miles from home—of the *natural* resources waiting for those who were ready to exploit them. Although most men of those agrarian days found their most precious natural asset in the fertile soil of America—with which we may associate a climate that kept them on their toes, granted them the boon of an adequate growing season, and made schemes of irrigation and thus tight political controls unnecessary—a few who had set their sights on modernity were already exulting in the seemingly limitless stores of coal, iron, copper, lead, and other minerals waiting for the pick-and-shovel industry. Still others were gratefully aware of the unharnessed surge of scores of rivers that ran down from the Appalachian heights and into tidewater. While abundant resources, we have noted, are as much a consequence as a cause of economic development, and while even a surfeit of resources is no guarantee of progress, we cannot overlook the immense natural advantages that a few nations have had over all others. Such a nation, surely, was the young United States. All Americans were prepared to agree with the redoubtable Harriet

Martineau—an unusual occurrence—when she wrote in the middle of the 1830's that "never was a country more gifted by nature."

The United States are not only vast in extent: they are inestimably rich in material wealth. There are fisheries and granite quarries along the northern coasts; and shipping from the whole commercial world within their ports. There are tanneries within reach of their oak woods, and manufactures in the north from the cotton growth of the south. There is unlimited wealth of corn, sugar-cane and beet, hemp, flax, tobacco, and rice. There are regions of pasture land. There are varieties of grape for wine, and mulberries for silk. There is salt. There are mineral springs. There is marble, gold, lead, iron, and coal. There is a chain of mountains, dividing the great fertile western valley from the busy eastern region which lies between the mountains and the Atlantic. These mountains yield the springs by which the great rivers are to be fed for ever, to fertilize the great valley, and be the vehicle of its commerce with the world. Out of the reach of these rivers, in the vast breadth of the north, lie the great lakes, to be likewise the servants of commerce, and to afford in their fisheries the means of life and luxury to thousands.[5]

Life and luxury not to thousands but to tens of millions—this had been the promise of America, which, generations before Miss Martineau lived among us disapprovingly, Abraham Lincoln hailed as "the fairest portion of the earth." [6] Students of American national development must never fail to recognize the magnitude of the promise.

Yet another happy accident that shaped the destiny of the young Republic was the *absence of overpowering enemies.* The facts of this situation, unusually fortunate in the history of developing and expanding nations, were a thinly settled and nonaggressive Canada, a weak, divided, and unstable Spanish America, an immensely outnumbered and demoralized indigenous population, and a distant, ever more preoccupied Spain, France, and England. The great powers were feared, especially in the first decades of American independence; they were feared, however, as seducers offering sly gold that might detach potential components of the continental Republic rather than aggressors pointing fearful cannon that might terminate this independence abruptly. We have already noted the most visible (or invisible?) consequence of

this pleasant security against invasion, conquest, and forced disunity: an army and navy in 1850 of 20,800 officers and men. The
proportions of military personnel (including trained militia) to
the total population and of military expenditures to the gross
national product were such tiny fractions of 1 per cent as to come
down, in terms of meaningful statistics, to almost zero.[7]

One could argue, of course, that the existence of only one powerful and threatening enemy, especially if it had been situated in
the western hemisphere, might have sharpened the sense of American nationalism and forced the pace of American industrial
progress, that such things as a more capable national government,
a high-level patriotic literature, a larger and better integrated
railroad network, a more abundant supply of trained engineers,
and a more progressive iron industry might have been some of the
beneficial results. Yet when one thinks of the dollars that were
not spent on nonproductive goods and services, the talents that
were *not* diverted into the military profession, the threat of a
military coup that did *not* harass the political system, and the
strains that were *not* visited upon a far-flung people (for whom
both wars of this period were highly sectional and therefore divisive in character),* one may judge the accidental security of the
new nation to have been a happy situation indeed. The Quest
went forward more smoothly because nature, demography, and
international politics joined hands and made the United States a
fortress that could not be subdued yet needed only a handful of
men to stand guard.

To the circumstance of common blood among white Americans, the product of an Anglo–Northern European flow of immigration for more than two centuries, we paid our respects in chapter 5. Only one observation need be added: The new nation of
those days was spared most of the grief that torments many new
and, indeed, old nations of these days because it harbored no
ethnic minorities that aspired to power or could demand and get
special protection, no irredentist areas that begged for release
from the bonds of Union or incorporation in some other country,
no scatter of tenacious men who owed their first loyalty to a coun-

---

* It is amusing if also embarrassing to learn that President Polk justified the
Mexican War to Congress as one whose successful conclusion would "tend
powerfully to preserve us from foreign collisions." [8]

try across the seas. In our twentieth-century eyes this scene of happy homogeneity is blotched by all those red, yellow, brown, and especially black faces that gaze accusingly across the generations, yet an exaggerated sense of present-mindedness must not obscure the primary fact that white America—the only America so far as better than four out of five Americans were concerned, not because they were wicked and cruel but because they lacked awareness, imagination, and information—was remarkably free from the soul-wasting, often death-dealing tensions of tribal or ethnic diversity.

About the final circumstance, the *common language* of the people, we can be almost as brief. In this matter, too, the lucky Americans escaped the disruptive pressures that today beset countries so different in character as South Africa, Canada, Ceylon, India, Spain, Belgium, and most new nations of black Africa. While old pockets of men who preferred to speak German, French, Spanish, or Dutch held out all through the years of the Quest, as did a smattering of newspapers to comfort some of them in their own tongue, and while new pockets of men who could speak only German, Spanish, Swedish, Norwegian, Chinese, Polish, Italian, or some other tongue sprang up after 1830, the English language won a total victory in all of public and most of private life. Although one consequence of the victory was to reinforce the cultural dependence of the young Republic on the mother from whom it had cut loose politically, this victory for English was a blessing for the cause of modern nationhood. The flow of ideas ran unimpeded by ignorance or hostility; no laws had to be passed stigmatizing a language like German or giving a language like Spanish a special status that irritated the rest of the people; the elite was not granted a special boost (as it has been in countries like India and Nigeria) by belonging to the tiny percentage of people able to speak the one common tongue; the absence of differences in language blunted the edge of differences in national origin. George Clinton's nephew DeWitt observed with satisfaction in 1814: "The triumph and adoption of the English language have been the principal means of melting us down into one people, and of extinguishing those stubborn prejudices and violent animosities which formed a wall of partition between the inhabitants of the same land." [9] Strange words from the mayor of what was then, as it is now, the nation's Tower of Babel—yet like any true Clinton he was simply exaggerating the truth to make sure that his audience understood it.

In all these matters—geography, distance from Europe, developments in Europe, natural resources, external security, the ascendancy of Anglo–Northern European blood, the dominance of the English language—Americans of the first generations of independence were lucky pawns of a fate for which they could take no credit, neither for themselves nor for their ancestors. Other blessings, however, were legacies of the colonial experience rather than aimless strokes of fortune, and we should not hesitate to praise the ancestors for amassing these legacies nor the men themselves for receiving them gratefully and then managing them resourcefully in the interest of their ambitious young nation.

The first such legacy was the foundation of a *political system* well suited to perform the tasks that fell to it in the early years. The tasks of these years, be it acknowledged, would have tested cruelly the most efficient system then in existence; resistance, rebellion, independence, war, legitimacy at home and abroad, unity, reconstruction, solvency, stability, and expansion. It speaks well for colonial America, and thus, in an odd sense, for imperial Britain, that many institutions and procedures of self-government were in working order on the eve of the Revolution, that they were republicanized swiftly in the midst of it, and that, in important matters of common concern, they were partly nationalized in the midst and fully in the aftermath. The system, moreover, had techniques, unsophisticated yet effective, for recruiting, training, and rewarding the men needed to operate it. The political culture of early America expected public service from time to time of all established men as a matter of course, and that fact alone was sufficient to compensate for the crude state of many aspects of the demanding art of self-government.

Supporting and supported by the political system was a functional, innovation-receptive, achievement-oriented society whose most prominent feature was a large, industrious, confident *middle class.* I am loath to follow the lead of some makers of the American Myth by cramming every citizen of the new nation into this class. While America had no peers, it had its "better sort": a top layer of 2 to 5 per cent of the population (depending on the definitions applied to the modest evidence in our grasp) made up of large landholders, rich merchants, highly successful lawyers and doctors, and their extended families. While it had few peasants, it had its "meaner sort": a bottom layer of 15 to 20 per cent made up of itinerant laborers, newly arrived servants, and hardscrabble farmers.[10] Yet something like three-fourths of the people —self-supporting farmers, competent shopkeepers, skilled artisans, moderately successful professionals, and their similarly extended families—were visibly and proudly of the "middling sort." Upon the ambition, self-respect, industry, pride in personal independence, capacity for social co-operation, and faith in themselves and their nation demonstrated by this middle class, men so different in temper as Jefferson, Madison, John Adams, and Hamilton found the promise of a special mission for the American Republic.

The middle class that emerged from the Revolution was to prove a major force in a process of modernization destined to sweep up the many, rather than the few, in its relentless train. The proximity and accessibility of this class to the one just below it did much to banish poverty, whether as fact or state of mind, from the American scene. At the same time, its existence made unnecessary the often bloody attempt to achieve the social restratification that is now said to be the first requisite of political and economic modernization in many countries of Latin America.[11] The immunity of early nineteenth-century America from the ravages of a class struggle was a blessing for the Quest, and most of that immunity stemmed from the pre-Revolutionary establishment and post-Revolutionary persistence of the middle class.

A third legacy for which men of progressive mind could be grateful, and could best express their gratitude by managing it with boldness rather than caution, was an *economic base* on which to build with a solid hope of success. The economy of newly independent America lagged far to the rear of that of England, yet it displayed features that developing nations in the modern world might look upon with envy:

a built-in capacity to take care of its own people by offering them an opportunity to live as human beings;

a similar capacity to feed them the staples of a decent life without reaching out like a beggar to external sources that might prove, for reasons political or natural, unreliable or domineering;

patterns of ingenuity and effort productive of a surplus to be marketed in whatever parts of the world could offer attractive goods, solid credit, or hard cash in return;

a willingness to trade, often in shrewd defiance of discriminatory laws and practices, with all those parts of the world;

a demand for both skilled and unskilled labor that in most years spared the new Republic the agonies of unemployment and the attritions, as well as the hypocrisies, of underemployment;

real wages for these workers that "exceeded by 30 to 100 percent" those paid to counterparts in England;[12]

a remarkably steady level of prices, except when the level was disrupted (as it has been always and everywhere) in the midst or aftermath of war;[13]

a brave beginning, certainly brave for an essentially agrarian-extractive-commercial society, in manufacturing; for example, the development of an iron industry in 1775 which, despite its crudity and organization in small units, is thought to have produced one-seventh of the world's supply;[14]

an ethic that heaped praise upon toil and innovation, that branded no calling as socially inferior, and that therefore encouraged men of good blood or vaulting aspirations to sweat and gamble.

The economy of the young Republic was notable for achievement, sound of function, and bursting with potential. Neither lavish nor stingy, this economy was already famous for the pay-off it delivered to the mass of the American people; and the pay-off was certain to grow larger as input climbed with the increase of population and output soared with the accumulation of new skills and introduction of new machines. The simplicity of the political and social systems was itself a promise of economic growth. Since neither system made exorbitant demands on the financial capacity of the American people, most of this capacity could be focused on the task of developing a viable economy. There is much to be said—although ideology and practice alike forbid us to say it in the twentieth century—for a stripped-down polity and an austere society as aids to rapid economic progress.

The American Situation: Pluses

At first glance, the *intellectual base* for American national development appears distinctly less impressive than the political, social, and economic bases we have just inspected. Yet in this matter, too, all the apparently threadbare beginnings added up to a solid blessing for which many new nations of our times would sell or trade anything except their own birthright to independence. Among the intellectual strengths upon which the nation of the Revolution could draw as it began the experiment in independence were these: a high degree of literacy among the people at large, a respectable fund of learning in the keeping of their leaders, nine colleges in a state of being and a half-dozen in the act of becoming, a spread of primary schools and scatter of academies, a family system more efficiently geared than ours to educate and discipline, law offices and countinghouses and factories offering a quality of on-the-job training that professional schools of today still have trouble matching, fifty or more newspapers that were uncensored and unperjured, bookstores and libraries and philosophical societies that sprouted like weeds. Whatever this system of training and enlarging the minds of free men lacked in sophistication it made up several times over in the increasingly indigenous character of its institutions and methods. America remained, as it had always been, yet would rarely admit, the child of Europe; the child, however, had begun to have a mind of its own.

So far we have been concentrating on those inherited blessings which held out the hope of modernity, yet the hope of nationhood, a historical and logical twin, also lay in the womb of colonial America; and it burst forth more than half-grown—the metaphor, I trust, is not too obstetrical or merely silly—under the fierce pressures of the fighting Revolution. The chief support of this second hope has never been given its due: Despite differences in everything from the pastimes of the better sort to the timing of the seasons, the thirteen colonies on the road to becoming thirteen states shared a rich store of *common institutions*. Not only blood and language bound South Carolina to Massachusetts and Virginia to New Hampshire, but political practice, social habit, commercial organization, distribution of property, learning, law, religion, values, taste, and style. Lawyers in Charleston were much like lawyers in Boston; Scotch-Irish farmers who faced the

255

Cherokee were much like Scotch-Irish farmers who faced the Iroquois; speakers who ranted and raved against the ministers of George III in the Great and General Court of Massachusetts were echoed by speakers in the House of Burgesses of Virginia; a scholar of William and Mary in 1776 read the same books as a scholar of Harvard. The colonizing and supervising hand of Britain, one admits both ruefully and gratefully, set *cluster nationalism* hard at work on the American scene long before the rise of the independent nation.[15] Otherwise, one may properly ask, how could the Stamp Act Congress of 1765 and the Continental Congress of 1774 have got on so expeditiously with their business? Otherwise, how could the Declaration of Independence have spoken so confidently of "these united colonies"?

One of the history-shaping qualities displayed in common by American ideas and institutions was negative in character; it was, in a sense, a quality of importance in that it did *not* exist. I refer, of course, to the *absence of feudalism* from the American scene, an absence commented upon favorably generations before Goethe (one of whose reasons for thinking America "had it better" was that the land was bare of "castles in ruins") and acclaimed in recent years by such scholars as Louis Hartz.[16] While much remains to be investigated about the effects of this absence, we know enough already to conclude that the special colonial status of America spared it many of the social conflicts of Europe and sent it largely unimpeded on the way to democracy. Ocean, wilderness, austerity, religious diversity, the scarcity of physical reminders like castles and cathedrals—these and other circumstances, both fortuitous and inherited, made certain that the fight to wipe out the strongholds of feudalism, which was a drag on the course of modernization in Europe, would be finished in America almost before it had begun. The Americans, in short, were uniquely fortunate—more fortunate, be it noted, than the men who had come to Quebec and Mexico, as well as the men who had stayed behind in Germany and France—to begin their experiment in independence without feudal tenures, a national church, centralized and autocratic government, hereditary stratification, and a privilege-ridden economy. They acknowledged their fortune by refusing, as their colonial ancestors had refused on several prophetic occasions,[17] to re-create a past that would in time have to be destroyed. "Weary," Hegel wrote, "of the historical lumber room of old Europe," [18] the choice spirits of the young Republic had their way eased into the future because of the scarcity of entrenched traditionalists they had to persuade, subdue, or exterminate.

The *elite* of the new nation has already claimed our attention in chapters 4, 6, and 7. I cannot, however, pass by this precious legacy, the leadership of the founding generation, without these few additional comments:

An elite did exist in both the upper and middle layers of society, and one is hard pressed to know how America could have taken off on an independent search for nationhood and modernity without the will, imagination, daring, endurance, and creativity it displayed at every stage of the Revolution and in the first years under the Constitution.

The elite was, we have noted, about as legitimate, accessible, functional, and adjusted—the very opposite, that is to say, of esoteric or alienated—as such a group can be. The select company of excellent Americans was always in close touch with the assumptions and aspirations of the great body of ordinary Americans.

All these qualities found support in the fact that many members of the second-level elite had risen from the bottom of American society and most members of the first-level elite from the middle. For that matter, some of the first-level men had gone all the way from the bottom to the top.

Finally, the upper or inner elite of the founding generation was *unusually political in character and interests.* The planters, lawyers, and merchants who made it up were also legislators, administrators, soldiers, judges, diplomats, and writers of constitutions, while college presidents, clergymen, and editors were all more active in the political arena than their counterparts (even college presidents) are today. The time had not come for a managerial, cultural, scientific, or military elite to flourish in America; the choice spirits of the new nation could give themselves over to politics with a rousing will at the one moment in our history when politics of the highest order was the first requisite of order and progress.

One observation remains to be made: The best of these choice spirits were not alone the best that crudely formed America had to offer; they were the best ever to flourish in the modern world. I must express the conviction, born of many years of reflection, that *the political genius of modern man flowered most profusely in Revolutionary America.* Giants like Washington, Franklin, Jefferson, Hamilton, Madison, John Adams, and Marshall; near giants like John Jay, James Wilson, Samuel Adams, George Mason, William Samuel Johnson, John Dickinson, Rufus King, Elbridge Gerry, Fisher Ames, Benjamin Rush, and the two Morrises; whole families of public men like the Lees, Pinckneys, Carrolls, Rutledges, Randolphs, Huntingtons, Trumbulls, and Livingstons—how could one remote, simple, sparsely settled, freshly independent nation have bred this array of political talent in so short a span of time? And, not to overlook a classic example of the vitality of the second-level elite, how could so many men in the small towns of Massachusetts have been such shrewd and sensible constitutionalists in 1776–1780? [19] No easy answer can be made to either of these related questions; a hope can be entertained that some of the rising generation of American social and political historians will consider them thoughtfully— and, if they feel the urge, hypothesize about them courageously or even outrageously.[20] The leadership of the American Revolution is a phenomenon that has been left, out of dullness of wit or embarrassment or timidity, in the largely untutored keeping of superpatriotic celebrants of a past that never was. The time has come for serious historians to acknowledge, probe, and ponder this phenomenon.

We arrive, finally, at the pluses of the Quest for which Americans of the first, second, and in some instances, third generations could take a great deal of credit. In addition to managing skillfully the political, social, economic, and intellectual legacies of the colonial experience, they made large contributions of their own, some of which were more conscious than others. The total gift was an ambience extremely favorable to national development.

The first was the *reduction of social strains*—tensions, cleavages, suspicions, antipathies, or whatever we may call them—that enabled the sections of America to hang together as one political community and set out boldly for the promised land of modernity. The post-Revolutionary acceleration of the movement toward mutual accommodation among religions was perhaps the longest stride toward social harmony. In this matter, as in many others, most parts of the Atlantic world were moving in the same direction, yet the young Republic, honoring the example of its most enlightened ancestral colonies, was well out in front of the straggling procession toward a future in which men would no longer burn or incarcerate or disenfranchise or despise or simply fear other men because of differences in religious conviction or behavior.

Being a Catholic in a predominantly Protestant country was, to be sure, not always pleasant, especially during the high tide of the Irish and German immigrations, yet the United States managed to combine diversity, common sense, principle, skepticism, and apathy in a social-intellectual formula that celebrated religious liberty as a central value of the new order of the ages. For the most part, moreover, the churches bestowed lavish blessings upon the Quest for nationhood and modernity. While Southern ministers came to question the sanctity of the Union and fundamentalist preachers warned credulous flocks against the vices of false progress (false, one suspects, because both sheep and shepherds were cheated of its rewards), the burden of proclaiming the message of the Protestant ethic fell squarely upon the willing shoulders of the Protestant clergy. And while the ethic itself invited every American to struggle with every other for profit and privilege, it also provided an underlying unity to the search for personal fulfillment and national glory. So crucial was the *Protestant ethic* for the development of the United States that we may properly isolate and salute it as a major plus.[21] Half-inherited, half-willed, this goad to achievement set much of the style of an almost obsessively achieving society.

Yet another circumstance contributing to the reduction of strains with which the new nation might have had trouble coping was the emergence of a *consensus* of political and social principle. Faced, in effect, with three grand choices among schools of thought, the American people spurned both the Conservatism of Burke and the Radicalism of Rousseau, then went ahead to convert the Liberalism of their own Jefferson into a national monument. While we must not exaggerate the unanimity of this choice, or fail to recognize that men of contradictory purposes could read the words inscribed on the monument in contradictory ways (one need only think, for example, of "all men are created equal"), we must also see how different were the Americans from the French, Germans, Russians, and Italians in pledging allegiance to a single national tradition. Such a tradition, it may be argued, was a flat necessity for the purposes of a new, diverse, and far-flung people; yet credit must not be lightly withheld from men who had the good sense to identify their overriding necessity and transform it into an encompassing virtue.

In a fourth favorable circumstance the founding generation had the decisive hand: the string of *political decisions* that gave substance to the rhetoric of the first sentence of the Declaration of Independence by enabling Americans "to assume among the powers of the earth the separate and equal status to which the Laws of Nature and of Nature's God" appeared at last to "entitle them," and that also opened up the road to freedom, prosperity, power, and greatness. The Declaration itself, the creation of a continental army in 1775 and a national domain in 1784, the treaty of alliance with France, the treaty of peace with England, the Northwest Ordinance, the Constitution, the precedents of Washington's Presidency, the successes of Hamilton's fiscal program, the stoutly republican measures of Jefferson and Madison, the Louisiana Purchase, John Marshall's mettlesome opinions, John Quincy Adams's single-minded diplomacy (under which we may include President Monroe's celebrated doctrine)— these were examples of political activity of which any new nation might be proud. The record was far from perfect, as fiascos like the failure of the Continental Congress to raise money, the passage of the ill-starred Alien and Sedition Acts, the resistance to Jefferson's embargo, and the behavior of almost everybody in office during the War of 1812 make uncomfortably clear. Any record that includes the creative political acts of 1787–1801, however, can bear the inspection of the most critical eye. Let me make the point in the person of one illustrious and durable man: When we think of the performance of James Madison in staging and then managing the Convention of 1787, persuading the Virginia ratifying convention of 1788, leading the First Congress,

and working with Jefferson and others to form the first genuine
political party in the world, we may forgive him his irresolute role
in the political, administrative, legislative, and military night-
mare known as the War of 1812.

Two political decisions of the early years invite special mention
as circumstances in which America took charge of its own destiny.
One was the policy of *neutrality* toward the warring powers of
Europe. This most venerable of American foreign policies, which
was something more dynamic than the isolationism of ancestral
folklore yet less pretentious than the "positive neutralism" of
contemporary folkways,[22] served the new nation effectively inside
as well as outside its borders. It kept America out of quarrels so
old and deep-seated as to defy peaceful resolution; it kept Americans, who were asked repeatedly to line up for Britian or France,
from the throats of other Americans.[23] The policy of neutrality
announced by Washington and carried forward by his successors
was not as casually fashioned a crutch as some historians would
have it. Newly independent America was racked by cold-war
strains in the 1790's as severely as any newly independent country
in the 1950's or 1960's, and once again credit must be awarded to
men who knew how to make a virtue out of necessity. By freeing
their minds if not their hearts of the passions of Francophiles and
subtleties of Anglophiles, they gave their nation two priceless
boons: space in which to maneuver during a savage moment in
European history, a defense against the assaults of ideology and
interest during a tricky moment in American history.

The second and more important of these politically created circumstances was *the Constitution*. The writing, ratifying, and
launching of this most successful of national charters in
1787–1789 was the principal action in uniting the American people and setting a stage for the search for modernity. While the
Framers put so high a priority on the cause of Union that later
generations were left to deal with the unjust anachronism of slavery, they laid a firm foundation for a new kind of nation with a
high potential for liberty-oriented progress. A vast and expansible free-trade area with one constitutional government to represent, defend, and oversee it was the essence of their political contribution to the American people. When we consider soberly the
choices open to them, as well as the consequences of the choices

they finally made, is it possible to deny that theirs was a contribution of the first magnitude? By the same token, we must honor Jefferson and his colleagues for their special contribution as a loyal opposition in the 1790's and a Constitution-accepting majority in 1801.

The last favorable circumstance over which the first generations had some control, and thus gave directions to every generation to follow, was the *flow of immigration* from Europe, not alone of men, but also of artifacts, inventions, machines, ideas, and money. The whole of America was the frontier of the whole of the Old World,[24] to be sure, and perhaps nothing could have stopped or deflected the relentless drives that pushed this frontier ever westward through the middle of North America. Nevertheless, the citizens of the early Republic deserve high marks, first, for not attempting to shut down the flow that spilled into their country and, second, for generating enough of the flow themselves to support the useful belief that America could take just about anything from Europe, for example, skilled workers, innovative processes, and ambitious capital, without jeopardizing its self-proclaimed status as the new and different order of the ages. The passage of men, things, and ideas from one world to the other was an essential element of American national development, and one must not underestimate the extent to which some men of the Quest expedited this passage in a forceful and positive way as contrasted with the acquiescent and negative way of standing aside and letting Europe do its best and worst. Indeed, small yet influential numbers journeyed physically or intellectually to the countries of their origin, especially to Britain, in order to stimulate the kinds of inward flow that might contribute to prosperity for themselves and progress for their nation.

All this flow was remarkably functional. The United States was not simply a convenient dump for weak men, superfluous artifacts, zany inventions, obsolescent machines, useless ideas, and soft money. Except for an occasional sad experience, like the unloading of a glut of British pots and pans on an avaricious yet impecunious America in the first months of peace in 1815, the new nation imported men, things, and ideas it could use and, in the case of most men, reward handsomely. Europe offered little of the worthless or exotic to America; America sought little of the worthless or exotic for itself. While the glad welcome Moses Brown gave in 1790 to Samuel Slater and his head full of ideas remains, symbolically and also substantively, the most consequential instance of selective importation in the early years,[25] one must not forget all the hopeful white men (and, indeed, the bewildered black men) who came in tens of thousands to build America. One must also not forget the many-faceted, many-personed kind of passage from Europe to America. I invite readers to consider a classic example: the movement in 1844 of the Best family along with its capital and skills from Mettenheim in civilized Germany to Milwaukee in raw Wisconsin, there to found what has since become the Pabst Brewing Company.[26] Only a churl or an anxious competitor would deny that this act of immigration made a major contribution to the flavor of American life.

The more diligently we go through the catalogue of fortuitous, inherited, and willed circumstances of a benevolent character at work in the first stage of American national development, the more respect we must have for *the Revolution* as the most influential of all. A host of historians (which appears to be self-replenishing) [27] has so exhaustively probed and tirelessly debated the causes, nature, and events of the American Revolution that we may fix full attention on the consequences. About them, it seems, there has been something close to a conspiracy of neglect. This modest beginning, I hope, will encourage energetic and knowledgeable historians to shift their gaze away from the prelude and the main event and toward the aftermath. The one opinion about the Revolution itself that I shall register here is this: It was *not a full-scale revolution* in the sense of being a violent break with the past and a great leap forward. It was, rather, a *war of independence,* a *struggle for political liberation* fought by men of progressive but by no means radical intent who had, in the words of Gordon Wood, "suddenly blinked" and seen their society "in a new perspective";[28] it was also, in one crucial sense, a *bloody civil war* between those who had blinked and those who had not or would not. Perhaps some of the fog of misunderstanding that hovers over the debate about the nature of the Revolution might blow away if the eminent participants would agree upon a fact of history so compelling as to be an axiom, perhaps even a law: *All revolutions are civil wars; not all civil wars are revolutions.*[29] To this fact let me add the proposition that neither a bloody civil war nor a limited revolution would have taken place in the American colonies in the late eighteenth century if the pressure for a war of independence had not mounted dramatically and then sought release.

Yet all three did take place, and together they helped as much as geography or natural resources to open wide the door of opportunity to the ambitions and energies of the American people. In the first place, while the Revolution brought the colonial experience to an abrupt end, it also put the seal of historical approval on many colonial developments, several of which had lain hidden beneath the surface, that pointed to the America of the future. In transforming thirteen dependent colonies into one independent country, it made certain that this America would be republican in the forms and purposes of politics, half-continental in area and fully continental in vision, fluid in social relations, self-conscious in culture, easygoing in religious faith and practice, and capitalist in the ownership and organization of the economy.

The consequences of the Revolution for American nationhood were enormous. Indeed, it may be said to have created the American nation in one grand gesture of resistance and rebellion, converting colonists with many loyalties or no loyalty at all to self-identified Americans in that blinking of the eye of history. Having aroused them from slumber and told them of their real identity, principally by stimulating an already lively sense of separateness from the Old World, the Revolution then forced them to make national decisions even before they had a national government, persuaded them to declare the United States a perpetual Union, provided a small but satisfactory package of national heroes and symbols, and finally, at the close of this period, convinced just enough voters and bystanders of the soundness of Hamilton's argument that a nation without a national government was "an awful spectacle." [30] The Constitution of 1787 was, in this view, the final act of the Revolution, for it put a stamp of unassailable, irrevocable legitimacy on the great legacies of 1776: independence, republicanism, an economy based on private property, expansion, and the Union. While the last of these was to prove an ambiguous legacy, there can be no doubt that the men of 1776 and 1787, including many who had qualms about 1776 and most who were outraged in 1787, thought of their "perpetual" and thereafter "more perfect" Union of states as a nation to be dealt with as a single entity by all other nations.

The consequences for modernity were equally enormous. The Revolution heralded an end to America's status as economic colony by demolishing the whole apparatus of the Navigation Acts, by creating a government that could begin to fight back against the discriminatory practices of England and other trading powers, by opening up the fertile lands and mighty rivers beyond the Appalachians to an impatient citizenry, and by unleashing economic forces sure to hurry the pace of progress toward a more productive, diversified, sophisticated, and balanced economy. At the same time, it cleared away a thicket of internal barriers to the flow of commerce and created the vast and expansible free-trade area of which we have already taken notice. By skimming off (to make the point crudely) a good deal of cream at the top in many colonies, the Revolution strengthened the position of the middle class; by forcing leaders to shift their pent-up energies, and thus in time their nascent loyalties, from a colony or region to an entire nation, it transformed a gaggle of petty elites into one elite with influence throughout the Atlantic world.

The circle of nationhood and modernity is once again closed if we recall that members of the Revolutionary elite were, with few exceptions, nation-oriented and future-conscious in interests, activities, and aspirations. Even those leading men who opposed ratification of the Constitution—George Clinton, Patrick Henry, Willie Jones, Albert Gallatin, and Richard Henry Lee come immediately to mind—were committed Americans, and thus were men dedicated to the Quest for modern nationhood. Unlike Washington, Madison, James Wilson, Hamilton, and even Jefferson, they could not understand why the *idea* of a progressive American nation had to come to fruition in the *fact* of an efficacious American national government. By such doubts, just as much as by the poisons of slavery, was the Quest to be plagued from 1790 to 1860. Yet if plagued it was, the Quest never halted or turned aside, not even when the nation faced dismemberment.

The American Quest

. . .

Let me top off this survey of an ambience that promised rich fulfillment to the dreams of the founding generation of Americans by stating a truth so plain that, were it not at the same time so important, it would be superfluous: We are probing the whats and hows and whys of *an instance of national development that took place more than a century ago.* Much of the uniqueness of the American experiment, as well as much of the skepticism about its usefulness as a model or even relevance as a case study, arises out of the implications of this truth. To put the matter another way, the *timing* of American independence may well have been the most important circumstance in the entire ambience. The Quest began long enough *after* the establishment of the European system of nation-states to encourage the American people to think in terms of progress as an independent nation; it began long enough *before* the explosive events and discoveries of the twentieth century that have encouraged peoples everywhere and in every condition to think in the same terms yet, in sad contrast to the lot of the fortunate Americans, have promised heart-rending failure as the result of too many efforts.

While the *after,* it may be argued plausibly, might have been stretched out even longer to the advantage of the American people, for example, by sending them forth on their independent search with more political, financial, social, and technological models available for adoption and adaption, the *before,* it can be asserted positively, was quite long enough. The new nation of the first decades of the nineteenth century found itself in an altogether different social-ideological-ecological ambience from that of the new nations of the last decades of the twentieth. Although it was leagues in front of other nations in the march toward democracy, its zestful brand of egalitarianism did not demand the immediate enfranchisement of men who were, through no fault of their own, untrained to make political decisions, nor did it insist upon launching schemes of social welfare that were beyond the competence of the nation to program, fund, staff, and manage. Although American ports were crowded with immigrants and American women were celebrated for their fecundity, the growth in population stayed within the limits of the nation's capacity to feed, educate, and employ. Here was one new nation—

266

and how differently it was situated in this critical matter from most new nations of today—for which birth control was a non-existent issue, for which, to the contrary, the central problem of population was to find more hands to clear land and tend machines rather than to arrange for fewer mouths to be fed.

It will not, I hope, be judged heartless to observe that the newly independent United States escaped many of the sorrows and frustrations of newly independent India because the "technology of public health," to borrow a phrase from Walt Rostow,[31] lagged far to the rear of the technologies of industry, agriculture, and transportation. Many Americans died before their appointed time; many more lived on to take part in an exercise of national development that was not condemned to failure by the sheer weight of the persons who climbed expectantly on board. While no decent man would advise a new nation of the twentieth century to wall itself off against the life-giving, life-saving bounties of modern medicine, no realistic man can deny that the chief consequence of this medicine, the grotesque increase in population, is even now swallowing up the gains and thus frustrating the hopes of modernizers all over the world.[32] Developing nations like India and Indonesia face this dilemma in its most agonizing form. My one concern in mentioning these countries has been to underscore the fact that the developing United States never had to face it.

One may go on and on listing the benefits, negative in nature yet positive in influence, of being a new nation in a more simple and less expectant world: no summit conferences at which George Washington would waste his time and the people's money; no United Nations in whose General Assembly John Adams would be tempted to pout and pose; no "politically overdeveloped youth," in Douglas Ashford's phrase, itching to harass the legitimate managers of an underdeveloped political system;[33] no rich nations growing richer at the expense of poor nations growing poorer; in sum, a world in which, Robert Heilbroner has pointed out, the young Republic "could afford to take its time" in a way "the new countries cannot." [34] All these circumstances, interacting with the others we have noted, created an ambience of national development in which economic capacity stayed in front of social demand, the "want-get" ratio was not distorted,[35] politics was not asked to perform feats of magic, and a disastrous "confrontation of authority and community" did not therefore take place.[36] In summing up his thoughts on modernization in the Middle East, Daniel Lerner has offered a useful dichotomy:

Where the increase of desirous individuals and the growth of opportunities are in balance, there the psychosocial conditions for stable growth are good. Where personal desires greatly exceed institutional capacities, there the prospects are for instability of a sort which impedes rational and cumulative modernization.[37]

The United States of the Quest had its share of misfortunes, yet they were not the vicious sort that plague the new nations of our century. In no nation in all history, it is safe to insist, did desire and opportunity interact in so favorable a conjunction. While the Republic demanded will, toil, and risk in exorbitant amounts, *it was situated by history and accident to pay off at a rate both satisfying to the ambitions of individuals and stimulating to the advance of the whole community.* That, surely, is the sum of all the pluses; that separates the United States of the Quest from all other new nations. The American ambience offered the American people a prospect of success that may never again be offered to any people. The challenge was enormous; so, too, was the promise.

10

The American Situation: Minuses

WHEN Goethe and like-minded men sang "America, you have it better," they did not mean that America "had it perfect." The circumstances in which the first new nation sought a lofty place in the world were, it bears repeating, unusually lucky. The American ambience held out promises of success denied to most new nations of our age. At the same time, this generally lucky situation was flawed with unlucky circumstances. Some of these worked as unpleasant influences on the course of modernization by slowing its pace, encouraging false starts, or diverting the energies of talented men into socially calamitous or morally reprehensible channels. Others were stiff challenges to the old hopes of Washington and Hamilton and new hopes of Webster and Douglas for a fulfilled American nationhood that no departure or event, inside or outside the country, could demolish. And one circumstance, the institution of slavery, turned out to be both: a drag on the process of modernization, an explosive charge placed in the edifice of nationhood.

While the purpose of this chapter is to provide an annotated catalogue of the minuses of the Quest, this purpose would be served poorly were we not to take note that most of the pluses just examined were not entirely favorable in influence. Two examples may suffice to show that forces and events could take away maliciously even as they gave lavishly:

The first is immigration, a saga about which historians should not wax too sentimental. Without it, obviously, there could have been no America, yet with it came a severe setback to some of the best achievements and ideals of the social order that emerged from the Revolution. The cities of Boston, New York, Philadelphia, and Baltimore, as I read their records sympathetically, were much less comfortable, manageable, safe, literate, sanitary, and humane places in 1860 than in 1820 because of the flood of immigrants that spilled into them, and also because of the unimaginative, indifferent, or downright cruel ways in which the established people of these cities dealt with the flood. In his *History of Public Health in New York City, 1625–1866* John Duffy gives the years after 1825 the stark label "The City Overwhelmed,"[1] and it is hard, indeed, to think of cities anywhere at any time in history that were pummeled so severely by the unintentional blows of uncontrolled immigration as were those of the Quest.

The second is the related phenomenon of internal migration. As the essential element in the pattern of flow, it made possible the expansion of the Republic and the nationalizing of the economy, yet it, too, put taut strains on the American experiment. It spread capital thinly, invited overbuilding of transportation facilities (which sometimes fell into ruins even before they could be used), and lowered the standard of living for millions of Americans. While the nation was ready to pay a short-run price for the long-run benefits of both immigration and internal migration, the price was steep and often painful. In contemplating these or any other circumstances of our national development, we should recognize that almost no blessing bestowed on the American people was unmixed in character and consequence.

If this were not a compelling truth of American history, if the pluses of the ambience were whole and pure, then those millions who took part in the Quest would not be in the position to receive admiring credit; and that, surely, would be an egregious error. The years between 1789 and 1861 were a bath of sweat, not a picnic. The men and women of this achieving society were not handed their individual and national rewards on a platter of comfort and idleness. They worked, gambled, and sacrificed to move onward and upward in a total effort that has rarely been equaled in modern history. We may come to a better understanding of the magnitude of both the effort and the rewards if we turn now to examine the harsh side of the ledgers of providence, heritage, and will. Let us run through a half-dozen or so of the most significant circumstances that promised failure rather than success to those men who dreamed of America as a great modern nation.

. . .

The first was a circumstance of geography: *the size of the enterprise.* The Republic grew, we have learned, from 890,000 to 3 million square miles in the years between the Treaty of Paris (1783) and the Gadsden Purchase (1854). In the spirited act of growing it found itself the owner of huge tracts of territory where rivers flowed across, rather than along, necessary lines of communication, annual rainfall dipped below the level of independent survival, mountains that made the Appalachians seem like foothills reared up menacingly, or the climate assaulted the health and morale of hard-working men in nearly every season of the year. To occupy the fairest portion of an entire continent was, of course, the free choice of the American people, into which they were prodded from time to time by the visions of men like John Quincy Adams and by their own urges to move westward. Their descendants of the twentieth century have much reason to be grateful for both the soaring visions and the earth-bound, indeed earth-hungry, urges. Nevertheless, the fact of unprecedented distance placed hazardous obstacles in the path of the United States.

If Karl Deutsch and others are right in their view that ease of communication is a mark of true political community, we may conclude that the young Republic was repeatedly in danger of biting off territory it could not digest as a united nation.[2] While the system of communication, of which the transportation of men and goods was a more important part than it is today, grew increasingly efficient, cheap, speedy, and thus distance-conquering, citizens of the Republic loaded it with increasingly demanding tasks. As a result, the lunge to the West brought about a break-off, at least temporarily, of many conversations on national topics, a distortion of messages that large-minded men wished to send smoothly in both directions, and a reduction of interest in and allegiance to the government at Washington. Prominent citizens argued that the government might be of some use in harassing Indians or selling public lands or discovering routes over the Rockies, but was of no use in making internal improvements on a generous and rational basis. All these developments boded ill for the continental nationalism of John Quincy Adams. It is worth pondering an alternative course of North American history in which a clutch of independent republics sprang up permanently west of the Mississippi or even the Appalachians.

As if these obstacles to nationalism were not enough of a burden for the United States, the overstretching of lines of communication in the early nineteenth century gave rise, as it had done from the beginning of our history, to a large class of subsistence farmers. Such men, in effect, sentenced themselves and their families to an indefinite term of banishment from the economic, social, intellectual, and political arenas of American life, and thus became questionable candidates for full American citizenship. In the final reckoning, of couse, the cardinal fact is that these once-and-future citizens, of whom an extra measure of loyalty was demanded, had no image of themselves in which they were not Americans; and sooner or later the power as well as the symbols of the Republic overhauled them and brought them back into the fold. The events of the 1780's teach us that small farmers in out-of-the-way places will not take the lead in *building* a nation; the events of the 1860's teach us that they will, however, do much of the dirty work of *preserving* one. The wonder must always be that, despite the strains of enormous expansion, a single nation was sitting there in 1860 for these quiet nationalists to preserve with their lives.

Distance also hampered the process of modernization. Migration, the cutting edge of distance, dispersed dangerously the material and human resources of the American Republic. As far back as 1827, Secretary of the Treasury Richard Rush advanced the "proposition too plain to require elucidation" that the "creation of capital is retarded, rather than accelerated, by the diffusion of a thin population over a great surface of soil."[3] Long before that date many settled areas of the East were being drained, to their economic detriment, of skilled men who had by no means become superfluous agents of development in their communities, and who too often finished as members of no community at all. The interaction of horizontal mobility, opportunity, vertical mobility, and democracy mentioned in chapter 6 is one of the elementary truths of early American development; this interaction, however, worked havoc on the course of orderly progress even as it hastened the emergence of a new style of life.

So it goes all up and down the catalogue of the criteria of modernity in those formative decades: Whether we consider the reversion of the mountain men to savagery,[4] the shriveling of culture and education in the newly settled areas, the special dimension of violence thrust into a society that granted equal status to the gun and the plow, the special dimension of uncertainty thrust into a financial system that operated always on the edge of chaos, the often staggering cost of moving raw and semiprocessed materials to market, or the exaggerated devotion of talent, energy, and capital to an outsized problem of transportation, we cannot fail to recognize the damaging effects of distance upon the course of modernization. When the Americans of the Quest undertook to have their progress and their expansion, too, they shouldered a burden much heavier, much more likely to drag them down to mediocrity, than many Western-minded historians would have us believe.

This is, perhaps, the most convenient place to deal with the tenacious question of the influence of *the frontier.* In dealing with it amidst a nest of minuses I do not mean to categorize it by implication as one of the unpleasant circumstances in the total American ambience. While I have never been persuaded by Turner or the Turnerians of the far-reaching extent and benevolent quality of the influence of the frontier as area or process,[5] I would not deny that it has been a primary force in the development of American democracy.[6] My purpose is not to plunge into the endless debate over the reasons why men made the risky journey to the frontier, what then befell them and their institutions, and what also befell the settled areas from which they came;[7] it is, rather, to consider in a preliminary and largely intuitive way what the existence of the frontier may have meant for modernity and nationhood. The comments that follow are an invitation to further study of the frontier and further debate about it. I shall be as glad as the next man to taste the fruits of the study and also to join, somewhere out on the fringes, in the debate; yet one sometimes wonders if American historians have not given attention to the frontier at the expense of other vital forces of American life.

If we confine our gaze to the first seven decades of the one century in which the frontier, we are told, existed as a living reality and not just a debated memory of independent America, we may find ourselves unable to decide whether it was a marginal plus, a marginal minus, or a fifty-fifty circumstance in the process of modernization. My own opinion is that the frontier—a context compounded of isolation, rawness, and underdevelopment, yet also of opportunity, exhilaration, and independence—was more a minus than a plus in these years. It was certainly not a helpful agent of modernization in the way the East Indies were for the Netherlands or the Congo for Belgium. The newly settled West was not milked systematically in behalf of the established East, and the reason was simple: The men who went to live in it were American citizens who could demand, if not always get, a fair price for their produce and a decent pay-off for their efforts. To fall back on a distinction we have made repeatedly, the frontier was a drag upon the short-run development of the United States; but, having acted as a drag while the United States bulled its way toward modernity, it surfaced many years after as a probable long-run benefit. I say "probable" because one can never be sure that an America confined to the boundaries of 1783, or even to the Proclamation Line of 1763, would not be every bit as modern as the America of fifty states.

Much the same judgment can be made about the influence of the frontier on the search for nationhood. By exaggerating the dangerous effects of distance, upsetting the balance of slave states and free states, and adding section after section to a Union already beset by the irritations of sectionalism, the western frontier hurt the development of American nationalism on a continental scale. At the same time, the frontier generated a self-conscious loyalty to the Union among many men who chose to wrestle with it, as the newspapers of the newly settled areas still bear witness. The act of moving west forced these men to think hard about what it meant to be American, and their conclusions were usually those of hopeful migrants rather than of sour expatriates. The frontier could not have produced this fresh sense of identity if the settlers had not been nation-minded Americans to begin with, or if they had not carried with them the constitutional promise of full citizenship that was embodied in the machinery for admitting new states into the Union on an equal footing with the old. One suspects that the baggage taken westward in men's minds—

expectations, memories, values, aspirations, patterns of behavior, institutions, and loyalties—was more important for the settlers' and our way of life than the experience undergone when they got there.

One of Turner's famous passages announced that "American democracy . . . was not carried in the Susan Constant to Virginia, nor in the Mayflower to Plymouth," rather, that it "came out of the American forest" and gained "new strength each time it touched a new frontier." [8] That announcement, even when qualified by fresh evidence and discounted for the hyperbole of eloquence, will remain a bone of contention among historians. What cannot be such a bone is the plain truth that both American nationalism and the American commitment to material progress, features of our way of life no less imposing than American democracy, came out of the East (in their embryonic forms, out of Europe) and did more to shape the frontier than the frontier did to shape them.

A related circumstance was *sectionalism.* Always a threat to the cause of full-fledged American nationhood, sectional differences finally became so domineering a fact of politics and so compelling a sentiment among the people that they put the existence of the nation in hazard.[9] Such differences had been a part of the American scene from the beginning, when the men of Jamestown undertook to do things in their way and the men of Plymouth to do things in theirs; and they were certain to grow more irritating if not indeed explosive in character with the passage of time. No country as large as the United States, whether in 1776 or 1783 or 1803 or 1819 or 1854 or, finally, 1860, has escaped the animosities of sectionalism. The interesting element in the American case is that these animosities were almost entirely a consequence of geography. Again I resort to that cautious "almost" because of the emphatically divisive effects of slavery, although this institution, too, was shaped in part by the hand of geography. In any event, it must be kept clearly in mind that the American brand of sectionalism was not first generated and thereafter sustained, as sectionalism has been in many parts of the world, by differences in ethnic origin, language, history, constitutional-legal practice, or religion. No matter how far west the people of the United States kept wandering, they had much more in common than the people of France or Spain in those days and India or Indonesia in these. Theirs was primarily a sectionalism of space, soil, rainfall, rivers, and mountains.

Sectionalism worked in three major ways to challenge American nationalism:

First and most obviously, it widened the gap between the South and the rest of the Union. It also kept the South, a section that was in fact a cluster of sections, in a state of tension. Little love was lost between, let us say, South Carolina and Tennessee, even less between Virginia and every other state, including the future state of West Virginia.

Second, it tempted many Americans in temporarily disaffected parts of the Union—New England in the years of Jefferson and Madison is a classic case—to act as unlawful resisters and think as antinational secessionists. War, we are told, is a mighty agent of nationalism, yet the wars and near wars of the first half of the nineteenth century in America were more sectional and therefore antinational in character than any we have fought in this century.

Finally, sectional interest made a mockery of most programs of national action in the national interest. It was, indeed, exactly this kind of action—undertaken by Hamilton in his financial proposals of 1790–1791 and by Jefferson in his attempts of 1806–1807 to keep America neutral politically by forcing it to disengage economically—that pushed hard-hit parts of the new nation to take up the posture of self-conscious sectionalism. The principal lesson we find in these events is the enduring power of sectionalism in a large country. No amount of talk about the national interest, however well-intentioned, will prevent many instances of action by a common government from seeming to favor some parts at the expense of others, and the result is too often a weakened allegiance to that government. Whatever the government of the United States did or did not do about roads, canals, and railroads in the 1820's and 1830's, it was fated, at least in the short run, to inflame sectional divisions. If it followed the advice of Henry Clay and went abuilding in the West, men in old regions that had done their own building would pay their share of the bill resentfully or not at all. If it followed the advice of Clay's opponents, men in new regions would begin to question, as some of them did in hurt tones, the benefits of participation in a spineless, fettered, stingy Union. One must probe deeply into the dogged nationalism-of-the-heart of a supporter of Clay like young Abraham Lincoln to understand why the sectionalism of interest did not tear the expanding nation into a dozen squabbling pieces. When the economist and the political scientist have said everything they can say together about the forces that created the nation of 1860, the historian and the psychologist may rise in unison to suggest that the most compelling of these forces were emotional or traditional in essence.

On the basis of the evidence available at this time, it is impossible to judge whether sectionalism slowed or speeded the pace of *modernization* in the decades before the Civil War. On one hand, because of the historically creative relationship between modernity and nationhood, it did damage to the cause of the first by doing damage to the cause of the second. On the other, it acted as a healthy warning that men determined to modernize a motley country in an equitable manner should be on guard against schemes promising quick gains at the peril of enduring disaffections. Modernization, let us recall, is a qualitative as well as quantitative process, and sectionalism may have been a crude yet effective guaranty that America would not lose its soul or style in an autocratic, consolidating rush toward the prizes of industrial progress.

Localism or, as I now choose to label it, *parochialism* turned out to be the most unpropitious circumstance of this general description in the years of the Quest. In chapter 8 we paid our respects to interregional, interstate, and intercity competition as a technique that stimulated the development of the American economy; here, perhaps, we should stand the technique on its head and see it as harmful to national development of an orderly character.

The railroad network of 1860 is the most vivid case in point. It was, we have noted, the product of an immense outpouring of human energy: a web of more than 30,000 miles of track that had conquered distance, stirred flow, and done more than any other material achievement to create a national economy, and thereby had helped to hold together a country tugged this way and that by strong centrifugal urges. It was also, however, the product of hundreds upon hundreds of separate and often bickering enterprises oblivious to the need for national or even regional planning. As a consequence, it was overbuilt in some areas, underbuilt in others, and badly built in most; and everywhere men and communities went bankrupt in witless attempts not merely to meet but also to beat their neighbors. Worse than that in terms of national integration, the pride and greed of local boosters had dictated wasteful discontinuity between different roads in many cities: Passengers and freight were unloaded at the end of one road, hauled a mile or two at a dawdling pace for an unnecessary price, then reloaded to journey onward to the next competitive city. Finally, one gazes with awe at a map of the American railroad network of 1860 until he discovers, on closer inspection, that eight or more gauges were in use, many the result of that same pride and greed rather than of honest differences of opinion over cost, speed, safety, and efficiency.[10] A classic case of this kind of artificial discontinuity was the "War of the Gauges" in Erie, Pennsylvania. The city fathers opposed the connection of two lines lest Erie lose the benefits of local transshipment; they were supported in their decision by the managers of the Pennsylvania Railroad and the city fathers of Philadelphia, all of whom were anxious to keep traffic off the most convenient route to New York City.[11]

Toward the end of this period of development gaps were being closed, small lines were being consolidated, techniques for converstion of rolling stock from one gauge to another were winning acceptance, and the need for a standard gauge throughout the United States was forcing itself upon public opinion. Still, the whole system had a kind of unnecessarily fragmented look; it would not become fully national for several decades, and only then at a huge price to the American people. It may be argued, of course, that a country like Australia (where several gauges are still in use) is no less a nation because of the fragmentation of its railroad network; yet the America of 1850 was hardly in the position of the Australia of 1970, which can shrug off the consequences of this element and symbol of disunity. Not only was its principal agency of flow chopped up into tinier bits and pieces; its antinational compulsions were more numerous and worrisome.

All these circumstances—the demands of distance, the austerities of the frontier, the tensions of sectionalism, the disorders of parochialism—put a dangerous amount of muscle into the long-standing threat to the Union posed by the ambiguous legacy of 1787. The social, economic, and emotional effects of these disruptive features of the ambience exaggerated, at least temporarily, the political-constitutional uncertainties of an uncertain nation. While the influence of the Union itself was more a plus than a minus in the Quest for both nationhood and modernity, no one can pass final judgment upon the quality of this influence unless he counts the guises in which the ambiguous legacy appeared to different men at different times in different parts of the country, and also listens to the babble of voices celebrating the beauties of the arrangement.[12] As Kalman Silvert and Willard Hanna have noted in commenting upon the interesting case of Sukarno's Indonesia, men do not chant ritualistically in praise of a nation unless they are worried sick about its continued existence.[13]

If the total record of the influence of the Union seems murky (a more pungent word, perhaps, for expressing the notion of ambiguity), we may find it consoling to recall what was said in chapter 5 about federalism, the one aspect of the balance of unity and diversity upon which all Americans (except for Alexander Hamilton out of the hearing range of the public) were agreed. Without the federal principle, which included the indelible fact of the states, the United States would never have expanded to become a continental republic; with it, however, the United States was forced to live through all these years under the guns of interposition, nullification, and threatened secession. The unique federalism of the United States is a reminder on a monumental scale of the ambiguities of the human condition. Successes and failures, blessings and troubles, advances and retreats, pluses and minuses —of such was the total contribution of federalism to the American experiment. Yet one cannot help concluding that the positive edged out the negative by a substantial margin. The United States of 1860 was an uncertain nation sustained by an uncertain nationalism. The nation nevertheless existed, as did also the nationalism; and those two facts, we shall see, were the deciding force in the hour of peril.

. . .

In order to make the point conclusively that all good things in the modern nation have bad aspects, let me call attention to the *rapidity of change* as a circumstance that hampered the progress of the United States toward the unabashedly proclaimed goal of being the most modern of the modern nations as well as the most civilized of the civilized. While the notion of planned obsolescence had not made its appearance to store up troubles for us and our own descendants by devouring natural resources and by littering the landscape with junk, change for the sake of change had taken hold of the emotions of millions of Americans; and far too many of them had fallen into the easy habit of equating change with progress. The cycle of boom and bust, needlessly shoddy products and services, and the decay of skills were all features of the American economy in 1860. A widespread sense of impermanence, the tensions of insecurity, the pressures of overwork and undercompensation, and the cruelties of unemployment were all features of American society. The fact that both economy and society were in a generally healthy condition should not blind us to the existence of these and other sore spots, such as the high incidence of individual and mob violence, which owed as much to the unprecedented mobility of American society as to the brutal nature of the Atlantic world, the imperatives of survival on the frontier, and the mingling of ethnic groups and religions long schooled in a suspicious posture. If Abraham Lincoln, a patriot to the marrow of his bones, could speak openly to his friends in 1838 of "savage Mobs," the "mobocratic spirit," and "mob law," [14] something was already rotten in the United States. One must fall back upon hunch, then propose candidly that the rapid pace of American life was a principal cause of American violence.

The price of modernization, we have come to realize, is a certain amount of dislocation and disruption, yet the Americans of the Quest could have reduced the price for themselves and their descendants if they had not been quite so anxious to get over the next ridge in the shortest possible time, if they had not been so willing to let "everything run to an excess," [15] if they had not been so deaf to the Jeffersonian call for self-discipline in their behavior as men and as a nation, and if they had not been so casual in permitting the laudable "ambition to get ahead" to swell into a rage. While the America of 1860 might have been a shade or two less modern—and how, by the way, can we bring even crudely quantitative evidence to the support of such a judgment?—it might also have been a more civilized society, one in which fewer tears of desperation were shed by persons who had exerted themselves earnestly and found only calamity. Such persons paid the hard way for having been caught up, in the words of Harriet Beecher Stowe, by the "headlong tide of business" of a "race more vehement and energetic than any of the old world ever saw," for having been trapped, in the words of a nameless citizen of New Orleans, by a situation in which "we have *over done* most of the things we have attempted." [16]

These observations are to a large extent gratuitous. Restless and therefore disruptive change was built into the American ambience by the interplay of an ethic of achievement-oriented men and the opportunities that nature and history had laid open to them. The Americans of the Quest had little choice except to move in one direction, and not much more choice except to move in it as fast as possible and with scant thought of the ill consequences that a simple-minded glorification of speed might visit upon their progeny. In this matter perhaps more acutely than in any other with which we have dealt, I recognize the occupational hazards of being read casually or misunderstood honestly; yet I feel obliged to say that two celebrated givens of the American situation, in which I, too, have gloried and will continue to glory, contributed heavily to the disruption of society. As a result, they must be assessed candidly as both minuses and pluses of the Quest.

The first of these was American-style *individualism*. Institutionalized as *capitalism*—or does the process run in the opposite direction?—this individualism, which came to life in the bouncy careers of tens of thousands of men like Robert J. Walker, worked wonders to build a modern nation. It also inflicted injuries upon the quality of life in the nation for which we still, more than a hundred years later, are mortgaging ourselves and our children. While this individualism bade Americans be up and doing, it frowned upon such kinds of associational effort as trade unions and co-operatives; and the result was to consign far too many men, women, and, worst of all, children to a condition—lonely, defenseless, cheerless, despairing—that William Graham Sumner himself would have judged inhuman. Here above all we must make a prodigious effort to think ourselves back into a world in which the kind of social welfare we take for granted in the latter half of the twentieth century was an activity "outside the range of common expectation." [17] While America had a scatter of social reformers who insisted that the sweep into the future need not be productive of racism, vulgarity, brutality, and suffering, the scatter was so thin, powerless, and itself individualistic that it could bring few of the disciplines of civility to bear upon the workings of the social order.

The immunity of this order from the controls of the community, in other words, the almost total victory of bumptious economic individualism over attempts to regulate it, began to show itself openly in the decades just before the Civil War: For the first time in American history a few men accumulated swollen fortunes while many other men slid inexorably downward, in most instances through no fault of their own, into a class that we would describe as the hard-core poor and our adversaries as the proletariat. Careful studies of the evolution of American society between the Revolution and the Civil War are likely to lend support to David Apter's largely intuitive conclusion that "unplanned development results in social inequalities, which can easily harden into more or less permanently organized classes." [18] Once again I seek not to be misunderstood, and for that reason take special pains to salute the achievements of early American individualism; once again, however, we should be conscious of the social costs of an effective yet essentially unbridled method of national development.

The second given—characteristically and healthily American yet also damaging to both nationhood and modernity in some respects—was *republicanism.* We have already looked painstakingly at this phenomenon as ideology and practice, and there is little to say except by way of repetition. The republicanism of all but a few apparently eccentric Americans like Alexander Hamilton and John Quincy Adams was flatly opposed to taxing, spending, subsidizing, operating, and planning, not to forget guiding, admonishing, chastising, and symbolizing; the Republic was therefore left to seek self-identity and progress through largely nonpolitical means.

This was not a totally unhappy state of affairs. Indeed, the mobilization of this people at this stage of history probably could not have proceeded half as effectively in any other way; a more intervening and controlling government might well have acted as a drag on the innovative exuberance of the American people. The leaders of the people were thoroughly instructed in the history of governments of every age and condition, and they knew of few instances in which anticipatory politics had lent a helping hand to economic and social progress. Still, a political system openly hostile to the modest kinds of national action mentioned on pages 227–229 was, despite its fine qualities of representativeness of public opinion and security for personal liberty, an inherited and thereafter willed circumstance that gave skimpy aid to the cause of modern nationhood. While the popular, constitutional republic has many virtues, it has a doubtful capacity for helping a country to find an identity or mobilizing resources on an equitable basis for a sharply accelerated drive into the future.

One final observation arises when we contemplate the commitment of the young nation to the ideology and practice of republicanism: It was precisely this commitment, exaggerated by the supposedly baleful effects of distance, austerity, and individualism, that led the nations of Europe to join without meaningful dissent in the comforting prediction that the United States of America would dissolve, explode, or wither away. We sometimes forget that in its early years this new nation was even more of an untried experiment than the poorest new nation is today. No proof existed anywhere on earth that a nonhereditary, representative, constitutional, and fundamentally noncoercive government could stay alive for even a few years in so enormous a room. The wise politicians of the Old World, in sharp contrast to both the wise politicians and simple people of the New, anticipated the demise of both the United States and its government; most of them relished the anticipation because the demise would confirm their own teachings about the politically impossible and ethically unthinkable.[19] It is interesting to contrast the position in the world at large of late twentieth-century Nigeria or India or Indonesia with that of early nineteenth-century America. Today, the hardheaded expectation of the established nations is failure for them, yet the warmhearted hope remains success; then, both expectation and hope were focused on failure. One wonders whether the attitude of the Old World was a plus or a minus for the American experiment; one then thinks back to the attitude of the Americans themselves, recalls how willing they were to push ahead, and concludes that this hostile attitude was most probably of no consequence one way or the other.

Every circumstance reviewed in this chapter was a mixed blessing, a bundle of pluses and minuses, in the years of the Quest. Few Americans would now insist that their ancestors were mistaken, even assuming they had any choice in these matters, to prefer a big nation to a little one, bravado to quiescence, the march to the bivouac, the self-chosen innovations of free men to the imposed habits of the herd, the permissive government to the controlling one. Indeed, it may be said quite properly that all we have been doing here is to rehearse the inescapable defects of a string of massive virtues. This cannot be said about the last negative circumstance of the American ambience, for it was an evil in the short run and the long run, an evil in essence and in consequence.

The circumstance was, of course, the institution of *slavery*. Like most other issues we come to grips with in this book, slavery has been examined by so many able scholars and from so many points of view, and will be until and beyond the end of the Republic, that I propose to fix attention only on the part it played in the evolution of American nationhood and the modernization of the American community. Let me open a recital of its specific influences, almost all of them injurious, with a generalized judgment: It was always a threat to the unity of the nation and became increasingly a drag upon the course of modernization. Whether the men of the Quest knew it or not, they had no more debilitating a burden to bear than the institution of slavery and the principles, prejudices, patterns of behavior, laws, and practices that propped it up.

This institution, noxious in itself and rendered doubly noxious by the way it interacted with the more distressing aspects of sectionalism, parochialism, and unbridled individualism, was a challenge to the fulfillment of American *nationhood* throughout this period. In 1787 the Framers shoved it under the carpet in the larger interest of forming a more perfect Union; in 1819–1820 the first great debate in Congress over its extension westward (and over the authority of Congress to forbid, ignore, or bless extension) set off a "fire-bell in the night" to warn nationalists that the threat it posed to the Union was growing with the demand of each newly settled area for admission as a state;* in 1850, 1854, and 1857 it goaded men to scorn each other and talk seriously of dissolution; in 1860–1861 it brought the challenge of slavery to a modern nation at last into the open and persuaded eleven states to make a counterrevolutionary attempt to leave the Union forever. The side-by-side existence and nonexistence of slavery was by no means the only difference between one part of the United States and all others; it was, however, so immediately or remotely the cause of other differences that I am ready to come full circle and join the old breed of historians who put overriding blame for the agonies of the Union on the institution of slavery.

In the first place, it helped to create a nation within the nation, a section clearly more separate, proud, defensive, and conscious of special identity than New England or the old Northwest or the Pacific slope. By sustaining a deviant and increasingly dissident American way of life, even for the swarming majority of whites who owned no slaves,† it threatened to make foolish fancies out of the prudent hopes of the great Virginia nationalists like Washington, Madison, and Marshall. By isolating the men of the South morally, not alone from the rest of the United States but from the whole Western world, it forced them to choose between defiance and submission; and nothing in the history of the South had taught it to submit. Tocqueville was only one of hundreds of travelers who saw and felt the "marked divergences" between North and South, and who traced them back accurately to their original, ever more vehemently flowing source.[22]

With every reality of a nation go the emotions of nationalism—

---

* It was Thomas Jefferson himself who heard the "fire-bell" in his retirement and confessed his "terror" in a letter to John Holmes dated April 22, 1820.[20]

† The census of 1860 counted 384,884 owners of Negro slaves in the United States; the total white population of the slave states was almost 8 million.[21]

and so they went in the Old South. As the institution of slavery sent its roots deeper into the economy, society, and politics, and as, in counterpoint, attacks upon it mounted in intensity, the sectionalism of this prickly part of the country took on the character of an incipient nationalism. In terms of the whole United States this nationalism was, of course, a form of antinationalism that boded ill for the cause of the more perfect Union. For all its pretensions to positive thinking about the rightness and utility of slavery, the South went heavily on the defense after 1820, and the defensive posture is notoriously hard on loyalties that are supposed to operate beyond the reach of one's own community. Hardly less damaging to the Union was the reaction of many Northerners to the rising nationalism of the South.When men in Alabama and South Carolina announced that they had a dwindling respect for the Union, men in Massachusetts and Wisconsin could be forgiven for expressing a dwindling sense of kinship with them. Indeed, if we poke carefully into the sentiments for a "Universal Yankee Nation" entertained by men like Robert Walsh,[23] we find that places were being set at the table for Ontario and Nova Scotia more cordially than for the fire-breathing Southern states. The social reformers of the 1840's and 1850's also waxed more anti-Southern in mood as the opinion of the world outside became less charitable toward a nation that harbored millions of slaves, and as the part of the nation that harbored them grew more adamant.[24]

We have already surveyed the damage done by the South-North schism. Suffice it to recall that this schism bludgeoned the government at Washington into a wasting preoccupation with the issue of the extension of slavery and converted almost every public problem into one that had to be dealt with, if not always frankly discussed, on the basis of whether it helped or harmed slavery. The "Irish Question" of the young Republic wrecked the party system, realigned it grotesquely, and held up all kinds of decisions that sooner or later would have to be made if the United States really intended to develop into a full-fledged nation. Worst of all, it transformed a politics of innovation into a politics of compromise, then rendered compromise itself, except at the most cynical level of bargaining, a flat impossibility. A special quality of irony was inflicted upon this sorry course of political deterioration by such countervailing facts as the growing economic interdependence of the South with other parts of the Union, the swarming of ambitious young Southerners, including John C. Calhoun himself, to the North for a better education than they could get at home,[25] and the always disproportionate number and influence of Southerners in the armed forces of the United States.[26] Moreover, as growth and expansion pushed the South into the position, real and imagined, of a one-down minority, the North began to resent the exaggerated political power, real and imagined, of the whites who ruled at home and, as they saw it, in Washington. Few Northerners were happy with the three-fifths rule of representation after 1820; few Southerners had ever been happy with it.

Whether as institution, idea, or myth, slavery did more than that to injure the cause of popular government, which in those wonderful departed days was the cause of the United States. The perpetuation of this anachronism tarnished the prestige of the new nation in most parts of the world—even, one learns to his chagrin, in Czarist Russia. The diplomacy of the United States was a perplexity for men as different in outlook as Castlereagh, Metternich, and Marx, not least because the common government of the nation was apparently forbidden to abolish slavery, was feeble in performing its self-proclaimed duty to suppress the slave trade,[27] and treated free Negroes in a hundred petty ways as third-class citizens (if citizens at all) of an equality-obsessed republic.[28] Was the United States the most progressive and morally elevated or most reactionary and morally debased of Western nations? Were the statesmen to understand and deal with the government of the United States in terms of the New England town meeting and its westward extensions or the laws of slavery in South Carolina and their westward extensions? America the Liberator, America the Enslaver, America cast by history in both roles—no wonder that diplomats of the caliber of John Quincy Adams had trouble advertising their country as a republican power.[29] However fervidly the indictment may have been denied, America was something of a "slave power" in the calculations of other nations all through the years of the Quest; and the indictment grew stickier as one after another took steps toward emancipation of slaves and suppression of the slave trade, thus gradually isolating the United States from the opinion of the civilized world on this fearful issue.[30] And who could believe in the validity of the American Mission when white Americans made slaves of black men and women from another part of the world—and slaves also of the black offspring of these men and women and the brown offspring of themselves and some of these women?

In chapter 5 we took candid note of the menace to popular cohesion embodied in the presence of black slaves in a predominantly white country, indeed in the presence of blacks of any description, whether kept in bondage, set free, or born free. About this matter, too, I am concerned not to repeat myself; rather, to indicate that the racial assumptions of whites did as much as the alien ways or cultural backwardness of Negroes to discourage attempts to digest them as the Germans, French, Scandinavians, and even, in due course, impoverished Irish were digested. Racism has become a vicious word in our vocabulary; yet it would be dishonest to deny that all but a handful of white Americans, taking their cue from Europe yet going much farther because for them the exotic had become the familiar,[31] were racists in this period. While writing in an objective and nonpejorative manner, I mean to assert candidly that our ancestors, however kind many of them may have been, assumed far more easily than we do the enjoyment of some sort of natural ineradicable, and therefore perpetual, superiority over men of African descent. The evidence amassed by Winthrop Jordan and Leon Litwack is enough to crush any dissent to this assertion,[32] and I have found to my own surprise that a racist strain even permeates the newspapers, speeches, and writings of dauntless abolitionists.[33] The achievement of the goal of popular cohesion commands, at the very least, admission to full citizenship of all persons living loyally within the boundaries of a nation. If Abraham Lincoln, under the prodding of Stephen A. Douglas, could speak in 1858 of the "probably" permanent "social and political" inferiority of the black race to the white, even while insisting upon the Negro's title "to all the natural rights enumerated in the Declaration of Independence," [34] the most sanguine of his listeners could hardly be blamed for continuing to look upon every Negro as a stranger in the land.

At the time he debated with Douglas, Lincoln was more concerned with the influence of slavery than with the condition of the slaves or the potential of all Negroes. In the celebrated "House Divided" speech at Springfield he had already expressed his belief in a kind of Gresham's Law of politics and society:[35] The bad in a nation, if not checked and ultimately eliminated, will sooner or later drive out the good. This belief was held strongly in the free states, in which, to tell the truth, one finds it hard in retrospect to decide whether the institution of slavery (because of immoralities and cruelties), the determination of the South to defend and extend this institution (because of the menace to free society), the great body of slaves (because of their "lack of civility"), or the special class of slaveowners (because of their "arrogant hypocrisy") was the principal offender. In any case, many men were stirred to question the value of a Union that, as Lincoln himself announced repeatedly, might "arrest the further spread" of a baleful institution yet leave it untouched where it already thrived. As they watched the Southern states suppress free speech, tamper with the mails, and harass white men who counseled charity and moderation, all the while flaunting their power in Washington, such men feared for the future of American democracy. Their fears encouraged them to entertain visions of a nation from which states unwilling even to think cautiously about the far-off demise of slavery might be excluded; they wondered if it might not be the wiser course to save the healthy parts of the American Republic than to see all of it racked by dissension, poisoned, and finally done to death. Such fears were a growing peril for the cause of fulfilled nationhood on a continental scale.

Slavery and modernity are so plainly incompatible in fact and principle that it hardly seems necessary to make an elaborate case for the proposition stated above: Slavery in the United States was increasingly a drag upon *modernization*. Having called attention to the leading role of cotton in the growth and expansion of the whole nation,[36] however, I am compelled to pick out a few details on the dark side of the moon. There is no intention to equate the production of cotton with the institution of slavery, for white men labored to grow a sizable portion of the annual crop and, had a single black slave never been carried to America, could sooner or later have grown it all.[37] Nevertheless, cotton claims special attention because, thanks in part to the genius of a Connecticut Yankee, it gave a new life to slavery just when men of good will all over America were dressing themselves (and thus justifying long-standing inaction) for a grand funeral.

First, we may read in the records that slavery was an inefficient means of organizing, training, and directing even unskilled labor. Whatever else a slave may be—and history is full of remarkable men who spent their lives in bondage—he is not, and cannot hope to be, a modern man. While Negro slaves were employed in considerable numbers in manufacturing throughout the South,[38] few performed other than menial tasks. While they contributed a stupendous amount of toil to the building of America, the toil was for the most part unimaginative and undignified. To give the average slave in Georgia the skills of the average factory worker in Massachusetts called for a measure of functional literacy that might open up spacious vistas of political freedom and social equality, and this course was exactly what the white South could not risk. The saddest aspect of a cruel situation was the way in which many of the unacceptable Americans came to believe in their unacceptability and resigned themselves to the status of inferior men who were simply not capable of matching the natural talents and nurtured skills of the white race.[39] That aspect, perhaps, is the clinching point in support of the argument that America sheltered one of the most degrading systems of slavery in the Atlantic world.

If most black slaves were deformed by being assigned chores so simple that immensely clever animals could have performed them, most white citizens were morally brutalized by dealing with human beings as if they were not fully human.[40] Modernity embodies (and, if it does not, it should) the notion of civilized behavior, and few white Southerners, prisoners of the usually vague and occasionally stark terror of insurrection, could manage to be civil, that is to say, respectful of human dignity, in day-to-day dealings with Negro slaves. White Northerners were every bit as uncivil, whether they lived in old areas and dealt with the uncomfortably situated free Negroes or journeyed to new areas and thereupon passed laws forbidding such Negroes to follow after. The confrontation of the races, moreover, raised the endemic violence of American life to an ever higher pitch of intensity.

Yet another drag upon modernization—saddled in this instance by the rancorous controversy over the nature and influence of slavery—was a wasteful diversion of intellectual energy. A nation should scrutinize, ponder, and discuss its great problems with care and at length, yet the debate over slavery had an especially debilitating effect upon the American mind. While historians of our political thought have been heard to thank this debate for producing (behind the smoke screen of the debate over the tariff) Calhoun's doctrine of the concurrent majority, this seems a ridiculous reward for the millions of man-hours that went into reviving the corpse of natural law in the North and joining Aristotle with Sir Walter Scott in unnatural matrimony in the South. An unhappy part of the stultifying burden borne by American literature was the necessity for everyone to have his say—in the nature of things a jaded or vulgar say—about slavery. James Russell Lowell did not attain the first rank of poetry, but he might have come closer to it if his conscience had not prodded him to write the falsely rustic *Biglow Papers*.

In the end, the South itself has a special fascination for students of national development, since it presents a classic case of one proud part of a rapidly modernizing country that fell farther and farther behind the other parts in the rush toward the future even as it helped them unwittingly to engage in the rush. Not only did it refuse to join the American chorus in praise of progress; it encouraged many of its notable men to excoriate progress and brand every departure from ancient ways an act of treason.

So many learned and loyal Southerners have spoken to this question that the Northerner is well advised to be silent and, above all, to resist the temptation to point a finger of scorn or condescension. In any case, the evidence is overflowing that in almost every field of endeavor the South lagged to the rear of the rest of the nation during the first half of the nineteenth century: standard of living, political capability, broad-mindedness of religion, output of literature, degree of literacy, quality and quantity of education, enjoyment of civil liberties, freedom and responsibility of the press, ease of communication and transportation, technological attitudes and achievements, and maintenance of a healthy rural-urban balance.[41] The economic lag was especially visible. It may have been comforting for Southerners to proclaim that, if the name of the game played diligently in Massachusetts was progress, they were glad to be left on the sidelines; yet there was, surely, something desperately wrong about a situation in which that one state alone manufactured 65 per cent more goods than all eleven states of the soon-to-be-formed Confederacy put together.[42] Moreover, the economy of slavery, in which cotton reigned unchallenged, was one from which the North extracted a good deal more than its fair share—in the best years, we are told, tens of millions of scarce dollars. By committing its natural and human resources to a largely agrarian, undiversified economy in which Northern merchants, manufacturers, financiers, and sea captains were delighted to lend a hand for a fat price, the South made itself, economically if not politically, a colony of the North; and who can blame the South for coming more and more to resent colonial status?

The increasingly subordinate and distrustful position of the South became a running sore in the otherwise healthy body of American nationalism, thus confirming again the existence of a link between modernity and nationhood. While the backwardness of Alabama and South Carolina may not have slowed the pace of development in Massachusetts and Illinois in this period, except by making these states a thin market for hawkers of machinery,[43] the slaveholding South counted roughly 35 per cent of the American people in 1860, and the 11 million persons whom this percentage represents were, after all, citizens or denizens of one nation.[44] To occupy so large a neo-traditionalist pocket of resistance was to snarl the progress of the whole United States; to set up a closed society in the midst of the most open society in history was to strain the bonds of the nation to the breaking point. While the South remained doggedly American—as contrasted, for instance, with Quebec or Cuba—it began to take relish in citing Calhoun and other separatists to the effect that men could live as Americans *outside* the Union.

We come, at the conclusion of a sad recital, to this central question: Why was a people dedicated to the goals of nationhood and modernity powerless to dismantle the barrier of slavery stone by stone or, if necessary, demolish it with one huge explosive charge? The answer is a mare's nest of complexity and ambiguity, the historical situation behind it one in which inertia, penury, custom, accident, greed, fear, myth, prejudice, cultural antipathy, false optimism, lack of imagination, lack of political capability, and, paradoxically, the ideology of egalitarianism dug in together and defied efforts to root out the institution peacefully.[45] Northerners doubted both the constitutionality and the practicality of emancipation under the supervision of the national government; Southerners, who might listen occasionally to a discussion of the profitability of slavery, were united in defending it as an instrument of social control of a potentially fractious minority; men of good will everywhere were at a loss to devise even small-scale schemes to give emancipated slaves the substance as well as the appearance of freedom. Indeed, as Tocqueville discerned, the widespread assumption of white superiority gave a depressing cast to most efforts to emancipate the slaves. "It is not for the good of the Negroes," he commented when he had returned to France and found time to reflect, "but for that of the whites, that measures are taken to abolish slavery in the United States." [46]

What was needed, of course, was daring public action funded by heavy federal taxation; and, even assuming that the will for an immense effort had existed, neither such action nor such taxation was possible in the political culture of the age. Even at the state level the white men of the South recognized abolition as a form of social revolution from which it was imperative to steer clear. The famous debate of 1831–1832 in the Virginia legislature over the possibility of gradual, compensated emancipation—the "final and most brilliant of the Southern attempts to abolish slavery" [47] —was hollow in nature, it seems to me, and a victory for the antislavery forces would also have proved hollow if not calamitous. Neither in the South nor anywhere else did men have a clear idea of the why and hows of freeing the slaves, then bringing them into the fullness of American citizenship. Every one of our model men of chapter 7 came in time to detest slavery; not one had any better plan than personal disengagement (Hamilton, Watson,

Walker[48]), a vague notion about diffusion (Jefferson[49]), or the deceiving dream of colonization (Adams*) for the triple-edged problem of freeing the Negro slaves legally, training them to the limits of their hitherto untapped talents, and protecting the nation against disorder while the freeing and training were under way. And even if one of these men had hammered out a plan in the most exhaustive, practical detail, how many of his fellow citizens would have been willing to give it the fifty-year-or-more chance needed for it to work successfully? By 1860 the institution of slavery was too deeply entrenched to be dislodged by other than violent means, and violence, alas, could be only the first hazardous step toward the final solution to the American problem of popular cohesion that continues to puzzle us more than one hundred years later.

As we cast the eye of detachment backward over the circumstances of young America's Quest for nationhood and modernity, we must be struck once again by the spectacle of a lucky country. Accident, heritage, and will interacted to give the people of the United States both a head start in pursuit of glory and a fair field in which to pursue it at an accelerating pace. The pluses of the American ambience were the lavish kind that promise success; the minuses were not the deadly kind that promise failure no matter how determined a people may be to seek a better future. Some, like the size of the enterprise, were likely to change from short-run liabilities into long-run assets if the Union (no trifling "if," to be sure) could survive the short run. Others, like sectionalism and parochialism, were interlocking parts of a totality of circumstance, and harsh suppression of their unpleasant influences would have caused severe damage to other, more benevolent parts. All the pluses had a small minus component; all the minuses had a plus component that was considerably larger.

All, that is to say, except the institution of slavery, which must now be judged by the entire nation, as it was then by only a

* It was, to be sure, a fitful dream of Adams, who expressed most of his disgust and fear of slavery by bewailing it from afar, defending the civil liberties of abolitionists, denouncing the slave trade, and, on one memorable occasion, securing freedom for a shipload of slaves who had struck out on their own and landed in a jail in New Haven.[50]

minority of farseeing black Americans and cranky white Americans, as a curse upon the hopes for unity and progress in the land. While we must reserve most of our pity for the slaves, we may also direct a sizable portion toward the United States itself: the most hopeful, progressive of human experiments to which the most hopeless, retrogressive of human conditions was tenaciously attached, the new order of the ages that harbored a system of labor and social control no longer tolerated by nations of the old order. Slavery was the great sin of a supposedly innocent people, which sinned against itself just as it did against the Africans and their descendants.

It was, at the same time, the great tragedy of this people, which may live forever with the consequences of racially oriented slavery. To ponder the ironic juxtaposition of liberty and slavery in the young Republic, of the "hope of all mankind" and mankind's most pernicious institution, is to wonder if Fate or Providence—some readers may wish to introduce God—had decreed that things not be made too easy for the citizens of the United States in their efforts to become and remain a modern nation. The establishment of all that remarkable machinery in that favorable setting, the flow of a chosen people to tend it imaginatively and productively, and then the tossing-in of the sand of another people remote of origin, dissimilar in culture, unwilling in the coming, oppressed in the staying—this is the kind of large-scale event that turns the thoughts of scholars toward a theology of history. Ulrich B. Phillips once described the determination of Southern whites to preserve a "white man's country" as "the central theme of Southern history." [51] Would it be presumptuous to suggest that this determination, wherever it could be found in 1850 and can be found today, is one of three or four central themes of all American history?

Since I am quite unqualified by training and temper to pose as a theologian of any description, and since I think it important to end this review of the pluses and minuses of the American ambience on an upbeat—the pluses, after all, were far and away more numerous, impressive, and enduring—let me point again to the element of timing. At the close of chapter 9 we took note of the benevolent results of the timing of the American experiment in the context of developments in Europe. Here I would stress the equally benevolent results of the *sequence of developments* in America itself. A half-dozen deserve special mention:

the consciousness of separateness before the strike for independence;

the consummation of independence before the flowering of nationalism;

political preparedness before political sovereignty;

constitutionalism before democracy;

a framework for republican expansion before expansion itself;

economic self-reliance before political independence.

One need only observe at first hand the torments of most new nations of the twentieth century originating in a string of perverse sequences—perverse because too often the exact opposite of American developments—to realize how fortunate the young Republic was to get these important things in, as it were, the correct order. The ambience in which the Americans embarked upon their Quest was both process and reality and in both they were favored "beyond the dreams of avarice." As an ambitious young lawyer put the issue prophetically in 1838:

> If destruction be our lot we must ourselves be its author and finisher. As a nation of freemen we must live through all time, or die by suicide.[52]

The Americans would, indeed, have no one to blame but themselves and nothing to rue but the defects of their own character if they were to fall short of the grand goals of the Quest.

11

Valedictory Musings on the Civil War

as an Ordeal of Nationhood and

a Crisis of Modernity

IT may be judged a feat of intellectual gamesmanship for a devoted Unionist, one who, gazing out from High-Water Mark at Gettysburg, sheds more tears for the Nineteenth Maine than for the First Virginia, to pretend that he can write objectively about the American Civil War. Indeed, so many issues of the Civil War have been probed deeply and debated brilliantly that he who proposes to beget a few thousand more words about it, and thereby to worry the yeas and nays again, runs the risk of being not only biased but stale. Yet write I must of this prodigious event. The Quest led to the Civil War; the war closed out the first stage of American national development; the United States thereupon went off on the next stage under rules that had been significantly amended. A rendering of the accounts of growth and expansion between 1789 and 1861 would be left inexcusably unfinished were it not carried forward to 1865.

Although our concern is with the Civil War as event rather than epic, as an ordeal of nationhood and a crisis of modernity that may in fact be studied objectively, I must acknowledge kinship with those historians who look upon it as a towering tragedy that one cannot begin to comprehend unless he is also willing to be subjective—to go beyond fact to feeling, beyond the statistical to the mystical, beyond prose to poetry. Tocqueville wrote from America in the first weeks of his visit that he had landed amidst a people bathed in a kind of "insipid happiness," a country in which "they have neither war, nor pestilence, nor literature, nor eloquence, nor fine arts, nor revolutions; no great excesses, nothing which wakes attention in Europe." [1] If he had visited us after the bath of fraternal blood in 1861–1865, he would not, surely, have been so condescending. He might have agreed with the most perceptive of latter-day Tocquevilles, Denis Brogan, that the Civil War put the Americans "decisively, once and for all, among the peoples who have lived in interesting times," [2] and with other scholars who see a hitherto innocent nation being propelled for the first time into the "fullness of history," [3] which is sometimes a record of triumph yet always a tale of woe. An extravagant price for a nation to pay in order to become interesting and savor the fullness of a history: the death of more than a half-million young men and the orgy of destruction and suffering that went with it. Yet a trial of such intensity can stir imagination even as it shocks sensibility. The Civil War remains the bloodiest act of the Great American Tragedy. As such an act it displays, paradoxically, an aspect of historical grandeur that has not always been present in our experiment.

The Civil War was an *ordeal of nationhood* that many men had talked of brazenly or vaguely, but that few had predicted soberly or confidently, ever since the founding of the Republic.[4] Like any properly conducted ordeal it was essentially a convergence of challenge and response. In the last analysis, the war was begun by the challenge of the South, which took the form of a shattering demand for independence, and was sustained by the response of the rest of the Union, which took the form of a fierce rejection of the demand.

The moment of challenge was the transformation in 1860–1861 of an exaggerated sectionalism into a self-conscious nationalism that could henceforth be content in the political realm with nothing short of full sovereignty. No longer was secession a muttered threat to be laughed off as the "old Mumbo Jumbo," [5] in James Russell Lowell's sneering phrase; it had suddenly become a blatant fact to be forcibly dealt with. "And the war came," Lincoln said pathetically in 1865,[6] and came chiefly because large numbers of men in a disenchanted part of the Union now agreed in principle, if not in every constitutional detail or emotional spasm, with fire-eaters of long standing like Edmund Ruffin, William L. Yancey, and Robert Barnwell Rhett. The slaveholding states had become, indeed may have always been, a separate nation with an admirable way of life and a high destiny of its own: to be "the proudest and most powerful country that ever flourished in the tide of time." [7] Doubts persist, even among historians friendly to the rebellion, about the quality of Southern nationalism; the conviction is strong that the centrifugal forces which took eleven states out of the Union, had they not been restrained by the power of the North, would have run on and on until the Confederacy itself disintegrated into a swarm of petty sovereignties. Yet the challenge of secession was real, perhaps not at first an assertion of full-blown Southern nationalism, yet certainly a refutation of American nationalism on a continental scale;[8] and one could argue that the eleven states of the Confederacy were as much a nation in fact and feeling in the summer of 1861 as the thirteen ex-colonies had been in the summer of 1776.[9] More than half the member states of the United Nations today are less conscious of their identity and less able to go it alone (if left alone) than were the Confederate States of America in 1861.

If the challenge was shockingly real, the response was unexpectedly explosive. One who looks back anew to the events of 1860–1861 may be surprised not so much by the decision of the South, whether fiery or reluctant, to pull out of the Union as by that of the North, whether vengeful or sober, to veto this decision by force of arms. One may be surprised not so much that Jefferson Davis, distinguished holder of national office in several administrations and soldier in the war with Mexico, should have elected to preside over a dissolution of the United States as that Abraham Lincoln, mediocre occupant of a seat in the House of Representatives for one term and critic of that war, should have elected to forbid the dissolution.

The pivotal facts for us to contemplate, and thereby transform surprise into understanding, are two: First, although then and now projected by the statistics of the election of 1860 as a sectional candidate for the Presidency, Lincoln was the most thoroughgoing American nationalist to occupy the office since John Quincy Adams. Indeed, he could never have hazarded the peace he treasured by moving in force against the Confederacy if he had not been a mystical as well as a constitutional nationalist, a public man for whom the Union was, as it was not for a public man like James Buchanan, an organic entity,[10] an inclusive and exclusive community of souls—some of them, to be sure, temporarily distressed—that was destined to be a nation just as plainly as was Britain or France. And second, Lincoln could take his nation-preserving actions of 1861 with confidence in the support of millions of plain Americans in the North, and also in the knowledge that thousands of leading Americans, including several ambitious governors, were chiding him for indecision and pushing ahead with their own plans to subdue the South. Behind the archetype of the humane nationalist stood an aroused nation that had quietly grown stronger in self-consciousness even as one part edged out into sullen orbit and contemplated an exhilarating dash into space.[11] In this fateful sense—the will and capacity to fight for American unity—the government of the United States was ready to do something in 1861 it could not possibly have done in 1790, 1798, 1814, or even 1832.

The Civil War was thus a huge paradox of history: an impressive challenge to the fact of American nationhood, an impressive display of the toughness of this fact in life as in law. The South's sense of separateness gave it the resolve to secede, then to rally its forces for a fight longer and bloodier than anyone, whether in the South or North or West or Europe, could have predicted; the North's feeling of oneness with the South gave it the resolve to declare secession a constitutional and social impossibility, then to rally its own forces for that kind of fight. Those who seek to understand the causes, conduct, and consequences of the Civil War must keep in mind this twofold reality: an alienated South ready to abandon the Union and break up the American nation, a stubborn North ready to prevent the abandonment forcibly. No mere fancy could have persuaded the majority of Southerners to cut loose from the Union; no mere spite could have persuaded the majority of Northerners to forbid the cutting, to insist, as the British could not insist in 1776, that the arena of controversy was "one nation, indivisible." I take pains to emphasize the double use of that word "majority"; for, just as plenty of Southerners remained loyal to the Union,[12] so plenty of Northerners reacted to the upsurge of nationalism in the South by falling back on a narrow version of the Universal Yankee Nation and reading the "wayward sisters" out of it forever. The belief in a comprehensive American nationhood went through less cruel an ordeal in the free states than in the slave states, yet the vivid spectacle of an aroused North should not blind us to the existence of a tenacious minority of dissenters in its midst. Such men were at last confirmed in the view that the reach of the true nation stopped abruptly at the line behind which slavery flourished pridefully. A few such men had reason to believe that the Civil War began not in 1861, or in 1854 or 1820 or 1787, but far back in 1619, when that first tiny band of miserable Africans was dropped off at Jamestown.

My conviction that the war arose out of the conflict of two nations—one uncertain but tested, the other uncertain and untested but rapidly taking form—refuses to be suppressed. To this faith a comment may be usefully appended: If the United States was more tenaciously a nation in 1861 than all but a handful of statesmen and poets had realized, the fierce clash of arms of the next four years was indeed a *civil* war. It was, moreover, the kind of civil war in which the clash of minds and hearts is every bit as fierce as that of arms, in which principles and emotions vie for influence as causes and determinants with economic conflicts and social divisions. This conclusion may place me among the dwindling band of historians who pay homage to the power of ideas to shake the world or make it over, a place I gladly accept.

The war was also a *crisis of modernity,* a point that many scholars have either overlooked casually or dealt with narrowly in Marxist or crypto-Marxist terms. Slavery, expansion, the extension of slavery, sectionalism, nationalism, the rise of Northern industrialism, the doggedness of Southern agrarianism, the decline of Southern political power, the anger of Northerners over the obdurate capacity of this power to block national undertakings, well-meaning blunders and savage feuds, agitation and counter-agitation, the escalation of wounded egos, the fall of the cards of American destiny—these are the most prominent "causes of the Civil War," [13] and each commands respectful attention. At the same time, I suggest that one other cause be added to the list: the widening gulf between a North perhaps too dedicated to the goals of modernity and a South perhaps scornful of these goals. As

Senator James M. Mason, of Virginia, declaimed boldly at the outset of this conflict, the Union and the Confederacy were embarking on "a war of sentiment and opinion," a war between "one form of society" and "another form of society." [14] Despite their common heritage and interests, the two societies had become different enough in style and purpose to force a bloody duel, and a large part of the difference arose out of the commitment of the one and antipathy of the other to a new, kinetic, industrial way of life.

We have already taken note of the backwardness of the South. Only one further observation needs to be made: As this proud section lagged farther and farther behind the rest of the country in just about every field but manners and marksmanship, it felt less and less kinship with other sections, which had succumbed greedily or mindlessly—such was the view from Charleston and even New Orleans—to the false lures of industrialization. In purpose, mood, and style the South of 1860 was a neo-traditional enclave within a developing country. Once again the concept of historical irony can help us to grapple with the consequences of the confrontation of a newly minted old order and an oldly ordained new order, to make sense out of the sad spectacle of a cheerful course of national development transformed overnight into a dreadful civil war. How else can we describe the situation in 1860 when, at the moment the American people were tensing for a great leap forward in every area of personal and social endeavor, a neo-traditional nation that had grown up within the body of the rapidly modernizing nation attempted to bring the whole structure down with a crash? How else can we describe a situation in which, while the political, social, intellectual, and emotional ties between the South and the rest of the Union had weakened with each passing year, the economic tie, in startling counterpoint, had grown steadily stronger? How else can we bestow a single plus on the institution of slavery, a circumstance of American life compounded of minuses, unless we recognize that this apparently firm foundation of an agrarian, dependent, neo-colonial economy fed, with cotton or cash or debt, the mills and ships of New England, the banks and trading enterprises of New York, and the farms and trading routes of the West?

The confrontation of North and South, which moved with

frightening speed from an exchange of pompous words to a duel of bloody wills, was at bottom a falling out between one part of a legally constituted nation racing into the future and another holding tightly to the values and institutions of a more serene past. While the North had pockets of backwardness and the South felt pressures for modernization, the over-all situation was one in which a gap was opening dangerously between the two— and becoming harder to accept complacently in the part that served as a kind of economic colony. In sum, *a principal cause of the Civil War was the uneven pace of modernization* in two sections of a nation already divided over the legitimacy, utility, and influence of Negro slavery. To put the matter in terms of the twofold concern of this study, *modernization* hastened the threatened day of secession even as *nationalism* prepared to spoil the day for the secessionists.

About the conduct of the war I need make only a few observations, conscious as I am, both painfully and gratefully, of the stupefying amount of energy wise men have poured into the task of setting forth the whats and hows and whys of a struggle without precedent in history. We may focus attention on the twin phenomena of nationhood and modernity in an effort to assess their influence upon the outcome of a war they had done much to ignite.

Let me reverse the customary order and point first to the fact that the more modern part of the divided nation—the more machine-centered, industrialized, opportunity-laden, fluid, literate, and innovative—had a clear-cut margin of superiority over the other part. Although few men in the opening phase of the war could grasp the meaning of the fact, we can see that the whip hand of modernity, if directed by a strong will, was bound to prove decisive in the long run, to prevail as the kind of advantage that no other combination of advantages such as morale, military skill, foreign sympathy, and geography could overcome. While the South drew ingeniously on untapped sources of talent to produce new weapons and skills in the course of the struggle, the North had a distinct edge in factories for boots and rifles, in techniques of supplying armies and summoning opinion to their support, and, to offer a specific example worth twenty or thirty divisions, in railroads that ran from here to there directly rather than from here to there by way of nowhere. At the end of the Civil War the Union had put the most modern armed forces ever known into the field and was backing them up with the second most modern organization of society. Looked at cold-bloodedly from this point of vantage, the South, despite all its valor and staying power, seems to have been doomed from the beginning.

By the same token, the enduring nationhood of the North proved impossible for the nascent nationhood of the South to overcome or even (the most realistic of Confederate hopes) to fight to a stalemate. Seizing again upon the revealing contrast in the quality of leadership of the two causes, I would suggest that the positive, encompassing, tradition-supported patriotism of Abraham Lincoln carried mightier weight than the negative, limited, tradition-shattering patriotism of Jefferson Davis, whether in the minds of each man's people or in the recesses of his soul. This kind of patriotism, multiplied millions of times over, steeled the Union for a long haul and thereby granted the material advantages of modernity an opportunity to assert themselves.

Neither side, we know, fought the war as a monolithic nation. Davis was harried by the pretensions to sovereignty of Georgia and Alabama; Lincoln could almost taste the fingers of Massachusetts and Illinois in the military pie.[15] The evidence is nevertheless conclusive that the Union commanded more vigorous support and suffered less debilitating inefficiency from its pattern of federalism than did the South from its pattern of confederacy. Federalism-as-principle encouraged millions of Northerners to have faith in their cause and led them, in the end, to the formula for peace; federalism-as-practice made possible, in defiance of the political culture of nineteenth-century America, the mustering of one of the largest forces in history. The principle and practice of confederacy, although finely tuned to the political culture of this special part of a lost America, prevented the South from mounting the concentrated, all-out effort that could have stamped the seals of long life and recognized legitimacy on the cause of secession. The Union held fast because it was a *federal nation;* the South faltered and finally collapsed because it was a *confederate nation*—a phrase that some historians and political scientists might wish to rewrite as *non-nation.*[16]

Valedictory Musings

The chief service of federalism to the cause of continental nationhood seems to have been, in retrospect, the incorporation of the West as an array of free states. The United States, we have learned, pushed its way triumphantly through the Appalachians, across the Mississippi, onto the Great Plains, over the Rockies, and down to the Pacific because it marched as a republican empire promising full equality to the communities that were sent ahead—or that went ahead in ignorance or defiance of its will. Thanks to the federal principle embodied in the Northwest Ordinance and the Constitution, the West was settled by Americans and for America; and, when the time of decision came for this America, the West rallied in exuberant might to swing the decision against the South; it provided, in the famous phrase, the cement of Union when the nation was in deepest peril.

One thinks—one can never be sure—that a United States confined to the coastal area, even to the eastern bank of the Mississippi, might have split in two with little agony in 1860–1861. The birth and flourishing of states like Iowa, California, and Minnesota, however, not only *forced* the issue in the form of political tussles over the admission of new states with slavery-protecting, slavery-outlawing, or slavery-ignoring constitutions; it *settled* the issue in the form of the free states that had gained admission. The settlement, as much of the Old World had to learn the hard way, was in favor of the continental nation. As the one major section that could not afford, economically or emotionally, to go it alone without the other two, the West—symbolized in the persons of Lincoln himself, of Grant and Sherman, of their legions, and of the "folks at home"—tipped the scales for the Union with a hard fist. Any young man of the Twentieth Maine or Thirteenth Vermont would have told us that the West did not win the war all by itself; yet this newest part of a New World, so new that the paint on its capitol domes had barely begun to dry, furnished the margin of victory in an otherwise dubious struggle. "The young giant that is growing up in the West," Michael Chevalier had foretold a generation before, "seems destined to fulfill the prophecy *the last shall be first,* and to hold together the North and the South in his vigorous grasp." [17] Was he thinking, we may wonder, of the upper Mississippi Valley or of its hero-in-hiding, Abraham Lincoln?

. . .

Not the causes or conduct but the consequences of the Civil War must be our chief interest, for they loomed enormously over the subsequent course of American national development. Like even the most just and necessary wars it left a bitter heritage: death, destruction, corruption, economic disarray, antagonism, the wasting of men and treasure and souls. The backward South was shoved farther to the rear of the American procession, and was also encouraged for a generation or longer to be more separatist in self-identity.[18] The North, too, had youthful dead to mourn, widening gaps between classes to contemplate, cynical politics to bewail, inflated prices to bring down, and eroded values to shore up. It had, moreover, as Thomas Cochran has proved to the satisfaction of most historians,[19] an economy that was damaged rather than stimulated as an immediate result.

Yet the war decided questions of immense historical importance that might have been left in the air as poisoning agents for decades to come, and decided them in a manner that permitted no appeal. The aborted revolution of 1861–1865 was like the fulfilled Revolution of 1765–1789: more earth-shaking in consequence than in intention, more remarkable for what it settled than for what men had taken up arms to settle. By removing or reordering huge piles of political, social, and intellectual debris that had cluttered the landscape of the Quest, it opened a new road to a new future of which some Americans were fearful, even in the victorious North, but about which most were confident as only Americans of those days could be.

In the first place, it *wiped out slavery* as a legal, social, and economic institution, first by withdrawing the support of the national government, then by doing the uncivilized institution to death with two swift blows. If the blows were not swift enough for all-out abolitionists like William Lloyd Garrison, Frederick Douglass, and Theodore Dwight Weld—or, more to the point, for the host of slaves—they were astonishingly abrupt and thus truly revolutionary in the long view of history. Emancipation did not, we know too well, incorporate the ex-slaves fully into the developing nation, solve our stickiest problem of popular cohesion, or eliminate white feelings of superiority and black feelings of inferiority.[20] Yet the war as finally understood and fought did things with the sword that all the haranguing and cajoling in the American political system had not been able to do: free the slaves, raise the problem of their long-standing servitude and sudden freedom to the national level at least temporarily, bring them suddenly more than halfway into the family (not yet "children," according to Douglass, but certainly "step-children" of America),[21] and put an end to the demeaning role of the United States as a slave power in the concert of nations. No one can be certain just when legal slavery in the South would have withered away had there been no Civil War; anyone who gets a sense of the power of the Southern commitment to this institution can be certain that it would have lasted a long time.[22] To have compressed that span of time to the few years between the formation of the Confederacy, February 4–March 11, 1861, and the proclamation of the Thirteenth Amendment, December 18, 1865, was an achievement of epic dimensions, the kind of achievement that war, alas, has too often brought off triumphantly where peace failed.

Second, the Civil War *tested the political system* of the United States mercilessly, and the system survived to answer "yes" to the long-debated question whether a continent could be governed on republican principles. While it had failed the American people by finding no peaceful solution to the twin problems of eliminating slavery and cementing the Union—or would one be more correct to say that the American people had failed it?—the system rose to the challenge of the South by feeling its way successfully into areas where American politics had never dared to go: It constructed and fueled the largest, most awesome machine of organized violence the world had known, kept the military managers of this machine out of the business of governing, and dismantled it abruptly when it was no longer needed. The national government demonstrated a hitherto untapped capability in the activities of famous men like Lincoln, Seward, Chase, Stanton, and Welles, as well as in those of the forgotten men and women who made the semiofficial Sanitary Commission a major force for victory; it demonstrated a hitherto untested obedience to the ground rules of constitutional democracy in the unprecedented elections of 1862 and 1864. These acts of obedience gave ordinary men an added reason to subscribe to the values embodied in the ground rules. While Henry James was right to judge that the war "introduced into the national consciousness a certain sense of proportion and relation, of the world being a more complicated place" than Americans had realized, he was wrong to add that "the future" now seemed "more treacherous" and "successes more difficult." [23] The democratic faith, reinforced by the substantial fact of victory and deepened by the splendid myth of Lincoln, would be more than a match, most Americans now believed, for any complications that might arise to plague their nation. The end of American innocence did not mean the end of American democracy.

It is not the province of these pages to speculate whether any war, even one fought under the direction of an Abraham Lincoln, can be described honestly as democratic. It should be enough to point out that American-style constitutional democracy flourished in the midst of this bloody war, helped both organizationally and spiritually to record a fateful victory, and emerged at the end stronger and more capable than ever before. If the political system weakened again in the Age of Enterprise, that was because the exuberant Americans who dominated the age lacked the will, rather than the capacity, to exercise public control of economic and social forces. Their faith in old-fashioned but newly oriented Jeffersonian democracy led them to believe that a government stripped down to a skeleton of inertia remained the best possible servant of liberty, equality, and progress.

The supreme test of both the durability of American democracy and the validity of its peculiar mission, the war also served as *the final layer of cement for the American Union,* which Lincoln rightly interpreted as the shield of democracy and vehicle of the mission. The ambiguous legacy of 1787 has never vanished completely from our minds and politics, yet the most dangerous feature of the ambiguity was eliminated when the doctrine of secession, if not that of states' rights, was buried alive at Appomattox and Durham's Station. Politically, constitutionally, and emotionally we have been a Union-in-perpetuity since 1865 as we were never, at any time, before 1861. Many citizens who cannot keep pace with the onward movement of America as a just, democratic, and cohesive nation may hate the government in Washington, yet from the most hate-filled of such people we no longer hear talk of secession as the ultimate solution to their problems; and secession

Valedictory Musings

is, after all, the cutting edge of any true belief in the existence of sovereign states. It is a strange turn of history that the only talk of political separatism today comes from the most hate-filled descendants of the men, the freed slaves of the decades that followed the war, at whose expense—let Americans not be afraid to face this ugly truth—the reconciliation of victorious North and defeated South was largely achieved.

At the same time, the Civil War did much to *confirm the nationhood of the United States.* It denied the petition of the South to separate and form a second American nation, and did so without alienating the affections of this section catastrophically or permanently. It gave a boost to the orators of self-conscious American nationalism; tied the economies of East and West together more tightly while leaving a place, although still a subordinate place, for the South; put tens of thousands of recent immigrants through an intensive course in Americanization; and at last, in the Fourteenth Amendment, gave American citizenship a properly national character. Perhaps most important, the voluntary withdrawal of the Southern delegations from Congress opened the floodgates that had been holding back the rising tide of demands for national legislation. The departure of men like former Senators Jefferson Davis and Robert Toombs (and, for that matter, former President James Buchanan) from Washington was a signal for creative action. Soon the Morrill Act providing for grants of land in support of new colleges, the Homestead Act, the National Bank Acts, the Pacific Railway Act, and the Act of 1862 establishing a Department of Agriculture came bursting forth to transform many areas of American life under the hand of a national government suddenly cured of paralysis.[24] While America's exaggerated "Irish Question" had taken on a new and menacing character in 1860–1861, its "Irishmen" had unwittingly given a new and exhilarating vigor to the political system by the simple act of taking themselves temporarily out of its councils.

In confirming the nationhood of the United States, the Civil War *resolved the crisis of modernity* and thus pledged the whole nation to the pursuit of every goal with redoubled intensity. The war was not itself an unusually forceful stimulus to industrialization. Yet as a violent contest between two ways of life in which one, the essentially industrial, overpowered the other, the essentially agrarian, it made sure that the first Quest would lead to an intensified second one. The preparations of the 1840's and 1850's would become the achievements of the 1870's and ever since; the process of national development would give way to a process of nation-building; relentless industrialization would go forward, as it were, under the Great Seal of the United States. Is it possible that Britain, the most modern of then existing nations, was sympathetic to the South because it recognized its own lost innocence and hostile to the North because now, for the first time, it faced the distressing prospect of being overtaken?

The most abiding consequence of the Civil War as comprehended and won by Lincoln and his friends—right down to the uncouth plowboy or prosaic mill hand who sensed why he had been summoned to die at Cold Harbor—was the *forging of an indissoluble American unity.* This easily overlooked but intractable unity has had two momentous meanings for the twentieth century: First, we were assured that no more wars would take place *inside* the United States, that classes might struggle, races glower, interests compete maliciously, and extremists mouth the vile language of revolution or reaction and go about smashing and bombing with relish, yet that section would no longer use brute force against section; and, second, both our friends and enemies *outside* were put on notice that when this continent was beckoned or enticed to throw its weight onto the scale of international politics, the weight would be thrown in one huge lump, as it was (unlike the weight of South America) in 1917, 1941, 1946, and 1950, and is (unlike that of South America) today. The basic fact about the position of the United States in the modern world, to which warm friends, hot enemies, and cool associates alike must adjust their policies of peace and war, is not that we are rich, modern, democratic, and powerful—although we have some right to think we are all these things—but that we are a nation, *one sovereign community* in a territory where two or three or five or perhaps ten might have come to life, endured, and gained membership in the United Nations, and then might have feared, bickered, and occasionally fought. The political, economic, and military results of any such development are fascinating but not pleasant for Americans to imagine.

If we set the sovereign United States against chopped-up South

America, think of the contrasting capacities of each continent to use its lush resources, and total up the contrasting amounts of power each can bring to bear for good or ill in the political, economic, and military affairs of the world, we may begin to fathom the true importance of Lincoln, not so much as democrat, statesman, commander, man of words, emancipator, and martyr, but as, first of all, preserver of the Union. We are seldom clearheaded about the virtues and deeds of our heroes, and I therefore always read the inscription behind the brooding figure of Lincoln in his Memorial in Washington as a refreshingly honest statement of historical truth. He sits in majesty not as the man who freed the slaves, but as the man who saved the Union. It was his real glory, his claim to have grasped the nettle of history, that he identified the Union with the American nation and both together with democracy. Only as Unionist, nationalist, and democrat could he have fought this bloody war to victory, indeed have steeled himself to fight it at all. This, we can be certain, was his essential contribution to history: He gave substance to the visionary premise of the lonely, forgotten Alexander Hamilton that the Union was a nation; and then he added, as Hamilton could never add, that to be a nation America had to be a democracy.

We come at last to take the measure of the Quest in the foggy yet exacting perspective of our own time. Several observations ought to be made before I say, after H. L. Mencken, "Thus ruminating, I subside."

First, to the extent that a jumbled chapter in the history of imperfect man can ever be one, the years from Washington to Lincoln were a success story. I lay myself open to the charge of arbitrariness in suggesting that four examples of national development—the Britain that bubbled its way from Henry VIII to and beyond the Duke of Bridgewater, the Japan of the Meiji, the Soviet Union of Lenin and Stalin, and the United States of the Quest—stand out above all others in achievement and interest. The charge of first-degree filiopietism may be tacked on when it is learned that I rank the United States first among these four. I take the risk calmly, however, because this judgment strikes me as fundamentally correct. The history of the world is full of unified nations that wanted to be developed societies and of developed societies that wanted to be unified nations. It is almost empty of countries that managed to become both—and scored the rare triumph as a constitutional democracy in the act of expanding as well as developing. The people that Washington led, Tocqueville observed, and both Lincoln and Davis called to battle has a special place in the record of human achievement.

The American record was flawed by one grievous fault and many unpleasant excesses, yet the story of every successful and notable people, like the career of every good and famous man, has streaks of weakness and failure. The achievements of nations, like those of men, are always pocked with lamentable blemishes or saddled with deferred payments. One must therefore judge them in a frame of mind that is conscious of both the possible and the impossible in the historical process. Thus judged, the United States of 1790–1860—an experiment without precedent in scale and intensity as a popular and voluntary commitment to innovation, expansion, growth, mobility, democracy, individualism, and nationalism—takes second place to no country in modern history, not even to the United States of later years; and for that United States, after all, it laid the solid foundation.

Odd but not absurd to relate, the Civil War remains the most convincing argument that the Quest had been successful. The pace of modernization in the free states did as much as the increase in population, the expansion to the West, or the attack on slavery to convince the South that it must at last transform secession from rhetorical threat into political fact; the growth of organic nationalism did more than the desire for vengeance or the traditional Northern interpretation of the Constitution to convince the rest of the country that secession was a blow to the hopes of the whole United States—and thus a blow to be countered with limitless force.

Much of the interest in the American experiment lies in the character of the American Method, in which politics slowed down as the economy and society speeded up. Except for the decisive actions of 1787 and the few years that followed, the fourth ingredient in the standard recipe for national development had less consequence than in any other success story in modern history. Not even the England of the Industrial Revolution, a classic arena in which the nongovernmental impulse could flex its muscles, gave such feeble political direction or thin political support to men bent on raising their country to the status of modern nationhood. This has been said before, yet it bears saying again in conclusion as the central theme of this study: While the nation boomed, its political system languished; while Americans mobilized for effervescent change in their economy and society, their government fell upon palsied days. We may think that Hamilton and Adams were more farsighted in their political prescriptions for glory than were Watson and Walker; we know that the Watsons and Walkers of the United States, especially men of the latter stripe, had their way. Since a retrospective view of the American ambience of the first half of the nineteenth century leads to the judgment that it was probably the only way, it may also have been the best way.

The over-all success of this unique method of achieving nationhood and modernity makes the United States of the Quest, somewhat paradoxically, *a nonmodel for the new nations of the twentieth century*. Our situation made it possible and perhaps even preferable to speed along the way with little help from politics; theirs, in which vague hopes have become immediate demands, deprives them of this option. We, in common parlance, had everything going for us, or nearly everything; they have little or nothing, whether of resources or skills or experience. Most important in the sight of history (and for the instruction of the historian who seeks to understand it), we could afford to take our time; they, under savage pressure to telescope centuries into decades and decades into years, simply cannot, lest desolation or chaos be their fate. If the new nations are to succeed in their own quests, they must brandish vigorously the one weapon of mobilization we were allowed to leave rusting in the scabbard. With the aid of government they may get nowhere or worse; without it they have no hope of achievement. In short, we were spared the agonies of a gamble they are forced to make—and which too many, alas, are doomed to lose because of crippling circumstance, incompetence, ignorance, apathy, intransigence, the dead weight of tradition, the lust for power, or the lack of a superhuman political capacity to perform tasks that would baffle the most skilled public servants in the developed world.

Yet if emerging America cannot serve as a general model for

the emerging nations of the twentieth century, it can provide specific warnings they might heed with profit. Three such warnings strike me as fateful and true, full of promise if heeded and full of calamity if disregarded by any would-be modern nation:

It must be *democratic* in the sense of involving and rewarding the whole body of the people.

It must be *constitutional* in the sense of injecting ample doses of regularity and predictability into its political procedures.

It must be *individualistic* in the sense of respecting the dignity of every man, unchaining his ambitions, acknowledging his rights, caring for his needs, and listening to his voice.

Each country of the twentieth century has its own definition, shaped by memory and reshaped by hope, of democracy, constitutionalism, and individualism; none that reaches out for nationhood and modernity can expect victory in the great gamble if it fails to make room for these things in its way of life. Indeed, in the overorganized world where some countries already dwell, the values and practices of democracy, constitutionalism, and individualism are more plainly than ever the indispensable ingredients of a humane way of life. They, too, are like fire and the sword: They may destroy the society in which they function, yet without their assistance no society worth preserving against destruction can arise to claim the allegiance of decent, self-respecting, modern men.

One last word, spoken from yesterday yet speaking to tomorrow: Although the nation may pass away and modernity be redefined in either more sophisticated or more austere terms, both will be remembered as the principal agents of a famous civilization of which the young United States was both forerunner and archetype. For that reason if for no other, the Quest commands the respect of history. The Americans went in search of something to which all but a few men aspire; they found a larger portion of it than all but a few will ever know.

Bibliography

Notes

Index

Bibliography

SHORT TITLES

AHR   *American Historical Review*
JAH   *Journal of American History*
JEH   *Journal of Economic History*
WMQ   *William and Mary Quarterly*

  B   substantial Bibliography
CB   substantial Critical Bibliography
BN   Footnotes with bibliography aids (not footnotes
        referring to quotes, etc.)

I. OFFICIAL, DOCUMENTARY, AND
PRIMARY SOURCES

American State Papers (Washington, 1832–1861)
    Foreign Relations, 6 vols.
    Indian Affairs, 2 vols.
    Finance, 5 vols.
    Commerce and Navigation, 2 vols.
    Military Affairs, 7 vols.
    Naval Affairs, 4 vols.
    Post Office, 1 vol.
    Public Lands, 8 vols.
    Claims, 1 vol.
    Miscellaneous, 2 vols.
Annual Report of the Secretary of the Treasury (Washington, 1837–)
Census of the United States (Washington, 1790–)
Congressional Directory (Washington, 1809–)
Executive Documents of the Senate and House of Representatives (New
    York, 1790–)
Historical Statistics of the United States (Washington, 1949)

The American Quest

Official Opinions of Attorneys-General (Washington, 1852)

Register of All Officers and Agents, Civil, Military, and Naval, in the Service of the United States (Washington, 1816–)

Register of Debates in Congress, also known as *Annals of Congress, Congressional Debates,* and *Congressional Globe* (Washington, 1834–)

James D. Richardson, ed., *A Compilation of the Messages and Papers of the Presidents,* 10 vols. (Washington, 1896)

United States Statutes at Large (Boston, 1850–)

United States Supreme Court Reports, which in earlier years bore the name of the reporter—Dallas, Cranch, Wheaton, Peters, Howard, Black, Wallace, Otto

PERIODICALS

The American Agriculturist (1842–)

American Railroad Journal (1832–)

The Continental Monthly: Devoted to Literature and National Politics (1862–1864)

De Bow's Commercial Review of the South and West (1846–1850); *De Bow's Review of the Southern and Western States* (1850–1852); *De Bow's Review and Industrial Resources, Statistics, etc.* (1853–1864); *De Bow's Review, Devoted to the Restoration of the Southern States* (1866–1867)

Harper's New Monthly Magazine (1850–)

Harper's Weekly (1857–)

Journal of the Franklin Institute (1826–)

The Knickerbocker; or, New York Monthly Magazine (1833–)

The Lady's Book (1830–1839); *Godey's Lady's Book and Ladies' American Magazine* (1840–1843); *Godey's Magazine and Lady's Book* (1844–1848); *Godey's Lady's Book* (1848–1854); *Godey's Lady's Book and Magazine* (1854–1883)

The Merchants Magazine and Commercial Review (1839–1850 and 1860–1870); *Hunt's Merchants' Magazine* (1850–1860)

North American Review (1815–)

Southern Quarterly Review (1842–)

The United States Magazine and Democratic Review (1837–1851); *The Democratic Review* (1852); *The United States Review* (1853–1855); *The United States Democratic Review* (1856–1859)

The Weekly Register (1811–1814); *Niles' Weekly Register* (1814–1837); *Niles' National Register* (1837–1849)

Bibliography

II. TRAVELERS' ACCOUNTS

Edward Strutt Abdy, *A Journal of Residence and Tour of the United States of North America,* 3 vols. (London, 1835)

Carl David Arfwedson, *The United States and Canada, in 1832, 1833, and 1834* (1834), 2 vols. (New York, 1969)

Francis Wright D'Arusmont, *View of Society and Manners* (1822) (Cambridge, 1963), Paul Baker, ed.

Gustave de Beaumont, *Marie, or Slavery in the United States: A Novel of Jacksonian America* (1835) (Stanford, 1958)

Karl Bernhard, Duke of Saxe-Weimar Eisenach, *Travels Through North America During the Years 1825 and 1826* (Philadelphia, 1828)

Morris Birkbeck, *Letters from Illinois* (Philadelphia, 1818)

———, *Notes on a Journey in America* (London, 1818)

Samuel Blodget, *Thoughts on Increasing Wealth and National Economy of the United States* (Washington, 1801)

Fredrika Bremer, *Homes of the New World,* 3 vols. (London, 1853)

Jacques Pierre Brissot de Warville, *New Travels in the United States of America, 1788* (1794) (Cambridge, 1964), Durand Echeverria, ed.

James Silk Buckingham, *America: Historical, Statistical and Descriptive,* 8 vols. (London, 1841)

George William Carlisle, *Travels in America* (New York, 1851)

Michael Chevalier, *Society, Manners, and Politics in the United States* (1839) (Garden City, 1961), John W. Ward, ed.

William Cobbet, *The Emigrant's Guide* (London, 1830)

———, *A Year's Residence in the United States,* 3 vols. (London, 1818)

Henry Steele Commager, ed., *America in Perspective* (New York, 1948)

Michel Guillaume Jean de Crèvecoeur, *Journey into Northern Pennsylvania and the State of New York* (1801) (Ann Arbor, 1964), Clarissa Spencer Bostelmann, trans.

Charles Dickens, *American Notes* (London, 1842)

———, *Martin Chuzzlewit* (New York, 1844)

Timothy Dwight, *Travels in New England and New York* (1821–1822) (Cambridge, 1969), Barbara Miller Solomon, ed.

Durand Echeverria, *Mirage in the West: A History of the French Image of American Society to 1815* (Princeton, 1957) CB

Isaac Fidler, *Observation on Professions, Literature, Manners, and Emigration in the United States* (New York, 1833)

Marvin Fisher, *Workshops in the Wilderness: The European Response to American Industrialization, 1830–1860* (New York, 1967)

Thomas Colley Grattan, *Civilized America* (1859), 2 vols. (New York, 1969)

Francis Joseph Grund, *The Americans in Their Moral, Social, and Political Relations* (1837) (New York, 1969)

———, *Aristocracy in America,* 2 vols. (London, 1839)

Basil Hall, *Travels in North America in the Years 1827–1828,* 3 vols. (London, 1829)

Thomas Hamilton, *Men and Manners in America,* 2 vols. (Philadelphia, 1833)

Oscar Handlin, ed., *This Was America* (Cambridge, 1949) B

Isaac Holmes, *An Account of the United States Derived from Actual Observation,* 4 vols. (London, 1823)

Axel Leonhard Klinckowstrom, *Baron Klinckowstrom's America* (1824) (Evanston, 1952), Franklin D. Scott, ed.

George W. Knepper, ed., *Travels in the Southland, 1822–1823: The Journal of Lucius Verus Bierce* (Columbus, 1966)

Sir Charles Lyell, *A Second Visit to the United States,* 2 vols. (New York, 1849)

———, *Travels in the United States,* 2 vols. (London, 1845)

Alexander Mackay, *The Western World, or, Travels in the United States in 1846–1847,* 3 vols. (London, 1850)

Frederick Marryat, *A Diary in America* (New York, 1839)

Harriet Martineau, *Retrospect of a Western Travel* (1838), 2 vols. (New York, 1969)

———, *Society in America,* 3 vols. (London, 1839)

Jane L. Mesick, *The English Traveller in America, 1775–1835* (New York, 1922) B

Francisco de Miranda, *The New Democracy in America* (1929) (Norman, 1963), Judson P. Wood, trans.

Frank Monaghan, *French Travellers in the United States, 1765 to 1932* (New York, 1933)

Moreau de Saint Méry, *American Journey* (Garden City, 1947), Kenneth and Anna M. Roberts, eds. and trans.

Achille Murat, *America and the Americans* (New York, 1849)

Charles Augustus Murray, *Travels in North America,* 2 vols. (London, 1839)

Allan Nevins, ed., *America Through British Eyes* (New York, 1948) B

———, *American Social History as Recorded by British Travellers* (New York, 1931) B

Frederick Olmstead, *The Cotton Kingdom: A Traveller's Observation on Cotton and Slavery in the American Slave States* (New York, 1861)

———, *A Journey in the Back Country* (New York, 1860)

Bibliography

————, *A Journey in the Seaboard Slave States with Remarks on Their Economy* (New York, 1856)

George W. Pierson, *Tocqueville in America* (Garden City, 1959) B

George E. Probst, ed., *The Happy Republic* (New York, 1962)

Friedrich Ludwig von Raumer, *America and the American People* (New York, 1846)

James Stirling, *Letters from a Slave State* (London, 1857)

James Stuart, *Three Years in North America*, 2 vols. (London, 1833)

Lady Emmeline Stuart-Wortley, *Travels in the United States* (New York, 1851)

Joseph Sturge, *A Visit to the United States in 1841* (London, 1842)

Alexis de Tocqueville, *Democracy in America* (1835), 2 vols. (New York, 1954), Phillips Bradley, ed.

Frances Trollope, *Domestic Manners of the Americans* (London, 1832)

Henry Theodore Tuckerman, *America and Her Commentators* (New York, 1864)

Sir Joseph Whitworth and George Wallis, *The Industry of the United States in Machinery, Manufactures, and Useful and Ornamental Arts* (London, 1854)

III. COLLECTED WORKS

Charles F. Adams, ed., *The Works of John Adams,* 10 vols. (Boston, 1850–1856)

Lyman H. Butterfield, ed., *Diary and Autobiography of John Adams,* 4 vols. (Cambridge, 1961)

Lester Cappon, ed., *The Adams-Jefferson Letters* (Chapel Hill, 1959)

Charles F. Adams, ed., *Memoirs of John Quincy Adams,* 12 vols. (Philadelphia, 1874–1877)

Worthington Chauncey Ford, ed., *Writings of John Quincy Adams,* 7 vols. (New York, 1913–1917)

Allan Nevins, ed., *The Diary of John Quincy Adams, 1794–1845* (New York, 1919)

Seth Ames, ed., *Works of Fisher Ames,* 2 vols. (Boston, 1854)

Thomas Hart Benton, *Thirty Years View,* 2 vols. (New York, 1854–1856)

Reginald McGrane, ed., *The Correspondence of Nicholas Biddle Dealing with National Affairs, 1807–1844* (Boston, 1919)

Richard Crallé, ed., *Works of John C. Calhoun,* 6 vols. (New York, 1851–1881)

Robert L. Meriwether, ed., *Papers of John C. Calhoun,* 4 vols. to date (Columbia, 1959–)

The American Quest

Calvin Colton, ed., *The Works of Henry Clay*, 6 vols. (New York, 1857)

William W. Campbell, *The Life and Writings of DeWitt Clinton* (New York, 1849)

E. W. Emerson, ed., *The Complete Works of Ralph Waldo Emerson*, 12 vols. (Boston, 1903–1904)

—— and W. E. Forbes, eds., *Journals of Ralph Waldo Emerson*, 10 vols. (Boston, 1909–1914)

Henry Adams, ed., *The Writings of Albert Gallatin*, 3 vols. (Philadelphia, 1879)

John C. Hamilton, ed., *The Works of Alexander Hamilton*, 7 vols. (New York, 1850–1851)

Henry Cabot Lodge, ed., *The Works of Alexander Hamilton*, 9 vols. (New York, 1885–1886)

Harold C. Syrett, ed., *Papers of Alexander Hamilton*, 15 vols. to date (New York, 1961–)

John S. Bassett, ed., *Correspondence of Andrew Jackson*, 7 vols. (Washington, 1926–1933)

Julian P. Boyd, ed., *Papers of Thomas Jefferson*, 17 vols. (Princeton, 1950–1965)

Paul Leicester Ford, ed., *The Writings of Thomas Jefferson*, 12 vols. (New York, 1904–1905)

Andrew A. Lipscomb, ed., *The Writings of Thomas Jefferson*, 20 vols. (Washington, 1903–1904)

C. R. King, *The Life and Correspondence of Rufus King*, 6 vols. (New York, 1894–1900)

Roy P. Basler, ed., *The Collected Works of Abraham Lincoln*, 8 vols. (New Brunswick, 1953)

Gaillard Hunt, ed., *The Writings of James Madison*, 9 vols. (New York, 1900–1910)

William T. Hutchinson and M. E. Rachal, eds., *Papers of James Madison*, 6 vols. to date (Chicago, 1962–)

John P. Roche, ed., *John Marshall: Major Opinions and Other Writings* (Indianapolis, 1967)

Stanislaus Murray Hamilton, ed. *The Writings of James Monroe*, 7 vols. (New York, 1898–1903)

Joseph Story, *Commentaries on the Constitution of the United States* (Boston, 1838)

——, *Miscellaneous Writings, Literary, Critical, Juridical and Political* (Boston, 1835)

John C. Fitzpatrick, ed., *The Writings of George Washington*, 39 vols. (Washington, 1931–1944)

Bibliography

Worthington Chauncey Ford, ed., *The Writings of George Washington*, 14 vols. (New York, 1889–1893)

Daniel Webster, *The Writings and Speeches of Daniel Webster*, 18 vols. (Boston, 1903)

IV. BIOGRAPHIES

Henry Adams, *The Life of Albert Gallatin* (Philadelphia, 1879)

Alexander Balinky, *Albert Gallatin: Fiscal Theories and Policies* (New Brunswick, 1958)

J. S. Bassett, *The Life of Andrew Jackson*, 2 vols. (New York, 1911)

Samuel F. Bemis, *John Quincy Adams and the Foundations of American Foreign Policy* (New York, 1949)

————, *John Quincy Adams and the Union* (New York, 1956)

Winfred E. A. Bernhard, *Fisher Ames: Federalist and Statesman, 1758–1808* (Chapel Hill, 1965) *CB*

Albert J. Beveridge, *The Life of John Marshall*, 4 vols. (Boston, 1916–1919) *BN*

Irving Brant, *James Madison*, 6 vols. (Indianapolis, 1948–1956)

Gerald M. Capers, *Stephen A. Douglas: Defender of the Union* (Boston, 1959)

John A. Carroll and Mary W. Ashworth, *George Washington, First in Peace* (New York, 1957)

William N. Chambers, *Old Bullion Benton, Senator from the New West* (Boston, 1956)

Alfred Dupont Chandler, Jr., *Henry Varnum Poor: Business Editor, Analyst and Reformer* (Cambridge, 1956) *CB, BN*

Thomas Childs Cochran, *Railroad Leaders, 1845–1890* (Cambridge, 1953)

Avery Craven, *Edmund Ruffin, Southerner: A Study in Secession* (1932) (Hamden, 1964)

William P. Cresson, *James Monroe* (Chapel Hill, 1946) *B*

Marcus Cunliffe, *George Washington, Man and Monument* (New York, 1960) *CB*

Richard N. Current, *Daniel Webster and the Rise of National Conservatism* (Boston, 1955) *CB*

————, *John C. Calhoun* (New York, 1963) *CB*

George Dangerfield, *Chancellor Robert R. Livingston* (New York, 1960)

Clement Eaton, *Henry Clay and the Art of American Politics* (Boston, 1957)

Robert Ernst, *Rufus King: American Federalist* (Chapel Hill, 1968) *BN*

Robert Kenneth Faulkner, *The Jurisprudence of John Marshall* (Princeton, 1968) *BN*

Hugh M. Flick, "Elkanah Watson, Gentleman-Promoter," unpublished Ph.D. dissertation (Columbia, 1958) *B*

Douglas S. Freeman, *George Washington,* 6 vols. (New York, 1948–1957) *CB*

Thomas P. Govan, *Nicholas Biddle: Nationalist and Public Banker* (Chicago, 1959) *B*

Constance Green, *Eli Whitney and the Birth of American Technology* (Boston, 1956) *B*

James B. Hedges, *The Browns of Providence Plantations: The Nineteenth Century* (Providence, 1968)

William W. Henry, *Patrick Henry: Life, Correspondence and Speeches,* 3 vols. (New York, 1891)

Marquis James, *Andrew Jackson: The Border Captain* (Indianapolis, 1933) *B*

————, *Andrew Jackson: Portrait of a President* (Indianapolis, 1937) *B*

Wheaton Lane, *Commodore Vanderbilt: An Epic of the Steam Age* (New York, 1942) *CB*

Gene D. Lewis, *Charles Ellet, Jr.: The Engineer as Individualist, 1810–1862* (Urbana, 1968)

George A. Lipsky, *John Quincy Adams: His Theory and Ideas* (New York, 1950) *B*

H. C. Lodge, *Life and Letters of George Cabot* (Boston, 1878)

Dumas Malone, *Jefferson and His Time,* 4 vols. to date (Boston, 1948–) *CB*

William H. Masterson, *William Blount* (Baton Rouge, 1954) *CB*

Theodore Maynard, *Orestes Brownson* (New York, 1943) *B*

Bernard Mayo, *Henry Clay* (Boston, 1937) *B*

Lawrence S. Mayo, *John Langdon of New Hampshire* (Concord, 1937)

John B. McMaster, *The Life and Times of Stephen Girard,* 2 vols. (Philadelphia, 1918)

John C. Miller, *Alexander Hamilton: Portrait in Paradox* (New York, 1959) *B*

Jeanette Mirsky and Allan Nevins, *The World of Eli Whitney* (New York, 1952) *B*

Broadus Mitchell, *Alexander Hamilton,* 2 vols. (New York, 1957–1962) *B, BN*

Frank Monaghan, *John Jay* (New York, 1935)

Samuel E. Morison, *Harrison Gray Otis: The Urban Federalist* (Boston, 1969) *CB*

Bibliography

Merrill D. Peterson, *Thomas Jefferson and the New Nation* (New York, 1970) *B*

Kenneth W. Porter, *John Jacob Astor: Business Man,* 2 vols. (Cambridge, 1931)

John H. Powell, *Richard Rush, Republican Diplomat* (Philadelphia, 1942)

James G. Randall, *Lincoln, the President,* 4 vols. (New York, 1945) *B*

Daniel Roselle, *Samuel Griswold Goodrich, Creator of Peter Parley: A Study of His Life and Works* (Albany, 1968) *B*

Clinton Rossiter, *Alexander Hamilton and the Constitution* (New York, 1964) *BN*

Kenneth W. Rowe, *Mathew Carey: A Study in American Economic Development* (Baltimore, 1933) *B*

Arthur M. Schlesinger, Jr., *Orestes A. Brownson* (1939) (New York, 1963) *CB*

Charles G. Sellers, *James K. Polk,* 2 vols. (Princeton, 1957–1966) *CB*

James P. Shenton, *Robert John Walker* (New York, 1961) *B*

Page Smith, *John Adams,* 2 vols. (New York, 1962)

Peter Tolis, *Elihu Burritt: Crusader for Brotherhood* (Hamden, 1968) *B*

Rhoda Truax, *The Doctors Warren of Boston: First Family of Surgery* (Boston, 1968) *B*

Glyndon G. Van Deusen, *The Life of Henry Clay* (Boston, 1937) *B*

――――, *William Henry Seward* (New York, 1967) *B*

Clarence L. Ver Steeg, *Robert Morris: Revolutionary Financier* (Philadelphia, 1954) *B*

Raymond Walters, Jr., *Albert Gallatin* (New York, 1957) *B*

John W. Ward, *Andrew Jackson: Symbol for an Age* (New York, 1955) *BN*

Harry R. Warfel, *Noah Webster, Schoolmaster to America* (New York, 1936) *B*

W. C. Watson, ed., *Men and Times of the Revolution; or Memoirs of Elkanah Watson,* 2nd ed. (New York, 1857)

Charles Wiltse, *John C. Calhoun,* 3 vols. (Indianapolis, 1944–1951)

V. NATIONALISM

Gottfried van den Bergh, "Contemporary Nationalism in the Western World," *Daedalus,* XCV (1966), 828

E. H. Carr, *Nationalism and After* (New York, 1945)

H. M. Chadwick, *The Nationalities of Europe and the Growth of National Ideologies* (Cambridge, England, 1945)

Karl Deutsch, *Interdisciplinary Bibliography on Nationalism* (Cambridge, 1956)

———, *Nationalism and Social Communication,* 2nd ed. (Cambridge, 1966) *B*

Leonard Doob, *Patriotism and Nationalism* (New Haven, 1964) *B*

S. N. Eisenstadt, *The Absorption of Immigrants* (London, 1955) *B*

Rupert Emerson, *From Empire to Nation* (Boston, 1962) *BN*

Ernst B. Haas, *Beyond the Nation-State* (Stanford, 1964) *BN*

Carlton J. H. Hayes, *Essays on Nationalism* (New York, 1926) *CB*

———, *The Historical Evolution of Modern Nationalism* (New York, 1931)

———, *Nationalism: A Religion* (New York, 1960)

Frederick Hertz, *Nationality in History and Politics* (New York, 1944) *BN*

Hans Kohn, *The Idea of Nationalism* (New York, 1961) *BN*

———, *Nationalism: Its Meaning and History* (Princeton, 1955)

———, *Prelude to Nation-States: The French and German Experience, 1789–1815* (Princeton, 1967)

Koppel S. Pinson, *A Bibliographical Introduction to Nationalism* (New York, 1935)

Royal Institute of International Affairs, *Nationalism: A Report* (London, 1939)

Boyd Shafer, *Nationalism: Myth and Reality* (New York, 1955) *B*

Louis Snyder, ed., *The Dynamics of Nationalism* (Princeton, 1964) *B*

———, *The Meaning of Nationalism* (New Brunswick, 1954) *CB*

———, *The New Nationalism* (Ithaca, 1968) *BN*

Jacob L. Talmon, *Political Messianism* (New York, 1961) *BN*

Richard B. Wernham, *Before the Armada: The Emergence of the English Nation, 1485–1588* (New York, 1966)

Arthur P. Whitaker and David C. Jordan, *Nationalism in Contemporary Latin America* (New York, 1966) *B*

VI. AMERICAN NATIONALISM

Yehoshua Arieli, *Individualism and Nationalism in American Ideology* (Cambridge, 1964) *BN*

Charles A. Beard, *The Idea of the National Interest* (New York, 1934)

E. M. Burns, *The American Idea of Mission* (New Brunswick, 1957) *B*

Merle Curti, *The Roots of American Loyalty* (New York, 1946) *CB*

Philip Davis, ed., *Immigration and Americanization* (Boston, 1920) *B*

Bibliography

Edward F. Humphreys, *Nationalism and Religion in America, 1774–1789* (Boston, 1924) *B*

Hans Kohn, *American Nationalism* (1957) (New York, 1961) *BN*

Seymour M. Lipset, *The First New Nation* (New York, 1963) *BN*

Frederick Merk, *Manifest Destiny and Mission in American History* (New York, 1963)

Richard L. Merritt, *Symbols of American Community, 1735–1775* (New Haven, 1966) *BN*

Paul C. Nagel, *One Nation Indivisible: The Union in American Thought, 1776–1861* (New York, 1964) *BN*

John H. Nef, *The United States and Civilization* (Chicago, 1967)

Timothy L. Smith, "Protestant Schooling and American Nationality," *JAH*, VIII (1967), 679

Fred Somkin, *Unquiet Eagle: Memory and Desire in the Idea of American Freedom, 1815–1860* (Ithaca, 1967) *B*

Robert E. Stauffer, ed., *The American Spirit in the Writings of Americans of Foreign Birth* (Boston, 1922)

Ernest Lee Tuveson, *Redeemer Nation: The Idea of America's Millennial Role* (Chicago, 1968)

W. Van Alstyne, *Genesis of American Nationalism* (Waltham, 1970)

Donald F. Warner, *The Idea of Continental Union* (Lexington, 1960)

Dixon Wecter, *The Hero in America* (New York, 1961) *BN*

Albert K. Weinberg, *Manifest Destiny: A Study of Nationalist Expansionism in American History* (Baltimore, 1935)

VII. MODERNIZATION

Robert Alexander, *A Primer of Economic Development* (New York, 1962) *CB*

Gabriel A. Almond, "Comparative Political Systems," *Journal of Politics*, XVIII (1956), 391

———— and James S. Coleman, eds., *The Politics of the Developing Areas* (Princeton, 1960)

———— and G. B. Powell, *Comparative Politics: A Developmental Approach* (Boston, 1966) *BN*

David E. Apter, *The Politics of Modernization* (Chicago, 1965) *BN*

————, *Some Conceptual Approaches to the Study of Modernization* (Englewood Cliffs, 1968)

Raymond Aron, *The Industrial Society* (New York, 1967)

Douglas E. Ashford, *National Development and Local Reform: Political Participation in Morocco, Tunisia, and Pakistan* (Princeton, 1967) *B, BN*

The American Quest

T. S. Ashton, *The Industrial Revolution, 1760–1830* (New York, 1964) *CB*

Edward C. Banfield, *The Moral Basis of a Backward Society* (Glencoe, 1958)

Arthur S. Banks and Robert B. Textor, *A Cross-Polity Survey* (Cambridge, 1963)

Peter Bauer and Basil Yamey, *The Economics of Underdeveloped Countries* (Chicago, 1957) *BN*

Reinhard Bendix, *Nation-Building and Citizenship* (New York, 1964) *BN*

Henry Bienen, *The Military Intervenes* (New York, 1968) *BN*

Knight Biggerstaff, "Modernization—and Early Modern China," *Journal of Asian Studies*, XXV (1966), 607

Leonard Binder, *Iran: Political Development in a Changing Society* (Berkeley, 1962)

C. E. Black, *The Dynamics of Modernization: A Study in Comparative History* (New York, 1966) *CB*

Pran Chopra, *Uncertain India: A Political Profile of Two Decades of Freedom* (Cambridge, 1969)

Colin Clark, *The Conditions of Economic Progress* (London, 1951)

I. L. Claude, *National Minorities* (Cambridge, 1955) *CB*

Robert A. Dahl, ed., *Political Oppositions in Western Democracies* (New Haven, 1966) *CB, BN*

R. E. Dawson and Kenneth Prewitt, *Political Socialization* (Boston, 1969)

Phyllis Deane, *The First Industrial Revolution* (Cambridge, England, 1965) *B*

Karl Deutsch, "Social Mobilization and Political Development," *American Political Science Review*, LV (1961), 493 *BN*

——— and William Foltz, eds., *Nation-Building* (New York, 1963) *B*

Harry Eckstein, *A Theory of Stable Democracy*, Research Monograph No. 10, Center of International Studies, Princeton University (Princeton, 1961)

S. N. Eisenstadt, *Essays on Sociological Aspects of Political and Economic Development* (The Hague, 1961) *BN*

———, *Modernization: Protest and Change* (Englewood Cliffs, 1966) *BN*

———, ed., *The Protestant Ethic and Modernization: A Comparative View* (New York, 1968) *B*

Amitai Etzioni, *Political Unification* (New York, 1965) *BN*

Lewis P. Fickett, Jr., *Problems of the Developing Nations* (New York, 1966) *B*

Bibliography

G. Lowell Field, *Comparative Political Development: The Precedent of the West* (Ithaca, 1967) *BN*

John Kenneth Galbraith, *Economic Development* (Cambridge, 1964)

Clifford Geertz, ed., *Old Societies and New States: The Quest for Modernity in Asia and Africa* (New York, 1963)

Frank H. Golay *et al.*, *Underdevelopment and Economic Nationalism in Southeast Asia* (Ithaca, 1969) *BN*

William Gutteridge, *Armed Forces in New States* (London, 1962)

Everett Hagan, *On the Theory of Social Change* (Homewood, 1962) *B*

J. L. and Barbara Hammond, *The Rise of Modern Industry* (New York, 1926) *BN*

Louis Hartz *et al.*, *The Founding of New Societies* (New York, 1964)

Robert L. Heilbroner, *The Great Ascent* (New York, 1964)

W. O. Henderson, *The Industrialization of Europe, 1780–1914* (New York, 1969) *B*

Albert O. Hirschman, *The Strategy of Economic Development* (New Haven, 1958)

Robert T. Holt and John E. Turner, *The Political Basis of Economic Development: An Exploration in Comparative Political Analysis* (Princeton, 1966) *B*

Irving L. Horowitz, *Three Worlds of Development* (New York, 1966) *BN*

Berthold F. Hoselitz, *Sociological Aspects of Economic Growth* (Glencoe, 1960)

Samuel P. Huntington, *Political Order in Changing Societies* (New Haven, 1968) *BN*

———— and Clement H. Moore, eds., *Authoritarian Politics in Modern Society: The Dynamics of Established One-Party Systems* (New York, 1969)

Herbert Hyman, *Political Socialization* (Glencoe, 1959) *BN*

Morris Janowitz, *The Military in the Political Development of New Nations* (Chicago, 1964)

John E. Johnson, ed., *The Role of the Military in Underdeveloped Countries* (Princeton, 1962)

Samuel L. Klausner, ed., *The Study of Total Societies* (New York, 1967)

Lillian Knowles, *Economic Development in the Nineteenth Century* (London, 1932) *B*

Simon Kuznets, "Quantitative Aspects of the Economic Growth of Nations," University of Chicago Research Center in Economic Development and Cultural Change, vols. 5 and 6 (Chicago, 1962)

The American Quest

Jacques Lambert, *Latin America: Social Structures and Political Institutions* (Berkeley, 1967) *B*
Joseph LaPalombara, ed., *Bureaucracy and Political Development* (Princeton, 1963) *B*
———— and Myron Weiner, eds., *Political Parties and Political Development* (Princeton, 1966) *B*
Harvey Leibenstein, *Economic Backwardness and Economic Growth* (New York, 1957)
Daniel Lerner, *The Passing of Transitional Society: Modernizing the Middle East* (New York, 1964)
———— and Wilbur Schramm, eds., *Communications and Change in the Developing Countries* (Honolulu, 1967) *B*
Marion J. Levy, Jr., *Modernization and the Structure of Society*, 2 vols. (Princeton, 1966)
Bernard Lewis, *The Emergence of Modern Turkey* (London, 1961) *B*, *BN*
William A. Lewis, *The Theory of Economic Growth* (London, 1955)
Colin Leys, ed., *Politics and Change in Developing Countries* (New York, 1969)
David McClelland, *The Achieving Society* (Princeton, 1961) *B*
William McCord, *The Springtime of Freedom* (New York, 1965) *CB*
John W. Mellor, *The Economics of Agricultural Development* (Ithaca, 1970) *B*
J. D. B. Miller, *The Politics of the Third World* (New York, 1967)
Max F. Millikan and Donald L. M. Blackmer, eds., *The Emerging Nations* (Boston, 1961) *B*
Barrington Moore, Jr., *Social Origins of Dictatorship and Democracy: Lord and Peasant in the Making of the Modern World* (Boston, 1966) *B*
Gunnar Myrdal, *Beyond the Welfare State* (New Haven, 1960)
E. Herbert Norman, *Japan's Emergence as a Modern State* (New York, 1940) *B*, *BN*
Ragnar Nurske, ed., *Problems of Capital Formation in Underdeveloped Countries*, 3rd ed. (Oxford, 1955)
A. F. K. Organski, *The Stages of Political Development* (New York, 1965) *B*
J. Roland Pennock, "Political Development, Political Systems, and Political Goods," *World Politics*, XVIII (1966), 415 *BN*
————, ed., *Self-Government in Modernizing Nations* (Englewood Cliffs, 1964)
John Plamenatz, *On Alien Rule and Self-Government* (London, 1960)
Lucian W. Pye, *Aspects of Political Development* (Boston, 1966) *BN*

Bibliography

——, ed., *Communication and Political Development* (Princeton, 1963) CB

——, *Politics, Personality, and Nation-Building* (New Haven, 1962)

—— and Sidney Verba, eds., *Political Culture and Political Development* (Princeton, 1965) BN

Robert Redfield, *Peasant Society and Culture* (Chicago, 1956)

Fred W. Riggs, *Administration in Developing Countries: The Theory of Prismatic Society* (Boston, 1964) BN

Arnold Rivkin, *Nation-Building in Africa* (New Brunswick, 1969)

E. A. G. Robinson, ed., *Economic Consequences of the Size of Nations* (London, 1960)

W. W. Rostow, *The Stages of Economic Growth* (Cambridge, England, 1960)

Bruce M. Russett *et al.*, *World Handbook of Political and Social Indicators* (New Haven, 1964)

Dankwart A. Rustow, *A World of Nations: The Dynamics of Modern Politics* (Washington, 1967) BN

Jacob Schmookler, *Invention and Economic Growth* (Cambridge, 1966) B

Lyle W. Shannon, *Underdeveloped Areas* (New York, 1957)

Edward A. Shils, *Political Development in the New States* (The Hague, 1962)

Kalman H. Silvert, *The Conflict Society: Reaction and Revolution in Latin America,* rev. ed. (New York, 1966) BN

——, ed., *Discussion at Bellagio* (New York, 1964)

—— *et al.*, *Expectant Peoples* (New York, 1963) CB

Neil Smelser, *Social Change in the Industrial Revolution* (Chicago, 1959) B

Thomas C. Smith, *Political Change and Industrial Development in Japan: Government Enterprise, 1868–1880* (Stanford, 1955) B

Eugene Staley, *The Future of Underdeveloped Countries* (New York, 1961) B

Barry E. Supple, ed., *The Experience of Economic Growth* (New York, 1963) B

Hugh Tinker, *Ballot Box and Bayonet: People and Government in Emergent Asian Countries* (New York, 1964)

Fred R. von der Mehden, *Politics of the Developing Nations* (Englewood Cliffs, 1964) B

Karl von Vorys, ed., "New Nations: The Problems of Political Development," *Annals of the American Academy of Political and Social Science,* CCCLVIII (1965)

The American Quest

Immanuel Wallerstein, *Africa: The Politics of Independence* (New York, 1961) *CB*

Barbara Ward, *The Rich Nations and the Poor Nations* (London, 1962)

Robert E. Ward and Dankwart A. Rustow, eds., *Political Modernization in Japan and Turkey* (Princeton, 1964) *B*

Myron Weiner, ed., *Modernization: The Dynamics of Growth* (New York, 1966) *B*

————, *The Politics of Scarcity* (Chicago, 1962)

Henry Wells, *Modernization of Puerto Rico* (Cambridge, 1969) *BN*

VIII. THE STUDY OF HISTORY

William O. Aydelotte, "Quantification in History," *AHR*, LXXI (1966), 803

Charles A. Beard, "Written History as an Act of Faith," *AHR*, XXXIX (1934), 219

Carl Becker, *Everyman His Own Historian* (New York, 1935)

Robert F. Berkhofer, *A Behavioral Approach to Historical Analysis* (New York, 1969) *BN*

Barton J. Bernstein, ed., *Towards a New Past: Dissenting Essays in American History* (New York, 1968) *BN*, with which might be read the communication of David Donald in *AHR*, LXXIV (1968), 531.

Marc Bloch, *The Historian's Craft* (New York, 1953), Peter Putnam, trans.

Herbert Butterfield, *Man on His Past* (Cambridge, England, 1955)

E. H. Carr, *What Is History?* (London, 1961)

Thomas C. Cochran, "Economic History, Old and New," *AHR*, LXXIV (1969), 1561 *BN*

————, *The Inner Revolution* (New York, 1964) *BN*

Alfred H. Conrad and John R. Meyer, *The Economics of Slavery and Other Studies in Econometric History* (Chicago, 1964) *BN*

Allen F. Davis and Harold D. Woodman, eds., *Conflict or Consensus in American History* (Boston, 1966) *B*

Martin Duberman, *The Uncompleted Past* (New York, 1969)

G. R. Elton, *The Practice of History* (New York, 1967)

Robert William Fogel, "Reappraisals in American Economic History—Discussion," *American Economic Review*, LIV (1964), 377

Patrick Gardiner, *The Nature of Historical Explanation* (Oxford, 1952)

————, ed., *Theories of History* (Glencoe, 1959) *B*

Bibliography

Louis Gottschalk, ed., *Generalization in the Writing of History* (Chicago, 1963) *B*

F. A. Hayek, ed., *Capitalism and the Historians* (Chicago, 1954)

J. H. Hexter, "Historiography: The Rhetoric of History," *International Encyclopedia of the Social Sciences*, VI (1968), 368

———, *Reappraisals in History* (New York, 1963) *BN*

John Higham, "Beyond Consensus: The Historian as Moral Critic," *AHR*, LXVII (1962), 609 *BN*

———, "The Cult of the 'American Consensus': Homogenizing Our History," *Commentary*, XXVII (1959), 93

———, ed., *The Reconstruction of American History* (New York, 1962) *CB*

——— *et al.*, *History* (Englewood Cliffs, 1965) *BN*

Sidney Hook, ed., *Philosophy and History: A Symposium* (New York, 1963) *BN*

Leonard Krieger, "The Horizons of History," *AHR*, LXII (1957), 62

Dwight E. Lee and Robert N. Beck, "The Meaning of 'Historicism,'" *AHR*, LIX (1954), 568 *BN*

Ved Mehta, *Fly and the Fly-Bottle* (Boston, 1962)

David W. Noble, *Historians Against History: The Frontier Thesis and the National Covenant in American Historical Writing since 1830* (Minneapolis, 1965)

David M. Potter, "The Historian's Use of Nationalism and Vice Versa," *AHR*, LXVII (1962), 924 *BN*

N. Rashevsky, *Looking at History Through Mathematics* (Cambridge, 1968) *B*

Nathan Rotenstreich, *Between Past and Present: An Essay on History* (New Haven, 1958)

Don Karl Rowney and James Q. Graham, eds., *Quantitative History: Selected Readings in the Quantitative Analysis of Historical Data* (Homewood, 1969)

Jennings B. Sanders, *Historical Interpretations and American Historianship* (Yellow Springs, 1966) *BN*

Edward N. Saveth, ed., *American History and the Social Sciences* (Glencoe, 1964) *BN*

Robert Jones Shafer, ed., *A Guide to Historical Method* (Homewood, 1969) *CB*

Page Smith, *The Historian and History* (New York, 1964) *B*

Social Science Research Council, *The Social Sciences in Historical Study*, Bulletin 64 (New York, 1954) *BN*

———, *Theory and Practice in Historical Study: A Report of the Committee on Historiography*, Bulletin 54 (New York, 1946) *B*

Fritz Stern, ed., *The Varieties of History* (Cleveland, 1956)
Cushing Strout, *The Pragmatic Revolt in American History: Carl Becker and Charles Beard* (Ithaca, 1966) B
Robert P. Swierenga, ed., *Quantification in American History: Theory and Research* (New York, 1970)
Paul Tillich, *The Interpretation of History* (New York, 1936)
William Henry Walsh, *An Introduction to Philosophy of History* (London, 1951)
Morton White, *Foundations of Historical Knowledge* (New York, 1965)
Robin W. Winks, *The Historian as Detective* (New York, 1969) *CB*
C. Vann Woodward, ed., *The Comparative Approach to American History* (New York, 1968) *CB*

IX. FROM INDEPENDENCE TO THE CIVIL WAR: USEFUL SURVEYS AND INTERPRETATIONS

R. A. Billington, *The Far Western Frontier, 1830–1860* (New York, 1956) *CB*
Marcus Cunliffe, *The Nation Takes Shape, 1789–1837* (Chicago, 1969) *CB*
George Dangerfield, *The Awakening of American Nationalism, 1815–1828* (New York, 1965) *CB, BN*
———, *The Era of Good Feelings* (New York, 1952) *B*
Carl N. Degler, *Out of Our Past* (New York, 1959) *CB*
Michael Kraus, *The United States to 1865: A Modern History* (Ann Arbor, 1959) *CB*
John Allen Krout and Dixon R. Fox, *The Completion of American Independence, 1790–1830* (New York, 1944) *CB*
Dumas Malone and Basil Rauch, *Crisis of the Union, 1841–1877* (New York, 1964) *CB*
———, *The Republic Comes of Age, 1789–1841* (New York, 1960) *CB*
John C. Miller, *The Federalist Era, 1789–1801* (New York, 1960) *CB*
H. B. Parkes, *The American Experience* (New York, 1947)
Francis S. Philbrick, *The Rise of the West, 1754–1830* (New York, 1965) *BN*
Marshall Smelser, *The Democratic Republic, 1801–1815* (New York, 1968) *B*
William A. Williams, *The Contours of American History* (Cleveland, 1961) *B*
Charles M. Wiltse, *The New Nation, 1800–1845* (New York, 1961) *CB*

Bibliography

X. FROM INDEPENDENCE TO THE CIVIL WAR: SPECIAL THEMES

H. C. Allen, *Bush and Backwoods* (Sydney, 1959) *BN*

———, *Great Britain and the United States* (London, 1954) *B*

R. A. Billington, ed., *The Frontier Thesis: Valid Interpretation of American History?* (New York, 1966) *CB*

———, *Westward Expansion: A History of the American Frontier* (New York, 1949) *CB*

Peter Brock, *Pacifism in the United States from Colonial Era to First World War* (Princeton, 1968), esp. chaps. 8–20 *B*

Ralph H. Brown, *Historical Geography of the United States* (New York, 1948) *B*

Roscoe C. Buley, *The Old Northwest: Pioneer Period, 1815–1850,* 2 vols. (Indianapolis, 1950) *CB*

Daniel H. Calhoun, *Professional Lives in America: Structure and Aspiration, 1750–1850* (Cambridge, 1965) *BN*

Thomas D. Clark, *Frontier America: The Story of the Western Movement* (New York, 1959) *B*

David P. Crook, *American Democracy in English Politics, 1815–1850* (New York, 1965) *B*

Merle Curti, *The American Peace Crusade, 1815–1860* (Durham, 1929) *B*

———, *Probing Our Past* (New York, 1955) *BN*

Bernard De Voto, *Across the Wide Missouri* (Boston, 1947) *B*

———, *The Year of Decision: 1846* (Boston, 1943)

David M. Ellis, ed., *The Frontier in American Development: Essays in Honor of Paul Wallace Gates* (Ithaca, 1969) *BN*

Thomas J. Fleming, *West Point: The Men and Times of the United States Military Academy* (New York, 1969) *B*

Charles N. Glaab and A. Theodore Brown, *A History of Urban America* (New York, 1967) *CB*

William H. Goetzmann, *Exploration and Empire* (New York, 1966) *BN*

Norman A. Graebner, *Empire on the Pacific* (New York, 1955)

John C. Greene, "American Science Comes of Age, 1780–1820," *JAH,* LV (1968), 22 *BN*

William T. Hagan, *American Indians* (Chicago, 1961) *CB*

W. Eugene Hollon, *The Great American Desert, Then and Now* (New York, 1966) *CB*

Haldvan Koht, *The American Spirit in Europe* (Philadelphia, 1949) *B*

The American Quest

George D. Lillibridge, *Beacon of Freedom: The Impact of American Democracy upon Great Britain, 1830–1870* (Philadelphia, 1954) *CB*

Leo Marx, *The Machine in the Garden: Technology and the Pastoral Ideal in America* (New York, 1964)

Thomas F. O'Dea, *The Mormons* (Chicago, 1957) *BN*

Frederick L. Paxson, *History of the American Frontier, 1763–1893* (Boston, 1924)

George W. Pierson, "The M-Factor in American History," *American Quarterly*, XIV (1962), 275

———, "A Restless Temper," *AHR*, LXIX (1964), 969

Francis P. Prucha, *American Indian Policy in the Formative Years* (Cambridge, 1962) *CB*

Samuel Rezneck, "The Depression of 1819–1822: A Social History," *AHR*, XXXIX (1933), 28

———, "The Social History of an American Depression, 1837–1843," *AHR*, XL (1935), 662

Robert E. Riegel, *America Moves West*, 3rd ed. (New York, 1956) *B*

Malcolm J. Rohrbough, *The Land Office Business: The Settlement and Administration of American Public Lands, 1789–1837* (New York, 1968) *B*

Ellen C. Semple, *American History and Its Geographic Conditions* (Boston, 1903)

Bernard W. Sheehan, "Indian-White Relations in Early America: A Review Essay," *WMQ*, XXVI (1969), 267 *BN*

Henry N. Smith, *Virgin Land: The American West as Symbol and Myth* (1950) (New York, 1957) *BN*

Robert Spencer et al., *The Native Americans* (New York, 1965)

Robert E. Spiller, *The American in England During the First Half Century of Independence* (New York, 1926) *B*

Marion L. Starkey, *The Cherokee Nation* (New York, 1946) *BN*

Cushing Strout, *The American Image of the Old World* (New York, 1963) *BN*

George R. Taylor, ed., *The Turner Thesis Concerning the Role of the Frontier in American History* (Boston, 1949)

Frank Thistlethwaite, *America and the Atlantic Community: Anglo-American Aspects, 1790–1850* (New York, 1963) *BN*

Frederick Jackson Turner, *The Significance of Sections in American History* (New York, 1932)

R. W. Van Alstyne, *The Rising American Empire* (New York, 1960) *BN*

Dale Van Every, *Ark of Empire: The American Frontier, 1784–1803* (New York, 1963) *B*

Bibliography

——, *The Final Challenge: The American Frontier, 1804–1845* (New York, 1964) *B*

XI. POLITICAL DEVELOPMENT

Herbert Agar, *The Price of Union* (Boston, 1950) *B*

Thomas B. Alexander, *Sectional Stress and Party Strength* (Nashville, 1967)

Lee Benson, *The Concept of Jacksonian Democracy: New York as a Test Case* (Princeton, 1961) *BN*

Wilfred E. Binkley, *American Political Parties* (New York, 1947) *B*

——, *President and Congress* (New York, 1947) *B*

Lynton K. Caldwell, *The Administrative Theories of Hamilton and Jefferson* (Chicago, 1944)

W. N. Chambers, *Political Parties in a New Nation: The American Experience, 1776–1809* (New York, 1963) *CB*

—— and Walter D. Burnham, *The American Party Systems: Stages of Political Development* (New York, 1967) *BN*

Joseph Charles, *The Origins of the American Party System* (Williamsburg, 1956)

Marchette Chute, *The First Liberty: A History of the Right to Vote in America, 1619–1850* (New York, 1969)

Noble E. Cunningham, Jr., *The Jefferson Republicans: The Formation of Party Organization, 1789–1801* (Chapel Hill, 1957) *CB*

——, *The Jeffersonian Republicans in Power: Party Operations, 1801–1809* (Chapel Hill, 1963) *CB*

——, ed., *The Making of the American Party System, 1789–1809* (Englewood Cliffs, 1965)

Manning Dauer, *The Adams Federalists* (Baltimore, 1953) *B*

A. Hunter Dupree, *Science in the Federal Government* (Cambridge, 1957) *CB*

Arthur A. Ekirch, Jr., *The Civilian and the Military* (New York, 1956) *BN*

Daniel Elazar, *The American Partnership* (Chicago, 1962) *B*

David H. Fischer, *The Revolution of American Conservatism: The Federalist Party in the Era of Jeffersonian Democracy* (New York, 1965) *BN*

Carl Russell Fish, *The Civil Service and the Patronage* (New York, 1905) *CB*

Eric Foner, *Free Soil, Free Labor, Free Men: The Ideology of the Republican Party Before the Civil War* (New York, 1970) *CB*

The American Quest

Henry J. Ford, *The Rise and Growth of American Politics* (1898) (New York, 1967)

Carter Goodrich, *Government Promotion of American Canals and Railroads* (New York, 1960) *B*

Constance Green, *Washington: Village and Capital, 1800–1878* (Princeton, 1962) *B*

Charles G. Haines, *The Role of the Supreme Court in American Government and Politics*, 2 vols. (Berkeley, 1944–1957) *BN*

Bray Hammond, *Banks and Politics in America from the Revolution to the Civil War* (Princeton, 1957) *B*

Oscar and Mary F. Handlin, *Commonwealth: A Study of the Role of Government in the American Economy: Massachusetts, 1774–1861*, rev. ed. (Boston, 1969) *CB*

Louis Hartz, *Economic Policy and Democratic Thought: Pennsylvania, 1776–1860* (Cambridge, 1948) *B*

Milton S. Heath, *Constructive Liberalism: The Role of the State in Economic Development in Georgia to 1860* (Cambridge, 1954) *B*

Homer C. Hockett, *The Constitutional History of the United States, 1776–1826*, 2 vols. (New York, 1939) *B*

Richard Hofstadter, *The American Political Tradition* (New York, 1948) *CB*

———, *The Idea of a Party System: The Rise of a Legitimate Opposition in the United States, 1780–1840* (Berkeley, 1969)

Michael Fitzgibbon Holt, *Forging a Majority: The Formation of the Republican Party in Pittsburgh* (New Haven, 1969) *B*

Samuel P. Huntington, *The Soldier and the State* (New York, 1957) *BN*

James Willard Hurst, *The Growth of American Law: The Lawmakers* (Boston, 1950) *CB*

———, *Law and the Condition of Freedom in the Nineteenth Century* (Madison, 1956) *BN*

John G. B. Hutchins, *The American Maritime Industries and Public Policy, 1789–1914: An Economic History* (Cambridge, 1941) *B*

Robert W. Johannsen, *Frontier Politics and the Sectional Conflict: The Pacific Northwest on the Eve of the Civil War* (Seattle, 1955) *B*

A. H. Kelly and W. A. Harbison, *The American Constitution* (New York, 1948) *CB*

Lewis H. Kimmel, *Federal Budget and Fiscal Policy, 1789–1958* (Washington, 1959) *BN*

David Kinley, *The History, Organization and Influence of the Independent Treasury of the United States* (New York, 1893)

Bibliography

Eugene P. Link, *Democratic-Republican Societies, 1790–1800* (New York, 1942) *B*

Robert A. Lively, "The American System," *Business History Review,* XXIX (1955), 81 *B*

Shaw Livermore, Jr., *The Twilight of Federalism: The Disintegration of the Federalist Party, 1815–1830* (Princeton, 1962) *B*

Richard P. McCormick, *The Second American Party System: Party Formation in the Jacksonian Era* (Chapel Hill, 1960) *CB*

A. C. McLaughlin, *A Constitutional History of the United States* (New York, 1935)

Lynn Marshall, "Strange Stillbirth of the Whig Party," *AHR,* LXXII (1967), 445 *BN*

Roy F. Nichols, *The Invention of the American Political Parties* (New York, 1967) *B*

Harry H. Pierce, *Railroads of New York: A Study of Government Aid, 1826–1875* (Cambridge, 1953) *B*

Kirk H. Porter, *A History of the Suffrage in the United States* (Chicago, 1918)

John H. Powell, *The Books of a New Nation: United States Government Publications, 1774–1814* (Philadelphia, 1957)

James N. Primm, *Economic Policy in the Development of a Western State: Missouri, 1820–1860* (Cambridge, 1945) *B*

Carl E. Prince, *New Jersey's Jeffersonian Republicans: The Genesis of an Early Party Machine, 1789–1817* (Chapel Hill, 1967) *BN*

Sidney Ratner, *American Taxation: Its History as a Social Force in States* (Ames, 1953) *B*

James A. Rawley, *Race and Politics: Bleeding Kansas and the Coming of the Civil War* (Philadelphia, 1969)

Robert V. Remini, *Andrew Jackson and the Bank War: A Study in the Growth of Presidential Power* (New York, 1967) *CB, BN*

———, *The Election of Andrew Jackson* (Philadelphia, 1963) *CB*

Wesley E. Rich, *The History of the United States Post Office to the Year 1829* (Cambridge, 1924) *B*

Norman K. Risjord, *The Old Republicans: Southern Conservatism in the Age of Jefferson* (New York, 1965) *B*

John P. Roche, *The Early Development of United States Citizenship* (Ithaca, 1949)

Lisle A. Rose, *Prologue to Democracy: The Federalists in the South, 1789–1800* (Lexington, 1968) *BN*

Harry N. Scheiber, *Ohio Canal Era: A Case Study of Government and the Economy, 1820–1861* (Athens, 1969) *BN*

Joel Silbey, *The Shrine of Party: Congressional Voting Behavior, 1841–1852* (Pittsburgh, 1967) *CB*

———, *The Transformation of American Politics, 1840–1860* (Englewood Cliffs, 1967) *CB*

Carl B. Swisher, *American Constitutional Development* (Boston, 1943) *BN*

Esther R. Taus, *Central Banking Functions of the United States Treasury, 1789–1941* (New York, 1943) *B*

Frank W. Taussig, *The Tariff History of the United States*, 8th ed. (New York, 1931) *BN*

Paul P. Van Riper, *History of the United States Civil Service* (Evanston, 1958) *BN*

Charles Warren, *The Supreme Court in United States History*, 2 vols. (Boston, 1947) *BN*

Russell F. Weigley, *History of the United States Army* (New York, 1967) *BN*

Leonard D. White, *The Federalists* (New York, 1948)

———, *The Jacksonians* (New York, 1954)

———, *The Jeffersonians* (New York, 1951)

Chilton Williamson, *American Suffrage from Property to Democracy, 1760–1860* (Princeton, 1960) *BN*

James Sterling Young, *The Washington Community, 1800–1828* (New York, 1966) *B, BN*

XII. ECONOMIC DEVELOPMENT

Robert G. Albion, *The Rise of New York Port, 1815–1860* (New York, 1939) *B*

———, *Square-Riggers on Schedule* (Princeton, 1938) *B*

Thomas S. Berry, *Western Prices Before 1861: A Study of the Cincinnati Market* (Cambridge, 1943) *B*

P. W. Bidwell and J. I. Falconer, *History of Agriculture in the Northern United States, 1620–1860* (Washington, 1933) *CB*

John L. Bishop, *A History of American Manufactures from 1608 to. 1860*, 3 vols. (Philadelphia, 1861–1868)

Stuart Bruchey, *The Roots of American Economic Growth, 1607–1861: An Essay in Social Causation* (New York, 1965) *B*

Norman S. Buck, *The Development of the Organization of Anglo-American Trade, 1800–1850* (New Haven, 1925) *B*

Roger Burlingame, *The March of the Iron Men* (New York, 1938) *B*

Guy S. Callender, "The Early Transportation and Banking Enterprises of the States in Relation to the Growth of Corporations," *Quarterly Journal of Economics,* XVII (1902), 111

———, *Selections from the Economic History of the United States, 1838* (Ithaca, 1962) *B*

Ralph C. H. Catterall, *The Second Bank of the United States* (Chicago, 1903) *B*

John W. Caughey, *Gold Is the Cornerstone* (Berkeley, 1948) *CB*

Alfred D. Chandler, Jr., ed., *The Railroads: The Nation's First Big Business* (New York, 1965) *B*

Hiram M. Chittenden, *The American Fur Trade of the Far West,* 2 vols. (Stanford, 1954) *CB*

John G. Clark, *The Grain Trade in the Old Northwest* (Urbana, 1966) *B*

Victor S. Clark, *History of Manufactures in the United States,* 3 vols. (Washington, 1929) *CB*

Frederick A. Cleveland and Fred W. Powell, *Railroad Promotion and Capitalization in the United States* (New York, 1909) *B*

Thomas C. Cochran and William Miller, *The Age of Enterprise,* rev. ed. (New York, 1961) *B*

Melvin T. Copeland, *The Cotton Manufacturing Industry of the United States* (Cambridge, 1912) *B*

Joseph S. Davis, *Essays in the Earlier History of American Corporations,* 2 vols. (Cambridge, 1917) *B*

L. E. Davis, J. R. T. Hughes, and D. M. McDougall, *American Economic History: The Development of a National Economy* (Homewood, 1961) *B*

Clive Day, *History of Commerce in the United States* (New York, 1925) *B*

Davis Rich Dewey, *Financial History of the United States,* 8th ed. (New York, 1922) *B*

Edwin M. Dodd, *American Business Corporations Until 1860* (Cambridge, 1954) *B*

J. R. Dolan, *The Yankee Peddlers of Early America* (New York, 1964)

Seymour Dunbar, *A History of Travel in America,* 4 vols. (Indianapolis, 1915) *B*

Howard N. Eavenson, *The First Century and a Quarter of American Coal Industry* (Baltimore, 1942) *B*

George H. Evans, Jr., *Business Incorporations in the United States, 1800–1943* (New York, 1948)

H. V. Faulkner, *American Economic History,* 8th ed. (New York, 1960) *B*

Albert Fishlow, *American Railroads and the Transformation of the Ante-Bellum Economy* (Cambridge, 1965) *B*

James T. Flexner, *Steamboats Come True: American Inventors in Action* (New York, 1944) *B, BN*

Robert W. Fogel, *Railroads and American Economic Growth: Essays in Econometric History* (Baltimore, 1964) *B*

John H. Frederick, *The Development of American Commerce* (New York, 1932) *B*

Paul W. Gates, *The Farmer's Age: Agriculture, 1815–1860* (New York, 1960) *CB*

——, *The Illinois Central Railroad and Its Colonization Work* (Cambridge, 1934) *B*

George Sweet Gibb, *The Saco-Lowell Shops* (Cambridge, 1950)

David T. Gilchrist, ed., *The Growth of the Seaport Cities, 1790–1825* (Charlottesville, 1967) *B*

H. J. Habakkuk, *American and British Technology in the Nineteenth Century* (Cambridge, England, 1962)

Louis M. Hacker, *The Course of American Economic Growth and Development* (New York, 1970) *BN*

——, *The Triumph of American Capitalism* (New York, 1940) *B*

Lewis H. Haney, *A Congressional History of Railways in the United States to 1850* (Madison, 1908) *B*

——, *A Congressional History of Railways in the United States, 1850–1877* (Madison, 1910)

Marshall Harris, *Origins of the Land Tenure System in the United States* (Ames, 1953) *B*

Seymour E. Harris, ed., *American Economic History* (New York, 1961) *B*

Blanche E. Hazard, *The Organization of the Boot and Shoe Industry in Massachusetts Before 1875* (Cambridge, 1921) *B*

Joseph E. Hedges, *Commercial Banking and the Stock Market Before 1863* (Baltimore, 1938) *B*

Paul C. Henlein, *Cattle Kingdom in the Ohio Valley, 1783–1860* (Lexington, 1959) *CB*

A. Barton Hepburn, *A History of Currency in the United States* (New York, 1915) *CB*

Ralph W. Hidy, *The House of Baring in American Trade and Finance: English Merchant Bankers at Work, 1763–1861* (Cambridge, 1949) *BN*

Brooke Hindle, *Technology in Early America* (Chapel Hill, 1966) *CB*

Archer B. Hulbert, *The Paths of Inland Commerce: A Chronicle of Trail, Road, and Waterway* (New Haven, 1920) *CB*

Bibliography

————, *Soil: Its Influence on the History of the United States* (New Haven, 1930)

Louis C. Hunter, *Steamboats on the Western Rivers: An Economic and Technological History* (Cambridge, 1949) *BN*

Leland H. Jenks, *The Migration of British Capital to 1875* (New York, 1927) *BN*

Emory R. Johnson, T. W. Van Metre, G. B. Huebner, and D. S. Hanchett, *History of Domestic and Foreign Commerce of the United States*, 2 vols. (Washington, 1915) *CB*

Edward C. Kirkland, *A History of American Economic Life*, 3rd ed. (New York, 1951) *CB*

————, *Men, Cities and Transportation: A Study in New England History, 1820–1900*, 2 vols. (Cambridge, 1948)

John H. Krenkel, *Illinois Internal Improvements, 1818–1848* (Cedar Rapids, 1958) *B*

Simon Kuznets, "National Income Estimates for the United States Prior to 1870," *JEH*, XII (1952), 115

William G. Lathrop, *The Brass Industry in the United States* (Mt. Carmel, 1926) *B*

Richard G. Lillard, *The Great Forest* (New York, 1947) *CB*

Shaw Livermore, *Early American Land Companies: Their Influence on Corporate Development* (New York, 1939) *B*

James W. Livingood, *The Philadelphia-Baltimore Trade Rivalry, 1780–1860* (Harrisburg, 1947) *B*

Rodney C. Loehr, "The Influence of English Agriculture on American Agriculture, 1775–1825," *Agricultural History*, XI (1937), 3

Raymond McFarland, *A History of the New England Fisheries* (New York, 1911) *B*

Caroline E. MacGill *et al.*, *History of Transportation in the United States Before 1860* (Washington, 1917) *B*

Paul F. McGouldrick, *New England Textiles in the Nineteenth Century: Profits and Investments* (Cambridge, 1968) *B*

Reginald C. McGrane, *Foreign Bondholders and American State Debts* (New York, 1935) *B*

————, *The Panic of 1837* (Chicago, 1924) *B*

Blake McKelvey, *Rochester, the Water-Power City, 1812–1854* (Cambridge, 1954)

Robert F. Martin, *National Income in the United States, 1799–1938* (New York, 1939)

Bruce Mazlish, ed., *The Railroad and the Space Program: An Exploration in Historical Analogy* (Cambridge, 1965)

Raymond Merritt, *Engineering in American Society, 1850–1875* (Lexington, 1970) *CB*

Nathan Miller, *The Enterprise of a Free People: Aspects of Economic Development in New York State During the Canal Period, 1792–1838* (Ithaca, 1962) *B*

William Miller, ed., *Men in Business* (New York, 1962) *B, BN*

Samuel E. Morison, *The Maritime History of Massachusetts* (Boston, 1941) *B*

Margaret G. Myers, *Origins and Development,* vol. 1 of *The New York Money Market,* 4 vols. (New York, 1931) *B*

National Bureau of Economic Research, *Output, Employment, and Productivity in the United States after 1800* (New York, 1966) *BN*

—————, *Trends in the American Economy in the Nineteenth Century* (Princeton, 1960)

Curtis P. Nettels, *The Emergence of a National Economy, 1775–1815* (New York, 1962) *B*

Allan Nevins, *History of the Bank of New York and Trust Company: 1784–1934* (New York, 1934)

Douglass C. North, *The Economic Growth of the United States, 1790 to 1860* (Englewood Cliffs, 1961) *B*

John W. Oliver, *History of American Technology* (New York, 1956) *B*

William Nelson Parker, *Commerce, Cotton, and Westward Expansion* (Chicago, 1964)

Rodman W. Paul, *California Gold: The Beginning of Mining in the Far West* (Cambridge, 1947) *B*

Henry V. Poor, *History of the Railroads and Canals of the United States of America* (New York, 1860)

B. U. Ratchford, *American State Debts* (Durham, 1941) *B*

Merl E. Reed, *New Orleans and the Railroads: The Struggle for Commercial Empire, 1830–1860* (Baton Rouge, 1966) *B*

Samuel Rezneck, "The Rise and Early Development of Industrial Consciousness in the United States, 1760–1830," *The Journal of Economic and Business History,* IV (1932), 184

Thomas A. Rickard, *A History of American Mining* (New York, 1932)

Roy M. Robbins, *Our Landed Heritage: The Public Domain, 1776–1936* (Princeton, 1942) *B*

Ross W. Robertson, *History of the American Economy,* 2nd ed. (New York, 1964) *B*

Murray N. Rothbard, *The Panic of 1819* (New York, 1962) *B, BN*

Stephen Salsbury, *The State, the Investor, and the Railroad: The Boston and Albany, 1825–1867* (Cambridge, 1967) *B*

Bibliography

Fred A. Shannon, *Economic History of the People of the United States* (New York, 1934) *CB*

Ronald E. Shaw, *Erie Water West: A History of the Erie Canal, 1792–1854* (Lexington, 1966) *CB*

Walter B. Smith, *Economic Aspects of the Second Bank of the United States* (Cambridge, 1953) *CB*

——— and A. H. Cole, *Fluctuations in American Business, 1790–1860* (Cambridge, 1935)

Robert Sobel, *Panic on Wall Street: A History of America's Financial Disasters* (New York, 1968) *B*

George Soule and Vincent Carosso, *American Economic History* (New York, 1957) *CB*

John F. Stover, *American Railroads* (Chicago, 1961) *CB*

George R. Taylor, *The Transportation Revolution, 1815–1860* (New York, 1951) *CB*

Peter Temin, *Iron and Steel in Nineteenth-Century America: An Economic Inquiry* (Cambridge, 1964) *B*

———, *The Jacksonian Economy* (New York, 1969) *B*

Holland Thompson, *The Age of Invention: A Chronicle of Mechanical Conquest* (New Haven, 1921) *CB*

Robert L. Thompson, *Wiring a Continent: The History of the Telegraph Industry in the United States, 1832–1866* (Princeton, 1947) *B*

Walter S. Tower, *A History of the American Whale Fishery* (Philadelphia, 1907) *B*

Rolla M. Tryon, *Household Manufactures in the United States, 1640–1860* (Chicago, 1917) *B*

Lloyd Ulman, *The Rise of the National Trade Union*, 2nd ed. (Cambridge, 1966)

U.S. Bureau of Labor Statistics, *History of Wages in the United States from Colonial Times to 1928*, Bulletin 499 (Washington, 1929)

———, *Wholesale Prices, 1890–1923*, Bulletin 367, Appendix F, "Wholesale Prices in the United States, 1801–1840" (Washington, 1925)

George W. Van Vleck, *The Panic of 1857: An Analytical Study* (New York, 1943) *B*

Caroline F. Ware, *The Early New England Cotton Manufacture* (Boston, 1931) *B*

Charles Warren, *Bankruptcy in United States History* (Cambridge, 1935) *BN*

G. F. Warren and F. A. Pearson, *Wholesale Prices for 213 Years, 1720–1932* (Ithaca, 1932) *B*

Chester W. Wright, *Economic History of the United States* (New York, 1941) *CB*

The American Quest

XIII. SOCIAL DEVELOPMENT

Thomas P. Abernethy, *From Frontier to Plantation in Tennessee* (Chapel Hill, 1932) *B*

Robert Berkhofer, Jr., *Salvation and the Savage: An Analysis of Protestant Missions and American Indian Response, 1787–1862* (New York, 1966) *CB*

Rowland T. Berthoff, "The American Social Order: A Conservative Hypothesis," *AHR*, LXV (1960), 495 *BN*

———, *British Immigrants in Industrial America, 1825–1950* (Cambridge, 1953) *BN*

R. A. Billington, *The Protestant Crusade, 1800–1860* (New York, 1938) *B*

Carl Bode, ed., *American Life in the 1840's* (New York, 1967) *B*

Arthur W. Calhoun, *A Social History of the American Family,* vol. 1 (Cleveland, 1918) *B*

Monte A. Calvert, *The Mechanical Engineer in America, 1830–1910: Professional Cultures in Conflict* (Baltimore, 1967) *B*

John R. Commons *et al., History of Labour in the United States,* 3 vols. (New York, 1918–1935) *B*

Mary Coolidge, *Chinese Immigration* (New York, 1909) *B*

Whitney R. Cross, *The Burned-Over District* (1950) (New York, 1965)

Albert L. Demaree, *The American Agricultural Press, 1819–1860* (New York, 1941)

Sigmund Diamond, ed., *The Creation of Society in the New World* (Chicago, 1963) *B*

John Duffy, *A History of Public Health in New York City, 1625–1866* (New York, 1968) *CB*

———, *Sword of Pestilence: The New Orleans Yellow Fever Epidemic of 1853* (Baton Rouge, 1966) *B*

Foster R. Dulles, *A History of Recreation: America Learns to Play,* 2nd ed. (New York, 1965)

———, *Labor in America: A History* (New York, 1949) *CB*

Robert Ernst, *Immigrant Life in New York City, 1825–1863* (New York, 1949) *B*

Henry P. Fairchild, *Immigration* (New York, 1913) *B*

Henry W. Farnam, *Chapters in the History of Social Legislation in the United States to 1860* (Washington, 1938) *B*

Dixon R. Fox, *The Decline of Aristocracy in the Politics of New York* (New York, 1918) *BN*

———, *Yankees and Yorkers* (New York, 1940)

Bibliography

Constance Green, *American Cities in the Growth of the Nation* (New York, 1965) *B*
————, *The Rise of Urban America* (New York, 1965)
Oscar Handlin, *Boston's Immigrants*, rev. ed. (Cambridge, 1959) *CB*
Marcus L. Hansen, *The Atlantic Migration, 1607–1860* (Cambridge, 1940)
Maldwyn A. Jones, *American Immigration* (Chicago, 1960) *CB*
Joseph F. Kett, *The Formation of the American Medical Profession: The Role of Institutions, 1790–1860* (New Haven, 1968) *CB*
John A. Krout, *The Origins of Prohibition* (New York, 1925) *B*
Roger Lane, *Policing the City: Boston, 1822–1885* (Cambridge, 1967)
Harold D. Langley, *Social Reform in the United States Navy, 1798–1862* (Urbana, 1967) *B*
Blake McKelvey, *American Prisons: A Study in American Social History Prior to 1915* (Chicago, 1936) *CB*
Edgar W. Martin, *The Standard of Living in 1860: American Consumption Levels on the Eve of the Civil War* (Chicago, 1942)
Lois K. Mathews, *The Expansion of New England: The Spread of New England Settlement and Institutions to the Mississippi River, 1620–1865* (Boston, 1909) *CB*
Douglas T. Miller, *Jacksonian Aristocracy: Class Democracy in New York, 1830–1860* (New York, 1967) *B*
Stuart C. Miller, *The Unwelcome Immigrant: The American Image of the Chinese, 1785–1882* (Berkeley, 1969) *BN*
Earl F. Niehaus, *The Irish in New Orleans, 1800–1860* (Baton Rouge, 1965) *BN*
Frank L. Owsley, *Plain Folk of the Old South* (Baton Rouge, 1949)
Thomas W. Page, "Distribution of Immigrants in the United States Before 1870," *Journal of Political Economy*, XX (1912), 676
Selig Perlman, *A History of Trade Unionism in the United States* (New York, 1922) *B*
Edward Pessen, *Most Uncommon Jacksonians: The Radical Leaders of the Early Labor Movement* (Yellow Springs, 1967) *BN*
————, *Society, Personality, and Politics: Jacksonian America* (Homewood, 1969) *CB*
Robert S. Pickett, *House of Refuge: Origins of Juvenile Reform in New York State, 1815–1857* (Syracuse, 1969)
John W. Reps, *The Making of Urban America: A History of City Planning in the United States* (Princeton, 1965) *B*
Robert E. Riegel, *Young America, 1830–1840* (Norman, 1949) *CB*
Charles E. Rosenberg, *The Cholera Years: The United States in 1832, 1849, 1866* (Chicago, 1962) *B*

Edwin C. Rozwenc, *Cooperatives Come to America* (Mt. Vernon, 1941) *B*

Arthur M. Schlesinger, *The American as Reformer* (Cambridge, 1950) *BN*

David M. Schneider, *The History of Public Welfare in New York State, 1609–1866* (Chicago, 1938)

Richard H. Shryock, *Medicine and Society in America: 1660–1860* (Ithaca, 1962) *BN*

Timothy L. Smith, *Revivalism and Social Reform in Mid-Nineteenth-Century America* (New York, 1957) *CB*

George M. Stephenson, *History of American Immigration, 1820–1924* (Boston, 1926)

Stephen Thernstrom, *Poverty and Progress: Social Mobility in a Nineteenth Century City* (Cambridge, 1964) *BN*

C. Warren Thornthwaite and Helen I. Slentz, *Internal Migration in the United States* (Philadelphia, 1934)

Alice F. Tyler, *Freedom's Ferment: Phases of American Social History from the Colonial Period to the Outbreak of the Civil War* (1944) (New York, 1962) *BN*

Richard C. Wade, *The Urban Frontier: The Rise of Western Cities, 1790–1830* (Cambridge, 1959)

Norman Ware, *The Industrial Worker, 1840–1860* (Boston, 1924) *B*

Adna F. Weber, *The Growth of Cities in the Nineteenth Century: A Study in Statistics* (1899) (Ithaca, 1963)

Bernard Wishy, *The Child and the Republic: The Dawn of Modern American Child Nurture* (Philadelphia, 1968) *B, BN*

Carl F. Wittke, *The Irish in America* (Baton Rouge, 1956) *B*

———, *We Who Built America: The Saga of the Immigrant* (New York, 1939) *BN*

XIV. CULTURAL AND INTELLECTUAL DEVELOPMENT

Wayne Andrews, *Architecture, Ambition and Americans* (New York, 1964) *B*

Carl Bode, *The American Lyceum* (New York, 1956) *CB*

Daniel J. Boorstin, *The Americans: The National Experience* (New York, 1965) *CB*

James T. Callow, *Kindred Spirits: Knickerbocker Writers and American Artists, 1807–1855* (Chapel Hill, 1967) *B*

Richard Chase, *The American Novel and Its Tradition* (Garden City, 1957)

Bibliography

E. P. Cubberley, *Public Education in the United States* (Boston, 1934) *CB*

Marcus Cunliffe, *The Literature of the United States* (London, 1954) *CB*

Merle Curti, *The Growth of American Thought* (New York, 1943) *CB*

Joseph Dorfman, *The Economic Mind in American Civilization, 1606–1865*, 2 vols. (New York, 1946) *BN*

Arthur A. Ekirch, *The Idea of Progress in America, 1815–1860* (New York, 1944) *B, BN*

Ruth Miller Elson, *Guardians of Tradition: American School Books of the Nineteenth Century* (Lincoln, 1964) *B*

James T. Flexner, *The Light of Distant Skies: American Painting, 1760–1835* (New York, 1954) *B*

Ralph H. Gabriel, *The Course of American Democratic Thought*, 2nd ed. (New York, 1956) *B*

Neil Harris, *The Artist in American Society: The Formative Years, 1790–1860* (New York, 1966) *CB, BN*

Louis Hartz, *The Liberal Tradition in America* (New York, 1955) *BN*

Richard Hofstadter, *Anti-Intellectualism in American Life* (New York, 1963) *BN*

——— and Walter P. Metzger, *The Development of Academic Freedom in the United States* (New York, 1955) *BN*

Howard Mumford Jones, *The Theory of American Literature* (Ithaca, 1965) *BN*

Michael B. Katz, *The Irony of Early School Reform: Educational Innovation in Mid-Nineteenth Century Massachusetts* (Cambridge, 1968)

Alfred Kazin, *On Native Grounds* (New York, 1942)

Henry A. Kmen, *Music in New Orleans: The Formative Years, 1791–1841* (Baton Rouge, 1966) *B*

E. W. Knight, *Education in the United States* (Boston, 1951) *B*

R. W. B. Lewis, *The American Adam* (Chicago, 1955)

Orie W. Long, *Literary Pioneers: Early American Explorers of European Culture* (Cambridge, 1935)

David Madsen, *The National University: Enduring Dream of the U.S.A.* (Detroit, 1966) *B*

F. O. Matthiessen, *American Renaissance: Art and Expression in the Age of Emerson and Whitman* (New York, 1941)

Marvin Meyers, *The Jacksonian Persuasion* (Stanford, 1957) *B*

James M. Miller, *The Genesis of Western Culture: The Upper Ohio Valley, 1800–1825* (Columbus, 1938) *B*

Lillian B. Miller, "Paintings, Sculpture, and the National Character, 1815–1860," *JAH*, LVII (1967), 696 *BN*

————, *Patrons and Patriotism: The Encouragement of the Fine Arts in the United States, 1790–1860* (Chicago, 1966) *B, BN*

Perry Miller, ed., *The Legal Mind in America from Independence to the Civil War* (New York, 1962)

————, *The Life of the Mind in America* (New York, 1965)

————, *The Raven and the Whale* (New York, 1956)

David W. Minar, *Ideas and Politics: The American Experience* (Homewood, 1964) *BN*

Richard D. Mosier, *Making the American Mind: Social and Moral Ideas in the McGuffey Readers* (New York, 1947) *B*

Frank Luther Mott, *American Journalism* (New York, 1947) *BN*

————, *A History of American Magazines* (New York, 1930), vols. I–II *BN*

R. B. Nye, *The Cultural Life of the New Nation, 1776–1830* (New York, 1960) *CB*

Stow Persons, *American Minds* (New York, 1958) *B*

Arthur H. Quinn *et al.*, eds., *Literature of the American People* (New York, 1951) *CB*

H. G. Richey, *The School in the American Social Order* (Boston, 1947) *B*

Woodbridge Riley, *American Philosophy, the Early Schools* (1947) (New York, 1958) *BN*

Frederick Rudolph, ed., *Essays on Education in the Early Republic* (Cambridge, 1965)

Charles L. Sanford, *The Quest for Paradise* (Urbana, 1961)

Arthur M. Schlesinger, Jr., and Morton White, eds., *Paths of American Thought* (Boston, 1963) *B*

Herbert W. Schneider, *A History of American Philosophy* (New York, (1946) *CB*

Robert Skotheim, *American Intellectual Histories and Historians* (Princeton, 1966)

Timothy L. Smith, *Revivalism and Social Reform* (New York, 1958) *CB*

Benjamin T. Spencer, *The Quest for Nationality: An American Literary Campaign* (Syracuse, 1957) *B*

Robert E. Spiller *et al.*, *Literary History of the United States,* 3 vols. (New York, 1953) *CB*

Dirk J. Struik, *Yankee Science in the Making* (Boston, 1948) *B, BN*

William Warren Sweet, *Revivalism in America* (New York, 1944) *B*

————, *The Story of Religion in America,* rev. ed. (New York, 1920) *B*

Donald G. Tewkesbury, *The Founding of American Colleges and Universities Before the Civil War* (New York, 1932) *B*

Bibliography

William P. Trent *et al., The Cambridge History of American Literature* (New York, 1917–1921)

Bernard A. Weisberger, *They Gathered at the River: The Story of the Great Revivalists and Their Impact upon Religion in America* (Boston, 1958) *BN*

Rush Welter, *Popular Education and Democratic Thought in America* (New York, 1962) *B*

XV. THE REVOLUTION AND THE CONSTITUTION

Randolph G. Adams, *Political Ideas of the American Revolution* (Durham, 1922) *B*

John R. Alden, *A History of the American Revolution* (New York, 1969) *CB*

Charles M. Andrews, *The Colonial Background of the American Revolution* (New Haven, 1924)

Hannah Arendt, *On Revolution* (New York, 1963) *B*

Bernard F. Bailyn, *The Ideological Origins of the American Revolution* (Cambridge, 1967) *BN*

———, *The Origins of American Politics* (New York, 1968) *BN*

Alice M. Baldwin, *The New England Clergy and the American Revolution* (Durham, 1928) *B*

Thomas C. Barrow, "The American Revolution as a Colonial War for Independence," *WMQ*, XXV (1968), 542 *BN*

Carl Becker, *The Declaration of Independence* (1922) (New York, 1942)

Samuel F. Bemis, *The Diplomacy of the American Revolution* (Bloomington, 1957) *CB*

George Athan Billias, ed., *The American Revolution: How Revolutionary Was It?* (New York, 1965) *CB*

Morton Borden, ed., *The Antifederalist Papers* (East Lansing, 1965)

Robert E. Brown, *Middle-Class Democracy and the Revolution in Massachusetts, 1691–1780* (Ithaca, 1955) *B, BN*

Richard Buel, Jr., "Democracy and the American Revolution: A Frame of Reference," *WMQ*, XXI (1964), 165 *BN*

Edmund C. Burnett, *The Continental Congress* (1941) (New York, 1964)

Trevor Colbourn, *The Lamp of Experience* (Chapel Hill, 1965) *BN*

Elisha P. Douglass, *Rebels and Democrats* (Chapel Hill, 1955) *CB*

Robert A. East, *Business Enterprise in the American Revolutionary Era* (New York, 1938) *B*

Paul Eidelberg, *The Philosophy of the American Constitution* (New York, 1968) *B*

E. James Ferguson, *The Power of the Purse: A History of American Public Finance, 1776–1790* (Chapel Hill, 1961) *CB*

Bernard Friedman, "The Shaping of the Radical Consciousness in Provincial New York," *JAH*, LVI (1970), 781 *BN*

L. H. Gipson, *The Coming of the Revolution, 1763–1775* (New York, 1954) *CB*

Jack P. Greene, "The Flight from Determinism: A Review of Recent Literature on the Coming of the American Revolution," *South Atlantic Quarterly*, LXI (1962), 235 *BN*

———, ed., *The Reinterpretation of the American Revolution: 1763–1789* (New York, 1968)

Alan Heimert, *Religion and the American Mind: From the Great Awakening to the Revolution* (Cambridge, 1966) *B*

Don Higginbotham, "American Historians and the Military History of the American Revolution," *AHR*, LXX (1964), 18 *BN*

John R. Howe, Jr., ed., *The Role of Ideology in the American Revolution* (New York, 1970) *CB*

J. Franklin Jameson, *The American Revolution Considered as a Social Movement* (1926) (Boston, 1956)

Merrill Jensen, *The Articles of Confederation* (Madison, 1940) *BN*

———, "Democracy and the American Revolution," *Huntington Library Quarterly*, XX (1957), 321

———, *The Founding of a Nation: A History of the American Revolution, 1763–1776* (New York, 1968)

———, *The New Nation* (New York, 1950)

Michael G. Kammen, *A Rope of Sand: The Colonial Agents, British Politics, and the American Revolution* (Ithaca, 1968) *CB*

Cecilia Kenyon, ed., *The Antifederalists* (Indianapolis, 1966)

Bernhard Knollenberg, *Origins of the American Revolution, 1759–1766* (New York, 1960) *B*

Michael Kraus, *The Atlantic Civilization: Eighteenth-Century Origins* (1949) (Ithaca, 1966) *CB*

———, *Intercolonial Aspects of American Culture on the Eve of the American Revolution* (New York, 1928) *B*

Jesse Lemisch, "Jack Tar in the Streets: Merchant Seamen in the Politics of Revolutionary America," *WMQ*, XXV (1968), 271 *BN*

David Lovejoy, *Rhode Island Politics and the American Revolution* (Providence, 1958)

Staughton Lynd, *Anti-Federalism in Dutchess County, New York* (Chicago, 1962)

Bibliography

————, *Class Conflict, Slavery, and the United States Constitution* (Indianapolis, 1967)

Forrest McDonald, *E Pluribus Unum: The Formation of the American Republic, 1776–1790* (Chicago, 1956) *BN*

————, *We the People: The Economic Origins of the Constitution* (Madison, 1958) *BN*

Andrew C. McLaughlin, *The Confederation and the Constitution* (New York, 1905) *CB*

Jackson T. Main, "Government by the People: The American Revolution and the Democratization of the Legislature," *WMQ*, XXIII (1966), 391

————, *The Social Structure of Revolutionary America* (Princeton, 1965)

————, *The Upper House in Revolutionary America* (Madison, 1967) *BN*

John C. Miller, *Origins of the American Revolution* (Boston, 1943)

Edmund S. Morgan, ed., *The American Revolution: Two Centuries of Interpretation* (Englewood Cliffs, 1965) *CB*

————, *The Birth of the Republic, 1763–1789* (Chicago, 1956) *CB*

———— and Helen Morgan, *The Stamp Act Crisis*, rev. ed. (New York, 1963)

Richard B. Morris, *The American Revolution Reconsidered* (New York, 1967) *BN*

————, *The Peacemakers: The Great Powers and American Independence* (New York, 1965)

William H. Nelson, *The American Tory* (Boston, 1961)

Allan Nevins, *The American States During and After the Revolution* (New York, 1924) *CB*

R. R. Palmer, *The Age of the Democratic Revolution*, 2 vols. (Princeton, 1959–1964) *BN*

Benjamin Quarles, *The Negro in the American Revolution* (Chapel Hill, 1961) *B*

Clinton Rossiter, *Seedtime of the Republic* (New York, 1953) *BN*

————, *1787: The Grand Convention* (New York, 1966) *B*

Max Savelle, "Nationalism and Other Loyalties in the American Revolution," *AHR*, LXVII (1962), 901 *BN*

————, *Seeds of Liberty* (New York, 1948)

Nathan Schachner, *The Founding Fathers* (New York, 1954) *B*

Arthur M. Schlesinger, *The Birth of a Nation: A Portrait of the American People on the Eve of Independence* (New York, 1968) *B*

————, *The Colonial Merchants and the American Revolution* (New York, 1917) *B*

William C. Stinchcombe, *The American Revolution and the French Alliance* (Syracuse, 1969) *B*

Charles S. Sydnor, *American Revolutionaries in the Making* (New York, 1965) *CB*

Carl Van Doren, *The Great Rehearsal* (New York, 1948)

Dale Van Every, *A Company of Heroes: The American Frontier, 1775–1783* (New York, 1962) *B*

Claude H. Van Tyne, *The Loyalists in the American Revolution* (Gloucester, 1902)

Franklin B. Wickwire, *British Subministers and Colonial America, 1763–1783* (Princeton, 1966) *CB*

Gordon S. Wood, *The Creation of the American Republic, 1776–1787* (Chapel Hill, 1969) *CB*

———, "A Note on Mobs in the American Revolution," *WMQ*, XXIII (1966), 635 *BN*

———, "Rhetoric and Reality in the American Revolution," *WMQ*, XXIII (1966), 3 *BN*

XVI. WAR AND DIPLOMACY

Francis F. Beirne, *The War of 1812* (New York, 1949) *B*

Samuel Flagg Bemis, *Jay's Treaty*, rev. ed. (New Haven, 1962) *CB*

———, *Pinckney's Treaty*, rev. ed. (New Haven, 1960) *CB*

J. Bartlet Brebner, *Canada: A Modern History* (Ann Arbor, 1960) *B*

———, *North Atlantic Triangle* (New York, 1945) *CB*

Harry L. Coles, *The War of 1812* (Chicago, 1965) *CB*

Gerald M. Craig, *The United States and Canada* (Cambridge, 1968) *CB*

Marcus Cunliffe, *Soldiers and Civilians: The Martial Spirit in America, 1775–1865* (Boston, 1968) *BN*

Alexander DeConde, *Entangling Alliance* (Durham, 1958)

James A. Field, *America and the Mediterranean World* (Princeton, 1969) *CB*

J. Mackay Hitsman, *The Incredible War of 1812: A Military History* (Toronto, 1965)

Reginald Horsman, *The War of 1812* (New York, 1969) *CB*

Frederick Merk, *The Monroe Doctrine and American Expansionism, 1843–1849* (New York, 1966) *BN*

———, *The Oregon Question* (Cambridge, 1967) *BN*

Bradford Perkins, *Castlereagh and Adams: England and the United States, 1812–1823* (Berkeley, 1964) *CB*

————, *First Rapprochement: England and the United States, 1795–1823* (Philadelphia, 1955) *CB*

————, *Prologue to War: England and the United States, 1805–1812* (Berkeley, 1961) *CB*

Francis Paul Prucha, *The Sword of the Republic: The United States Army on the Frontier, 1783–1846* (New York, 1969) *B*

Charles Ritcheson, *British Politics and the American Revolution* (Norman, 1954) *B*

Otis Singletary, *The Mexican War* (Chicago, 1960) *CB*

C. C. Tansill, *The United States and Santa Domingo, 1798–1873* (Baltimore, 1938) *BN*

Robert M. Utley, *Frontiersmen in Blue: The United States Army and the Indian, 1848–1865* (New York, 1967) *B*

Donald F. Warner, *The Idea of Continental Union: Agitation for the Annexation of Canada to the United States, 1849–1873* (Lexington, 1960)

XVII. SLAVERY AND ANTISLAVERY

Hugh C. Bailey, *Hinton Rowan Helper: Abolitionist-Racist* (University, Ala., 1965) *B*

Eugene H. Berwanger, *The Frontier Against Slavery: Western Anti-Negro Prejudice and the Slavery Extension Controversy* (Urbana, 1967) *B*

Alfred H. Conrad *et al.,* "Slavery as an Obstacle to Economic Growth in the United States: A Panel Discussion," *JEH,* XXVII (1967), 518

———— and John R. Meyer, "The Economics of Slavery in the Ante Bellum South," *Journal of Political Economy,* LXVI (1958), 95

Philip D. Curtin, *The Atlantic Slave Trade: A Census* (Madison, 1969) *B*

David B. Davis, *The Problem of Slavery in Western Culture* (Ithaca, 1966) *BN*

Merton Dillon, *Benjamin Lundy and the Struggle for Negro Freedom* (Urbana, 1966) *CB*

Martin Duberman, ed., *The Antislavery Vanguard: New Essays on the Abolitionists* (Princeton, 1965) *BN*

William E. B. Du Bois, *The Suppression of the African Slave-Trade to the United States of America, 1638–1870* (1896) (New York, 1954) *B*

Dwight L. Dumond, *Antislavery Origins of the Civil War in the United States* (Ann Arbor, 1959)

The American Quest

——, *Bibliography of Antislavery in America* (East Lansing, 1961)

Stanley Elkins, *Slavery,* 2nd ed. (New York, 1968) *BN*

Louis Filler, *The Crusade Against Slavery, 1830–1860* (New York, 1960) *CB*

Roger A. Fischer, "Racial Segregation in Ante Bellum New Orleans," *AHR,* LXXIV (1969), 926

John Hope Franklin, *From Slavery to Freedom: A History of American Negroes,* 2nd ed. (New York, 1963) *CB*

Eugene D. Genovese, *The Political Economy of Slavery: Studies in the Economy and Society of the Slave South* (New York, 1965) *CB, BN*

Winthrop Jordan, *White Over Black* (Chapel Hill, 1968) *CB*

Herbert S. Klein, *Slavery in the Americas: A Comparative Study of Cuba and Virginia* (Chicago, 1967) *BN*

Lawrence Lader, *The Bold Brahmins: New England's War Against Slavery, 1831–1863* (New York, 1961) *B*

Leon F. Litwack, *North of Slavery: The Negro in the Free States, 1790–1860* (Chicago, 1961) *CB*

Alma Lutz, *Crusade for Freedom: Women of the Antislavery Movement* (Boston, 1968) *B*

Robert McColley, *Slavery and Jeffersonian Virginia* (Urbana, 1964) *BN*

Edgar J. McManus, *A History of Negro Slavery in New York* (Syracuse, 1966)

Donald G. Mathews, *Slavery and Methodism: A Chapter in American Morality, 1780–1845* (Princeton, 1965) *B*

Russel B. Nye, *Fettered Freedom: Civil Liberties and the Slavery Controversy, 1830–1860* (East Lansing, 1964) *B*

Ulrich B. Phillips, *American Negro Slavery* (1918) (Baton Rouge, 1966) *BN*

——, *Life and Labor in the Old South* (Boston, 1929) *BN*

Benjamin Quarles, *Black Abolitionists* (New York, 1969)

——, *Lincoln and the Negro* (New York, 1962) *CB*

Lorman Ratner, *Powder Keg: Northern Opposition to the Antislavery Movement, 1831–1840* (New York, 1968) *B*

John H. Russell, *The Free Negro in Virginia, 1619–1865* (Baltimore, 1913) *B*

Elbert B. Smith, *The Death of Slavery: The United States, 1837–1865* (Chicago, 1967) *CB*

Kenneth M. Stampp, *The Peculiar Institution: Slavery in the Ante-Bellum South* (New York, 1964)

Robert Starobin, *Industrial Slavery in the Old South* (New York, 1970) *CB*

Bibliography

P. J. Staudenraus, *The African Colonization Movement* (New York, 1961)

Bernard C. Steiner, *History of Slavery in Connecticut* (Baltimore, 1893)

Richard C. Wade, *Slavery in the Cities: The South, 1820–1860* (New York 1964) *B*

Arthur Zilversmit, *The First Emancipation: The Abolition of Negro Slavery in the North* (Chicago, 1967) *CB*

XVIII. THE SOUTH

Stuart Bruchey, ed., *Cotton and the Growth of the American Economy: 1790–1860* (New York, 1967) *B*

Jesse T. Carpenter, *The South as a Conscious Minority, 1789–1861* (New York, 1930) *B*

W. J. Cash, *The Mind of the South* (New York, 1941)

Avery Craven, *The Growth of Southern Nationalism* (Baton Rouge, 1953) *CB*

———, *Soil Exhaustion as a Factor in the Agricultural History of Virginia and Maryland, 1606–1860* (Urbana, 1925) *B*

Clement Eaton, *The Freedom-of-Thought Struggle in the Old South* (New York, 1964) *BN*

———, *The Growth of Southern Civilization, 1790–1860* (New York, 1961) *CB*

———, *The Mind of the Old South* (Baton Rouge, 1964) *CB*

John Hope Franklin, *The Free Negro in North Carolina, 1790–1860* (Chapel Hill, 1943) *B*

———, *The Militant South, 1800–1861* (Cambridge, 1956) *CB*

William W. Freehling, *Prelude to the Civil War: The Nullification Controversy in South Carolina, 1816–1836* (New York, 1966) *CB*

Lewis C. Gray, *History of Agriculture in the Southern United States to 1860*, 2 vols. (New York, 1933) *B, BN*

M. B. Hammond, *The Cotton Industry: An Essay in American Economic History* (1897) (New York, 1966) *B*

Arthur S. Link and Rembert W. Patrick, eds., *Writing Southern History* (Baton Rouge, 1966) *B, BN*

Thomas H. O'Connor, *Lords of the Loom: The Cotton Whigs and the Coming of the Civil War* (New York, 1968) *B*

Ulrich B. Phillips, *The Slave Economy of the Old South: Selected Essays in Economic and Social History* (Baton Rouge, 1968), Eugene D. Genovese, ed.

David M. Potter, *The South and the Sectional Conflict* (Baton Rouge, 1968) *BN*

The American Quest

Joseph C. Robert, *The Road from Monticello: A Study of the Virginia Slavery Debate of 1832* (Durham, 1941) *BN*
———, *The Tobacco Kingdom: Plantation, Market, and Factory in Virginia and North Carolina, 1800–1860* (Durham, 1938) *B*
Robert R. Russel, *Economic Aspects of Southern Sectionalism, 1840–1861* (New York, 1960) *B*
Harold S. Schultz, *Nationalism and Sectionalism in South Carolina, 1852–1860* (Chapel Hill, 1950) *B*
Joseph C. Sitterson, *Sugar Country: The Cane Sugar Industry in the South, 1753–1950* (Lexington, 1953) *CB*
Charles S. Sydnor, *The Development of Southern Sectionalism, 1819–1848* (Baton Rouge, 1948) *CB*
James L. Watkins, *King Cotton: A Historical and Statistical Review, 1790–1908* (New York, 1908) *B*
Harold D. Woodman, ed., *Slavery and the Southern Economy* (New York, 1966) *B*
C. Vann Woodward, *The Burden of Southern History*, rev. ed. (Baton Rouge, 1968)
———, "The Southern Ethic in a Puritan World," *WMQ*, XXV (1968), 343

XIX. THE CIVIL WAR

Ralph Adreano, ed., *The Economic Impact of the American Civil War* (Cambridge, 1967) *CB*
Curtis A. Amlund, *Federalism in the Southern Confederacy* (Washington, 1966)
Herman Belz, *Reconstructing the Union: Theory and Policy During the Civil War* (Ithaca, 1968) *CB*
James H. Brewer, *The Confederate Negro: Virginia's Craftsmen and Military Laborers, 1861–1865* (Durham, 1969) *B, BN*
Denis Brogan, *American Aspects* (New York, 1964)
Arthur C. Cole, *The Irrepressible Conflict, 1850–1865* (New York, 1934) *CB*
E. M. Coulter, *The Confederate States of America* (Baton Rouge, 1950) *CB*
Avery Craven, *The Coming of the Civil War*, 2nd ed. (Chicago, 1957) *BN*
———, *Reconstruction: The Ending of the Civil War* (New York, 1969) *B*
Richard N. Current, *Lincoln and the First Shot* (Philadelphia, 1963) *B*

Bibliography

Leonard P. Curry, *Blueprint for Modern America: Nonmilitary Legislation of the First Civil War Congress* (Nashville, 1968) *B*

David H. Donald, *Excess of Democracy: American Civil War and Social Process* (New York, 1960)

Dwight L. Dumond, *The Secession Movement, 1860–1861* (New York, 1931) *B*

Clement Eaton, *A History of the Confederacy* (New York, 1954) *BN*

George Fredrickson, *The Inner Civil War: Northern Intellectuals and the Crisis of the Union* (New York, 1965) *BN*

Paul W. Gates, *Agriculture and the Civil War* (New York, 1965)

David T. Gilchrist and David Lewis, eds., *Economic Change in the Civil War Era* (Greenville, 1965)

Burton J. Hendrick, *Lincoln's War Cabinet* (Boston, 1946)

William B. Hesseltine, *Lincoln and the War Governors* (New York, 1948) *B*

Margaret Leech, *Reveille in Washington* (New York, 1941) *B*

James McCague, *The Second Rebellion: The Story of the New York City Draft Riots of 1863* (New York, 1968) *B*

William Q. Maxwell, *Lincoln's Fifth Wheel: The Political History of the United States Sanitary Commission* (New York, 1956) *B*

Eugene Murdock, *Patriotism Limited, 1862–1865* (Kent, 1967)

Allan Nevins, *The Emergence of Lincoln*, 2 vols. (New York, 1950) *CB*

———, *The Ordeal of the Union*, 2 vols. (New York, 1947)

———, *The War for the Union*, 2 vols. (New York, 1959–1960) *B*

———, James I. Robertson, Jr., and Bell I. Wiley, eds., *Civil War Books: A Critical Bibliography*, 2 vols. (Baton Rouge, 1967–1969)

Roy F. Nichols, *The Disruption of American Democracy* (New York, 1948) *B*

Frank L. Owsley, *King Cotton Diplomacy* (Chicago, 1959) *B*

Thomas J. Pressly, ed., *Americans Interpret Their Civil War* (New York, 1964) *CB, BN*

Charles P. Roland, *The Confederacy* (Chicago, 1960) *CB*

F. A. Shannon, *The Organization and Administration of the Union Army*, 2 vols. (Cleveland, 1928) *B*

Kenneth M. Stampp, *And the War Came* (Baton Rouge, 1950) *B*

———, ed., *The Causes of the Civil War* (Englewood Cliffs, 1959)

C. J. Stille, *History of the United States Sanitary Commission* (Philadelphia, 1866)

Georgia Lee Tatum, *Disloyalty in the Confederacy* (Chapel Hill, 1934) *B*

The American Quest

William H. Townsend, *Lincoln and the Bluegrass: Slavery and Civil War in Kentucky* (Lexington, 1955) *BN*

G. E. Turner, *Victory Rode the Rails* (Indianapolis, 1953)

Frank E. Vandiver *et al., Essays on the American Civil War* (Austin, 1968) *B, BN*

Jacque Voegeli, *Free But Not Equal: The Midwest and the Negro During the Civil War* (Chicago, 1967) *CB*

T. Harry Williams, *Lincoln and the Radicals* (Madison, 1941) *B*

Notes

CHAPTER 1

1. Henry James, *Hawthorne* (1879) (Ithaca, 1956), 34.
2. (Hudson, N.Y.) *Balance and Columbian Repository*, March 5, 1818.
3. Taylor, *Transportation Revolution*, esp. 102–103, 132 ff., 248–249, 396–398.
4. These and other statistics of growth may be found (and then handled with care) in *Historical Statistics of the United States*.
5. Fourth Annual Message to Congress, December 5, 1848, in Richardson, *Messages and Papers of Presidents*, IV, 629.
6. James, *Hawthorne*, 33.
7. Eisenstadt, *Modernization*, iii.
8. Haas, *Beyond the Nation-State*, 462, makes a persuasive case for the argument that, while nationalism may be something of a luxury in the overdeveloped West, the rest of the world sees it as a necessity of life.
9. Hexter, *Reappraisals in History*, 194.
10. See generally the thoughtful critiques of John Higham listed in the bibliography under the heading "The Study of History" and also such case studies as Lynd, *Anti-Federalism in Dutchess County*, esp. 1–9.
11. Rossiter, *1787: The Grand Convention*, 19.
12. Arnold, "The Scholar Gipsy" (1853), in *The Works of Matthew Arnold* (London, 1903), I, 236.
13. Arthur Rimbaud, *Une Saison en Enfer* (1873), in *Complete Works, Selected Letters* (Chicago, 1966), 209.
14. Twain, *Life on the Mississippi* (Boston, 1883), 437.

CHAPTER 2

1. In Renan's *Oeuvres Complètes* (Paris, n.d.), I, 887. The quotations in this chapter can be found on pp. 887–906.

2. For some of the more useful books on nationalism and national development, see pp. 325–332.
3. Moore, *Political Power and Social Theory* (Cambridge, 1958), 89 ff.
4. Deutsch, *Nationalism and Social Communication*, 89.
5. From the Farewell Address, September 19, 1796, in *Writings of Washington*, XXXV, 231.
6. See generally K. H. Silvert, *Chile Yesterday and Today* (New York, 1965), esp. 51 ff., 118 ff.; F. B. Pike, *Chile and the United States* (Notre Dame, 1963), esp. 1 ff., 159 ff. For an interesting if, in my opinion, wrongheaded Marxist analysis of the problem, see A. G. Frank, *Capitalism and Underdevelopment in Latin America* (New York, 1967), 55 ff.
7. Hertz, *Nationality*, chap. 5.
8. Renan, *Oeuvres Complètes*, I, 904.
9. Arthur Clutton-Brock, *Essays on Religion* (London, 1926), 80–110.
10. Quoted in C. J. Friedrich, *Man and His Government* (New York, 1963), 556.

CHAPTER 3

1. Hyman, *Political Socialization*, esp. 18–25; Almond and Coleman, *Politics of the Developing Areas*, 26–31.
2. Almond and Coleman, *Politics of the Developing Areas*, 33–45.
3. Apter, *Politics of Modernization*, esp. 22 ff., 36, 357 ff., 391 ff.
4. Pye, *Politics, Personality, and Nation-Building*, esp. xiii ff., 212 ff.
5. LaPalombara and Weiner, eds., *Political Parties and Political Development*, esp. 298 ff.
6. My own use of this concept is somewhat more narrowly focused than that of Almond, "Comparative Political Systems," 396–397, or Pye, *Politics, Personality, and Nation-Building*, 122–125, to both of which discussions I am much in debt.
7. Silvert *et al.*, *Expectant Peoples*, 435; Apter, *Politics of Modernization*, 433.
8. Supple, *Experience of Economic Growth*, 11 ff., 52 ff.; Rostow, *Stages of Economic Growth*, 1 ff.; Heilbroner, *Great Ascent*, 14 ff.
9. Hacker, *Course of American Economic Growth and Development*, xiii.
10. Hirschman, *Strategy of Economic Development*, chaps. 6–7.
11. Heilbroner, *Great Ascent*, esp. chaps. 3–5.
12. Merle Fainsod, *How Russia Is Ruled*, rev. ed. (Cambridge, 1967), chap. 16.
13. McCord, *Springtime of Freedom*, chap. 4.

Notes

14. Deutsch, *Nationalism and Social Communication,* esp. chap. 4.
15. I have been impressed and instructed by Kalman Silvert's discussion of Argentina in Silvert *et al., Expectant Peoples,* 347–372, as well as by Robert E. Scott's chapter in Deutsch and Foltz, eds., *Nation-Building,* 73–83.
16. Silvert *et al., Expectant Peoples,* viii.
17. Eisenstadt, *Modernization,* 60.
18. Bettelheim, *The Children of the Dream* (New York, 1969), esp. 13, 165 ff., 175 ff. See also Melford E. Spiro, *Kibbutz: Venture in Utopia* (New York, 1963), chap. 5.
19. Deutsch, *Nationalism and Social Communication,* 97.
20. Butterfield, *The Origins of Modern Science* (London, 1949), esp. chap. 10.

CHAPTER 4

1. Renan, *Oeuvres Complètes,* I, 904.
2. Sir William Watson, "Our Eastern Treasure," in *The Poems of William Watson* (London, 1893), 81.
3. McClelland, *Achieving Society,* esp. chaps. 1–4. See also Deutsch, *Nationalism and Social Communication,* 25–26, 165 ff.; Hertz, *Nationality,* 13, 233 ff.; Ashford, *National Development and Local Reform,* chaps. 10–12.
4. Dickinson, *The Greek View of Life* (London, 1929), 248.
5. Kohn, *Idea of Nationalism,* 16.
6. To the Convention of 1787, in *Papers of Hamilton,* IV, 216.
7. The bibliography of Indian democracy is endless. I have been especially impressed by the point of view of Chopra, *Uncertain India,* 244 ff.
8. Bienen, ed., *The Military Intervenes,* xiii–xiv.
9. See the studies of Turkey listed in the bibliography at pp. 330–332, especially Ward and Rustow, eds., *Political Modernization in Japan and Turkey,* 328–388, as well as Janowitz, *The Military in the Political Development of New Nations,* 30 n.
10. Janowitz, *The Military,* 67.
11. Huntington, *Political Order in Changing Societies,* 237 ff.
12. For this discussion I have drawn on my *Marxism: The View from America* (New York, 1960), 244 ff., as well as on the works cited at pp. 323–324 of that book.
13. V. I. Lenin, *What Is to Be Done?* (1902) (New York, 1929), 12, 15, 61, 75, 82, 94 ff., 105, 110 ff., 168.

CHAPTER 5

1. John Mein, *Sagittarius's Letters* (Boston, 1775), 20.
2. For a useful if somewhat strained introduction to the British-American Whig theory of the significant role of conspiracy in history, see the note in Bailyn, ed., *Pamphlets of the Revolution* (Cambridge, 1965), 86 ff.
3. (Little Rock) *Arkansas Gazette,* July 2, 1822.
4. See the table in Allen, *Great Britain and the United States,* 59, which shows that Britain accounted for 50 per cent of American exports and 40 per cent of American imports in the period 1846–1850.
5. (Portsmouth) *New Hampshire Mercury,* August 23, 1787. See generally the famous strictures of Lord Sheffield, *Observations on the Commerce of the American States,* 2nd ed. (London, 1784).
6. See especially the works of Bruchey, Hacker, North, Parker, and Taylor in the bibliography at pp. 340–345. This is one of those areas in which plentiful and reliable statistics would seem to be, but are definitely not, easy to assemble.
7. Thistlethwaite, *America and the Atlantic Community,* chaps. 1, 6.
8. Allen, *Great Britain and the United States,* chap. 5.
9. See especially Webster's preface to *A Grammatical Institute of the English Language . . . Part I* (Hartford, 1784); Ingersoll's *A Discourse Concerning the Influence of America on the Mind* (Philadelphia, 1823); Channing, *The Works of William Ellery Channing* (Boston, 1869), I, 243–280; and Emerson's Phi Beta Kappa address of 1837 in *Emerson's Complete Works* (Boston, 1886), I, 81–115.
10. H. L. Mencken, *The American Language,* 4th ed. (New York, 1946), 130 ff.
11. *Edinburgh Review,* XXXI (December 1818), 144.
12. For several extreme assertions of continuing American artistic dependence, see the works cited in Lipset, *First New Nation,* 71 n.
13. Although the date of the Gadsden Purchase is generally given as 1853, I prefer 1854, as the year in which, on June 29, to be exact, the treaty with Mexico was finally ratified.
14. *Louisville* (Ky.) *Public Advertiser,* December 11, 1824.
15. March 1, 1825, *Register of Debates in Congress* (18th Cong., 2nd Sess., Senate), I, 712.
16. *Memoirs of J. Q. Adams,* IV, 437–439.
17. *Memoirs of J. Q. Adams,* VI, 250–251. An excellent presentation of the Adams point of view is to be found in Walter LaFeber, ed., *John Quincy Adams and American Continental Empire* (Chicago, 1965), esp. 35–46.

Notes

18. De Voto, *Year of Decision*, 467–484.
19. January 9, 1812, *Annals of Congress* (12th Cong., 1st Sess., House), 712.
20. (Little Rock) *Arkansas Gazette*, November 25, 1825.
21. Merk, *Manifest Destiny*, esp. chap. 10.
22. For an introduction to the enduring problem of Canada, see Allen, *Great Britain and the United States*, 177 ff., as well as the passages quoted from Brebner, *North Atlantic Triangle*.
23. H. P. Johnston, ed., *The Correspondence and Public Papers of John Jay* (New York, 1890–1893), III, 154.
24. O'Dea, *Mormons*, 79 ff.; De Voto, *Year of Decision*, 235 ff., 312 ff., 368 ff.; Billington, *Far Western Frontier*, 182–183.
25. Farnam, *History of Social Legislation to 1860*, 223–224.
26. Rossiter, *Hamilton and the Constitution*, esp. 194 ff.
27. Nagel, *One Nation Indivisible*, esp. 117, 136–137.
28. *The Writings of Daniel Webster*, VI, 181–238.
29. Story, *Commentaries on the Constitution*, I, 318–343, esp. 329.
30. *Texas* v. *White*, 7 Wallace 700, 725 (1869).
31. August O. Spain, *The Political Theory of John C. Calhoun* (New York, 1968), 184 ff.
32. Nagel, *One Nation Indivisible*, esp. 3–9.
33. Fox, *Yankees and Yorkers*, esp. chaps. 1, 3, 8.
34. Rossiter, *Seedtime of the Republic*, 150–156, and works cited at 497, n. 11.
35. *Historical Statistics*, 83.
36. *Historical Statistics*, 57, 59, 61.
37. And also on American politics. See Silbey, *Transformation of American Politics*, esp. 8 ff.
38. Billington, *Protestant Crusade*, esp. chaps. 11–13.
39. *Works of Adams*, IX, 546; *Writings of Jefferson* (Lipscomb), XII, 277.
40. *Historical Statistics*, 11.
41. For an overpowering argument on this point, see Jordan, *White Over Black*, esp. chaps. 1, 5–6, 12–15.
42. *Historical Statistics*, 9; Coolidge, *Chinese Immigration*, chap. 1; Miller, *Unwelcome Immigrant*, 167 ff.
43. Hagan, *American Indians*, 71–76, 80–81, and works cited on 179; Starkey, *Cherokee Nation*, 282 ff. A somewhat countervailing view of this whole problem (as well as an introduction to recent literature) is Sheehan, "Indian-White Relations in Early America."
44. Litwack, *North of Slavery*, esp. chaps. 3–5.
45. Farnam, *History of Social Legislation to 1860*, 218–221.

46. Merritt, *Symbols of American Community,* chap. 1; Kohn, *American Nationalism,* chaps. 2–3.
47. From the jointly written commencement address of Philip Freneau and H. H. Brackenridge at the College of New Jersey (Princeton), September 25, 1771, in F. L. Pattee, ed., *The Poems of Philip Freneau,* 3 vols. (Princeton, 1902–1907), I, 80.
48. The phrase is from the Rev. William Smith, *A Sermon on the Present Situation* (Philadelphia, 1775), 23, which was delivered to members of the Continental Congress. See especially the development of the theme of an "Arcadia-Enterprise" ambivalence in Meyers, *Jacksonian Persuasion,* 11 ff., 123, 203–209.
49. *Works of Lincoln,* I, 108.
50. *Works of Lincoln,* IV, 271.
51. Gabriel, *Course of American Democratic Thought,* 93 ff., a kind yet essentially debunking interpretation. A contrary view is Curti, *Roots of American Loyalty,* chap. 5.
52. Cunliffe, *Washington, Man and Monument,* esp. chaps. 1, 5; Wecter, *Hero in America,* chaps. 1, 3–8; Van Alstyne, *Genesis of American Nationalism,* 135 ff.
53. Hartz, *Liberal Tradition,* chaps. 4–7; C. Rossiter, *Conservatism in America,* 2nd ed. (New York, 1962), 117 ff.
54. To Thomas Dwight, October 26, 1803, in Ames, ed., *Works of Fisher Ames,* I, 328.
55. Strout, *American Image of the Old World,* 1.
56. *American Railroad Journal,* I (1832), 375; Stanley T. Williams, *The Life of Washington Irving* (New York, 1935), II, 334, n. 2.
57. James, *Hawthorne,* 121.
58. Arieli, *Individualism and Nationalism,* chaps. 9–10.
59. Curti, "Francis Lieber and Nationalism," in *Probing Our Past,* 119–151.
60. (Little Rock) *Arkansas Gazette,* January 1, 1820; *Louisville* (Ky.) *Public Advertiser,* April 27, 1825.
61. Strout, *American Image of the Old World,* chap. 3; Palmer, *Age of Democratic Revolution,* I, 263 ff., 282.
62. (St. Stephens, Ala.) *Halcyon,* July 3, 1820.
63. For these and other statements of the American mission, as well as for more elaborate discussions of the concept, see C. Rossiter, "The American Mission," *The American Scholar,* XX (1950–1951), 19; Burns, *American Idea of Mission,* esp. chaps. 1–4; Tuveson, *Redeemer Nation,* esp. chaps. 5–6, which stresses the religious origins of the concept; Gabriel, *Course of American Democratic Thought,* 22 ff.; Nagel, *One Nation Indivisible,* chap. 5; Strout, *American*

Notes

Image of the Old World, chap. 3; James H. Smylie, "Protestant Clergymen and American Destiny," *Harvard Theological Review,* LVI (1963), 217, which is especially useful for its emphasis on the connection made by the clergy between the new Republic and ancient Israel; Van Alstyne, *Genesis of American Nationalism,* 65, 169 ff.

64. Farrand, *Records of the Convention* (New Haven, 1966), I, 423–424, the language of the reporter, Madison himself, and also of Hamilton, having been changed from the third to the first person. Other expressions of this idea during and after the Convention of 1787 may be found in Farrand, *Records,* I, 405, 515, 519, 529; II, 249; III, 37, 449.

65. Richardson, *Messages and Papers of Presidents,* I, 45.

66. Ford, *Writings,* VIII, 158–159.

67. Story, *Miscellaneous Writings,* 86.

68. Farewell Address, March 4, 1837, in Richardson, *Messages and Papers of Presidents,* III, 308.

69. Mosier, *Making the American Mind,* 40–41; Kohn, *American Nationalism,* 72.

70. Bancroft, *Memorial Address on the Life and Character of Abraham Lincoln* (Washington, 1866), reprinted as *Abraham Lincoln: A Tribute* (New York, 1908), 5, 7.

71. Merk, *Manifest Destiny and Mission,* esp. 24 ff., 215 ff.

CHAPTER 6

1. Joseph P. Bradley, *Progress: Its Grounds and Possibilities* (New Brunswick, 1849), 14–15.

2. Weber, *The Theory of Social and Economic Organization,* A. R. Henderson and Talcott Parsons, trans., (London, 1947), 297 ff.

3. Lipset, *First New Nation,* 16 ff.; Cunliffe, *Washington, Man and Monument,* chap. 4.

4. Jefferson to John Adams, August 30, 1787, in *Adams-Jefferson Letters,* I, 196.

5. 6 Peters 515 (1832); Warren, *Supreme Court,* I, 753–769, 776–777.

6. *American State Papers: Finance,* V, 502.

7. See especially the works of Agar, Benson, Binkley, Chambers, Charles, Cunningham, Fischer, Hofstadter, Holt, Livermore, McCormick, Nichols, Prince, Silbey, and Young in the bibliography, pp. 337–340.

8. Hofstadter, *Idea of a Party System,* esp. chaps. 5–6.

9. *Historical Statistics,* 737.

10. For a review of the second Bank's activity as a central bank (and a dissenting point of view), see Temin, *Jacksonian Economy*, 44 ff.
11. See White's hard yet understanding assessment in *The Jacksonians,* 14–17.
12. *Historical Statistics,* 7, 705, 721; Martin, *National Income,* 1–6; Dewey, *Financial History of U.S.,* 110, 123, 168, 246, 267.
13. Taylor, *Transportation Revolution,* 355.
14. For evidence of administrative inefficiency in a leading state (Pennsylvania), see Hartz, *Economic Policy and Democratic Thought,* 33, 148 ff., 267, 292 ff.
15. Hartz, *Economic Policy and Democratic Thought,* 126 ff., 175 ff., 309 ff.
16. Henry (with the aid of Brooks) Adams, *The Degradation of the Democratic Dogma* (New York, 1920), 42.
17. Young, *Washington Community,* 41 ff., 250 ff., who makes the point brilliantly if also extravagantly; Green, *Washington,* esp. 152 ff., 383.
18. Edward Bates, in *Opinions of the Attorneys-General,* VIII, 166, quoted and discussed in Roche, *Early Development of United States Citizenship,* 23.
19. Rostow, *Economic Growth,* I, 38; Benson, *Jacksonian Democracy,* 13 n.; Fogel, *Railroads and American Economic Growth,* chap. 4; Bruchey, *Roots of American Economic Growth,* 85–91, a discussion of this whole topic; Hacker, *Course of American Economic Growth and Development,* 69 ff., 139 ff., 172 ff.
20. Cochran, *Inner Revolution,* 53.
21. *Historical Statistics,* 302, 312, 349, 355 ff., 366 ff., 409, 427–428, 445 ff., 538 ff., 623 ff., 647, 672. I have also found the following tables especially useful and reliable: Taylor, *Transportation Revolution,* 79, 123, 163, 249, 325, 440–452; North, *Economic Growth,* 219 ff.; Robert E. Gallman, "Gross National Product in the United States," *Studies in Income and Wealth* (National Bureau of Economic Research), XXX (1966), 3 ff.; Bruchey, *Roots of American Economic Growth,* 80, 81, 82, 148, 149; Harris, ed., *American Economic History,* 105; Hacker, *Course of American Economic Growth and Development,* 80, 82, 100–104, 117, 122, 135.
22. Martin, *National Income,* 6; Taylor, *Transportation Revolution,* 294–295, 393, and studies there cited.
23. *Historical Statistics,* 115 ff., 127.
24. See generally *Eighth Census: Manufactures,* 733–742.
25. Whitworth and Wallis, *Industry of the U.S.,* viii.
26. Gates, *Farmer's Age,* 279–293.
27. Cochran and Miller, *Age of Enterprise,* 56.

Notes

28. Taylor, *Transportation Revolution*, 206; *Historical Statistics*, 538.
29. Ware, *Early New England Cotton Manufacture*, 129–130; Taylor, *Transportation Revolution*, 236–238; Hedges, *Browns of Providence Plantations*, chaps. 7–12.
30. Taylor, *Transportation Revolution*, esp. chaps. 7–8; Cochran and Miller, *Age of Enterprise*, 57.
31. Cochran and Miller, *Age of Enterprise*, 56.
32. Taylor, *Transportation Revolution*, 132 ff., 442.
33. Chevalier, *Society in the United States*, 204.
34. "Is not space annihilated?" Cornell wrote to his wife jubilantly in 1844 after the first public trial of the telegraph, which he had strung between Baltimore and Washington for Samuel F. B. Morse. Morris Bishop, *A History of Cornell* (Ithaca, 1962), 17.
35. See the interesting essay on Poor by Alfred C. Chandler, Jr., in Miller, ed., *Men in Business*, 254 ff.
36. *American Railroad Journal*, XXVII (1854), 147–148.
37. Whitworth and Wallis, *Industry of the U.S.*, 158–159.
38. *Historical Statistics*, 647–648; Harris, ed., *American Economic History*, 103–111; Taylor, *Transportation Revolution*, 324–330; Hepburn, *History of Currency in U.S.*, chaps. 5–10.
39. Whitney's pre-eminence has been disputed but not seriously challenged. See Hindle, *Technology in Early America*, 21 ff., 47–48.
40. *Historical Statistics*, 562–565; North, *Economic Growth*, 219–220.
41. Bruchey, *Roots of American Economic Growth*, 153 ff.
42. *Journals of Emerson*, VII, 201.
43. *Historical Statistics*, 547; Taylor, *Transportation Revolution*, 451.
44. Tocqueville, *Democracy in America*, I, 3 ff., 48 ff.
45. Matthew Arnold, *Civilization in the United States* (Boston, 1888), 85.
46. Birkbeck, *Notes on a Journey in America*, 37.
47. Rossiter, "American Mission," 24.
48. Ware, *Industrial Worker*, xii ff., 26 ff., 106 ff.; Dulles, *Labor in America*, 36, 73 ff. For a contrary view, see Hayek, ed., *Capitalism and the Historians*, esp. 9 ff.
49. Chevalier, *Society in the United States*, 97.
50. See generally Shryock, *Medicine and Society in America*, esp. chap. 4; Kett, *Formation of American Medical Profession*, esp. chap. 6.
51. *Historical Statistics*, 24, 26.
52. Tocqueville, *Democracy in America*, I, 198 ff.
53. Kett, *Formation of American Medical Profession*, 170.
54. Tryon, *Household Manufacture*, chaps. 7–8.
55. Calhoun, *Social History of the American Family*, chaps. 3, 5.

56. Gabriel, *Course of American Democratic Thought,* 7.
57. Commons, *History of Labour,* I, pts. 3–4; Dulles, *Labor in America,* chaps. 4–5; Taylor, *Transportation Revolution,* chaps. 12–13; Ware, *Industrial Worker,* chaps. 14–15; Maurice Neufeld, "Realms of Thought and Organized Labor in the Age of Jackson," *Labor History,* X (1969), 5, 11–12.
58. *Historical Statistics,* 14, 74; Solomon Fabricant, "The Changing Industrial Distribution of Gainful Workers," in *Studies in Income and Wealth* (National Bureau of Economic Research), XI (1949), 3, 41–44; Gates, *Farmer's Age,* 420. Fabricant puts the "gainful workers" in agriculture in 1860 at about 60 per cent; Gates, at 40 per cent. Under the kindly goad of Professor Gates I have retraced his pioneering steps through the census of 1860 and have arrived at a mid-point between his calculations and those of Fabricant. See also the estimates of Stanley Lebergott in *Studies in Income and Wealth,* XXX (1966), 117 ff.
59. Bishop, *History of Cornell,* 33, 37; Hofstadter and Metzger, *Academic Freedom,* 219.
60. Tewkesbury, *Founding of American Colleges,* 28; Hofstadter and Metzger, *Academic Freedom,* 211–212. This is one area in which the statistics printed in the census of 1860 are positively misleading —and one therefore in which much spadework of the most fatiguing kind remains to be done.
61. Farnam, *History of Social Legislation to 1860,* chap. 12; Cubberley, *Public Education in the United States,* chap. 8; Knight, *Education in the United States,* 173 ff.; Richey, *School in the American Social Order,* chaps. 7–10.
62. To Col. Charles Yancey, January 6, 1816, in *Writings of Jefferson* (Lipscomb), XIV, 385.
63. Welter, *Popular Education and Democratic Thought,* 1–6, 116–117.
64. Gates, *Farmer's Age,* 362–366.
65. Curti, *Growth of American Thought,* 355 ff.
66. Eaton, *Freedom-of-Thought Struggle,* chap. 3.
67. *Historical Statistics,* 206; Cross, *Burned-Over District,* 93, 98–100, 360.
68. Welter, *Popular Education and Democratic Thought,* 105.
69. Hofstadter, *Anti-Intellectualism in American Life,* 87 ff.; Weisberger, *They Gathered at the River,* 20 ff.; Smith, *Revivalism,* esp. chap. 1; Cross, *Burned-Over District,* esp. chaps. 10–12, 17, 20.
70. See especially Miller, *Life of the Mind in America,* vii, 34, 40, 88–95.
71. A definitive history of early American science remains to be written. In the meantime, Struik, *Yankee Science in the Making,* esp. pt.

III, remains in a class by itself. See also Curti, *Growth of American Thought,* chap. 13.

72. Elkins, *Slavery,* 27–32, 81, 142 ff., 151, 165; Berthoff, "American Social Order," 499–502, 507, 514.
73. (Ithaca, N. Y.) *American Journal,* July 26, 1820, whose editorialist found it not surprising that "there appears to be something wanting."
74. Allen, *Great Britain and the United States,* 151.
75. Lawrence Thompson, *Young Longfellow* (New York, 1938), 317.
76. *Edinburgh Review,* XXXIII (1820), 79.
77. On the unique dilemma of the American writer, see Cunliffe, *Literature of the United States,* 9 ff., 43 ff.
78. Spencer, *Quest for Nationality,* x; Nye, *Cultural Life of the New Nation,* 235 ff.; Jones, *Theory of American Literature,* 48 ff.
79. Quoted in Spencer, *Quest for Nationality,* 183.
80. In Theodore S. Fay, ed., *Crayon Sketches* (New York, 1833), I, 212.
81. See Harris, *Artist in American Society,* vii ff., 25 ff., 33 ff., 298, as well as his essay-review, "The Persistence of Portraiture," *Perspectives in American History,* I (1967), 380.
82. Spiller *et al., Literary History of U.S.,* chap. 33; Trent *et al., Cambridge History of American Literature,* chaps. 15–16; Boorstin, *The Americans: The National Experience,* 307 ff.
83. Quoted in Kohn, *American Nationalism,* 34–35.
84. (Little Rock) *Arkansas Gazette,* November 20, 1819.
85. *Historical Statistics,* 7 ff., 14, 57, 152, 402, 409; Gates, *Farmer's Age,* 160, 168; *Eighth Census: Statistics,* xi–xv; North, *Economic Growth,* 165.
86. *Historical Statistics,* 427, 497, 500, 563 ff., 608; Thompson, *Wiring a Continent,* 241.
87. R. R. Palmer *et al., Atlas of World History* (Chicago, 1957), 193.
88. *The Times* (London), September 2, 1851, p. 4; Herbert L. Stone, *The "America's" Cup Races* (New York, 1930), chaps. 1–3.
89. *The Times* (London), September 2, 1851, p. 4; Curti, "America at the World Fairs," in *Probing Our Past,* 246 ff.; Cochran and Miller, *Age of Enterprise,* 58.
90. Chevalier, *Society in the United States,* 94.
91. See generally Whitworth and Wallis, *Industry of the U.S.*
92. Hindle, *Technology in Early America,* 70; Habakkuk, *American and British Technology,* 4 ff., 105–106, 170–171.
93. Lillibridge, *Beacon of Freedom,* esp. 19 ff.; Crook, *American Democracy in English Politics,* 40 ff., 73 ff.

94. F. Wharton, ed., *Diplomatic Correspondence of the American Revolution* (Washington, 1889), VI, 150.
95. James, *Hawthorne*, 112.

CHAPTER 7

1. Hamilton to Robert Morris, April 30, 1781, in *Papers of Hamilton*, II, 633; Polk to Congress, December 5, 1848, in Richardson, *Messages and Papers of Presidents*, IV, 629; Lincoln's "Proclamation of Thanksgiving," October 3, 1863, in *Works of Lincoln*, VI, 496.
2. (Portland, Me.) *Eastern Argus*, September 15, 1803.
3. (Boston) *New England Galaxy*, March 15, 1822. For a sample of similar comments, see (Boston) *Massachusetts Centinel*, January 10, March 4, 1789; (Halifax) *North Carolina Journal*, January 30, 1793, and December 7, 1795; (Newark, N.J.) *Centinel of Freedom*, November 23, 1796; (Annapolis) *Maryland Gazette*, April 14, 1803; (Nashville) *Tennessee Gazette*, August 17, 1803; *Carlisle* (Pa.) *Gazette*, July 6, 1804; (Vincennes, Ind.) *Western Sun*, September 2, 1809; *Nashville Whig*, July 18, 1815.
4. See again McClelland, *Achieving Society*, esp. 149–151.
5. Important references of a confident nature may be found in Farrand, *Records of the Convention*, I, 85, 161, 398 ff.; III, 138. A few sour or simply cautionary notes are sounded in Farrand, *Records*, I, 48, 372; II, 3.
6. I base this judgment on the results of an exacting job of research into the opinions voiced in more than forty newspapers of the years 1787–1825, which was undertaken in my behalf by Robert M. Johnstone, Jr.
7. See especially the opinions delivered and remarks collected in Kenyon, ed., *Antifederalists*, lvi, cvii, 11, 46, 48, 152, 255 ff., 378.
8. Joel Barlow, *The Columbiad* (London, 1809), 39.
9. James Wilson to the Pennsylvania ratifying convention, November 24, 1787, in Farrand, *Records*, III, 138.
10. To John Parish, January 20, 1801, in Jared Sparks, *The Life of Gouverneur Morris* (Boston, 1832), III, 144.
11. (Fredericksburg) *Virginia Herald*, February 10, 1791.
12. Watson, ed., *Men and Times of the Revolution*, 523. See also the prediction of John Adams to Count Sarsfield, February 3, 1786, in *Works of Adams*, IX, 546.
13. To Robert Morris, April 30, 1781, in *Papers of Hamilton*, II, 617–618.

Notes

14. From Burke's Speech on Conciliation with America, March 22, 1775, in *The Works of Edmund Burke* (Boston, 1839), II, 28.
15. See especially Stiles, *The United States Elevated to Glory and Honor* (New Haven, 1783), 23, 52; Dwight, *Columbia: An Ode* (Philadelphia, 1794), 6 ff.
16. Timothy Dwight, "Columbia" (1777), in Elihu Smith, ed., *American Poems, Selected and Original* (Litchfield, Conn., 1793), 63.
17. The phrase is from the Massachusetts Constitution of 1780, which was drafted by John Adams, in *Works of Adams,* IV, 259.
18. Montesquieu, *The Spirit of the Laws,* T. Nugent, ed., I, (New York, 1949), 20–21.
19. July 4, 1778, in H. Niles, ed., *Principles and Acts of the Revolution* (Baltimore, 1822), 64.
20. (Elizabethtown) *New Jersey Journal,* April 8, 1789.
21. March 25, 1764, in A. H. Smyth, ed., *The Writings of Benjamin Franklin* (New York, 1906), IV, 193.
22. Morse, *An American Geography* (Elizabeth, 1789), 64.
23. A. C. Fraser, ed., *The Works of George Berkeley* (Oxford, 1871), III, 232.
24. Ames, *An Astronomical Diary for the Year 1758* (Boston, n.d.).
25. Pattee, ed., *Poems of Philip Freneau,* I, 82.
26. To John Jay, May 8, 1785, in *Works of Adams,* VIII, 246.
27. *Penn Yan Herald,* March 30, 1819. See also (New) *Orleans Gazette and Commercial Advertiser,* February 23, 1819.
28. John Trumbull (1770), in S. G. Goodrich, ed., *The Poetical Works of John Trumbull* (Hartford, 1820), II, 158. See generally Van Alstyne, *Genesis of American Nationalism,* 3 ff., 61, 64, 96.
29. To James McHenry, June 21, 1799, in B. C. Steiner, *The Life and Correspondence of James McHenry* (Cleveland, 1907), 395.
30. "The Perpetuation of Our Political Institutions," January 27, 1838, in *Works of Lincoln,* I, 109.
31. *Columbiad,* 331.
32. December 2, 1815, in *Niles' Weekly Register,* IX, 238; Emerson, *Complete Writings* (New York, 1929), I, 113. A suggestive note of skepticism has been sounded in Page Smith, "Anxiety and Despair in American History," *WMQ,* XXVI (1969), 416, as well as by Somkin, *Unquiet Eagle,* esp. 45.
33. (New) *Orleans Gazette and Commercial Advertiser,* August 6, 1819.
34. *North American Review,* XXXIV (1832), 228.
35. A useful corrective to any tendency toward extremism in applying the concept of elitism to early American history is provided by

Jesse Lemisch, "American Revolution from the Bottom Up," in Bernstein, ed., *Towards a New Past*, 3 ff.

36. Bigelow, *Elements of Technology* (Boston, 1829), 7.
37. Franklin, *Slavery to Freedom*, chap. 14, as well as 161–163, 222–223, 237.
38. Miller, *Life of the Mind in America*, 109 ff.; Calhoun, *Professional Lives in America*, 4 ff., 179–180, 188 ff.; Merritt, *Engineering in American Society*, esp. chaps. 1–3.
39. Kohn, *American Nationalism*, 42, 63–64.
40. *Papers of Hamilton*, X, 1–340; Rossiter, *Hamilton and the Constitution*, 9–10, 21–24, 81, 164–165, 179–182, 252–253, and references there cited, especially the writings of Broadus Mitchell.
41. Richardson, *Messages and Papers of Presidents*, II, 299 ff., esp. 311–317; Bemis, *Adams and the Union*, 25, 60 ff., 75–76, 89, 102, 147, 150–151, 248, 271, 441, and references there cited; Lipsky, *Adams*, 146 ff.; Adams, *Degradation of the Democratic Dogma*, chaps. 1–2.
42. See the vigorous case for Washington's primacy as an economic nationalist in Nettels, *Emergence of a National Economy*, 104–108, as well as the tribute of the Adamses in *Degradation of the Democratic Dogma*, 13 ff.
43. Ver Steeg, *Robert Morris*, 120, 199. No major figure of the founding generation, except perhaps the other Morris, from New York, is more desperately in need of a full-scale, modern biography than Robert Morris of Philadelphia.
44. *Papers of Hamilton*, X, 10–12.
45. Brant, *Madison*, esp. III, 11 ff., and VI, 393 ff. The satirical thrust was made by John Randolph. See Brant, *Madison*, VI, 403.
46. April 8, 1808, in *American State Papers, Miscellaneous*, I, 724–741; Adams, *Life of Gallatin*, 350–352; Goodrich, *Government Promotion*, 27 ff.
47. Mayo, *Clay*, 277 ff.; Eaton, *Clay*, chap. 3; Van Deusen, *Clay*, esp. 46–48, 110–115, 119–120, 160–166, 237–238, 248–266, 277–289.
48. Gabriel, *Course of American Democratic Thought*, 81 ff.; Dorfman, *Economic Mind*, II, 566 ff., 575 ff., 865 ff., 936 ff.
49. I have used the more complete edition of *Men and Times* published in 1857. The Watson papers, most of which are deposited in Albany, are rich enough to encourage the writing of a modern biography of an extraordinary man. Although this may have the ring of gratuitous advice, I would hope that Hugh Flick, who wrote his doctoral dissertation at Columbia on Watson (1958), would turn his considerable talents to the task.
50. Flick, "Watson," 326.

51. Walker is the subject of a competent biography written by James P. Shenton, to whose scholarly labors I am greatly indebted. The bulk of Walker's papers, which are in fact distressingly few and unrevealing for so incredible a man, may be found in the Library of Congress. See also the colorful pamphlets and speeches listed in Shenton, *Walker*, 274, 277–278, as well as the *Continental Monthly*, a journal published by Walker and James R. Gilmore to provide support for the Union cause.

52. December 3, 1845, in *Executive Documents* (29th Cong., 1st Sess., Doc. No. 6), II, 4 ff., esp. 8–14; December 10, 1846, in *Executive Documents* (29th Cong., 2nd Sess., Doc. No. 7), II, 7–13; December 8, 1847, in *Executive Documents* (39th Cong., 1st Sess., Doc. No. 6), II, 24–35; December 11, 1848, in *Executive Documents* (39th Cong., 2nd Sess., Doc. No. 7), II, 6–14.

53. By H. D. Jordan in the entry on Walker in the *Dictionary of American Biography*, XIX, 356.

54. Shenton, *Walker*, 199–202.

55. D. D. Egbert and Stow Persons, eds., *Socialism and American Life* (Princeton, 1952), I, 175 ff.

56. *Writings of Jefferson* (Lipscomb), XIV, 387–392.

57. For Walker's advanced views on the importance of profit-sharing for the success of both capitalism and republicanism, see *Executive Documents* (30th Cong., 1st Sess., Doc. No. 6), II, 24–25.

58. To John Adams, October 28, 1813, in Cappon, ed., *Adams-Jefferson Letters*, II, 388.

59. Walker, in *Executive Documents* (30th Cong., 2nd Sess., Doc. No. 7), II, 9.

60. *Papers of Hamilton*, X, 317.

61. For a somewhat different view of Jefferson's opinion of the role of the national government, see Bruchey, *Roots of American Economic Growth*, 114–122.

62. Walker, *Men and Times*, 452 ff.

63. Jefferson to John Cartwright, June 5, 1824, in *Writings of Jefferson* (Lipscomb), XVI, 46.

64. See generally the documents in *Writings of Jefferson* (Ford), VIII, 241–249, and the letters in *Writings of Jefferson* (Lipscomb), X, 407, 415, 417.

65. Bemis, *Adams and the Foundations of American Foreign Policy*, esp. chaps. 16, 25.

66. See especially the letters to President Madison (April 27, 1809) and President Monroe (October 24, 1823) in *Writings of Jefferson* (Lipscomb), XII, 277; XV, 477–480.

67. For Jefferson's serene vision of separate, friendly nations in the West, see his letter to John Breckinridge, August 12, 1803, in *Writings of Jefferson* (Lipscomb), X, 409–410.
68. To Abigail Adams, June 30, 1811, in *Writings of J. Q. Adams*, IV, 128. On this whole question, see generally Dangerfield, *Awakening*, chap. 2.
69. Bemis, *Adams and the Union*, 65–70.
70. Meyers, *Jacksonian Persuasion*, esp. chaps. 1–2.

CHAPTER 8

1. Thompson, *Wiring a Continent*, vii.
2. For these and other studies of the role of politics in economic development in this period, see the bibliography, pp. 337–340, as well as the studies listed in Taylor, *Transportation Revolution*, 401–403, 407–410, 432–435. Robert A. Lively's "The American System" is a thoughtful survey of this whole problem.
3. Billington, *Far Western Frontier*, chap. 5, and references at pp. 299–301; Goodrich, *Government Promotion*, 122–126, and references there cited; W. J. Lane, *From Indian Trial to Iron Horse: Travel and Transportation in New Jersey, 1620–1860* (Princeton, 1939), chaps. 8–9.
4. Taylor, *Transportation Revolution*, 98.
5. Namier, *England in the Age of the American Revolution*, 2nd ed. (London, 1961), 131.
6. I *Stat.* 131, 605; II *Stat.* 806; III *Stat.* 417, 679; IV *Stat.* 139, 275; V *Stat.* 618; X *Stat.* 219; XI *Stat.* 32.
7. Taylor, *Transportation Revolution*, 360–366, and references there cited; North, *Economic Growth of U.S.*, 156; Cochran and Miller, *Age of Enterprise*, 18, a partially dissenting opinion.
8. Dangerfield, *American Nationalism*, 204.
9. Hammond, *Banks and Politics*, esp. chaps. 17–19.
10. V *Stat.* 304, 626; X *Stat.* 61.
11. Rossiter, *Hamilton and the Constitution*, 153–163.
12. Richardson, *Messages and Papers of Presidents*, II, 312.
13. *Historical Statistics*, 737.
14. Hindle, *Technology in Early America*, 47 ff., offers a somewhat different appraisal.
15. Medicine, too, drew heavily on the older countries. See Shryock, *Medicine and Society in America*, 123 ff.
16. Hindle, *Technology in Early America*, 18 ff., 79, 88 ff., and references there cited. See also Allen, *Great Britain and the United*

States, 121 ff., for examples of a two-way flow of ideas and institutional arrangements in the area of social relations.

17. Chevalier, *Society in the United States; General Report of the British Commission on the New York Industrial Exhibition, British Sessional Papers* (1854), XXXVI, and also Whitworth and Wallis, *Industry of the U.S.*

18. *Papers of Hamilton,* VII, 236 ff.; Hammond, *Banks and Politics,* 128–129; Huntington, *Soldier and State,* 197, and references there cited; Sidney Forman, *West Point* (New York, 1950), 43–44, 51–58.

19. IV *Stat.* 604; V *Stat.* 551, 727.

20. IV *Stat.* 22; V *Stat.* 257.

21. IX *Stat.* 466; X *Stat.* 8, 155; XI *Stat.* 17–21, 195.

22. I have made my own calculations, which are too elaborate and, to tell the truth, too finely shaded to spread through these pages, from such sources as *Historical Statistics of the U.S.,* esp. 710–711; *Register of Officers and Agents . . . in the Service of the U.S.* (1820–1860); the *Congressional Directory; U.S. Statutes at Large; U. S. Supreme Court Reports;* and *Annual Report of the Secretary of the Treasury.*

23. Gates, *Farmer's Age,* chaps. 3–4; White, *Jeffersonians,* chap. 33; Rohrbough, *Land Office Business,* 49, 51 ff., 271 ff.

24. Thompson, *Wiring a Continent,* esp. 16–34, 56.

25. Report of the Postmaster General, December 1, 1845, in *Executive Documents* (29th Cong., 1st Sess., Doc. No. 2), 860; Report of the Postmaster General, December 1, 1846, in *Executive Documents* (29th Cong., 2nd Sess., Doc. No. 4), 689.

26. Gates, *Farmer's Age,* chaps. 3–4, a judicious summary and assessment of an extremely confusing question.

27. Dupree, *Science in the Federal Government,* esp. chaps. 3, 5.

28. Dupree, *Science in the Federal Government,* chap. 4.

29. III *Stat.* 488; IX *Stat.* 127, 149, 220; X *Stat.* 715; Hansen, *Atlantic Migration,* 12 ff., 93 ff., 102, 106, 253 ff.; Fairchild, *Immigration,* 61–62, 81–87; Farnam, *History of Social Legislation,* 242–252.

30. Du Bois, *Suppression of the African Slave-Trade,* 158 ff., 178 ff.; Stampp, *Peculiar Institution,* 271–273, and references there cited.

31. II *Stat.* 19, 248; V *Stat.* 440, 614; Warren, *Bankruptcy in U.S. History,* 13–21, 70–85.

32. Sidney Fine, *Laissez Faire and the General Welfare State* (Ann Arbor, 1956), chap. 1; Hartz, *Economic Policy and Democratic Thought,* chap. 7, who somewhat overstates an interesting thesis.

33. *American State Papers: Public Lands,* VIII, 910. For two splendid

official expressions of the antistatist ideology, see Jackson's peroration to his veto of the act rechartering the Bank of the United States (1832) and Van Buren's peroration to his message to a special session of Congress (1837), in Richardson, *Messages and Papers of Presidents,* II, 578; III, 344.

34. Huntington, *Soldier and State,* 144, 147, 153 ff.
35. *Annals of Congress* (14th Cong., 1st Sess.), 1801, as well as 183–194, 199–204, 1127–1134, 1158–1188.
36. *Annals of Congress* (14th Cong. 2nd Sess.), 1278, as well as 10, 22, 23, 31, 83, 85, 90, 92, 232, 243, 483–693 (a fascinating debate on representative government), 712–713.
37. *Congressional Globe* (34th Cong., 1st Sess.), 2079–2084.
38. Welter, *Popular Education and Democratic Thought,* 6, 53, 60 ff., 74 ff., 86–87, 109.
39. For evidence of the "collapse" of state efforts to regulate the practice of medicine, see Kett, *Formation of American Medical Profession,* esp. vii–ix, 1 ff., 165 ff.
40. IX *Stat.* 466.
41. IX *Stat.* 462.
42. December 3–22, 1849, in *Congressional Globe* (31st Cong., 1st Sess.), 4–67; December 3, 1855–February 2, 1856, in *Congressional Globe* (34th Cong., 1st Sess.), 3–343.
43. Joseph Schumpeter, *Business Cycles* (New York, 1939), I, 294–296.
44. See the map and table in Goodrich, *Government Promotion,* 34–35.
45. Dupree, *Science in the Federal Government,* 94.
46. April 28, 1846, in *Congressional Globe* (29th Cong., 1st Sess.), 738; Dupree, *Science in the Federal Government,* 62–63; Bemis, *Adams and the Union,* 514–515, 521.
47. See again Arieli, *Individualism and Nationalism, passim.*

CHAPTER 9

1. Julius Zeitler, ed., *Goethe Handbuch* (Stuttgart, 1916), I, 38–39; Walter Wadepuhl, *Goethe's Interest in the New World* (Jena, 1934), esp. 64–65. See also Hegel's approving observations on America as the "land of the future" and the "land of desire" in *Lectures on the Philosophy of History* (London, 1902), 90.
2. Echeverria, *Mirage in the West,* esp. chaps. 1, 5, presents a useful introduction to many of the issues in this debate.
3. *Nashville Whig,* July 18, 1815.
4. *Historical Statistics,* 48 ff., 57.

Notes

5. Martineau, *Society in America,* I, 159–160.
6. January 27, 1838, in *Works of Lincoln,* I, 108.
7. *Historical Statistics,* 7, 9, 719, 737.
8. December 5, 1848, in Richardson, *Messages and Papers of Presidents,* IV, 633.
9. Quoted in Jones, *American Immigration,* 76.
10. See the revealing statistics and persuasive conclusions in Main, *Social Structure of Revolutionary America,* esp. 197 ff., 270 ff. Prominent among the unpersuaded are Jesse Lemisch, "American Revolution from the Bottom Up," in Bernstein, ed., *Towards a New Past,* esp. 32–33; Staughton Lynd, "Who Should Rule at Home?," *WMQ,* XVIII (1961), 332; and Aubrey C. Land, "Economic Base and Social Structure: The Northern Chesapeake in the Eighteenth Century," *JEH,* XXV (1965), 639. The suspicion grows that the ongoing accumulation of evidence in the field of American social history will lead to more, rather than less, scholarly disagreement over such questions as the identity, size, and role of the middle class in the years of the Quest.
11. See the comments of George Blanksten in Almond and Coleman, eds., *Politics of the Developing Areas,* 474.
12. R. B. Morris, *Government and Labor in Early America* (New York, 1946), 45.
13. *Historical Statistics,* 115–116, 119 ff.
14. *Historical Statistics,* 761–765; Rossiter, *Seedtime of the Republic,* 66 ff., and references there cited.
15. For evidence of the power of this phenomenon in the political field, see Michael Kammen, *Deputyes and Liberties* (New York, 1969) esp. 10.
16. *Goethe Handbuch,* I, 39; Hartz, *Liberal Tradition in America,* 3 ff.; Hartz *et al., Founding of New Societies,* esp. 26 ff.
17. For examples, see Charles M. Andrews, *The Colonial Period of American History* (New Haven, 1934–1938), I, 320, 343, 400–429; III, 212–226.
18. Hegel, *Lectures on the Philosophy of History,* 90.
19. See the useful compilation of genuine grass-roots opinion in Robert J. Taylor, ed., *Massachusetts, Colony to Commonwealth* (Chapel Hill, 1961).
20. Of several recent explorations of one of the darkest continents of American social and political history I have found John J. Waters, Jr.'s *The Otis Family* (Chapel Hill, 1968) the most engaging in method and rewarding in content.
21. Crucial, yes, but still resistant to analysis, as one may read for him-

self in Eisenstadt, ed., *Protestant Ethic and Modernization*, esp. 3 ff. (Eisenstadt's introduction) and 67 ff. (Ephraim Fischoff).

22. Evidence that neutrality was by no means synonymous with isolationism abounds in Field, *America and the Mediterranean World*, esp. chaps. 1–3, 6.

23. This important point is especially well made in Lipset, *First New Nation*, 62–66.

24. W. P. Webb, *The Great Frontier* (Boston, 1952), esp. 7 ff.

25. Hedges, *Browns of Providence Plantations*, 161–166.

26. T. C. Cochran, *The Pabst Brewing Company* (New York, 1948), 1 ff.

27. For a judicious introduction to the debate, see the writings of Morgan, Higginbotham, Wood, Greene, and Barrow listed in the bibliography, pp. 351–354, as well as W. F. Craven's contribution to Higham, ed., *Reconstruction of American History*, 46–63, 223–224. My own views, for what they are worth, are stated in *The First American Revolution* (New York, 1956), esp. 4–6, 234–239; *Seedtime of the Republic*, esp. 4–5, 448; *Conservatism in America*, 86–87; *1787: The Grand Convention*, 29–30, 36–38.

28. Wood, "Rhetoric and Reality in the American Revolution," *WMQ*, XXIII (1966), 3, 13.

29. For a general introduction to the problem of revolution, see Carl J. Friedrich's observations (as well as the works he cites of Crane Brinton, George S. Pettee, and Hannah Arendt) in Friedrich *et al.*, *Revolution* (New York, 1966), 3 ff.

30. *Federalist*, 527.

31. Rostow, *Stages of Economic Growth*, 140.

32. McCord, *Springtime of Freedom*, 124 ff., makes this point with special clarity.

33. Ashford, *National Development and Local Reform*, 258 ff.; Eisenstadt, *Modernization*, 26 ff.

34. Heilbroner, *Great Ascent*, 125.

35. Lerner, *Passing of Traditional Society*, vii, 4 ff. (observations of David Riesman).

36. Ashford, *National Development and Local Reform*, 270 ff.

37. Lerner, *Passing of Traditional Society*, 401.

CHAPTER 10

1. Duffy, *History of Public Health in New York City*, esp. 271–278.

2. Somkin, *Unquiet Eagle*, 91 ff., has many interesting things to say

Notes

about the ambivalent feelings of perceptive Americans toward space, their "least valuable resource."

3. Robbins, *Landed Heritage*, 42; Cochran and Miller, *Age of Enterprise*, 39–40.
4. Billington, *Far Western Frontier*, 41 ff.
5. Billington, *Westward Expansion*, 9.
6. Rossiter, *Seedtime of the Republic*, 9–11.
7. For an introduction to the debate, see the summaries, articles, and bibliographies in Billington, *Westward Expansion*, esp. 8 ff.; Billington, *Frontier Thesis;* and Taylor, ed., *Turner Thesis.* I found the article by Stanley Elkins and Eric McKitrick, "Turner Thesis: Predictive Model," in Saveth, ed., *American History and the Social Sciences*, 379–399, as well as Allen, *Bush and Backwoods*, esp. chaps. 7–8, unusually fresh contributions to an often stale debate, yet even they offer few clues to an understanding of the total influence of the frontier. See also William Coleman, "Science and Symbol in the Turner Frontier Hypothesis," *AHR*, LXXII (1966), 22.
8. Turner, *The Frontier in American History* (New York, 1920), 293.
9. For a somewhat contrary, powerfully argued view of the relative strengths of sectionalism and nationalism, see Silbey, *Shrine of Party*, esp. 5 ff., 142 ff.
10. See the excellent maps at the end of George R. Taylor and Irene D. Neu, *The American Railroad Network, 1861–1890* (Cambridge, 1956).
11. Goodrich, *Government Promotion*, 283.
12. See again Nagel, *One Nation Indivisible*, esp. 235 ff.
13. Silvert *et al., Expectant Peoples*, 136, 176, 428.
14. *Works of Lincoln*, I, 109, 111.
15. (New) *Orleans Gazette and Commercial Advertiser*, August 6, 1819.
16. Stowe, *Uncle Tom's Cabin* (1852) (Boston, 1882), 168, in which she is speaking of the Mississippi; (New) *Orleans Gazette and Commercial Advertiser*, August 6, 1819.
17. Harold Laski, *The American Presidency* (New York, 1940), 37.
18. Apter, *Politics of Modernization*, 13.
19. A garland of anti-American statements may be found in Henry Pelling, *America and the British Left* (London, 1956), 2 ff., a book that also points to the early attractiveness of America for British Radicalism.
20. *Writings of Jefferson* (Lipscomb), XV, 249.
21. *Historical Statistics*, 9–13; Franklin, *Slavery to Freedom*, 185.
22. Tocqueville, *Democracy in America*, I, 30 ff., 376 ff., 410 ff.

23. Livermore, *Twilight of Federalism*, 95 ff.; Stampp, ed., *Causes of Civil War*, 44–45.
24. Craven, *Growth of Southern Nationalism*, 3 ff., 158 ff.
25. Eaton, *Freedom-of-Thought Struggle*, 229 ff.
26. Huntington, *Soldier and State*, 211 ff.
27. Du Bois, *Suppression of the African Slave-Trade*, esp. 181–183.
28. Litwack, *North of Slavery*, 30 ff., 40 ff., 49–50, 279.
29. Bemis, *Adams and the Union*, esp. 384 ff.
30. Elkins, *Slavery*, 34–35, 140.
31. Jordan, *White Over Black*, esp. 3 ff.
32. Jordan, *White Over Black*, 482 ff.; Litwack, *North of Slavery*, vii–ix, 15 ff., 29, 47, 64, 71, 157, 223 ff., 247, 257, 279.
33. Litwack, *North of Slavery*, 216 ff. Since my own point of view forbade me to agree unreservedly with Professor Litwack (even though I knew him to be a reputable scholar), I made a careful investigation into the public and private attitudes of leading abolitionists toward the potential of the Negro race. My only complaint about his conclusions is that they were not severe enough in condemning white attitudes.
34. At Ottawa, Ill., August 21, 1858, in *Works of Lincoln*, III, 16.
35. June 16, 1858, in *Works of Lincoln*, II, 461 ff.
36. Above, pp. 158–159.
37. Gates, *Agriculture and Civil War*, 4–5, and *Farmer's Age*, 139–140; Hammond, *Cotton Industry*, 62 ff., 94 ff.
38. Stampp, *Peculiar Institution*, 60–67, 397–398, and works there cited.
39. See the enlightening, if somewhat less than fully convincing, observations of Elkins, *Slavery*, esp. chap. 3.
40. Woodman, ed., *Slavery and Southern Economy*, 113 ff.
41. On this point, see especially the table (compiled from the census of 1860) in North, *Economic Growth*, 258.
42. *Eighth Census: Manufactures*, 13, 22, 60, 81, 204, 257, 283, 438, 558, 578, 594, 637, 729.
43. But not, it would seem, for farm machinery, in which the sugar-refining, cotton-ginning South had a large investment. See the interesting statistics compiled from the Eighth Census in Gates, *Farmer's Age*, 291.
44. *Historical Statistics*, 11, 13.
45. On the last of these reasons for the failure of emancipation, see Rossiter, *1787: The Grand Convention*, 32, which derives much from Hartz, ed., *Founding of New Societies*, 53 ff. (Hartz) and 143–144 (R. M. Morse).
46. Tocqueville, *Democracy in America*, I, 375.

47. Robert, *Road from Monticello*, v, 12–18; Eaton, *Growth of Southern Civilization*, 226 ff.
48. Hamilton's approach to slavery is well known; for the less familiar Watson, see *Men and Times*, 66, 72, and for Walker, see Shenton, *Walker*, 2, 113, 125, 135, 154–155, 172, 179–180, 183, 189, 193, 195, 197.
49. Dangerfield, *Awakening*, 125. See the exhaustive analysis of Jordan, *White Over Black*, chap. 12.
50. Bemis, *Adams and the Union*, chaps. 17, 19; Jordan, *White Over Black*, 546 ff.
51. Phillips, "The Central Theme of Southern History," *AHR*, XXXIV (1928), 30. On the role of Phillips in the historiography of slavery, the South, and the Civil War, see Pressly, ed., *Americans Interpret Their Civil War*, 265 ff., and the observations of Eugene D. Genovese in the paperback edition of Phillips, *American Negro Slavery*, vii ff.
52. Abraham Lincoln to the Young Men's Lyceum, Springfield, Ill., January 27, 1838, in *Works of Lincoln*, I, 109.

CHAPTER 11

1. Pierson, *Tocqueville in America*, 234.
2. Brogan, *American Aspects*, 22.
3. Brogan, *American Aspects*, 22–23.
4. As representative samples of hundreds of discussions of this issue, see Stampp, *And the War Came*, chap. 1; Coulter, *Confederate States*, 2 ff.; Cochran and Miller, *Age of Enterprise*, 92–104; Sydnor, *Southern Sectionalism*, 177 ff., 222 ff., 294 ff., 315 ff.; Curti, *Growth of American Thought*, 451–453.
5. *The Complete Works of James Russell Lowell* (Boston, 1910), V, 41.
6. March 4, 1865, in *Works of Lincoln*, VIII, 332.
7. From the *Montgomery Weekly Mail*, January 11, 1861, quoted in Coulter, *Confederate States*, 57–58. See also Sydnor, *Southern Sectionalism*, chap. 15.
8. Craven, *Southern Nationalism*, 34, 83, 85, 130, 204; Genovese, *Political Economy of Slavery*, esp. 3 ff., 13 ff.
9. On Southern nationalism (or, as some may still prefer, "nationalism"), see the discussions cited immediately above in note 8, as well as Arieli, *Individualism and Nationalism*, 294 ff.; Craven, *Southern Nationalism*, esp. 7 ff.; Eaton, *Growth of Southern Civilization*, 205 ff.; Roland, *Confederacy*, 1 ff., 15 (a judgment with which I fully agree), 27, 38 ff.

10. For the contrast of the nationalisms of Lincoln and Buchanan, see Stampp, *And the War Came,* 46 ff., 69, 98, 123 ff., 147, 165–167.
11. See the impressive evidence gathered by Fredrickson, *Inner Civil War,* esp. 1 ff., 53 ff., 65 ff.
12. For a special view of the Southern Unionists, see Eaton, *Freedom-of-Thought Struggle,* chap. 15.
13. For three useful introductions to this never-ending discussion, see Pressly, *Americans Interpret Their Civil War,* esp. 7–20; Potter, *South and Sectional Conflict,* chap. 4; and Howard K. Beale, in *Theory and Practice in Historical Study* (Social Science Research Council), 55 ff.
14. Quoted in S. E. Morison and H. S. Commager, *The Growth of the American Republic,* 4th ed. (New York, 1950), I, 652.
15. A somewhat exaggerated, yet still instructive, discussion of the force of states' rights in the North in Shannon, *Organization of the Union Army,* I, 15 ff., 259 ff., 295.
16. On the obstacle to a Southern victory presented by the principle and practice of states' rights, see Roland, *Confederacy,* 51 ff., 125 ff., 143, 191 ff.
17. Chevalier, *Society in the United States,* 112.
18. This point is made with subtle vigor in Woodward, *Burden of Southern History,* chaps. 1–2, countered in the same style in Potter, *South and Sectional Conflict,* 63 ff. On the ambivalence of Southern loyalties, see Kohn, *American Nationalism,* 106 ff.
19. Cochran, *Inner Revolution,* 39 ff., to which many of the pieces collected in Adreano, ed., *Economic Impact of the Civil War* are thoughtful rejoinders or qualifications.
20. Voegeli, *Free But Not Equal,* esp. 1 ff., 160 ff.
21. From Douglass's oration (1876) in memory of Abraham Lincoln in H. J. Storing, ed., *What Country Have I?* (New York, 1970), 49.
22. Stampp, *Peculiar Institution,* esp. 19 ff.
23. James, *Hawthorne,* 114.
24. XII *Stat.* 392, 489, 503, 807; XIII *Stat.* 340, 365.

Index

Academy of Sciences, U.S.S.R., 94
activeness: as mark of political efficacy, 50
activeness, U.S.: as mark of political efficacy, 141–143
Adams, Brooks, 374
Adams, Henry, 368, 374
Adams, John, 104, 119, 130, 132, 188, 192, 193, 194, 373
Adams, John Quincy, 104, 110, 119, 130, 141, 201, 220, 230, 233, 253, 271, 282, 293–294, 294n, 299, 313, 376; First Annual Message (1825), 201, 220
Adams-Onís Treaty, 110
Adreano, Ralph, 384
Africa, 96, 142, 251
Agar, Herbert, 367
Agassiz, Louis, 166
agriculture, 72, 88, 150–152, 248
Algeria, 33
Allen, H. C., 364, 365, 371, 376–377, 381
Almond, Gabriel, 49, 362, 379
America, yacht, 181
American Railroad Journal, 155, 156
Americans: attitudes of, 127, 128, 254, 282–283, 288, 300; hostility to political power, 229–231; virtue and, 192
Ames, Fisher, 127, 192
Ames, Nathaniel, 193, 373
Andrews, Charles M., 379
Apter, David, 50, 53, 94, 236, 282, 362, 381
Arabs, 24, 43
architects, 175
Argentina, 36, 77

Arieli, Yehoshua, 129, 366, 378, 383
Aristotle, 47
armed forces, U.S., 142, 220–221, 229, 230, 250, 304; military surveys, 238
army: ruling, 91–92
Arnold, Matthew, 19, 161, 361, 369
art, 31, 176, 177
artists, American, 176
Ashford, Douglas, 267, 363, 380
Ataturk, Kemal, 90–91
Atlantic Ocean, 247
atomic bomb, 15
Australia, 30, 36, 37, 77, 121, 278
authority, political, 35, 86, 112; transfer of, 48, 139
authors: American, 107, 172–173; British, 174
autocratic control: as technique of national development, 90–92, 94

Bache, Alexander D., 144
Bailyn, Bernard, 364
balance of abodes: as mark of social integration, 64
balance of abodes, U.S.: as mark of social integration, 165–166
Bancroft, George, 125, 134, 144, 199, 367
banks and banking, 142, 156, 218, 223, 227–228, 238
Barlow, Joel, 195, 372
Barrow, Thomas C., 380
Basques, 24, 32
Bates, Edward, 368
Beale, Howard K., 384
Beaumont, William, 146

Index

Index

Index

Index

Index

outsiders, 36–37

Pabst Brewing Company, 263
Paine, Thomas, 104
Pakistan, 246
Palmer, R. R., 371
Palmerston, Henry, Lord, 103
Panic of 1857, 106
Parker, William Nelson, 364
Parsons, Talcott, 25
patent system, U.S., 144
patriotism, 19, 39, 42, 85, 86, 214, 304
Paulding, James K., 173
Pelling, Henry, 381
penal reform, 146
Perry, Comm. Oliver Hazard, 144
Persons, Stow, 375
Phillips, Ulrich B., 295, 383
Pierson, George W., 383
Pike, F. B., 362
Planck, Max, 97
Poe, Edgar Allan, 174
Pogodin, Mikhail, 178
political efficacy: as goal of modernity, 27, 54, 79; marks of, 47–53; opposition to, 265; in U.S., 138–148, 178
political parties, 49, 50–51, 94; in U.S., 130, 141
political response: as technique of national development, 86–88, 94, 314
political response, U.S.: as technique of national development, 216–219, 224, 225, 307, 314
political science, 9, 33
politics: as essential to national development, 82–83, 94
politics, U.S.: as essential to national development, 142–143, 199–200, 234–236, 237–238, 282–283, 286; creative decisions in, 260–261; role in national development, 200, 213–214
Polk, James K., 5, 141, 189, 202, 250
Poor, Henry Varnum, 155, 156
popular cohesion, 87; as goal of nationhood, 27, 35–39
popular cohesion, U.S.: as goal of nationhood, 115–123, 178, 248, 288
population, U.S., 4, 116, 120–122, 149, 165–166, 190–191, 221, 266, 267; national origins of, 116
populations, native, 36–37
populism, 145

postal service, U.S., 51n, 143, 154
Potter, David M., 157, 384
poverty, 62
Prescott, William H., 174
Presidency, U.S., 141, 144, 223; transferral of power in, 139
Pressly, Thomas J., 383, 384
Prince, Carl E., 367
private enterprise, 94; as technique of national development, 84–86
private enterprise, U.S.: as technique of national development, 214–215, 224
productivity: as mark of economic viability, 55–56
productivity, U.S.: as mark of economic viability, 113–114
professionalization, in U.S., 155–156, 198
property, 162
Protestant ethic, 259
public health, 63, 72; in U.S., 146, 267, 270
public lands, 14; in U.S., 140, 144, 218, 228, 235
public service: U.S. standards of, 143
Pye, Lucian, 362

Quebec, 24, 119

Radicalism, 126
railroads, 4, 150; in U.S., 150, 153, 155, 226, 236, 238, 277–278
Ramsay, David, 192
Randolph, John, 111, 374
regional diversity, 35, 113; in U.S., 158
religion, 38, 44, 78; as mark of social integration, 65–66
religion, in U.S., 168–169; Roman Catholic, 118
Renan, Ernest, 39, 41, 76–77, 361, 362, 363
representativeness: as mark of political efficacy, 49
representativeness, U.S.: as mark of political efficacy, 140–141
repression, political, 53
revenues, U.S., 140, 145
Revolution, American, 11, 12–13, 15, 29, 105, 131, 182; nature of, 263–264; consequences for nationhood,